A

BE A BETTER READER

EIGHTH EDITION

W9-AZC-617

NILA BANTON SMITH

PEARSON

Research References for the *Be A Better Reader* Professional Development Articles:

Banton Smith, N. (1963). *Reading instruction for today's children.* Englewood Cliffs, NJ: Prentice-Hall.

Erickson, H. (2002). *Concept-based curriculum and instruction: Teaching beyond the facts* (p. 106). Thousand Oaks, CA: Corwin Press.

Freeman, D., Freeman, Y. S., and Mercuri, S. (2002). *Closing the achievement gap: How to reach limited-formal-schooling and long-term English learners* (p. 55). Portsmouth, NH: Heinemann.

Keene, E. and Zimmerman, S. (2007). *Mosaic of thought: The power of comprehension strategy instruction* (p. 27). Portsmouth, NH: Heinemann.

Lewis, C. W., Cobb, R. B., Winokur, M., Leech, N., Viney, M. and White, W. (2003). The effects of full and alternative day block scheduling on language arts and science achievement in a junior high school. *Education Policy Analysis Archives, 11(41),* 1.

National Council of Teachers of English (NCTE) Commission on Reading. (2004). *A call to action: What we know about adolescent literacy and ways to support teachers in meeting student's needs.* Retrieved October 31, 2007, from ww.ncte.org/about/over/positions/category/literacy/118622.htm.

National Institute of Child Health and Human Development. (2000). *Report of the National Reading Panel: Report of the Subgroups. Teaching children to read: An evidence-based assessment of the scientific research literature on reading and its implications for reading instruction* (p. 45). (NIH Publication No. 00-4769). Washington, DC: U.S. Government Printing Office.

National Writing Project and Nagin, C. (2006). *Because writing matters: Improving student writing in our schools* (p. 47). San Francisco, CA: Jossey-Bass.

Perkins-Gough, D. (2003). Creating a timely curriculum: A conversation with Heidi Hayes Jacobs. *Educational Leadership, 61(4),* 16.

Pressley, M. (2002). "Improving comprehension instruction: A path for the future." In C. C. Block, L. B. Gambrell, and M. Pressley (Eds.), *Improving comprehension instruction: Rethinking research, theory, and classroom practice* (p. 387). San Francisco, CA: Jossey-Bass.

Routman, R. (2000). *Conversations: Strategies for teaching, learning, and evaluating* (p. 130). Portsmouth, NH: Heinemann.

Acknowledgments: [Additional acknowledgments appear on page 2.]
Grateful acknowledgment is made to the following for copyrighted material: **John Wiley & Sons, Inc.:** "Skin" from *Webster's New World Dictionary, Basic School Edition.* Copyright © 1989 by John Wiley & Sons, Inc. Reprinted by permission of John Wiley & Sons, Inc. Note: Every effort has been made to locate the copyright owner of material reproduced in this component. Omissions brought to our attention will be corrected in subsequent editions.

Photo Credits: Cover images, clockwise from top left: © Getty Images, © Steffen Foerster Photography/Shutterstock, © Juicedrops, Charmaine Whitman/Pearson, © PhotoSky 4t com/Shutterstock, © hfng/Shutterstock, © Art Explosion, © Juice Drops, © Kirill Roslyakov/Shutterstock, © Brand X Pictures; Cover background: © Juice Drops; Lesson and unit opener: © Stockbyte.

Staff Credits: Joshua Adams, Melania Benzinger, Karen Blonigen, Laura Chadwick, Andreea Cimoca, Katie Colón, Nancy Condon, Barbara Drewlo, Kerry Dunn, Marti Erding, Sara Freund, Daren Hastings, Ruby Hogen-Chin, Mariann Johanneck, Julie Johnston, Mary Kaye Kuzma, Mary Lukkonen, Carol Nelson, Carrie O'Connor, Marie Schaefle, Julie Theisen, Chris Tures, Mike Vineski, Charmaine Whitman, Sue Will

ISBN-13: 978-0-7854-6663-5

ISBN-10: 0-7854-6663-0

1 2 3 4 5 6 7 8 9 10   12 11 10 09 08

1-800-992-0244
www.pearsonschool.com

Contents

Be A Better Reader

Students Succeed With The Premier Content-Area Reading Program

Be A Better Reader consists of eight leveled worktexts for content-area reading. This time-tested and research-based program makes it possible to provide students in middle school and high school with reading selections and skills instruction at their appropriate instructional level. Direct skill instruction before reading prepares all students for success. Four reading selections per theme-based unit cover literature, social studies, science, and mathematics. These core lessons are followed by brief skill lessons and end with a real-life skill lesson.

The Annotated Teacher's Edition for each level provides complete teaching support and additional assessment material. The *Assessment Manual* helps you place students in the appropriate level of *Be A Better Reader* and identifies those students who require practice in specific reading skills, while helping you track ongoing student progress.

With *Be A Better Reader*, Eighth Edition, you can:

- Guide students more easily with full teacher support for each lesson.

- Transition your students at reading levels 3 and 4 from *Caught Reading* to *Be A Better Reader* with the *Starting Out* component, which now includes an additional unit of material.

- Track students' mastery of key skills with the *Assessment Manual*.

- Help your ESL/ELL students and reluctant readers gain the skills they need to read and succeed in the content areas.

With *Be A Better Reader*, Eighth Edition, students will:

- Learn specific reading skills with immediate application and reinforcement.

- Apply reading skills to high-interest, relevant content directly related to literature, social studies, science, and mathematics.

- Relate new reading skills to essential life skills at the end of each unit.

Ensure Success by Starting Each Lesson With Relevant Instruction.

Provides easy-to-find lessons and skills; the lesson title states the skill being taught. For a complete list of skills, see the Scope and Sequence on pages T14–T16.

For ESL/ELL support, see highlighted words, page T86, and pages T28–T30.

LESSON 26

Skill: Cause and Effect

For lesson support, see page T86.

BACKGROUND INFORMATION

Offers students a head start with **Background Information**, which tells them what the selection is about and provides them with important content, cultural background, and historical information.

"Animals Among Us" is about wild animals moving into our communities. In recent years, many wild animals that were once endangered have become more common. The numbers of deer, falcons, foxes, coyotes, and other species are steadily increasing. These animals are now a common sight in suburbs and even in cities. Wildlife delight many people. At the same time, problems can arise when people and wild animals get too close for comfort.

SKILL FOCUS: Cause and Effect

Encourages student success as they read because **Skill Focus** instruction comes before they read.

When one event makes another event happen, the process is called **cause and effect**. A **cause** is an event that makes something happen. An **effect** is what happens as a result. In a cause-and-effect relationship, either the cause or the effect can be stated first.

Look for the cause and the effect in these sentences. Then look at the chart that follows.

Hunting and trapping are forbidden in cities. So these foxes are safe from human predators.

Helps students organize and record their ideas using **graphic organizers**.

Cause	Effect
Hunting and trapping are forbidden in cities.	These foxes are safe from human predators.

Certain words and phrases can signal a cause-and-effect relationship. These signal words include *so*, *because*, *as a result*, *due to*, and *that is why*. Looking for these signal words will help you find causes and effects.

▶ Circle the cause-and-effect signal words in the sentences below. Then write the cause and the effect on the chart at the top of the next column.

Coyote attacks on humans and pets are very rare. However, coyotes have been rapidly extending their range…. (As a result,) coyote attacks on pets and young children are increasing.

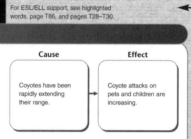

Cause	Effect
Coyotes have been rapidly extending their range.	Coyote attacks on pets and children are increasing.

CONTEXT CLUES: Synonyms

Some context clues are **synonyms**. Synonyms are words with the same or similar meanings.

Read the following sentences. What synonym explains the meanings of the underlined word?

*Foxes are **wily**. These clever creatures can usually avoid people.*

If you don't know the meaning of *wily*, the word *clever* in the next sentence will help you. The words *wily* and *clever* are synonyms.

▶ Read the following sentences. Circle the synonym that shows the meaning of the underlined word.

*The last 50 years have been a time of suburban **expansion**. This (growth) has cut into the foxes' natural habitat.*

While you read the next selection, look for synonym context clues. Use the synonyms to figure out the meanings of the underlined words *forsake*, *scavenge*, and *voraciously*.

Helps students deal successfully with new words in the reading selection with vocabulary support right up front.

> **Strategy Tip**
>
> As you read "Animals Among Us," look for words that signal cause-and-effect relationships. Recognizing causes and effects will help you understand the ideas in the selection.

LESSON 26 Cause and Effect **73**

Level A, Annotated Teacher's Edition Lesson 26

ESL/ELL

Features extra support for ESL/ELL students with references right on the Annotated Teacher Edition page.

Aids students' understanding of the selection through the **Strategy Tip**, which tells them how to apply the lesson skill while reading.

Practice New Skills on a Reading Selection.

Engages students and introduces the lesson focus immediately with the high-interest opener.

Helps students learn new words with phonetic pronunciations.

Adds interest and aids comprehension through relevant photographs and captions.

Alerts students to new vocabulary through boldfaced words.

Challenges students to identify the main idea.

Reminds students to look for context clues—in this case, synonyms—with underscored words.

Provides easy access to content-area lessons in each unit with margin tabs.

Alerts teachers to wording that may be unfamiliar to ESL/ELL students with shaded words and phrases.

(READING A SCIENCE SELECTION)

Animals Among Us

Falcons swoop down from New York City skyscrapers. Red foxes dig dens under porches in Washington, D.C. Black bears wander onto golf courses. Canada geese take over New Jersey soccer fields. All over the country, wild animals are moving from the countryside into our towns. Why is this happening? Let's look at some of the reasons.

Urban Falcons

Peregrine (PAIR ə grin) falcons are the fastest birds in the world. They can travel the length of a football field in a single second. Normally these birds live in rugged mountain areas. Why, then, are peregrine falcons nesting in skyscrapers? At least 12 breeding pairs and their chicks were living in New York City in 2001.

In some ways, tall city buildings are an ideal habitat for peregrine falcons. Skyscrapers offer the birds a high perch for hunting. There is also a steady supply of animals to hunt, including city birds such as sparrows, starlings, and pigeons. The city also allows peregrine falcons to escape their own **predators** (PRED ə tərz). In the wild, raccoons and owls feed on falcon eggs and chicks.

Ledges on skyscrapers provide good nesting spots and hunting perches for falcons.

74 LESSON 26 Cause and Effect

The increase in urban falcons has another cause, too. Nearly 40 years ago, the birds were in danger of dying out. That is because too many farmers were using a chemical called DDT. DDT killed insects and it also kept falcon eggs from hatching. So the U.S. government banned DDT, and scientists began raising peregrine falcons in captivity. When the scientists released these birds, many settled in and around cities.

The Foxes Go to Town

Foxes are wily. These clever creatures can usually avoid people. In addition, foxes hunt mainly at night. As a result, no one has ever been able to count how many foxes there are in U.S. cities. We do know that people are seeing foxes more often, however. Golfers in Minneapolis, Minnesota, recently watched some fox cubs dash onto the green and steal a golf ball. In Toronto, Canada, officials say there are at least 40 fox dens in that city.

Why would foxes forsake the open meadows? Why would they abandon their meadows in the country for the crowded city? One reason is that there are not as many open meadows as there used to be. The last 50 years have been a time of suburban expansion. This growth has cut into the foxes' natural habitat. Many foxes have been forced to find new homes.

Moving to the city was a practical move for some foxes. Foxes are **territorial** (TAIR ə TOR ee əl) animals. Each fox marks its own area and fights off other foxes. Because most city neighborhoods have not been claimed by foxes yet, it is easy for foxes to find "open territory" there.

Also, cities make a good habitat for foxes. Empty city lots are full of moles and mice, a fox's favorite foods. Hunting and trapping are not allowed in cities, so these foxes are safe from human predators. ✗ In the city, foxes are good citizens. They go about their business silently, usually unseen. Weighing only about 12 pounds, foxes do not attack cats or dogs. They run away from young children. Foxes don't scavenge for garbage, either, unlike raccoons or dogs.

Instead of searching for a free meal, they hunt, getting rid of pests such as mice and rats.

The Bear Raiders

The voters in Cross City, Michigan, got a big surprise one recent Election Day. A 400-pound black bear kept them from leaving the building where they were voting. That same fall, more than a dozen bears entered Colorado homes. Most of the bears headed straight for the kitchen.

In autumn, bears prepare to sleep away the winter. To survive the coming winter, they eat voraciously. They hungrily gobble up wild fruits and nuts. If the summer has been very dry, there will not be enough fruits and nuts for them all.

When bears cannot find enough food in the forest, they turn to dumpsters, landfills, garbage cans, and bird feeders in cities and suburbs. As a result, people often see bears in the autumn.

If food is scarce in forests in the fall, bears might raid garbage cans to fatten up for the winter.

Bear attacks on humans are very rare. Still, these powerful animals can be dangerous to city residents. So wildlife managers in cities trap bears and release them in the wild. They may also try to scare the bears away by shooting them with stinging rubber bullets. However, some bears return time after time, hoping to find an easy meal.

The Geese Mess

In the 1800s, many people hunted Canada geese for their meat. By 1900, the geese were very rare. Then in the 1960s, scientists found a group of Canada geese in Minnesota. The excited scientists took pairs of the birds to many different areas around the country.

They hoped the geese would start new flocks. The Canada geese loved their new homes. They were protected from hunters. They had plenty of grass, their favorite food. People also fed them bread. In fact, there was so much food that the geese no longer needed to migrate in winter. Because the geese had plenty of food and no predators, their numbers increased.

The goose population on golf courses, playgrounds, and parks began to skyrocket. Geese live for 20 years or more. A pair of geese can produce 100 new birds in just five years. At certain times of the year, more than 500 geese might gather in one place.

Goose droppings can make parks unsafe. They **pollute** (pə LOOT) ponds and drinking water, and cleaning up the mess is expensive. To limit the number of geese, some cities and parks now use herding dogs to keep the geese from nesting. Officials also discourage the feeding of geese. Even so, the solution to the goose problem has not been found.

Problems and Solutions

As the human population increases, people will have more encounters, or run-ins, with wild animals. Some encounters are more frightening than others. Coyote attacks on humans and pets are very rare. However, coyotes have been rapidly extending their range. They have spread from the central United States to all of the lower 48 states, Alaska, and Canada. As a result, coyote attacks on pets and young children are increasing.

In the West, people have begun building houses in remote areas where mountain lions live. People are beginning to spot mountain lions in and around parks and other public places. Attacks by mountain lions are very rare. Still, getting too close to these powerful creatures could be deadly.

Can people live in peace with wildlife? Most wildlife experts urge us to try. Some towns are setting aside special paths and areas for wild animals. Others use special fences and chemical sprays to keep wildlife away.

Experts urge people to enjoy wild animals only from a distance. Approaching or feeding them can be dangerous or can cause wild animals to become pests. Experts say that it is always better to keep the "wild" in wildlife.

LESSON 26 Cause and Effect **75**

SCIENCE

ESL/ELL

Level A, Annotated Teacher's Edition

Reinforce Learning Immediately With Review Questions.

Helps students focus on the important facts and tests their literal understanding of the text with **Comprehension questions**.

Offers quick and easy reference with a skill label and answer for each question in the Annotated Teacher's Edition.

Helps students evaluate their ability to infer information not explicitly stated in the text with **Critical Thinking questions**.

Checks students' understanding of the lesson skill with **Skill Focus exercises**. In the "Skill Focus" section at the beginning of the lesson, students learned about the lesson skill. Now they complete a written activity that applies the skill to the reading selection.

Offers students an opportunity to apply information from the lesson to their own lives, communities, or interests as they write, through the **Reading-Writing Connection**.

COMPREHENSION

Recalling details
1. Why are cities a good habitat for peregrine falcons?
Skyscrapers make good perches for hunting. There are lots of other birds in the city for the falcons to hunt. There are fewer of the falcon's own predators in the city.

Recalling details
2. What are some of the predators that attack falcon eggs and chicks in the wild?
Raccoons and owls feed on falcon chicks and eggs in the wild.

Identifying cause and effect
3. Why is it difficult to count all the foxes that are living in cities?
The foxes are clever and can usually avoid people. They also come out mainly at night.

Recalling details
4. How do wildlife managers in cities deal with bears?
They trap them and release them into the wild or try to scare them away by shooting them with rubber bullets.

Comparing and contrasting
5. How has the size of the Canada goose population changed from the early 1960s to today?
In the 1960s, scientists found one small group of Canada geese. Today, the population has skyrocketed.

Identifying cause and effect
6. What is the effect of using herding dogs in parks?
Herding dogs can reduce the number of Canada geese in the parks. The dogs prevent the geese from nesting.

Identifying main idea
7. Find the paragraph on page 74 that is marked with an **X**. Underline the sentence in that paragraph that states the main idea.

Identifying cause and effect
8. Why have people in the West begun seeing more mountain lions recently?
People have begun building houses in remote areas where mountain lions live.

Identifying cause and effect
9. Which of the following is *not* a reason why foxes are good citizens in cities? Circle the letter next to the correct answer.
   a. They are quiet and rarely seen.
   b. They help get rid of mice.
   c. They eat garbage.
   d. They do not attack pets.

Using context clues
10. Write the letter of the correct synonym next to each word.
   __b__ voraciously   a. abandon
   __a__ forsake   b. hungrily
   __c__ scavenge   c. search

CRITICAL THINKING

Inferring cause and effect
1. What effect might an increase in the falcon population have on a city's pigeon population?
An increase in falcons might lead to a decline in the pigeon population because falcons hunt pigeons.

Inferring cause and effect
2. Tell what might happen trapped or being shot a
Answers will vary. The bear

76 LESSON 26 Cause and

Comparing and contrasting
3. Which would you rather have living in your neighborhood, foxes or coyotes? Use details from the selection to support your answer.
Answers will vary. Foxes would make better neighbors because they do not attack children or pets, while coyotes occasionally do.

Inferring cause and effect
4. Explain how the growth of suburbs has led to more contacts between people and wild animals.
As suburbs fill up, people have begun building houses in remote areas that were once wild. As people take over the habitats of wild animals, the animals are forced to live closer to people and to invade their yards and houses in search of food.

SKILL FOCUS: CAUSE AND EFFECT

Answers will vary.
1. Write one or more possible causes for each of the following effects.
   a. The population of geese in a local park increases rapidly each year.
   The geese have no predators in the park and can find plenty of food there. People like to feed bread to the geese.
   b. More and more red foxes are digging dens in city areas.
   The cities may be the only territory open to the foxes. The cities have mice to hunt.

Answers will vary.
2. Write one or more possible effects of each of the following causes.
   a. Hunting and trapping is forbidden in city neighborhoods.
   Without hunters and trappers, foxes have an easier time surviving.
   b. Wildlife managers shoot stinging rubber bullets at bears in city neighborhoods.
   Bears find the bullets so unpleasant that they leave the area and return to the woods.

3. In the following sentences, underline the *cause* once. Underline the *effect* twice. Then circle the signal word or phrase that shows a cause-and-effect relationship.
   a. Bears often enter cities in the fall because they cannot find enough food in the forest to fatten themselves up for winter.
   b. Herding dogs disturb the nesting of Canada geese in a park. As a result, the geese leave the park.

Reading-Writing Connection
Research a wild animal that lives in or near your community. Find out more facts about its habitat and diet. On a separate sheet of paper, write a short report about the animal, based on your findings.

LESSON 26 Cause and Effect 77

Reinforce Skills With Brief Skills Lessons.

Focuses on one important skill in concise **Skill Lessons**. Students are introduced to the lesson concept and then are guided to formulate rules and generalizations.

Gives students the opportunity to apply their new reading skills to a valuable high-interest topic—**a practical life skill**—the subject of the last lesson in each unit.

Prepares students with techniques they can use to read and understand ads and other real-life materials.

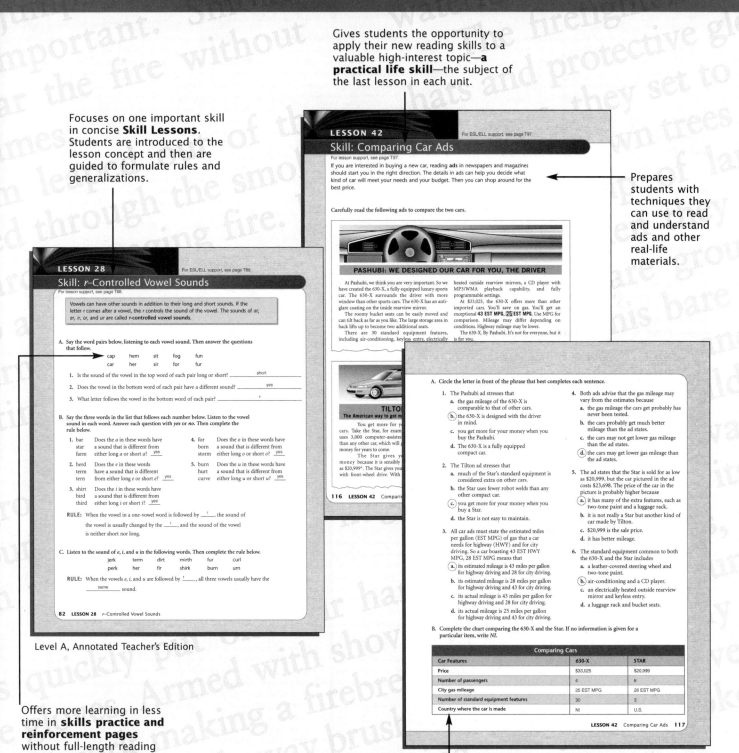

Level A, Annotated Teacher's Edition

Level A, Annotated Teacher's Edition

Offers more learning in less time in **skills practice and reinforcement pages** without full-length reading selections. In *Starting Out* and Levels A, B, and C, phonics skills are reviewed.

Provides opportunities, through **charts and graphs**, to extract information from the text, draw new conclusions, and enhance comprehension.

Teaching Support Gives a Recipe for Success With Comprehensive Lesson Pages.

Highlights the skill, context clue words, ESL/ELL words, and graphic organizer.

Guides you through activating prior knowledge, identifying the objectives and previewing the text, and gives a purpose-setting question with helpful Before Reading suggestions.

Gives you step-by-step ideas for teaching each skill, including explanations and active learning suggestions.

ESL/ELL

Provides support for ESL/ELL through suggestions in ESL/ELL Strategies for each core lesson.

ESL/ELL

Supports your English Language Learners with an ESL/ELL Activity in each skill and life skill lesson.

Reinforces skills in creative ways in Extension Activities for each skill and life skill lesson.

Offers support for each skill and life skill lesson.

Helps you stay focused on the lesson purpose with During Reading reminders.

Applies the lesson content and expands on the Reading-Writing Connection with ideas offered in After Reading.

LESSON 26

Skill: Cause and Effect (pages 73–77)
SCIENCE SELECTION: **Animals Among Us**
OBJECTIVES
▸ Identify cause and effect
▸ Use synonyms as context clues

CONTEXT CLUE WORDS: *forsake, scavenge, voraciously*
ESL/ELL WORDS: *in the wild, in captivity, spot*
GRAPHIC ORGANIZER: Cause-and-Effect Charts, p. T54

SELECTION SUMMARY
"Animals Among Us" explains why wild animals are becoming more common in suburban and urban settings. It looks at the rise in falcon and fox populations in downtown city areas and explores why Canada geese, black bears, and mountain lions have increasing numbers of contacts with people. It suggests how people can coexist with wildlife.

▸ **BEFORE READING**
Have students read the Background Information about wildlife on page 73. Then discuss different forms of wildlife seen in students' neighborhoods. Ask students to speculate on the causes for the animal's sudden appearance and to predict some problems that might arise as a result.

Teaching Cause and Effect
1. Review that a cause is what makes something happen and an effect is what happens as a result. Explain that in a cause-and-effect relationship, one event makes another event happen.
2. Ask a question about a recent local sporting event. For example: *Why did our basketball team lose last weekend?* Write the response on the chalkboard. For example: *Our basketball team lost because our best player was sick.* Underline the word *because,* and explain that it always signals a cause-and-effect relationship. Then ask students to identify the cause and the effect in the sentence. Draw a small Cause-and-Effect Chart like the one on page 73. Write the cause (Our best player was sick.) and the effect (Our basketball team lost.) in the correct boxes.
3. Have students read the Skill Focus on page 73 and complete the activity.

Teaching Context Clues
1. Point out that synonyms are words with similar meanings. Ask students to name some words that are synonyms, and list them on the chalkboard. For example: *good, wonderful, fantastic,* and *terrific.*
2. Explain that synonyms can help you figure out the meaning of new words and might appear before or after the unknown word. Write these sentences on the chalkboard: *He walked quietly. He tiptoed.* Ask students to circle the synonym for *tiptoed.* (walked quietly)
3. Have students read the Context Clues section on page 73 and complete the activity.
4. Write the context clue words *forsake, scavenge,* and *voraciously* on the chalkboard or word wall. Remind students to find synonyms for these words as they read.

Previewing the Text
Have students preview the section headings and photos to predict cause-and-effect relationships in the selection. Then distribute copies of the Cause-and-Effect Charts, and ask students to record causes and effects as they read.

Purpose-Setting Question
What are some of the reasons that wild animals are showing up in populated areas?

▸ **DURING READING**
As students read, remind them to identify cause-and-effect relationships. Also have them look for synonyms that explain the meanings of the underlined words.

▸ **AFTER READING**
Ask volunteers to share their Cause-and-Effect Charts and to answer the purpose-setting question. Then have students complete the activities on pages 76–77.

Reading-Writing Connection
Have students talk to local police officers, park rangers, animal control officers, or veterinarians to find out about wild animals in the community. Students prepare fact cards about each animal, listing details about its physical appearance, diet, habitat, and the precautions people should take in handling it.

ESL/ELL Strategy
PERSONALIZING THE LESSON Have partners write riddles about animals who live amon[...] garbage can before I take a lo[...] (a bear) Partners ask other par[...]

LESSON 28

Skill: r-Controlled Vowel Sounds (page 82)
OBJECTIVE:
▸ Identify *r*-controlled vowel sounds

Teaching the Skill
1. Ask students to pronounce each pair of words as you write them on the chalkboard: *cat/cart, ten/tern, bid/bird, pot/port, bun/burn.* Invite volunteers to circle the *r* in each pair and note how the short vowel sound in the first word of each pair changes when it is followed by the letter *r.* Ask students to provide other word pairs, such as *pat/part, pet/pert, skit/skirt, spot/sport,* and *hut/hurt.*
2. Read the paragraph at the top of page 82. Then call on volunteers to read aloud each pair of words in boldface type. Answer items 1–3 in Exercise A with the class.
3. Write the words *car, her, sir, for,* and *fur* on the chalkboard and circle the *r* and the *r*-controlled vowel in each.
4. Direct students to complete Exercises B and C and the rules independently.

ESL/ELL Strategy
USING MANIPULATIVES Invite students to draw pictures that contain at least five objects whose names have an *r*-controlled vowel sound. Then have partners exchange papers and write the words with the *r*-controlled vowel sounds.

Extension Activity
Make a rhyming dictionary available to students. Ask them to find rhymes for the boldface words in Exercise C on page 82. Challenge them to write poems that use these rhymes at the end of lines.

LESSON 42

Skill: Comparing Car Ads (pages 116–117)
OBJECTIVE:
▸ Compare and contrast ads for information

Teaching the Skill
1. Review that comparing is finding similarities between two things and that contrasting is finding differences.
2. Distribute handouts of two newspaper or magazine ads for two different types of cars. Ask students to note ways in which the cars are similar or different. Have them compare and contrast such features as size, design, cost, and special features.
3. Ask students to discuss how the ads might be useful if they were planning to buy a car. Point out that in addition to using persuasive techniques that appeal to emotions, ads often contain useful facts. Have students point out examples of facts in the ads.
4. Read the paragraph at the top of page 116. Then direct students to carefully read the ads for the Pashubi and Tilton cars. Direct students to complete the exercises on page 117.

ESL/ELL Strategy
[US]ING REALIA Provide partners with car ads from a local [ne]wspaper or magazine. Ask students to circle facts and [use]ful details about the cars with a red pencil. Suggest [that] they discuss what these facts mean and list them in [ch]art form.

Extension Activity
[Ha]ve small groups create their own car ads. Urge students [to] make their ads persuasive while including facts and [de]tails that would help a consumer learn more about the [ca]r. When groups are finished, have them display the ads [on] a bulletin board. Students can compare and contrast the [a]ds for type of car, different facts and figures shown, type [of] persuasive language, and so on.

Level A,
Annotated Teacher's Edition

Determine Placement and Monitor Progress With Easy-to-Use Assessment Materials.

Evaluates students' mastery of skills at each level with the reproducible **Assessment Test** in the Annotated Teacher's Edition.

Prepares students for state and standardized tests with the four-choice multiple-choice format.

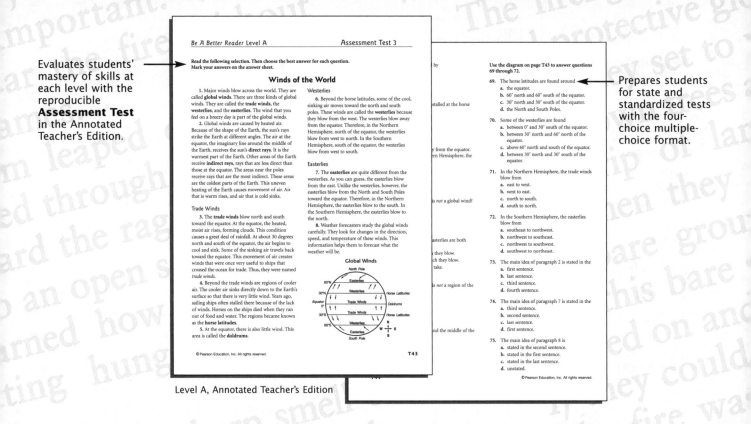

Level A, Annotated Teacher's Edition

With the *Assessment Manual* you can:

- Place each student confidently at the appropriate instructional level with the Placement Test.

- Verify Placement Test results quickly and identify where each student needs help, using the Diagnostic Tests and the coded Answer Key.

- Evaluate reading ability in a particular content area effectively and efficiently.

- Use the reproducible tests for ongoing monitoring of students' achievement.

- Help students bolster weak skills with the Reteaching the Skills section, which includes instructions for using reproducible graphic organizers.

- Track each student's progress and overall class performance with reproducible Student Performance and Class Performance Charts.

- Facilitate testing with complete instructions for administration and assessment.

Pacing Suggestions

Pacing suggestions are based on the class-period time allotments shown. Adjust the schedule, using additional teaching options, to accommodate longer time periods or block scheduling.

▶ PACING FOR A FULL-YEAR SCHEDULE (36 Weeks; 50–90 minute daily class periods)

Weeks	1–6	7–12	13–18	19–24	25–29	30–36
Unit	1	2	3	4	5	6

During each block of time, complete one unit. Provide direct instruction for the introduction page of each core lesson in the unit: literature, social studies, science, or mathematics. Then choose the combination of instructional elements below that works best for your class.

- **Reading and Practice:** For all core lessons, use the selections and question pages that follow.
- **Writing:** For all core lessons use "Reading-Writing Connections."
- **Skill Practice:** Use additional skill lessons from each unit.
- **Assessment and Reteaching:** Use "Progress Monitors" and "Reteaching the Skill" in the *Assessment Manual.*
- **Independent Reading:** Use the *Starting Out* Student Readers, *Amazing Insects* and *The World of Inventions.*

ADDITIONAL TEACHING OPTIONS
Use related programs from Pearson.

Independent Reading: *Adapted Classics, FastBacks, Globe Reader's Collection, Freedom Fighters, Multicultural Literature Collection*

Writing Skills and Practice: *Success in Writing, Writing Across the Curriculum, World of Vocabulary*

Reading-Writing Connections: *Stories Without Endings, Plays Without Endings*

▶ PACING FOR A SUMMER SCHOOL SCHEDULE
(6 Weeks; 90–120 minute daily class periods)

Each week, complete one unit. During each week, complete all four core lessons and additional skill lessons.

Weekly Schedule		
Day	Core Lessons	Skill Lesson (Remaining Lessons of Each Unit)
1	Reading Literature	Choose one or more relevant skill lessons based on students' needs.
2	Reading Social Studies	Choose one or more relevant skill lessons based on students' needs.
3	Reading Science	Choose one or more relevant skill lessons based on students' needs.
4	Reading Mathematics	Choose one or more relevant skill lessons based on students' needs.
5	Assessment: Use "Progress Monitors" and "Reteaching the Skill" in the *Assessment Manual*. Use the *Starting Out* Student Readers for independent reading. Choose from Additional Teaching Options below.	

ADDITIONAL TEACHING OPTIONS

Use related programs from Pearson.

Independent Reading: *Adapted Classics, FastBacks, Globe Reader's Collection, Freedom Fighters, Multicultural Literature Collection*

Writing Skills and Practice: *Success in Writing, Writing Across the Curriculum, World of Vocabulary*

Reading-Writing Connections: *Stories Without Endings, Plays Without Endings*

Scope and Sequence

	Starting Out	A	B	C	D	E	F	G
Word Analysis								
Compound Words	✓							
Contractions	✓							
Syllables	✓	✓	✓	✓	✓	✓	✓	
Accented Syllables		✓	✓	✓	✓	✓	✓	
Letter Patterns	✓							
Phonics								
Consonants	✓	✓						
Consonant Blends	✓	✓						
Consonant Digraphs		✓						
Long and Short Vowel Sounds	✓	✓						
Vowel Digraphs	✓							
Vowel Diphthongs	✓			✓				
Vowel-Consonant Combinations				✓				
r-controlled Vowel Sounds	✓	✓						
Schwa Sound	✓	✓	✓	✓	✓	✓	✓	
Silent Letters	✓		✓					
Hard and Soft c and g	✓		✓					
Rhyming Words	✓							
Content-Area Reading								
Reading a Diagram	✓	✓	✓	✓	✓	✓	✓	✓
Reading a Flowchart						✓	✓	
Reading a Graph	✓		✓	✓	✓	✓		
Reading a Map	✓	✓	✓	✓	✓		✓	✓
Reading a Timeline			✓	✓				
Reading a Table	✓	✓						✓
Content-Area Vocabulary	✓	✓	✓	✓	✓	✓	✓	✓
Reading Math Terms and Symbols	✓	✓	✓	✓	✓	✓	✓	✓
Reading and Solving Word Problems	✓	✓	✓	✓	✓	✓	✓	✓
Using Statistics					✓	✓	✓	
Using a Spreadsheet					✓			
Critical Thinking								
Analyzing								✓
Classifying		✓	✓	✓	✓		✓	
Comparing and Contrasting	✓	✓	✓	✓	✓	✓	✓	✓
Evaluating Opinions				✓				
Fallacies in Reasoning								✓
Making Generalizations	✓			✓	✓	✓	✓	

	Starting Out	A	B	C	D	E	F	G
Comprehension								
Cause and Effect	✓	✓	✓	✓	✓	✓	✓	✓
Drawing Conclusions	✓							
Context Clues	✓	✓	✓	✓	✓	✓	✓	✓
Fact and Opinion	✓	✓	✓	✓	✓	✓	✓	✓
Following Directions		✓	✓	✓		✓	✓	✓
Making Inferences	✓	✓	✓	✓	✓	✓	✓	✓
Main Idea—Stated or Unstated	✓		✓	✓	✓	✓	✓	
Main Idea and Supporting Details	✓	✓	✓	✓	✓	✓	✓	✓
Sequence of Events	✓	✓						✓
Recognizing Propaganda				✓	✓			✓
Vocabulary Development								
Analogies						✓	✓	✓
Denotation and Connotation								✓
Etymology								✓
Multiple-Meaning Words	✓	✓	✓	✓		✓	✓	✓
Nouns, Plural and Possessive	✓							
Prefixes, Suffixes, and Base Words	✓	✓	✓	✓	✓	✓	✓	✓
Synonyms and Antonyms					✓		✓	
Word Parts	✓					✓	✓	
Understanding Word Origins	✓		✓					
Transitional Words and Phrases							✓	
Context Clues	✓	✓	✓	✓	✓	✓	✓	✓
Study Skills								
Alphabetical Order		✓	✓					
Using a Dictionary	✓	✓	✓	✓	✓	✓	✓	
Using the Library		✓	✓	✓				
Encyclopedia		✓						
Using Guide Words		✓	✓					
Outlining			✓	✓	✓	✓	✓	✓
Using Parts of a Book	✓	✓	✓	✓	✓		✓	
Using Reference Books			✓	✓				
Skimming for Information			✓					
Taking Notes				✓	✓			✓
Summarizing					✓			✓
Using a Primary Source		✓				✓	✓	✓
Improving Reading Rate				✓	✓		✓	✓

	Starting Out	A	B	C	D	E	F	G
Life Skills								
Using the Yellow Pages	✓		✓					
Reading Information on the Internet	✓							
Comparing Car Ads		✓						
Reading a Job Application				✓				
Reading a Bank Statement					✓			
Reading a Loan Application						✓		
Reading a Résumé							✓	
Completing an Employment Application								✓
Shopping Online				✓				
Literary Genres								
Short Story	✓	✓	✓	✓	✓	✓	✓	✓
Fable	✓							
Folktale			✓					
Myth				✓				
Biography			✓		✓			✓
Play			✓	✓			✓	
Article	✓	✓	✓	✓	✓	✓	✓	✓
Poem					✓	✓	✓	✓
Letter						✓		
Science Fiction	✓			✓	✓		✓	
Journal	✓			✓				
Literary Elements and Skills								
Character	✓	✓	✓	✓	✓	✓	✓	✓
Conflict and Resolution	✓	✓	✓	✓	✓	✓	✓	✓
Imagery					✓			
Plot	✓	✓	✓	✓	✓	✓	✓	✓
Setting	✓	✓	✓	✓	✓	✓		✓
Theme	✓	✓	✓	✓		✓	✓	✓
Point of View			✓	✓	✓		✓	
Mood				✓				✓
Tone						✓		✓
Satire							✓	
Figures of Speech			✓			✓		✓

PROFESSIONAL DEVELOPMENT

The *Be A Better Reader* Lesson Plan

"WHAT THE RESEARCH SAYS"

We know from studies that "...there are unique differences in skills used in different subject matter fields; and that while 'general reading ability' is operative in all reading to a certain extent, there is also definite need for the development of specific skills to use in the different curricular areas."

Nila Banton Smith
(see page T2)

At every level and in every lesson, *Be A Better Reader* emphasizes developing background information, acquiring reading skills, comprehension, and moving beyond a text to think critically and make new connections. To achieve these goals, each lesson follows a classic three-part format: Before Reading, During Reading, and After Reading.

▶ BEFORE READING

Prereading is a time to motivate students to read the selection while equipping them with information, skills, and strategies to maximize the benefits of the reading experience.

While the Background Information section of the student text will help students access the selection, a background-building prereading discussion is ideal for generating relevant information from the students' own knowledge and experience. Often, graphic organizers can be used to elicit and record background information and relate ideas—and many of the lessons include such organizers.

The Skill Focus section is another key element of prereading. Each Skill Focus introduces a reading skill that is vital for comprehending and interpreting the reading selection. The Skill Focus provides examples drawn from the selection itself and also gives the student an opportunity to practice a given skill before beginning to read.

Because using context clues is essential for success in comprehension and vocabulary development, each prereading page of the lesson provides instruction for a particular type of context clue, such as comparisons, details, synonyms, in-text definitions, and so on. Examples of vocabulary context clues are drawn directly from the text that students are about to read. Furthermore, students are directed to use the introduced skill to identify the meaning of specific vocabulary words, thus helping them to prepare for the new vocabulary they will encounter.

The Strategy Tip that completes the prereading page of each student lesson is another valuable feature. By giving students a concrete suggestion for how to use a newly acquired skill in the text they are about to read, students get a head start in their quest for comprehension.

The lesson support on pages T68–T112 also provide valuable prereading suggestions that will further student comprehension. The purpose-setting question, for example, gives students a formal reason for reading that will help them focus on the text and identify the main points and ideas of the selection. Making predictions is another important prereading skill, and this Annotated Teacher's Edition makes specific suggestions for previewing the text by scanning the title, illustrations, diagrams, maps, photos, and text of a selection to predict what the story or article might be about.

▶ DURING READING

In *Be A Better Reader*, students will find timely, high-interest reading selections that will naturally engage their interest. The readability of each selection in each level of the program has been carefully controlled to help ensure successful comprehension. Illustrations, photographs, and other graphics have been chosen to complement the text, enhance meaning, and add to the overall appeal.

If students are working with graphic organizers, for example, lesson-support pages remind them to add details and information to these as they read. If visuals are prominent in a selection, students are asked to study these closely. Attention is paid to section headings that might appear in the selection and students are reminded of the underscored vocabulary words introduced in the Context Clues section for which they must figure out the meaning while reading.

▶ AFTER READING

After students finish reading a selection, they can complete the Comprehension, Critical Thinking, and Skill Focus questions and activities that appear at the end of each core lesson. As the name indicates, the Comprehension questions assess students' literal comprehension of the text. The answers to these questions, which can usually be stated in a few words or a sentence, are stated directly in the text. Students should realize that a close rereading of portions of the text will yield the answers for these items.

The answers to Critical Thinking questions are not stated directly in the text. Instead, students must use higher-level thinking skills, along with information in the text, to infer appropriate answers. The answers to these questions often require students to use specific reading skills, such as making inferences, comparing and contrasting, or identifying cause and effect—skills that have already been taught in the level. The students' answers to the Critical Thinking questions will vary somewhat, and suggested answers are provided in the Annotated Teacher's Edition.

The Skill Focus activities offer an opportunity to practice the specific reading skill introduced in the Skill Focus section during prereading. Since these questions are based on information in the text, they also test overall comprehension. Some students may benefit from a quick review of the lesson's Skill Focus before attempting to complete the activities.

After-reading oral activities are also important. Individually or in groups, students formally answer the purpose-setting question. They compare and discuss their predictions or any graphic organizers that they have completed. Such activities can contribute markedly to overall comprehension.

Each lesson ends with a feature called the Reading-Writing Connection. This activity, a springboard to writing about the selection, asks students to respond to new information and ideas in a thoughtful and personal way. In addition to providing beneficial writing practice, the activity aids in the long-term retention of the skills and information taught in the lesson.

"**WHAT THE RESEARCH SAYS**"

Strategies are the thinking, problem-solving mental processes that the learner deliberately initiates, incorporates, and applies to construct meaning....When teaching for strategies, we build on the child's existing foundation of what he knows and show him how to connect that knowledge to new situations.

Regie Routman
(see page T2)

Reading comprehension is a process that begins with word recognition. It does not end, however, until students have derived meaning from the ideas both stated and implied in the text and have been able to evaluate and respond to these ideas.

In *Be A Better Reader*, each lesson focuses on a specific reading skill that helps students recognize and understand a text pattern that is typical of a content area or of other reading materials that students encounter in their daily lives.

▶ COMPREHENSION SKILLS

Comprehension questions help students process information that is stated explicitly in the text. These questions require students to recall from memory or to select from the text specific answers—in other words, to reproduce what has been stated in the text. These questions provide opportunities for students to:

1. Identify the stated main idea.
2. Identify the stated main idea and details.
3. Recall details.
4. Identify the stated cause and effect.
5. Recognize a sequence of events.
6. Recognize fact and opinion.
7. Recognize elements of a short story, such as plot, character, setting, and theme.
8. Recognize a variety of nonfiction text types or literary genres, such as plays, short stories, biographies, articles, reports, and essays.
9. Compare and contrast.

▶ CRITICAL THINKING AND COMPREHENSION

Numerous activities and questions are included to encourage students to probe for deeper meanings that are implied but not explicitly stated in the text. These questions require students to think about the meanings that can be derived from their reading. Inferential and critical comprehension begins with literal meanings, but it advances to higher-level thinking and reasoning skills that help students to:

1. Infer unstated main idea.
2. Infer cause and effect.
3. Infer details.
4. Infer conclusions.
5. Infer comparisons and contrasts.
6. Distinguish fact from opinion.
7. Infer information about elements of a short story, such as plot, character, setting, and theme.
8. Make generalizations.
9. Evaluate validity of ideas.
10. Predict outcomes.
11. Draw conclusions.
12. Identify a point of view.

Certain basic skills are called for in all subject areas in order to study and understand information. As students work with selections in literature, social studies, science, and mathematics, *Be A Better Reader* provides instruction and practice in the following study skills.

▶ PREVIEWING

Previewing a selection results in an organized "picture" or understanding of the structure of the selection. In *Be A Better Reader*, students learn to preview a selection by noting headings of sections, main ideas, and visuals.

▶ LOCATING INFORMATION

The skill of locating information includes activities that range from using a table of contents and an index to using a dictionary, an encyclopedia, and the library catalog. In *Be A Better Reader*, lessons on locational skills are self-contained and include representative examples of typical dictionary and encyclopedia entries, indexes, and tables of contents.

▶ SELECTING AND EVALUATING INFORMATION

Textbooks in the content areas contain many questions and directions that call for selection and evaluation skills. The skill of selecting and evaluating information requires students to select a piece of information and judge its worth in meeting the specifications of an activity or question. In *Be A Better Reader*, lessons on fact and opinion, primary sources, and propaganda teach students selection and evaluation skills.

▶ ORGANIZING INFORMATION

The skill of organizing information is important because of the frequency with which students must apply it when studying the material in textbooks, listening in class, writing papers, and taking tests. Organizing information calls for systematically putting together items or ideas that belong to a whole. *Be A Better Reader* includes lessons on the procedures most often used when organizing information: (1) classifying, (2) outlining, and (3) summarizing.

▶ READING VISUALS

Most content-area textbooks require students to read a variety of visuals, such as maps, timelines, diagrams, and graphs. Throughout *Be A Better Reader*, in all content areas, students are taught how to extract specific information from visuals and how to compress textual information into a brief visual presentation.

▶ FOLLOWING DIRECTIONS

Reading to follow directions is a fundamental skill needed in all content areas. In *Be A Better Reader*, students complete specific lessons in following directions. They acquire abundant experience in reading and following directions throughout each level of the program.

▶ READING SPECIAL MATERIALS

Students must be able to read special materials that they encounter outside the classroom. The last lesson in each unit of *Be A Better Reader* provides specific directions on how to read the Yellow Pages, a recipe, a floor plan, a travel brochure, an advertisement, a schedule, and so on.

▶ READING RATE

Studies indicate that most students are ready for a variety of reading rates by the end of fifth grade. Students who have acquired reading skills by only reading fiction need to learn that there are different rates at which they should read different content. In *Be A Better Reader*, emphasis is placed on adjusting the rate of reading to both the content and the purpose of the material.

❝ WHAT THE RESEARCH SAYS ❞

If word recognition is difficult, then much consciousness is consumed by it, reducing the amount of capacity available for comprehension and thus reducing comprehension.

Michael Pressley
(see page T2)

Students need specific instruction in word recognition to ensure that they have a variety of word-attack strategies needed to read an unfamiliar word. In *Be A Better Reader*, direct instruction is provided for the following skills.

Phonetic Analysis: recognizing and identifying the sounds of consonants, consonant blends, and digraphs; recognizing and identifying vowel sounds and their variant spellings

Structural Analysis: recognizing root words, prefixes and suffixes, compound words, multisyllabic words, accent marks, and syllabication

Context Clues: determining word meaning from a particular context clue

Respellings, Footnotes, and Other Word Helps: using vocabulary aids typical of content-area textbooks

▶ VOCABULARY INSTRUCTION

Extensive reading opportunities are key to developing new vocabulary. However, in addition to independent reading, teacher-directed vocabulary instruction is needed. Teachers can assist students in developing etymological, historical, and morphological knowledge. Such instruction in word derivation is especially important as students encounter content-laden terms in science, social studies, and mathematics.

▶ WORD ANALYSIS

As students encounter more multisyllabic words, they need to learn strategies to decode these words. Structural features such as prefixes and suffixes should be studied. Then base words can be identified and studied. Students who are not reading at grade level should receive continued explicit instruction in decoding multisyllabic words and technical terminology.

▶ CONCEPT WORDS

In lessons that feature social studies, science, and mathematics selections, words that are unique to the content and whose meanings are essential to the selection are treated as concept words. These words appear in boldface type and are often followed by a phonetic respelling and a definition.

▶ ESL/ELL WORDS AND PHRASES

Be A Better Reader provides additional vocabulary support for English language learners. Idioms, expressions, and words with more than one meaning are highlighted for each literature, social studies, science, and mathematics lesson. These words and phrases can be reviewed with students before students read a selection. You may wish to have students use notebooks in which to record the words and phrases and add additional ones of their own. These word books would contain individual vocabulary entries, each with a definition as used in context and an illustration, as appropriate, for each word or phrase. The word book could serve as an ongoing vocabulary tool to be used throughout the school year.

"WHAT THE RESEARCH SAYS"

Through extensive reading of a range of texts, supported by strategy lessons and discussions, readers become familiar with written language structures and text features, develop their vocabularies, and read for meaning more efficiently and effectively.

National Council of Teachers of English (NCTE) Commission on Reading

(see page T2)

Reading research has shown that different types of text require specialized reading skills. During the preparation of *Be A Better Reader*, textbooks in literature, social studies, science, and mathematics were analyzed for text patterns, visual programs, and study aids typical of each content area. The specific skills situations that occurred most often in each content area were selected for inclusion and direct instruction.

▶ LITERATURE

The literature selections in *Be A Better Reader* were carefully selected to appeal to student interest and were written or selected at appropriate reading levels. The basic goals of the lessons with literature selections are threefold: (1) to acquaint students with a variety of literary genres; (2) to increase students' awareness of the literary elements; and (3) to provide practice in applying comprehension skills to reading literature.

Each level of *Be A Better Reader* provides a lesson that develops one of the following literary elements required in understanding and appreciating literature.

Plot

Most short stories have a plot, or sequence of events. They have a beginning, a middle, and an end, and events are arranged to build to a climax. As students read stories, they need to keep the events in order, to notice how one event leads to the next, and to be able to identify the climax, or turning point of the story.

Character

Students need to be able to identify the main character, or protagonist, in a story. They should think about what motivates characters to act as they do. They should also notice how characters develop and change by contrasting how the characters behave at the beginning of a story with how they behave at the end.

Conflict

Students should be able to recognize a story's central conflict, or problem. Most stories are built around one of three common conflicts: (1) The main character is in conflict with himself or herself. (2) The main character is in a conflict with other characters. (3) The main character is in conflict with nature, society, or some outside force over which he or she may not have any control.

Setting

Setting is the time and place of the events in a story. Awareness of setting is essential to an understanding of the characters and their conflicts.

Theme

The theme, or central message, of a story is usually the most difficult concept for students to formulate by themselves. Students need to use higher-level comprehension skills to infer the theme—the author's underlying message.

▶ SOCIAL STUDIES

Social studies texts have their own characteristic text patterns that require special reading skills. For example, social studies texts include frequent references to visuals, such as maps, graphs, and pictures. These references may require students to find information in a specific visual and then combine that information with information in the text.

Many social studies texts require students to interpret material critically. Students are expected to make inferences from facts, to distinguish fact from opinion, to analyze propaganda, to interpret primary sources, to draw conclusions and make generalizations, and to answer open-ended questions. *Be A Better Reader* provides specific instruction and practice in these skills so that students can learn to probe for deeper meanings and respond to higher-level questions.

Be A Better Reader teaches some of the following skills that aid in the comprehension of the patterns typical in social studies textbooks.

Cause and Effect

While the cause-and-effect text pattern occurs to some extent in most content areas, it occurs with the highest frequency in social studies, especially history. Every major event in history comes about as the result of some cause or set of causes, and when the event happens, its effect or effects are felt. Sometimes the effect of one event becomes the cause of another event. Thus, the student often encounters a chain of causes and effects. Students who are adept at recognizing cause-and-effect patterns will find this to be a valuable asset in studying social studies textbooks.

Sequence of Events

Another text pattern encountered in social studies presents events in specific time sequences accompanied by dates. Students should read this pattern for two purposes: (1) to grasp the chronological order of large periods or whole blocks of events; (2) to grasp times of important happenings within each period or block to associate events with dates and to think about how each event led to others.

Social studies textbooks include several kinds of visual aids designed to help students understand time relationships. These aids include charts of events and dates, chronological summaries, timelines, outline maps with dates and events, and so on. Each of these visual aids requires special reading skills.

Comparison and Contrast

A text pattern calling for the comparison of likenesses and/or the contrast of differences is common in social studies textbooks. This pattern occurs most frequently in discussions of such topics as the theories of government or policies of different leaders; physical features, products, or industries of different countries; and so on. Students who recognize a comparison and contrast chapter or section of a text can approach it with the foremost purpose of noting likenesses and differences.

Detailed Statements of Fact

Much social studies text contains many details and facts. Facts, however, are usually included within one of the characteristic text patterns already discussed. The facts in social studies textbooks are not as dense as they usually are in science textbooks, nor are they as technical. Because they are often associated with sequential events or with causes and effects, they are more easily grasped.

Combination of Patterns

A single chapter in a social studies book may contain several text patterns. For example, a chapter may contain biographical material similar to the narrative pattern, a chronology of events during a certain time period, maps and charts depicting those events, and cause-and-effect relationships. If students who start to study such a chapter have not acquired the skills necessary to recognize and process each of these text patterns and instead use the same approach in reading all of them, the resulting understandings of the concepts presented will be extremely limited.

Visuals in Social Studies

Pictures in social studies textbooks are selected to depict historical concepts and events. The ability to read pictures and the captions that accompany them allows students to gain information and implied meanings that go beyond the text. Reading pictures requires close attention to detail.

Reading maps and graphs is a highly specialized kind of reading skill. Map reading requires the recognition and interpretation of symbols for geographical features, towns and cities, boundary lines, and such features as scales of miles, color keys, and meridians. When reading graphs, students need to know how to extrapolate data and use it to make generalizations, thereby supplementing information in the text.

▶ SCIENCE

Science texts call for the use of such comprehension skills as identifying main ideas and making inferences. However, an analysis of science textbooks reveals text patterns unique to science that demand other approaches and special reading skills.

As in social studies textbooks, science texts include frequent references to such visuals as diagrams and pictures. Students need continued practice in combining text reading with visual reading in order to process all the information that is available on a science text page.

Be A Better Reader provides lessons on the following special reading skills that are needed for science textbooks.

Classification

In this pattern, living things, objects, liquids, gases, forces, and so on are first classified in a general grouping that has one or more elements in common. This group is further classified into smaller groups, each of which varies in certain respects from every other group in the general grouping. Students who recognize the classification text pattern will learn to concentrate on understanding the basis of the groupings and the chief characteristics of each one.

Explanation of a Technical Process

Another text pattern particularly characteristic of science is the explanation of a technical process. Explanation is usually accompanied by diagrams, necessitating a very careful reading of the text with continuous references to diagrams.

Cause and Effect

In this pattern, the text gives information that explains why certain things happen. In reading this type of pattern, students first read to find the causes and effects. A careful rereading is usually necessary to determine how and why the causes had such effects.

Following Directions for an Experiment

This text pattern consists of explicit directions or instructions that must be carried out exactly. The common study skill of following directions is essential in reading this science pattern, but experiments also call for the mental activities of making discriminating observations, understanding complex explanations, and drawing considered conclusions.

Detailed Statements of Fact

This pattern in science frequently involves dense facts and a definition or statement of principle. In reading this text pattern, students can make use of the reading skill of finding the main ideas and supporting details. Students first locate the most important thought or main idea in each paragraph; then they proceed to find details that reinforce the main idea—noting particularly any definitions or statements of principles.

Descriptive Problem-Solving Situations

This text pattern describes problem-solving situations by taking the reader through a series of scientific experiments conducted by one or by many people. Students should approach this pattern with the idea of finding out what each successive problem was and how it was solved.

Combination of Patterns

As in social studies textbooks, a single chapter of a science text may contain several text patterns. If students who start to study such a chapter have not acquired the skills necessary to recognize and process each of these patterns and instead use the same approach in reading all of them, then the resulting understandings of the concepts presented will be extremely limited.

Science textbooks usually contain many diagrams. Students need to learn how to go from the text to the diagrams and back to the text if they are to understand the meaning of scientific concepts. Reading diagrams requires an understanding of the purpose of diagrams, the ability to interpret color and other visual devices used to highlight parts of a diagram, and the comprehension of labels.

▶ MATHEMATICS

The reading skills needed for reading mathematics are sharply different from the skills needed in other content areas. Many students who read narrative text with relative ease have great difficulty in reading mathematics, especially word problems and abstract mathematical symbols. The mathematics selections in *Be A Better Reader* are not included for the purpose of teaching mathematics. Their function is to give students practice in reading the different types of text and symbols used in mathematics textbooks, and to apply basic reading skills to mathematics text.

One of the special characteristics of mathematics text is compactness. Every word and every symbol is important. Unlike reading in other content areas, skipping an unfamiliar word or guessing its meaning from context will impair students' progress in mathematics. Students should be aware of this difference.

Another adjustment students may have to make in reading mathematics is a change in basic left-to-right eye movement habits. Mathematics text often requires vertical or left-directed eye movements for rereading portions of the text for better understanding or for selecting certain numbers or symbols.

Reading in mathematics makes heavy demands on the comprehension skills that call for interpretation, critical reading, and creative reading. Students must weigh relationships and discover principles as a result of studying pictures and diagrams.

The inferential reading skills and the study skills of reading pictures and diagrams emphasized throughout *Be A Better Reader* should transfer to the following skills and attitudes specifically needed in working with mathematics.

Word Problems

Because problem solving is a priority in mathematics, *Be A Better Reader* includes one or two lessons on solving word problems in each level. A five-step strategy is used throughout the series. The steps in the strategy closely parallel the steps used in most mathematics textbooks. However, *Be A Better Reader* emphasizes the reading and reasoning skills necessary to solve word problems.

Explanation

Mathematical explanations are comparatively short and often contain symbols. They are usually accompanied by or are preceded by a series of exercises or questions designed to guide students in discovering the principle or process. This text pattern calls for careful reading and rereading until the process is understood.

Visuals in Mathematics

In mathematics, students must read sentences composed of word symbols and number symbols, such as equations. Recognizing and understanding symbols of various types is reading, and it should be taught as such in mathematics.

In reading equations, students have to recognize the meaning of the entire mathematical sentence, as well as the various symbols. In addition to symbols for operations, other symbols are used frequently.

Other distinctive visual elements in mathematics texts are graphs, such as bar graphs and circle graphs. While these visual aids are used in social studies and science, they almost always represent mathematical concepts.

To get the most information from a graph, students should: (1) read the title to determine exactly what is being compared; (2) read the numbers or labels to determine what the figures or labels stand for; (3) study the graph to compare the different items that are illustrated; and (4) interpret the significance of the graph as a whole.

" WHAT THE RESEARCH SAYS "

The goal of an integrated curriculum should be "integrated thinking"—seeing the patterns and connections of knowledge at a conceptual and transferable level of understanding

H. Lynn Erickson
(see page T2)

Good readers connect and use information and ideas from a variety of life and literary experiences. Thematic instruction fosters this process in a number of ways.

When students explore a topical theme in-depth, they tend to apply it to "real world" contexts. That is, thematic lessons from the classroom are likely to relate to and enrich various events of a student's own life. This synergy often improves the student's ability to make decisions and solve problems both inside and outside the classroom setting.

Thematic instruction is also flexible and multifaceted. Students explore a topic using different types of texts, each approaching the theme from a different perspective. Students might work individually, in small groups, or as a whole class. Each broad theme also provides a rich variety of extension activities—writing tasks, discussions, and projects.

To maximize the advantages of teaching with themes, and to tap the storehouse of information and experience that students bring to the classroom, each unit of *Be A Better Reader* is organized around a different theme. A unit theme such as "The Ocean," "Flight," or "Communications," unites the subject matter in the literature, social studies, science, and mathematics selections of the unit and develops some aspect of that theme.

To maximize the benefits of the program's thematic organization, use some of the following classroom activities as students progress through *Be A Better Reader*.

▶ THEME INTRODUCTIONS

When beginning a new unit, introduce its theme. Discuss students' associations with the theme and invite them to suggest topics that might be included in it. Have them speculate how the selections in the unit might relate to the unit theme. Let them share movies and books they know about that relate to the theme.

▶ THEME BOOKS

Provide a selection of theme-related books and magazine articles for students to peruse. When beginning a unit on "Flight," for example, provide a biography of the Wright brothers and other pioneers in flight, a short history of ballooning, a field guide to birds, magazine articles about space stations and planned flights to Mars, and books about stars and constellations. Encourage students to read some of these materials and write short book reports or critiques during the period of time you study the theme.

▶ THEME WORDS

At the beginning of a unit, provide a place for students to record theme-related vocabulary. After each reading session, ask students to record at least three new theme-related words that they have learned. When you finish a theme, review the words. Students can play a picture dictionary game. Assign different words to teams and ask them to illustrate each one. Teams challenge each other to guess the words and provide their meanings.

▶ THEME ESSAYS

At the end of a unit, have students write essays expressing their personal views of, or reactions to, some aspect of the theme. Construct essay topics based on the theme. For example, for "Challenges," you might pose the essay "What challenges do the characters in this unit successfully face?"

▶ THEME BULLETIN BOARDS

While students are working on a unit, create a theme bulletin board. The items on the bulletin board might include current-event articles, photographs, original poems, drawings, and objects that illustrate some aspect of the theme. Ask each student to write a few sentences on a notecard that explain the theme connection. Post each one on the bulletin board below the item.

❝ WHAT THE RESEARCH SAYS ❞

Students in both forms of block scheduling—4X4 and AB—[outperform] students in traditional scheduling and AB block scheduling has the largest positive impact on low-achieving students.

Chance W. Lewis, R. Brian Cobb, Marc Winokur, Nancy Leech, Michael Viney, and Wendy White

(see page T2)

The term "block scheduling" refers to a way of organizing the school day for intermediate and high school students. Traditional scheduling generally calls for six, seven, or eight single periods of study of about 40–50 minutes each per day. With block schedules, students take fewer, but longer, classes daily. Within each block, a variety of related classroom activities take place.

In recent years, many schools have initiated block schedules with great success. Some schools use an alternating day plan, with students and teachers meeting in three to four 90- to 120-minute classes every other day. The "4 × 4" semester plan is another popular model, with students enrolling in four 90-minute courses that meet every day of the week for a semester. There is also a trimester plan, in which students take two or three 120-minute classes for 60 days, along with two or three traditional-length classes.

▶ BENEFITS OF BLOCK SCHEDULES

Block scheduling provides a significantly different classroom experience than traditional class periods. Some benefits of block scheduling for teacher and students are shown in the chart below.

Teacher Benefits	Student Benefits
1. can focus on more activities; more varied than straight lecture	1. increased possibilities for in-depth study
2. fewer courses to prepare each day	2. fewer classes that students must attend and prepare for each day and/or each term
3. longer blocks of time that allow and encourage the use of active teaching strategies and greater student involvement	3. fewer class changes during the school day and less of the disruption that occurs during these changes
4. more time to adapt to different learning styles	4. more time for students to learn, without lowering standards and without punishing those who need more or less time to learn

▶ BLOCK SCHEDULING AND *BE A BETTER READER*

In block scheduling, teachers need to determine the most effective way for teaching students, considering their individual learning styles. Using selected portions of the block for formal student instruction is crucial. However, interspersed with these segments, other activities can be included that facilitate active student involvement. These include discussions, cooperative groups for projects, independent research, extra skill practice, brainstorming a writing assignment, and opportunities for advanced study. The following are suggestions for ways to use *Be A Better Reader* within the framework of a block schedule.

- Incorporate the skills presented in the literature selections of *Be A Better Reader* into instruction of other stories, novels, and plays that students are reading.

- Use the social studies, science, and mathematics articles in *Be A Better Reader* in conjunction with social studies, science, and mathematics textbooks to develop and extend key concepts.

- Use the suggestions in the Reading-Writing Connection found in the lesson plans of the Annotated Teacher's Edition to provide students with additional activities.

- Use the ESL/ELL Strategy with groups of students who need additional access to lessons.

- Use the "Progress Monitors" in the *Assessment Manual* to track students' ongoing progress toward mastery of key skills.

" WHAT THE RESEARCH SAYS "

Even though many students with limited formal schooling and many long-term English learners have not developed the academic concepts and language proficiency of other students their age, they are capable. What they need are activities that will stretch them....Without a challenging curriculum, older English learners will not develop the academic English they need to close the achievement gap.

David E. Freeman, Yvonne S. Freeman, and Sandra P. Mercuri

(see page T2)

In order to raise the achievement level of English language learners (ELL), this edition of *Be A Better Reader* includes strategies that have been designed to be compatible with SDAIE (Specially Designed Academic Instruction in English) and CALLA (Cognitive Academic Language Learning Approach). These approaches to teaching grade-level subject matter in English to English language learners use strategies tailor-made to help speakers of other languages access content. The goal of incorporating these strategies is to assist ELL students of intermediate fluency or higher in benefiting from instruction in complex academic content delivered through readings and accompanying instruction in specific, proven classroom strategies.

Some curriculum designers slot subjects into a continuum of challenge to English language learners based on the content area's dependency on language. The following chart represents this continuum.

Core Content and English Language Proficiency

Physical Education, Art, Music	Dependency on language alone to convey meaning is relatively low. Reliance is on modeling and demonstration. As movement strategies and artistic techniques are introduced, language proficiency becomes more important.
Mathematics	Comprehension of basics is not completely dependent on language proficiency. Through math symbols, tools (calculators and computers), real-life applications, projects, and manipulatives, content becomes more explicit. Language proficiency is more important for solving word problems.
Science	Dependence on language to convey meaning is fairly high. Nomenclature, along with concepts students may not encounter in everyday life, makes science more abstract. Use demonstration, lab partnering, hands-on experimentation, media support, science software, and videos to make comprehension more accessible.
Social Studies	Dependence on language to convey meaning is high. Many abstract and complex concepts rely heavily on language to convey meaning; primary source documents written in archaic language add to the challenge. Use simulation games, group projects, graphic organizers, and field trips.
Literature/ Reading	Dependence on language to convey meaning for vocabulary, semantics, and cultural literacy to appreciate nuances that enrich stories, poetry, and plays is almost exclusive. Beginning reading is often made easier when students bring to English the ability to read in their primary language; higher-level critical-thinking skills transfer to English, such as understanding cause and effect, main idea, and sequencing. Students learning to read in a language other than their primary language need teacher techniques and materials for those nontransferable aspects of language.

▶ STRATEGIES FOR ENGLISH LANGUAGE LEARNERS

Techniques and strategies which make abstract concepts more readily understood by English language learners include the following:

1. **Building background** to move students from the known to the new.

2. **Previewing vocabulary** to identify and teach students essential words and terms before they encounter them in the text. These are often more than the new "key terms" in a content lesson; they are often words and phrases that native English speakers at the grade level already know.

3. **Using illustrations and visuals** including photographs, drawings, artwork, posters, graphs, maps, videos, computer programs, and reproductions of documents to provide a context for learning. Students new to English literacy can focus on reading captions and labels in their textbooks, which often capture the main ideas of a lesson.

4. **Using realia** (real objects and materials) to reduce abstractions and make new concepts more explicit. Use of realia helps ELL students relate classroom teaching to real life and their own prior knowledge and experience.

5. **Using graphic organizers** including matrices, Venn diagrams, tables, charts, story maps, outlines, study guides, and webs to maximize comprehension, visually organize information into meaningful conceptual groupings, and foster a collaborative, interactive style of learning. Study guides for individual lessons, similar to computer derived handouts, can also be distributed to students to use in organizing notes as they read.

6. **Using manipulative materials/hands-on activities** including props, multimedia presentations, experiments, building models, and demonstrations to build background and context.

7. **Using nonverbal cues**, such as gestures, body language, and slowed pace of speech, to aid student comprehension.

8. **Using repetition and review** of concepts and vocabulary. Provide bilingual dictionaries.

9. **Group activities** including team projects, cooperative learning, and peer tutoring to promote interaction between class members. These strategies assure that students get adequate practice speaking the new language rather than teacher lecture as the only model of learning.

▶ ESL/ELL STRATEGIES AND *BE A BETTER READER*

There are a number of specific strategies and approaches you can use to adapt *Be A Better Reader* to help ESL/ELL students gain access to the lesson structure.

1. Preview the *Be A Better Reader* lessons from the English language learner's point of view. Introduce the three ESL/ELL words for each selection, highlighted in the Annotated Teacher's Edition. Look for additional idioms or words with double meanings that should be clarified. Preteach the new vocabulary and idioms. Further clarify new vocabulary when it appears in the text to reinforce language acquisition while teaching content.

2. You may wish to have students create word books in which they collect words they don't know. Students can draw illustrations of idioms and then write their meanings below the pictures. Explain idiomatic expressions, simplify grammatical structures, and summarize/paraphrase material into shorter, simpler passages, where necessary.

3. Establish context and build background to personalize lessons by eliciting prior knowledge and experience. (See Background Information in the Student Edition. It is found on the first page of each selection lesson.)

4. When introducing content that is completely new or abstract, read complex material aloud to aid clarity. Talk about context clues in each selection. (See Context Clues in the Student Edition.) Have ELL students retell or summarize the text orally while you record on chart paper. This simplified text can become material that can be used as a language experience chart to teach basic English reading as well as to provide a summary of the content.

5. Use leveled questions to engage English language learners at the various levels of English proficiency in the class. In *Be A Better Reader*, the series of Comprehension questions may prove less challenging than the Critical Thinking questions.

6. Teach students key study skills and the use of textbook aids, such as visuals and graphics, which are found in *Be A Better Reader*. You can also designate one of your more fluent English students each week to be the class scribe. Course notes can then be photocopied for less proficient English language learners so they can devote complete attention to listening to and comprehending the lesson.

7. Use the ESL/ELL strategy found on the teacher support page of every *Be A Better Reader* lesson.

Elizabeth Jimenez
CEO, GEMAS Consulting
Trainer, Los Angeles County Office of Education
California Association for Bilingual Education

" WHAT THE RESEARCH SAYS "

An effective writing assignment does more than ask students to write about what they have read or experienced. It engages students in a series of cognitive processes, such as reflection, analysis, synthesis, so that they are required to transform the information from the reading material in order to complete the writing assignment.

National Writing Project and Carl Nagin

(see page T2)

Understanding and using the writing process allows virtually every student to write more fluently and effectively. This process consists of five steps. The following paragraphs review these steps and provide helpful suggestions for how students can benefit from them.

Step 1: Prewriting The novelist Ernest Hemingway once wrote, "My working habits are simple: long periods of thinking, short periods of writing." His remark speaks to the importance of prewriting—all the thinking and planning should occur before students begin a first draft.

During prewriting, students brainstorm, choose, and narrow a topic. They also decide how they will develop the topic, organizing their ideas and details into a logical outline or plan. Class discussions and brainstorming sessions are excellent sources of prewriting ideas. For today's students, graphic organizers, such as those provided on pages T53–T67, are an invaluable prewriting aid.

Step 2: Drafting During the drafting stage of the writing process, students rely on the prewriting work they have done as a source of ideas and details. They decide whether they have a workable subject or whether they need to go back and rethink their ideas.

The goal during drafting is to get the best ideas down on paper without worrying too much about phrasing, spelling, grammar, usage, and mechanics of writing. While drafting, students move logically from one thought to the next, using their prewriting notes as a guide but departing from them when necessary. Students need to stop frequently and read over their drafts to get ideas about how to move logically from

one idea to the next. They need to be aware that there will be time later to add or delete ideas as necessary.

Step 3: Revising Revising means "seeing again," and this step of the writing process requires students to take a new look at a written draft and find ways to make it better. Many writers put away their first drafts for awhile before revising. In this way, they have a fresh outlook and can more easily see what needs to be improved.

During revision, students check primarily for unity and coherence. If a piece of writing is unified, readers will not be distracted by paragraphs or sentences that stray from the main idea. If the writing has coherence, readers can take in the ideas with smooth progressions. In order to revise for unity and coherence, students may need to add some ideas and details and eliminate or rephrase others. They may also need to add transition words and phrases, such as *next, later on,* and *in the end,* so that the sentences and paragraphs flow.

Step 4: Proofreading Proofreading is the careful rereading of a revised draft to correct mistakes in spelling, grammar, usage, and mechanics. Students should be aware that proofreading will eliminate mistakes that might distract their readers or lessen the overall effectiveness of what they have written.

To proofread, students carefully read each word. They may benefit by focusing on one line at a time, using a sheet of paper to cover adjacent lines. Peer proofreading—exchanging drafts with partners—is an effective way to find errors. When students are unsure about corrections, encourage them to use a dictionary or a grammar and usage handbook. You might have students create a proofreading checklist that lists the typical errors that writers make.

Step 5: Publishing Publishing is the final step of the writing process. When a student publishes work, he or she presents it in neat, corrected final form to an audience. Oftentimes, the intended audience is the teacher. At other times, it may be classmates or other members of the school community. Studies show, however, that writings reaching new or varied authentic audiences, such as letters to an editor, are often a powerful stimulus for students to improve their writing.

Encourage students to explore new ways to publish their writing. Display work on bulletin boards and in folders in the library. Impromptu sessions in which students read aloud their work to small groups is another valuable publishing outlet. Suggest that students submit their writing to the school newspaper or literary magazine, or help them prepare writing for essay contests.

▶ THE RECURSIVE NATURE OF WRITING

Help students understand that writing is a recursive, not a lockstep, process. The five-step writing process is a valuable guide to better writing skills. All writers spend some time preparing to write, writing, revising, proofreading, and sharing their work. However, writers do not compose in exactly the same way.

Encourage students to write recursively; at any step of the writing process, students can return to an earlier step. (See page T33.) Some students might pause in revision, for example, and return to prewriting to gather more information. Other students might stop during proofreading to take more time for further revision. One of the best features of the writing process is that it allows students to use new ideas while they are creating and improving their work.

▶ THE WRITING PROCESS AND EVALUATION

Many students have difficulty suiting their writing to a purpose, clarifying a main idea, elaborating a composition with adequate details, or organizing details in logical order. Self-evaluation or peer evaluation that occurs

midway through the writing process can address these and other stumbling blocks to effective communication.

After students have written their first drafts, suggest that they use a checklist, such as that shown below, to identify possible problems in their work.

❏ Is the subject interesting? Does it address the writing task?

❏ Is the main idea clearly stated?

❏ Is the main idea supported by adequate details?

❏ Are the details logically organized?

Many students find it helpful to work in pairs to evaluate each other's draft. One student can read his or her draft aloud while the other listens. In this way, both listener and writer can hear how the piece sounds and can detect areas in which revisions are needed.

▶ WRITING AND *BE A BETTER READER*

Writing is an essential part of *Be A Better Reader*. The Reading-Writing Connection activities that follow the four core lessons in every unit are a treasury of writing ideas designed to help students become better writers and more thoughtful readers. These activities deepen the students' understanding of the processes of reading by requiring them to return to the text and look more closely at its structure.

The writing tasks in *Be A Better Reader* are also springboards to self-expression. Reading aloud and discussing their writing will lead to animated classroom discussions and a general exchange of ideas that will enable students to better express their views on a wide range of topics.

Finally, the Reading-Writing Connection activities show that writing, when closely linked with reading, can become a powerful road to learning. To this end, the writing tasks often require students to activate prior knowledge, summarize and extend their understanding of the text, or offer a personal response.

Name _____ **Date** _____

STEPS OF THE WRITING PROCESS

Check each step in the Writing Process as you complete it. Remember that you can go back to a previous step if you need to.

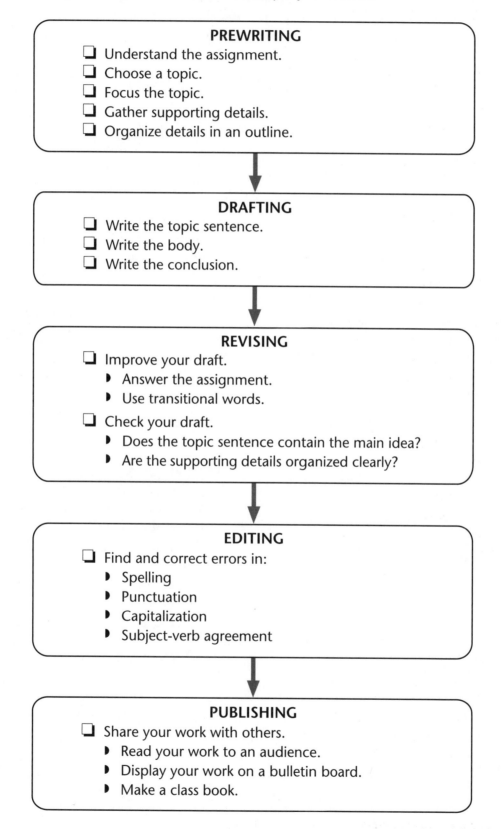

PREWRITING
❑ Understand the assignment.
❑ Choose a topic.
❑ Focus the topic.
❑ Gather supporting details.
❑ Organize details in an outline.

DRAFTING
❑ Write the topic sentence.
❑ Write the body.
❑ Write the conclusion.

REVISING
❑ Improve your draft.
▶ Answer the assignment.
▶ Use transitional words.

❑ Check your draft.
▶ Does the topic sentence contain the main idea?
▶ Are the supporting details organized clearly?

EDITING
❑ Find and correct errors in:
▶ Spelling
▶ Punctuation
▶ Capitalization
▶ Subject-verb agreement

PUBLISHING
❑ Share your work with others.
▶ Read your work to an audience.
▶ Display your work on a bulletin board.
▶ Make a class book.

T33

❝ WHAT THE RESEARCH SAYS ❞

The one subset of skills that's requisite for any test or any assessment is literacy....Schools can't lose when they help students become more discriminating and discerning readers; more critical responders in their writing; and more effective speakers, reflective listeners, and active note-takers.

Deborah Perkins-Gough

(see page T2)

TWO TYPES OF TESTS

Nonstandardized tests, often designed by teachers, measure a student's periodic progress in a particular subject. They provide information to both teacher and student as to whether the student is keeping up with the class, needs extra help, or is ahead of other students. To the extent that teacher-made tests assess the learning objectives determined at the outset of the learning period and the material taught, they are precise tools. The results of these tests are often the basis for report-card grades.

Standardized tests, by contrast, use certain measurable standards to assess student performance across an entire district, city, or state. Students take the same test according to the same rules, making it possible to measure each student's performance against that of the larger population.

POLICIES AND PRACTICE

Students will benefit by knowing your policies for "teacher-made" tests as well as the school's policies and practices for standardized tests and the use of test scores. Early in the school year, review with students the kinds of tests they will be taking during the year and the schedule for standardized tests. Ongoing practice in taking standardized tests will also help students perform better by becoming familiar with test directions and formats.

AVOIDING TEST ANXIETY

A technique for reducing test anxiety is to discuss test-taking strategies. (See page T35.) Regular reinforcement of such strategies helps students approach tests in a more relaxed manner. Also remind students to space their studying over days or weeks in order to learn the material well. Point out that cramming before a test might interfere with clear thinking. Encourage a good night's sleep before the test and an early arrival at class the next day.

AFTER THE TEST

Students need to review their test results as soon as practically possible. A graded exam paper shows students not only where they had difficulty, but why. Take time to discuss incorrect answers with your students and find out why they answered as they did. Explore situations in which students misunderstood the wording of a question or misinterpreted what was asked. Make sure students understand any comments made on their test papers, especially in responses to essay-type answers. Have students use a checklist such as that shown below to evaluate their test performance.

❑ Did I use my time during the test well?

❑ What was asked that I didn't expect?

❑ What part of the test was most difficult for me? Why?

❑ What should I do differently in preparing for the next test?

TEST-TAKING STRATEGIES

The assessment component of *Be A Better Reader* provides a wide variety of testing opportunities. Placement tests in the *Assessment Manual* determine the ideal level of the program at which each student should work. Four Assessment Tests included with each level of the Annotated Teacher's Edition assess students' progress during the year and evaluate how well they can apply particular skills. These tests can be used as pretests and/or posttests, depending on students' needs and your classroom management style. In addition to the program's formal tests, Comprehension, Critical Thinking, and Skill Focus questions appear at the end of each core lesson. These provide practice in such test formats as multiple-choice, fill-in, and matching. There are also a number of short and longer essay-type questions—all valuable preparation for standardized tests.

20 WAYS TO BOOST YOUR TEST PERFORMANCE

Check the tips that work best for you as you study for a test and take it.

As You Study

❑　1.　Make a list of the test topics you need to review.

❑　2.　Write a list of questions you think will be asked on the test. Then answer them.

❑　3.　Turn the titles of sections you are studying into questions. Look for the answers as you review.

❑　4.　Make flashcards for studying key words and phrases. Write a word or phrase on one side and the definition on the other.

❑　5.　Make an outline for the materials you need to study.

❑　6.　Look for key words in a chapter you are studying. Be sure you know what they mean. Use a dictionary to find words you do not understand.

❑　7.　Write important vocabulary words you are studying in sentences.

❑　8.　Look back at the photos, charts, and maps. Reread the captions to remember ideas about the topic.

❑　9.　List the main ideas of the subjects you are studying.

❑　10.　Be sure you know how to spell the names of people and events in the chapter. Practice writing each of them several times.

❑　11.　When you are looking for details in the text, look through the material quickly. Look for names, dates, and facts that will help you answer questions.

❑　12.　Try studying with a friend. Ask one another questions from your textbook.

Taking the Test

❑　13.　Before you begin the test, look it over. Decide how much time you can spend on each question.

❑　14.　Read the test directions carefully. Underline or circle the important words in the questions.

❑　15.　Focus on one question at a time.

❑　16.　In a multiple-choice test, cross out answers that you know are not correct.

❑　17.　In an essay test, reread what you wrote to be sure you answered the question.

❑　18.　Try to check all your answers before handing in your test paper.

❑　19.　Skip questions that you are unsure of. Then go back after you have answered the rest of the questions.

❑　20.　Keep a positive attitude. Decide to do your best and focus on the material you know.

**Read the following selection. Then choose the best answer for each question.
Mark your answers on the answer sheet.**

The Captive

1. From the day that she learned to walk, Katie's parents had warned her not to wander past the wire fence. The fence divided the Cavanaughs' farm from the open prairie that stretched for miles like a dusty, green sea. A child could get lost in the high, waving grass. Katie's mother would remind her about her sister Hannah. "Hannah was no older than you the day that she disappeared," Mama would say. Then for a week or two, Katie would stay close to home. She couldn't think of anything worse than to be separated from her mother and father.

2. Katie had never seen her sister. Hannah had been lost before Katie was even born. Katie often thought about the fun that they might have had together. She liked to imagine that one day a beautiful stranger would come driving up the road in a buggy, and it would be Hannah. Katie's mother told her that it was foolish to hope for the impossible. Yet, Katie thought that sometimes even her mother hoped that Hannah was not lost forever.

3. Now, more than twelve years after her disappearance, Hannah was coming home! Major Hawkins rode out from Sioux Falls with the wonderful news. His cavalry unit had found Hannah at a Sioux village many miles away. A Lakota woman told them how she had found the lost child many years ago. She had carried her home and raised Hannah like one of her own children.

4. Katie's father and Major Hawkins would bring Hannah back the next day, but the major warned them about Hannah's return. "Hannah might not be able to settle down easily," he said. "She probably has no memory of her childhood before she disappeared. Remember, this is not her real home." Katie found that difficult to believe. How could Hannah not want to live with her real family?

5. Katie and her mother kept busy all day. They dusted and polished the spare bedroom. They set the white china pitcher and the best towels on the washstand. Katie put her own silver-backed mirror and brush on the dresser. She made the big bed with fresh, clean sheets. She also laid out her newest nightgown for Hannah. Then she and her mother dug up a small wild rosebush that was growing on the other side of the fence. They put the plant in a clay pot on the mantelpiece in Hannah's room. The lovely marble mantelpiece had been bare. Now, centered above the fireplace, the roses made the room look pretty.

6. The next day Hannah arrived with her father, Major Hawkins, and an interpreter. Katie flung open the front door and raced out into the yard, her arms open wide. As she came closer to the tall, young woman, her arms dropped. The cry of welcome died in her throat. Hannah had sun-browned skin and her pale hair hung in a long braid. She had a blanket pulled around her shoulders and beaded moccasins on her feet. She stood staring, looking helpless, as Katie's mother moved forward to embrace her.

7. At that moment, Katie remembered the rabbit that she had caught in her trap last winter. It was still alive when she found it. Katie had carried it home gently. She had built a sturdy pen and filled it with fresh wood shavings. The next morning the rabbit was gone. "It was used to freedom," her mother had explained. Katie wondered if her mother remembered that now.

8. Hannah stayed at her new home for almost a month. She never slept in the soft bed or wore the nightgown or used the silver hairbrush. She seldom came out of her room. Whenever Katie went into Hannah's room, she always found Hannah looking out the window. Katie's mother and father kept telling her that it was just a matter of time. Hannah would get used to their ways. "After all," Mama said, "we're her real family."

9. Then one night, when Katie went in to say good night, Hannah was gone. Her window was open wide. Katie looked around the empty room. It looked just as it had the day Hannah came, except that the wild roses on the mantelpiece had withered and turned brown. Katie started to run down the stairs to call her mother and father, but then she stopped. The wild roses reminded Katie of the rabbit that she had caught. She would not tell. She would let her parents discover Hannah's absence in the morning. Then Hannah would have had a head start on her long journey back to her family.

1. Who is the main character in this story?
   a. Katie's mother
   b. Major Hawkins
   c. Katie
   d. Hannah

2. What does the main character most want at the beginning of the story?
   a. to have her sister back
   b. to live on the prairie
   c. to clean the spare bedroom
   d. to catch a rabbit

3. Which words best describe the main character?
   a. kind and understanding
   b. selfish and unkind
   c. shy and unhappy
   d. helpless and scared

4. By the end of the story, the main character
   a. has not changed in any important way.
   b. understands more than she did at the beginning of the story.
   c. understands less than she did at the beginning of the story.
   d. does not understand why Hannah left.

5. The first important event in the story is when
   a. Katie is told not to walk past the fence.
   b. The rabbit was gone from its sturdy pen.
   c. Katie cleans the spare bedroom.
   d. Major Hawkins tells Katie's family that Hannah has been found.

6. The most important event in the middle of the story occurs when
   a. Hannah comes home.
   b. Katie puts the rosebush on the mantelpiece.
   c. Katie remembers her rabbit.
   d. Katie goes out into the prairie.

7. The climax of the story occurs when
   a. Katie sees that the roses have withered.
   b. Hannah sleeps in the soft bed.
   c. Katie finds Hannah's room empty.
   d. Hannah speaks in English.

8. The story ends when
   a. Hannah leaves the Cavanaughs' home.
   b. Katie says goodnight to Hannah.
   c. Katie gets a new rabbit.
   d. Katie gives Hannah a head start.

9. The story takes place
   a. in the present.
   b. about 150 years ago.
   c. about 1,000 years ago.
   d. in the future.

10. The setting of the story is
    a. a Sioux village.
    b. an army camp.
    c. a farm on the prairie.
    d. a large city.

11. The scene described in paragraph 6 takes place
    a. at the back door of the house.
    b. in the yard right outside the house.
    c. on the prairie.
    d. in the Sioux village.

12. Hannah's room is described in paragraph 5. What change in this setting is mentioned when the room is described again in paragraph 9?
    a. The white china pitcher was missing.
    b. The rosebush had withered and turned brown.
    c. The window was shut.
    d. One moccasin was torn.

13. Katie's experience with the rabbit that she caught helps her to believe that people
    a. belong where they are most comfortable.
    b. are cruel to animals.
    c. should not run away.
    d. should have pets.

14. Katie's mother believes that Hannah
   a. is free.
   b. is not her real daughter.
   c. should stay for awhile.
   d. belongs with her real family.

15. Because of a *difference of opinion*, there is conflict between
   a. Katie and Hannah.
   b. Katie and her mother.
   c. Katie and Major Hawkins.
   d. Katie and the Lakota woman.

16. How is the conflict resolved?
   a. Katie and Hannah become friends.
   b. Katie decides not to tell her parents that Hannah has run away.
   c. Katie understands why the rabbit ran away.
   d. Katie runs away.

17. The title of this story best describes
   a. Hannah when she lived in the Sioux village.
   b. the rabbit when it was in the pen.
   c. Hannah when she returned to the farm.
   d. Major Hawkins' cavalry unit.

18. By the end of the story, Katie has learned that
   a. it is best to live out on the prairie.
   b. her family is right about Hannah.
   c. it is dangerous to wander past the fence.
   d. it is wrong to interfere in other people's lives.

19. By having Hannah escape from the Cavanaughs' house, the author hints that
   a. Hannah belonged with the people who brought her up.
   b. Hannah did not want a sister.
   c. Hannah made a mistake when she ran away.
   d. Hannah went to find the rabbit.

20. Which statement best expresses the story's theme?
   a. It is always wrong to hate anybody.
   b. It is difficult to grow up on the prairie.
   c. It is sometimes more important to think of another person's happiness than one's own.
   d. It is never safe to wander alone.

21. What can you infer about the way Katie feels about Hannah in paragraph 2?
   a. Katie has never seen her sister.
   b. Katie wishes her sister had never been lost.
   c. Katie thinks about the fun that she could have had with her sister.
   d. Katie is glad she's the only child.

22. What can you infer about Katie and Mama in paragraph 5?
   a. Katie and Mama want to make Hannah comfortable when she comes home.
   b. Katie and Mama clean the spare bedroom every week.
   c. Katie and Mama are afraid that Hannah will be unable to settle down easily.
   d. Katie and Mama hate to clean.

23. What can you infer about Hannah in paragraph 8?
   a. Hannah misses her rabbit.
   b. Hannah does not like Katie.
   c. Mama understands Hannah better than Katie does.
   d. Hannah is not happy at the farm.

24. Choose the definition of the word *captive* that best fits the title of the story.
   a. a person who is held in prison
   b. a person held against his or her will
   c. a person who is forced to listen
   d. a person who is interested in something

25. In paragraph 1, a *prairie* is
   a. a fenced-in area around a farm.
   b. an ocean.
   c. the name of a baby cow.
   d. a broad area of grass with no trees.

26. In paragraph 5, a *mantelpiece* is a
   a. rough blanket.
   b. clay pot for plants.
   c. shelf above a fireplace.
   d. washstand.

Read the following selection. Then choose the best answer for each question. Mark your answers on the answer sheet.

Balloning

1. People fly balloons for fun and adventure. Weather forecasters use balloons to collect weather information. Scientists use balloons to study space. While hot-air balloons are used for short flights, gas balloons are used for long flights. Balloons are used for many purposes.

2. What makes a balloon go up? A balloon rises because the heated air or the gas inside the balloon is lighter than the air outside the balloon. The heated air or lighter gas rises to the top of the balloon bag. This makes the balloon look like a big, upside-down pear. The pilot has some control over the upward movement of a balloon. The pilot can drop ballast, such as sandbags. By dropping weight, the pilot makes the balloon lighter, and it rises.

3. What makes a balloon go down? The pilot can also control the downward movement of a balloon. On a gas balloon, the pilot opens a valve and lets gas out of the balloon. On a hot-air balloon, the pilot controls the burners that heat the air. Cooler air makes the balloon go down.

4. Wind determines the speed and direction of a balloon. A strong wind increases the speed of a balloon. A weak wind slows its speed. Pilots study the skies and weather reports, searching for winds that will take them in the direction they want to go.

5. Ballooning began in France. The first balloon flight with a pilot took place near Paris on November 21, 1783. The balloon flew for more than five miles (almost nine kilometers). The next day, a Paris newspaper ran this headline: "Balloons are a promising invention."

6. In a short time, balloons were carrying mail. It wasn't long before armies used balloons to watch enemy troop movements. Balloons were used by armies in the American Civil War.

7. Many people have been hurt or killed in balloon accidents. Leaks were a big problem with early balloons. Many balloons exploded in flight. Because most of today's balloons are made of strong nylon, they are less likely to develop leaks. However, some balloons still explode in flight. At times, clouds block the view of the ground. When this happens, the pilot flies "blind." Sometimes storms blow balloons off course, and balloon crews have had to land in icy seas and other dangerous places.

8. The dangers of ballooning have not stopped people from trying long flights. For more than a hundred years, people tried to fly balloons across

Flight of the *Double Eagle II*

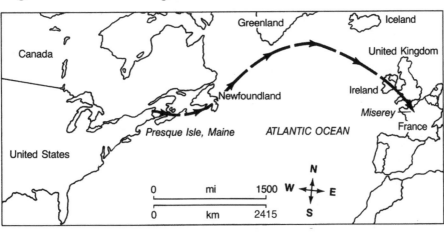

the Atlantic Ocean. But all the flights failed. Then on August 11, 1978, the *Double Eagle II* lifted off from Presque Isle, Maine. The balloon was piloted by three Americans, Ben Abruzzo, Max Anderson, and Larry Newman. Five and a half days later, the balloon landed near the small village of Miserey in France. The *Double Eagle II* had flown 3,120 miles (4,992 kilometers).

27. Because heated air inside a balloon is lighter than the air outside the balloon, the balloon becomes
   a. smaller and goes down.
   b. lighter and rises.
   c. heavier and floats.
   d. "blind" and blows off course.

28. Today's balloons are less likely to develop leaks because
   a. they are made of strong nylon.
   b. they are sewed tightly.
   c. they are made of steel wool.
   d. they are shaped like an upside-down pear.

29. When weight is removed, a balloon becomes
   a. smaller and goes down.
   b. heavier and floats.
   c. lighter and rises.
   d. "blind" and blows off course.

30. How are gas balloons different from hot-air balloons?
   a. Gas balloons are for long flights; hot-air balloons are for fast flights.
   b. Gas balloons are for short flights; hot-air balloons are for long flights.
   c. Gas balloons are for long flights; hot-air balloons are for short flights.
   d. Gas balloons are made of rubber; hot-air balloons are made of nylon.

31. How are today's balloons different from earlier balloons?
   a. Today's balloons do not explode.
   b. Today's balloons are only used by forecasters.
   c. Today's balloons cannot be blown off course.
   d. Today's balloons are less likely to develop any leaks.

32. Which problem do today's balloon pilots share with past pilots?
   a. The hours are long and the pay is low.
   b. Clouds often block the view of the ground.
   c. People do not appreciate the dangers that balloon pilots face.
   d. Pilots cannot make the balloons go up and down.

33. How did the flight of the *Double Eagle II* differ from earlier balloon flights across the Atlantic Ocean?
   a. During the flight, the *Double Eagle II* was lost.
   b. The flight of the *Double Eagle II* was a failure.
   c. The flight of the *Double Eagle II* was a success.
   d. The *Double Eagle II* landed in Ireland.

34. Another word for *ballast* in paragraph 2 is
   a. weight.
   b. sandbag.
   c. gas.
   d. balloon.

35. Which of the following statements is a fact?
   a. Balloons are shaped like upside-down pears.
   b. Ballooning is over two hundred years old.
   c. Neither statement is a fact.
   d. Both statements are facts.

36. Which of the following statements is an opinion?
   a. Balloons are lighter than air.
   b. Balloons have been used for watching enemy troop movements.
   c. Balloons are a beautiful sight.
   d. Wind determines the speed and direction of a balloon.

37. *American balloon pilots are better than French balloon pilots.* This statement is
   a. a fact.
   b. an opinion.
   c. neither of the above.
   d. both of the above.

T40

38. *The* Double Eagle II *landed near Miserey, France.* This statement is
    a. a fact.
    b. an opinion.
    c. neither of the above.
    d. both of the above.

39. Balloons were used by armies for watching enemy troop movements
    a. after the year 1783.
    b. 400 years ago.
    c. in recent times.
    d. while they were delivering mail.

40. Why do you think balloons were invented before airplanes?
    a. Balloons are more difficult to make.
    b. Balloons are easier to make.
    c. People like balloons.
    d. Metal hadn't yet been discovered.

41. To remain on course, a pilot needs to be concerned most about
    a. leaks.
    b. low ballast.
    c. broken valves.
    d. wind changes.

42. The *Double Eagle II* took over five days to reach Europe because
    a. it made several stops.
    b. it was blown off course.
    c. its speed depended on wind speed.
    d. it had a leak.

43. The *Double Eagle II* was a
    a. lighter balloon.
    b. gas balloon.
    c. hot-air balloon.
    d. motor-powered balloon.

44. The main idea of paragraph 1 is stated in the
    a. first sentence.
    b. second sentence.
    c. third sentence.
    d. last sentence.

45. The main idea of paragraph 4 is stated in the
    a. first sentence.
    b. second sentence.
    c. third sentence.
    d. last sentence.

46. The main idea of paragraph 5 is stated in the
    a. first sentence.
    b. second sentence.
    c. third sentence.
    d. last sentence.

47. Which detail below supports the main idea of paragraph 1?
    a. Children like balloons.
    b. Scientists use balloons to study space.
    c. Balloons have been flown for many years.
    d. Balloons are used for many purposes.

48. Which detail below supports the main idea of paragraph 4?
    a. A strong wind increases the speed of a balloon.
    b. Wind determines what the weather will be.
    c. Wind determines how high a balloon will go.
    d. Wind determines the speed and direction of a balloon.

49. Which detail below supports the main idea of paragraph 7?
    a. Many people have been hurt or killed in balloon accidents.
    b. Balloons are safe to fly.
    c. The dangers of ballooning have not stopped people from trying long flights.
    d. Many balloons exploded in flight.

50. Choose the correct definition for the word *block* as it is used in the sixth sentence of paragraph 7.
    a. to stop movement
    b. to shape or mold
    c. to get in the way of
    d. a wooden cube

51. Choose the correct definition for the word *course* as it is used in the eighth sentence of paragraph 7.
    a. part of a meal
    b. direction taken
    c. line of action
    d. progress of time

52. Choose the correct definition for the word *movements* as it is used in the second sentence of paragraph 6.
    a. organized activities
    b. motions of a person
    c. changes in location
    d. rhythms

53. Which document mentioned in the selection is a primary source?
    a. speech
    b. magazine
    c. letter
    d. newspaper

54. What is the date of this primary source?
    a. 1783
    b. 1883
    c. 1983
    d. 2002

55. In which country was this document written?
    a. United States
    b. England
    c. France
    d. Ireland

56. What fact did you learn from this document?
    a. People had high hopes for ballooning.
    b. People thought that ballooning was dangerous.
    c. People believed ballooning was only for scientists.
    d. People thought that ballooning was a passing fad.

Use the map on page T39 to answer questions 57 through 61.

57. For the last half of its trip, the *Double Eagle II* flew
    a. southwest.
    b. southeast.
    c. northeast.
    d. northwest.

58. According to the scale of miles, about how many kilometers is equal to 1,500 miles?
    a. 1,500
    b. 900
    c. 450
    d. 2,400

59. The *Double Eagle II* flew over the islands of
    a. Iceland, United Kingdom, and Greenland.
    b. Iceland, Ireland, and United Kingdom.
    c. Presque, Newfoundland, and Greenland.
    d. Newfoundland, Ireland, and United Kingdom.

60. Counting the country it left from and the country it arrived in, the *Double Eagle II* flew over
    a. three countries.
    b. four countries.
    c. five countries.
    d. six countries.

61. The *Double Eagle II* did *not* fly over which of the following countries?
    a. Iceland and Greenland
    b. Canada and the United Kingdom
    c. Greenland and Ireland
    d. France and the United States

Read the following selection. Then choose the best answer for each question.
Mark your answers on the answer sheet.

Winds of the World

1. Major winds blow across the world. They are called **global winds**. There are three kinds of global winds. They are called the **trade winds**, the **westerlies**, and the **easterlies**. The wind that you feel on a breezy day is part of the global winds.

2. Global winds are caused by heated air. Because of the shape of the Earth, the sun's rays strike the Earth at different angles. The air at the equator, the imaginary line around the middle of the Earth, receives the sun's **direct rays**. It is the warmest part of the Earth. Other areas of the Earth receive **indirect rays**, rays that are less direct than those at the equator. The areas near the poles receive rays that are the most indirect. These areas are the coldest parts of the Earth. This uneven heating of the Earth causes movement of air. Air that is warm rises, and air that is cold sinks.

Trade Winds

3. The **trade winds** blow north and south toward the equator. At the equator, the heated, moist air rises, forming clouds. This condition causes a great deal of rainfall. At about 30 degrees north and south of the equator, the air begins to cool and sink. Some of the sinking air travels back toward the equator. This movement of air creates winds that were once very useful to ships that crossed the ocean for trade. Thus, they were named *trade winds*.

4. Beyond the trade winds are regions of cooler air. The cooler air sinks directly down to the Earth's surface so that there is very little wind. Years ago, sailing ships often stalled there because of the lack of winds. Horses on the ships died when they ran out of food and water. The regions became known as the **horse latitudes**.

5. At the equator, there is also little wind. This area is called the **doldrums**.

Westerlies

6. Beyond the horse latitudes, some of the cool, sinking air moves toward the north and south poles. These winds are called the **westerlies** because they blow from the west. The westerlies blow away from the equator. Therefore, in the Northern Hemisphere, north of the equator, the westerlies blow from west to north. In the Southern Hemisphere, south of the equator, the westerlies blow from west to south.

Easterlies

7. The **easterlies** are quite different from the westerlies. As you can guess, the easterlies blow from the east. Unlike the westerlies, however, the easterlies blow from the North and South Poles toward the equator. Therefore, in the Northern Hemisphere, the easterlies blow to the south. In the Southern Hemisphere, the easterlies blow to the north.

8. Weather forecasters study the global winds carefully. They look for changes in the direction, speed, and temperature of these winds. This information helps them to forecast what the weather will be.

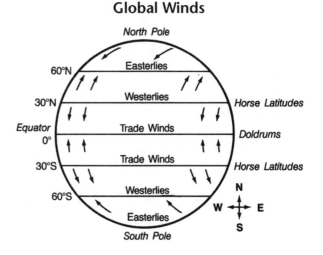

Global Winds

62. Global winds are caused by
   a. heated air.
   b. mountain ranges.
   c. oceans.
   d. the equator.

63. Sailing ships were often stalled at the horse latitudes because of
   a. warm air.
   b. torn sails.
   c. running out of fuel.
   d. the lack of winds.

64. The westerlies blow away from the equator. Therefore, in the Northern Hemisphere, the westerlies blow from
   a. west to south.
   b. west to north.
   c. west to east.
   d. north to west.

65. Which of the following is *not* a global wind?
   a. trade
   b. easterly
   c. horse latitude
   d. westerly

66. The westerlies and the easterlies are both named for the
   a. direction from which they blow.
   b. direction toward which they blow.
   c. direction they finally take.
   d. direct ways.

67. Which of the following is *not* a region of the earth?
   a. horse latitudes
   b. doldrums
   c. equator
   d. westerlies

68. The imaginary line around the middle of the earth is called the
   a. equator.
   b. horse latitudes.
   c. hemisphere.
   d. doldrums.

Use the diagram on page T43 to answer questions 69 through 72.

69. The horse latitudes are found around
   a. the equator.
   b. 60° north and 60° south of the equator.
   c. 30° north and 30° south of the equator.
   d. the North and South Poles.

70. Some of the westerlies are found
   a. between 0° and 30° south of the equator.
   b. between 30° north and 60° north of the equator.
   c. above 60° north and south of the equator.
   d. between 30° north and 30° south of the equator.

71. In the Northern Hemisphere, the trade winds blow from
   a. east to west.
   b. west to east.
   c. north to south.
   d. south to north.

72. In the Southern Hemisphere, the easterlies blow from
   a. southeast to northwest.
   b. northwest to southeast.
   c. northwest to southwest.
   d. southwest to northeast.

73. The main idea of paragraph 2 is stated in the
   a. first sentence.
   b. last sentence.
   c. third sentence.
   d. fourth sentence.

74. The main idea of paragraph 7 is stated in the
   a. third sentence.
   b. second sentence.
   c. last sentence.
   d. first sentence.

75. The main idea of paragraph 8 is
   a. stated in the second sentence.
   b. stated in the first sentence.
   c. stated in the last sentence.
   d. unstated.

76. The main idea of paragraph 4 is that there is an area beyond the trade-wind area, called the horse latitudes, that has very little wind. What detail supports this main idea?

    a. Sailing ships often stalled in this area.

    b. Years ago, horses were carried onboard ships.

    c. This area has very rough water.

    d. Cool winds killed horses there.

77. Which detail supports the main idea of paragraph 7?

    a. The easterlies blow in a northern direction.

    b. The easterlies blow toward the equator.

    c. The easterlies are found in both the Northern and Southern Hemispheres.

    d. The easterlies form into westerlies at the North Pole.

78. Choose the correct definition of the word *trade* as it is used in the sixth sentence of paragraph 3.

    a. a bargain or deal

    b. a kind of work or occupation

    c. a track or path

    d. a business of buying or selling

79. Choose the correct definition of the word *stalled* as it is used in the third sentence of paragraph 4.

    a. came to a standstill

    b. were kept in a stall

    c. avoided action

    d. spoke hesitantly

Questions 80 through 83 are word problems. Use another sheet of paper for your calculations.

80. In one desert, daytime temperatures rise to 120°F. Nighttime temperatures drop to 30°F. What is the difference between the day and night temperatures?

    a. 40°F

    b. 90°F

    c. 120°F

    d. 150°F

81. Camel A traveled 27 kilometers in one day. Camel B traveled twice as far. How many kilometers did camel B travel?

    a. 34 km

    b. 13.5 km

    c. 29 km

    d. 54 km

82. An airplane is flying at 300 kilometers per hour. The wind behind it is blowing at 60 kilometers per hour, making it move that much faster. How fast is the plane actually moving?

    a. 360 kph

    b. 1,800 kph

    c. 240 kph

    d. 300 kph

83. An airplane is flying at 325 kilometers per hour. A wind is blowing from directly ahead at 70 kilometers per hour, making it move that much slower. How fast is the plane actually moving?

    a. 2,275 kph

    b. 255 kph

    c. 395 kph

    d. 325 kph

A. Study the following dictionary entry. Then answer questions 84 through 87.

> **skin** (skin) *n.* **1** the tissue covering the body of persons and animals. **2** the hide or pelt of an animal [Early settlers made coats from beaver *skins*] **3** the outer covering of some fruits and vegetables [tomato *skin*]. **4** something like skin in looks or use. ◆*v.* **1** to remove the skin from [to *skin* a rabbit; to *skin* one's elbow by falling]. **2** to cheat or swindle; *used only in everyday talk.* —**skinned, skin´ning** —**by the skin of one's teeth,** by the smallest possible margin; barely. —**have a thin skin,** to be easily hurt by blame, insults, etc. —**save one's skin,** to keep one's self from getting killed or hurt; *used only in everyday talk.* —**skin´less** *adj.*

84. How many verb meanings are given?

    a. two

    b. four

    c. six

    d. one

85. Which of the following is the respelling of the entry word?

    a. skinless

    b. save one's skin

    c. skinned

    d. skin

86. Which of the following is a noun meaning?

    a. by the smallest possible margin

    b. the hide or pelt of an animal

    c. to cheat or swindle

    d. to remove skin from

87. The expression "have a thin skin" is

    a. a definition.

    b. an idiom.

    c. used only in everyday talk.

    d. a noun.

B. Study the following encyclopedia index. Then answer questions 88 through 91.

CANADA
  Agriculture **C:** 50–54
    government and **C:** 55–56
    honey **B:** 76
    irrigation **I:** 150
    wheat **C:** 50, **W:** 82 (tables)
  Climate **C:** 54
    Arctic **N:** 147–148
    rainfall **N:** 150 *with map*
  Education
    agricultural education **A:** 132
    colleges and universities **U:** 260
    primary and secondary schools **E:** 68–69
  Furs and fur trade **F:** 223–228, **C:** 56
    Hudson's Bay Co. **H:** 350
    seals **S:** 78–79
  Geological history **N:** 152–153
  History. *See in Index* Canadian history
  Indians **I:** 52, 53–54, 62
    art **A:** 214–217
    folktales **F:** 136–139

88. Where would you find information about agricultural education in Canada?

    a. **C:** 50–54

    b. **U:** 260

    c. **I:** 150

    d. **A:** 132

89. Where would you find a map showing rainfall in Canada?

    a. **N:** 150

    b. **C:** 54

    c. **N:** 147–148

    d. **I:** 150

90. Where would you find a table showing wheat production in Canada?

    a. **C:** 50

    b. **C:** 50–54

    c. **W:** 82

    d. **A:** 132

91. Where else in the index would you look for references to the history of Canada?
   a. under geological history
   b. under Hudson's Bay Co.
   c. under Canadian history
   d. under education

92. Choose the base word in *truthfulness*.
   a. truth
   b. ful
   c. truthful
   d. fulness

93. Choose the base word in *infielder*.
   a. in
   b. fielder
   c. infield
   d. field

94. Choose the suffix that will make the word *slow* mean "in a slow manner."
   a. -ness
   b. -ly
   c. -ful
   d. -er

95. Choose the suffix that will make the word *preach* mean "one who preaches."
   a. -er
   b. -en
   c. -able
   d. -ful

96. Choose the prefix that will make the word *fair* mean "not fair."
   a. pre-
   b. in-
   c. re-
   d. un-

97. Choose the prefix that will make the word *historic* mean "before history."
   a. pre-
   b. re-
   c. un-
   d. in-

98. Choose the prefix that will make the word *do* mean "do again."
   a. in-
   b. re-
   c. pre-
   d. un-

99. Choose the correct way to divide the word *unhappy* into syllables.
   a. un hap py
   b. un happ y
   c. un ha ppy
   d. unhap py

100. Choose the correct way to divide the word *simple* into syllables.
   a. si mple
   b. simp le
   c. sim ple
   d. si mp le

Assessment Tests for Level A are designed to measure students' level of achievement in each of the important comprehension and study skills that receive emphasis in all levels of *Be A Better Reader*. The tests may be used in conjunction with the tests provided in the *Assessment Manual* as pretests and/or posttests, depending on students' needs and your particular classroom management style. Combined with an overview of students' performance on each lesson, the tests should enable you to refine your assessment of students' performance and determine students' readiness to advance to the next level. The four tests in Level A can be administered separately or at one time, depending on the time available. Because directions are provided for each test, students should be able to take the tests independently. The skill for each test item is identified in the Answer Key below. Following the skill is the number of the lesson or the lessons in Level A where that skill is treated as a Skill Focus. To simplify the scoring process, you can use the Answer Key to make a scoring mask, which when placed over the answer sheet, reveals only those items that are correct. The total score is equal to the number of correct items. Criterion scores are not specified in this book, but you can refer to the Scoring Rubric in the *Assessment Manual* for more information on grading.

Test 1

1. c Understanding character (43)
2. a Understanding character (43)
3. a Understanding character (43)
4. b Understanding character (43)
5. d Recognizing sequence of events (1)
6. a Recognizing sequence of events (1)
7. c Recognizing sequence of events (1)
8. d Recognizing sequence of events (1)
9. b Identifying setting (13)
10. c Identifying setting (13)
11. b Identifying setting (13)
12. b Identifying setting (13)
13. a Identifying conflict and resolution (24)
14. d Identifying conflict and resolution (24)
15. b Identifying conflict and resolution (24)
16. b Identifying conflict and resolution (24)
17. c Inferring theme (33)
18. d Inferring theme (33)
19. a Inferring theme (33)
20. c Inferring theme (33)
21. b Making inferences (49, 57)
22. a Making inferences (49, 57)
23. d Making inferences (49, 57)
24. b Recognizing multiple meanings of words (59)
25. d Using comparison context clues (13)
26. c Using detail context clues (33, 44, 45)

Test 2

27. b Identifying cause and effect (2, 26)
28. a Identifying cause and effect (2, 26)
29. c Identifying cause and effect (2, 26)
30. c Comparing and contrasting (25)
31. d Comparing and contrasting (25)
32. b Comparing and contrasting (25)
33. c Comparing and contrasting (25)
34. a Using synonym context clues (1, 24, 26, 43, 46)
35. d Distinguishing fact from opinion (39)
36. c Distinguishing fact from opinion (39)
37. b Distinguishing fact from opinion (39)
38. a Distinguishing fact from opinion (39)
39. a Making inferences (49, 57)
40. b Making inferences (49, 57)
41. d Making inferences (49, 57)
42. c Making inferences (49, 57)
43. b Making inferences (49, 57)
44. d Identifying the main idea (6, 17, 18)
45. a Identifying the main idea (6, 17, 18)
46. b Identifying the main idea (6, 17, 18)
47. b Identifying the main idea and supporting details (40, 45)
48. a Identifying the main idea and supporting details (40, 45)

49. d Identifying the main idea and supporting details (40, 45)
50. c Recognizing multiple meanings of words (59)
51. b Recognizing multiple meanings of words (59)
52. c Recognizing multiple meanings of words (59)
53. d Using a primary source (44)
54. a Using a primary source (44)
55. c Using a primary source (44)
56. a Using a primary source (44)
57. b Using a map (14, 54, 56)
58. d Using a map (14, 54, 56)
59. d Using a map (14, 54, 56)
60. c Using a map (14, 54, 56)
61. a Using a map (14, 54, 56)

Test 3

62. a Identifying cause and effect (2, 26)
63. d Identifying cause and effect (2, 26)
64. b Identifying cause and effect (2, 26)
65. c Classifying (3)
66. a Classifying (3)
67. d Classifying (3)
68. a Using appositive context clues (15, 56)
69. c Reading text with diagrams (15, 35)
70. b Reading text with diagrams (15, 35)
71. c Reading text with diagrams (15, 35)
72. a Reading text with diagrams (15, 35)
73. a Identifying the main idea (6, 17, 18)
74. d Identifying the main idea (6, 17, 18)
75. b Identifying the main idea (6, 17, 18)

76. a Identifying the main idea and supporting details (40, 45)
77. b Identifying the main idea and supporting details (40, 45)
78. d Recognizing multiple meanings of words (59)
79. a Recognizing multiple meanings of words (59)
80. b Solving word problems (4)
81. d Solving word problems (4)
82. a Solving word problems (4)
83. b Solving word problems (4)

Test 4

84. a Using a dictionary entry (52)
85. d Using a dictionary entry (52)
86. b Using a dictionary entry (52)
87. b Using a dictionary entry (52)
88. d Using an encyclopedia (62)
89. a Using an encyclopedia (62)
90. c Using an encyclopedia (62)
91. c Using an encyclopedia (62)
92. a Recognizing base words (29)
93. d Recognizing base words (29)
94. b Adding suffixes to words (29, 61)
95. a Adding suffixes to words (29, 61)
96. d Adding prefixes to words (29, 60)
97. a Adding prefixes to words (29, 60)
98. b Adding prefixes to words (29, 60)
99. a Dividing words into syllables (30, 31, 38, 47, 48)
100. c Dividing words into syllables (30, 31, 38, 47, 48)

Name _____

STUDENT ANSWER SHEET

	Test 1					Test 2					Test 3					Test 4			
	a	b	c	d		a	b	c	d		a	b	c	d		a	b	c	d
1.	○	○	○	○	27.	○	○	○	○	62.	○	○	○	○	84.	○	○	○	○
2.	○	○	○	○	28.	○	○	○	○	63.	○	○	○	○	85.	○	○	○	○
3.	○	○	○	○	29.	○	○	○	○	64.	○	○	○	○	86.	○	○	○	○
4.	○	○	○	○	30.	○	○	○	○	65.	○	○	○	○	87.	○	○	○	○
5.	○	○	○	○	31.	○	○	○	○	66.	○	○	○	○	88.	○	○	○	○
6.	○	○	○	○	32.	○	○	○	○	67.	○	○	○	○	89.	○	○	○	○
7.	○	○	○	○	33.	○	○	○	○	68.	○	○	○	○	90.	○	○	○	○
8.	○	○	○	○	34.	○	○	○	○	69.	○	○	○	○	91.	○	○	○	○
9.	○	○	○	○	35.	○	○	○	○	70.	○	○	○	○	92.	○	○	○	○
10.	○	○	○	○	36.	○	○	○	○	71.	○	○	○	○	93.	○	○	○	○
11.	○	○	○	○	37.	○	○	○	○	72.	○	○	○	○	94.	○	○	○	○
12.	○	○	○	○	38.	○	○	○	○	73.	○	○	○	○	95.	○	○	○	○
13.	○	○	○	○	39.	○	○	○	○	74.	○	○	○	○	96.	○	○	○	○
14.	○	○	○	○	40.	○	○	○	○	75.	○	○	○	○	97.	○	○	○	○
15.	○	○	○	○	41.	○	○	○	○	76.	○	○	○	○	98.	○	○	○	○
16.	○	○	○	○	42.	○	○	○	○	77.	○	○	○	○	99.	○	○	○	○
17.	○	○	○	○	43.	○	○	○	○	78.	○	○	○	○	100.	○	○	○	○
18.	○	○	○	○	44.	○	○	○	○	79.	○	○	○	○					
19.	○	○	○	○	45.	○	○	○	○	80.	○	○	○	○					
20.	○	○	○	○	46.	○	○	○	○	81.	○	○	○	○					
21.	○	○	○	○	47.	○	○	○	○	82.	○	○	○	○					
22.	○	○	○	○	48.	○	○	○	○	83.	○	○	○	○					
23.	○	○	○	○	49.	○	○	○	○										
24.	○	○	○	○	50.	○	○	○	○										
25.	○	○	○	○	51.	○	○	○	○										
26.	○	○	○	○	52.	○	○	○	○										
					53.	○	○	○	○										
					54.	○	○	○	○										
					55.	○	○	○	○										
					56.	○	○	○	○										
					57.	○	○	○	○										
					58.	○	○	○	○										
					59.	○	○	○	○										
					60.	○	○	○	○										
					61.	○	○	○	○										

	Test 1	Test 2	Test 3	Test 4			
Number Possible	26	35	22	17	Total	100
Number Incorrect	_____	_____	_____	_____	Total	_____
Score	_____	_____	_____	_____	Total	_____

CLASS RECORD-KEEPING CHART

Test Item	Skill	Name									
1–4	Understanding character										
5–8	Recognizing sequence of events										
9–12	Identifying setting										
13–16	Identifying conflict and resolution										
17–20	Inferring theme										
21–23, 39–43	Making inferences										
24, 50–52, 78–79	Recognizing multiple meanings of words										
25–26, 34, 68	Using context clues										
27–29, 62–64	Identifying cause and effect										
30–33	Comparing and contrasting										
35–38	Distinguishing fact from opinion										
44–46, 73–75	Identifying the main idea										
47–49, 76–77	Identifying the main idea and supporting details										
53–56	Using a primary source										
57–61	Using a map										
65–67	Classifying										
69–72	Reading text with diagrams										
80–83	Solving word problems										
84–87	Using a dictionary entry										
88–91	Using an encyclopedia										
92–100	Recognizing base words, prefixes, suffixes, and syllables										
	Total Incorrect										
	Score (subtract total incorrect from 100)										

"WHAT THE RESEARCH SAYS"

Teaching students to organize the ideas that they are reading about in a systematic, visual graph benefits the ability of the students to remember what they read and may transfer, in general, to better comprehension.

National Institute of Child Health and Human Development

(see page T2)

Research in reading since the early 1980s has led to some major inroads in helping readers comprehend more effectively. This research shows that building on a learner's schema, or prior knowledge, together with scaffolding, or support mechanisms, enables readers to make the necessary connections that improve comprehension. The graphic organizer, used in tandem with a reader's background knowledge, provides the necessary support that allows learners to bridge gaps in their understanding.

According to David Hyerle (*Visual Tools for Constructing Knowledge,* 1996) graphic organizers foster a collaborative, interactive style of learning. Hyerle introduces the term *visual tools*, which he feels broadens the concept of the term *organizer* beyond the sole purpose of helping students organize information. Indeed, visual tools can be used for brainstorming and facilitating dialogue, open-ended thinking, mediation, metacognition, theory development, and self-assessment. The real value of introducing graphic organizers or visual tools is to provide students with a lifetime set of skills that they can use independently to become problem solvers and learn to read, write, and think with greater facility and meaning.

Be A Better Reader incorporates the strategic use of graphic organizers into the selection lessons in every level of the program. Once students begin internalizing these organizers, they can learn to use them as their own visual tools when encountering similar reading and thinking problem-solving situations.

Graphic organizers used in *Be A Better Reader*:
- *Cause-and-Effect Charts*
- *Character Traits Map*
- *Classification Chart*
- *Comparison-and-Contrast Chart*
- *Details About Setting Map*
- *Drawing Conclusions Map*
- *Fact-and-Opinion Chart*
- *Flowchart*
- *Generalization Chart*
- *Idea Web*
- *Inference Chart*
- *KWL Chart*
- *Main Idea and Supporting Details Map*
- *Outline*
- *Plot Diagram*
- *Prediction Chart*
- *Pros and Cons Chart*
- *Story Map*
- *Sequence Chart*
- *Steps in a Process Map*
- *Venn Diagram*
- *Who, What, Where, When, Why Chart*

This comprehensive set of organizers, used throughout *Be A Better Reader*, provides scaffolding activities to support the improvement of all students' literacy development. They are particularly useful for struggling readers and English language learners who will learn to use organizers to guide them on the way toward independent reading, learning, and problem solving.

John Edwin Cowen, Ed.D.
Peter Sammartino School of Education
Fairleigh Dickinson University

Name _____ Date _____

SEQUENCE CHART

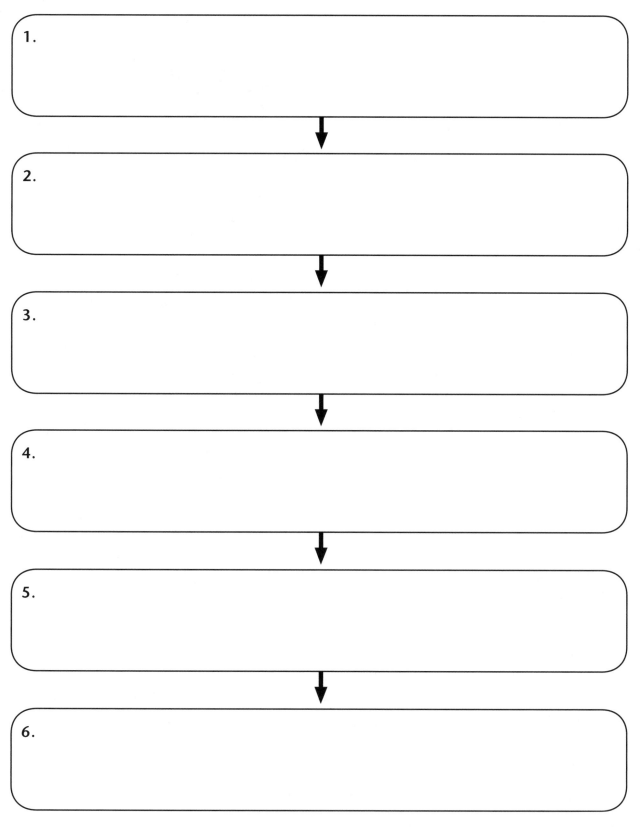

1.

2.

3.

4.

5.

6.

CAUSE-AND-EFFECT CHARTS

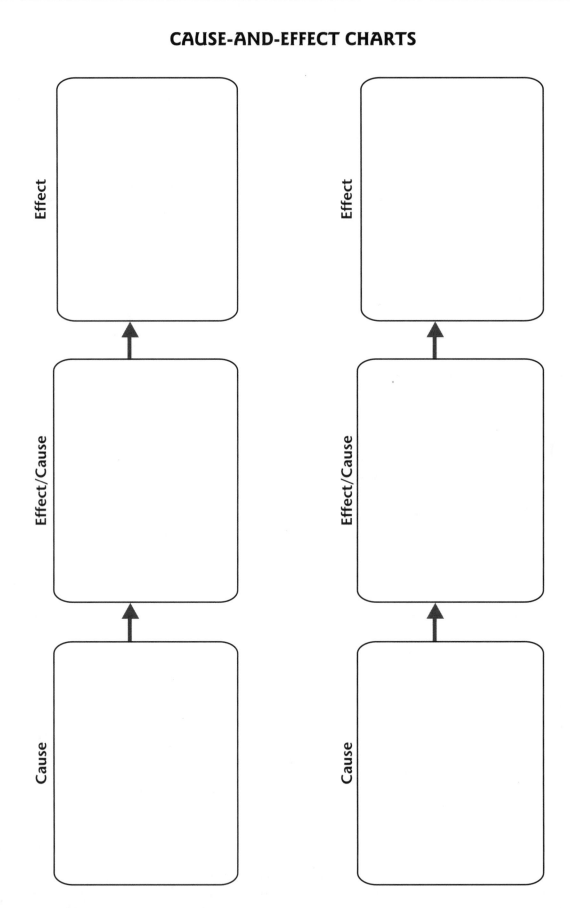

IDEA WEB

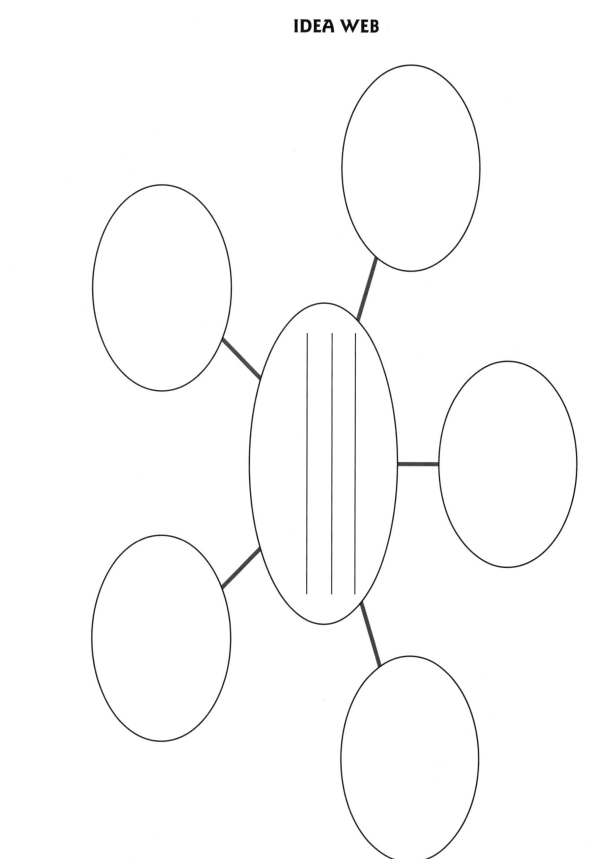

DETAILS ABOUT SETTING MAP

Topic: _____

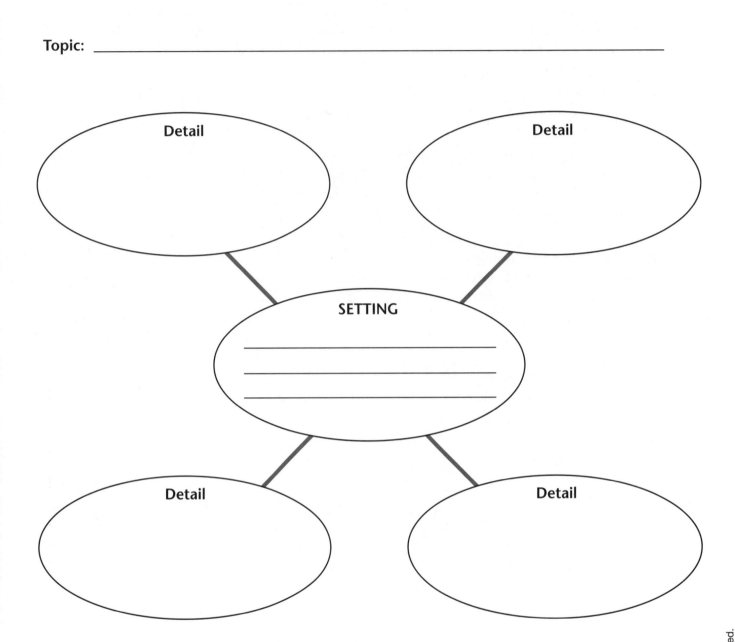

Detail

Detail

SETTING
_____
_____
_____

Detail

Detail

KWL CHART

K What I Know	W What I Want to Know	L What I Learned

Name _____ Date _____

PREDICTION CHART

Page	What I Predict	What Happens

COMPARISON-AND-CONTRAST CHART

Things Being Compared	How They Are Alike	How They Are Different

VENN DIAGRAM

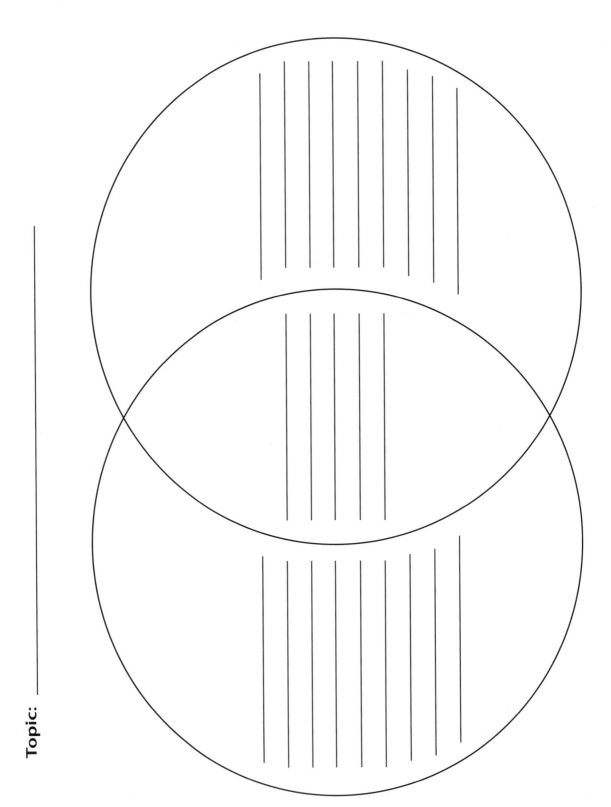

Topic: _____

Name _____   Date _____

MAIN IDEA AND SUPPORTING DETAILS MAP

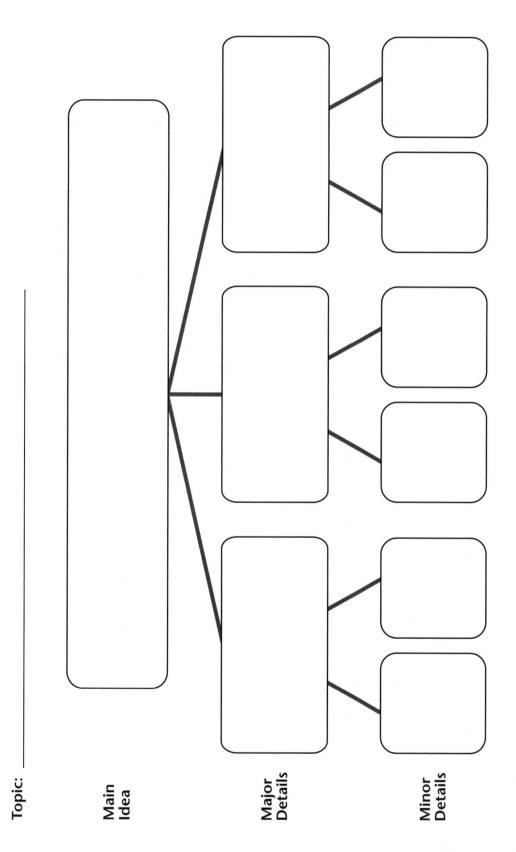

Topic: _____

Main Idea

Major Details

Minor Details

Name _____ **Date** _____

INFERENCE CHART

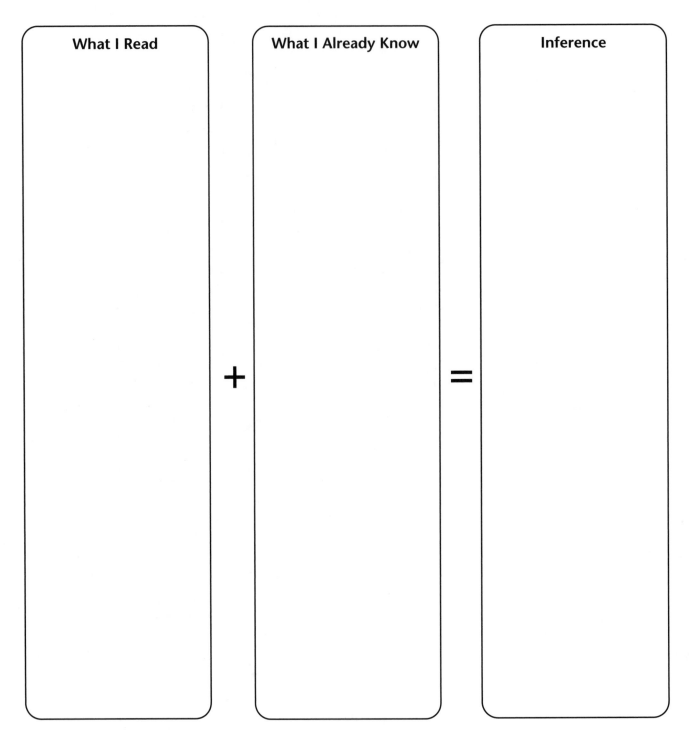

What I Read

+

What I Already Know

=

Inference

CHARACTER TRAITS MAP

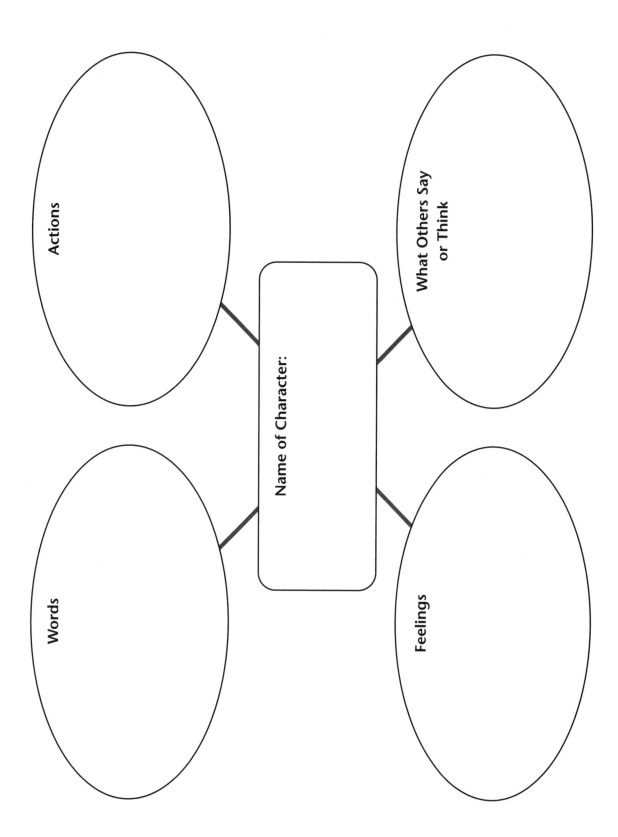

Actions

What Others Say
or Think

Name of Character:

Words

Feelings

Name _____ **Date** _____

STORY MAP

Story Title: _____

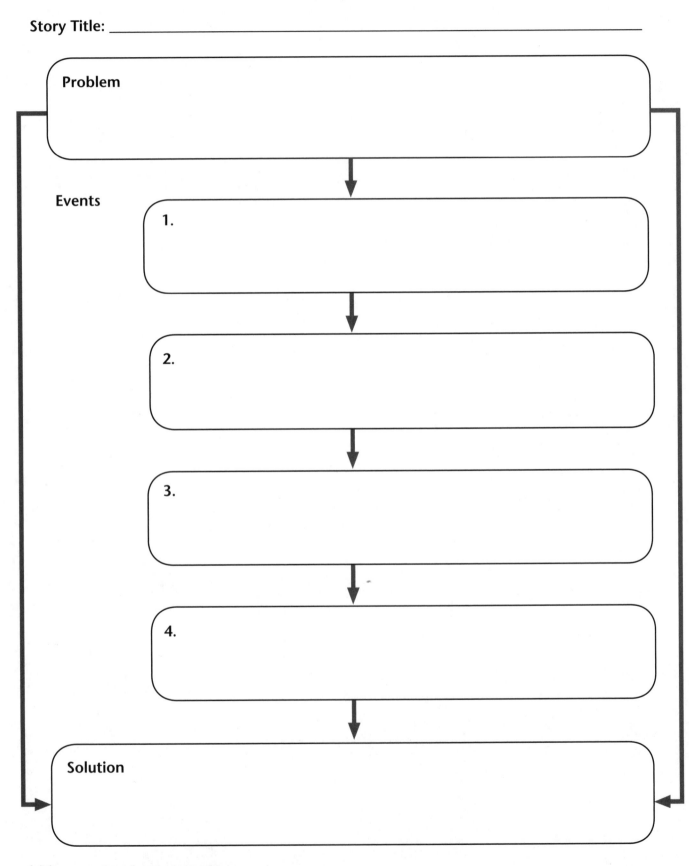

Problem

Events

1.

2.

3.

4.

Solution

Name _____   Date _____

OUTLINE

Topic: _____

I. _____

    A. _____

        1. _____

        2. _____

    B. _____

        1. _____

        2. _____

    C. _____

        1. _____

        2. _____

II. _____

    A. _____

        1. _____

        2. _____

    B. _____

        1. _____

        2. _____

    C. _____

        1. _____

        2. _____

Name _____   Date _____

PROS AND CONS CHART

Topic: _____

Pros	Cons

WHO, WHAT, WHERE, WHEN, WHY CHART

WHO?	
WHAT?	
WHERE?	
WHEN?	
WHY?	

LESSON 1

> **Skill: Sequence of Events** (pages 6–11)
>
> **LITERATURE SELECTION: Broken Voyage**
>
> **OBJECTIVES:**
> ▶ Recognize sequence of events
> ▶ Use synonyms as context clues
>
> **CONTEXT CLUE WORDS:** *course, charts, flare*
>
> **ESL/ELL WORDS:** *cabin, on deck, frozen*
>
> **GRAPHIC ORGANIZER:** Sequence Chart, p. T53

_____ **SELECTION SUMMARY** _____

"Broken Voyage" is the true story about the Robertsons, an English family who set out to sail around the world. In the Pacific Ocean, however, their boat was rammed and sunk by killer whales. Escaping into a small raft and lifeboat, the three teenaged children and their parents drifted for five weeks until they were finally rescued by a Japanese fishing vessel.

▶ BEFORE READING

Have students read the Background Information about sailing around the world on page 6. Invite volunteers to share what they know about taking a sea voyage on a sailboat. *What dangerous events might happen?* (storms, getting lost, shark attacks)

Teaching Sequence of Events

1. Review that stories have a beginning, a middle, and an end. We get to know the characters and setting in the beginning of the story. In the middle, we see the problems and difficulties the characters face. At the end, we see how these problems are solved.

2. Invite a volunteer to briefly retell the events of a familiar childhood tale, such as "Goldilocks and the Three Bears," as you list the events in correct sequence on the chalkboard. Have students group the story events into the beginning, the middle, and the end. Point out that you need a logical sequence of order of events for the story to make sense.

3. Direct students to complete the sequence chart in the Skill Focus on page 6.

Teaching Context Clues

1. Explain that synonyms are words with the same or similar meanings. Write the word *big* on the chalkboard, and ask students to name its synonyms. (large, huge, gigantic, mammoth)

2. Write *girl, boy, male, female.* Ask students to match the synonyms. Then ask students to provide synonym pairs of their own.

3. Have students read the Context Clues section on page 6 and complete the activity using synonyms in context.

4. Write the context clue words *course, charts,* and *flare* on the chalkboard or a word wall, and remind students to find synonym clues for these words as they read the selection.

Previewing the Text

Have students preview the selection, studying the title, map, and photo to predict what will happen. Then distribute a copy of the Sequence Chart for students to complete as they read, noting the sequence of events in the Robertsons' journey.

Purpose-Setting Question

Why is this story called "Broken Voyage"?

▶ DURING READING

As students read, remind them to complete their Sequence Charts and to look for synonyms that explain the meanings of the three underlined words.

▶ AFTER READING

Ask students to share the events they listed on their Sequence Charts. Then have students answer the purpose-setting question and complete the activities on pages 9–11.

Reading-Writing Connection

Before students write their lists of items to take on the life raft, have small groups brainstorm a master list to choose from.

> **ESL/ELL Strategy**
>
> **ROLE-PLAYING** Have pairs of students take turns retelling the story as if they were Neil, Sandy, or Douglas Robertson. Encourage them to use first-person pronouns.

Skill: Cause and Effect (pages 12–16)

SOCIAL STUDIES SELECTION: The Whaling Industry

OBJECTIVES:
▸ Identify cause and effect
▸ Use definitions as context clues

CONTEXT CLUE WORDS: *harpoons, spermaceti, ambergris*

ESL/ELL WORDS: *washed up, buggy whips, school*

GRAPHIC ORGANIZER: Cause-and-Effect Charts, p. T54

_____ **SELECTION SUMMARY** _____

"The Whaling Industry" traces the history of whaling from ancient times to the present. Whale oil and other whale products played an important economic role in the eighteenth and nineteenth centuries until international efforts to ban the hunting of endangered whales caused its decline in the twentieth century.

▸ BEFORE READING

Have students read the Background Information on the whaling industry on page 12, and ask them to share any knowledge they have about whales. Discuss why it is important to protect endangered animals such as whales.

Teaching Cause and Effect

1. Review that a cause is a reason something happens. An effect is what happens as a result. Explain that the question "What happened?" will help in recognizing effects. The question "Why did it happen?" will help in finding a cause.

2. Discuss a recent event in your school or community. Ask: *What happened? Why did it happen?* On the chalkboard, draw and label two small boxes—one box *Cause* and the other *Effect*. Write the cause in the first box and the effect in the other. Draw an arrow between the two boxes to give students a visual understanding of the cause-and-effect relationship.

3. Direct students to complete the Cause-and-Effect Charts in the Skill Focus activity on page 12.

Teaching Context Clues

1. Review that definitions provide meanings for words, and that sometimes a new word is defined in a sentence following its first use in a selection.

2. Write the following on the chalkboard: *Many groups tried to ban whaling. To ban something is to stop it by making it illegal.* Have students point out the definition of *ban*. (to stop something by making it illegal)

3. Have students read the Context Clues section on page 12 and complete the activity.

4. Write the context clue words *harpoons, spermaceti,* and *ambergris* on the chalkboard or word wall. Remind students to look for definition clues for these words as they read "The Whaling Industry."

Previewing the Text

Have students preview the selection, studying the title, the section headings, and the illustrations. Ask students to think about possible causes and effects for each section headings. Then distribute copies of the Cause-and-Effect Charts, and remind students to list causes and effects as they read.

Purpose-Setting Question

Why did the American whaling industry grow quickly in the eighteenth century and then decline in the nineteenth century?

▸ DURING READING

As students read, remind them to look for causes and effects. Also have them look for the definitions of the three underlined words.

▸ AFTER READING

Have students share some of the causes and effects listed on their charts. Then invite them to answer the purpose-setting question and complete the activities on pages 15–16.

Reading-Writing Connection

Have groups of students debate the issue of outlawing whaling before writing their opinions on the subject. List on the chalkboard any facts, examples, or reasons mentioned. Encourage students to use these details as they write.

ESL/ELL Strategy

SUMMARIZING Have pairs of students use their completed Cause-and-Effect Charts to orally summarize the selection's main ideas.

Skill: Classifying (pages 17–21)

SCIENCE SELECTION: Three Groups of Water Animals

OBJECTIVES:

▶ Classify information

▶ Use pictures as context clues

CONTEXT CLUE WORDS: *scallops, lobsters*

ESL/ELL WORDS: *scales, fins, joints*

GRAPHIC ORGANIZER: Idea Web, p. T55

_____ **SELECTION SUMMARY** _____

"Three Groups of Water Animals" focuses on the distinctive features of fish, mollusks, and crustaceans that scientists use to classify these animals. By focusing on these three categories, students gain practice with classifying.

▶ BEFORE READING

Have students read the Background Information on page 17. Then, list on the chalkboard students' suggestions of life forms that reside in the world's oceans. Explain that scientists have ways of deciding how to classify animals. Ask students to suggest some ways. (whether they have skeletons or shells; whether they have legs; how they breathe; how they eat; where they live)

Teaching Classifying

1. Ask students to name some ways in which they classify or group items in everyday life. For example, music CDs might be classified as rock, rap, country, or jazz. Explain that in order to classify, we think about how items in the same group are alike and how they are different from items in other groups.

2. Have students classify these animals into two groups: dog, fox, cat, hamster, bear, skunk. Have them explain how they made their decisions. (A dog, a cat, and a hamster are all pets. A fox, a bear, and a skunk are all wild.)

3. Direct students to read the Skill Focus on page 17 and complete the charts to classify water animals.

Teaching Context Clues

1. Explain that photographs or illustrations in a science and social studies textbook often contain clues to the meanings of words.

2. Preview the photographs in the selection, and ask students what they can learn about haddock, scallops, and lobsters by studying the photographs. (Haddock have scales. Scallops have a shell. Lobsters have an exoskeleton.) List the information on the chalkboard.

3. Have students read the Context Clues section and complete the activity.

4. Write the context clue words *scallops* and *lobsters* on the chalkboard or word wall, and remind students to find picture clues for them as they read the selection.

Previewing the Text

Have students preview the selection, by making the connection between the section headings and the photos. (Each photo represents one of the three groups of water animals outlined in each section.) Distribute three copies of the Idea Web to each student. Have students write *Fish* in the center of one web, *Mollusks* in the second web, and *Crustaceans* in the third web. Ask students to fill in the webs with details about each type of ocean animal as they read.

Purpose-Setting Question

What are some important differences between fish, mollusks, and crustaceans?

▶ DURING READING

As students read, have them classify by adding details to their Idea Webs. Remind them to study the photos to learn more about the underlined words.

▶ AFTER READING

Have students share details from their Idea Webs. Then have them answer the purpose-setting question and complete the activities on pages 19–21.

Reading-Writing Connection

Before sending students to the library or the Internet to research the importance of fish as food, ask: *What important nutrients do fish provide? In which parts of the world do people eat the most fish? Why?* Encourage students to find answers to these questions before they start writing their reports.

ESL/ELL Strategy

USING VISUALS Have pairs of students make sketches of imaginary fish, mollusks, and crustaceans. Their creatures should show the distinctive features of each category. Students can invent names for their animals and discuss what they look like.

Skill: Word Problems (pages 22–25)

MATHEMATICS SELECTION: Solving Word Problems

OBJECTIVES:
- Solve word problems
- Use word clues to determine mathematical operations

ESL/ELL WORDS: *label of measurement, diagram, key word*

GRAPHIC ORGANIZER: Sequence Chart, p. T53

_____ **SELECTION SUMMARY** _____

"Solving Word Problems" uses information about whales and the ocean to introduce and explain the five-step process of solving word problems. The focus is on simple problems that involve addition or subtraction.

▶ BEFORE READING

Have students read the Background Information on page 22, and ask them to recall some recent real-life situations in which they needed to use their math skills to solve a problem. Students might draw examples from sports, games, travel, home projects, shopping, and so on. Did they need to add, subtract, multiply, or divide to solve the problem?

Teaching Word Problems

1. Review that a word problem suggests a situation that requires one or more mathematical operations to solve. Point out that there are five steps to complete them.

2. Have volunteers read aloud and explain the five steps in the Skill Focus on page 22. List these on a classroom chart for student reference.

3. Ask students to think about the following word problem: *There are 25 students in the class. Thirteen returned permission slips for a field trip. How many more students still need to return permission slips?* Ask students to solve the problem (12 students) and explain how they did so. (Subtract 13 from 25.)

4. Have students answer the question in the Skill Focus section.

Teaching Word Clues

1. On the chalkboard draw two columns. List the words associated with addition (*in all, together, total,* and *sum*) in one column and those with subtraction (*difference, less, more, shorter, longer, left,* and *change*) in the other columns.

2. Call on volunteers to give examples of word problems that contain these signal words. Have other students decide whether they need to add or subtract and explain their decisions.

3. Have students read the Word Clues section on page 22 and complete the activity.

4. Remind students to look for the signal words as they read the selection.

Previewing the Text

Have students preview the selection, studying the diagrams and the section headings, which correspond to the five steps to solve word problems. Distribute copies of the Sequence Chart. As they read each word problem in the selection, have students fill in the chart with the five steps that are to be followed in order to solve it.

Purpose-Setting Question

What are the steps to follow to solve word problems?

▶ DURING READING

As students read, stress that the section headings are the five steps to follow when solving a word problem. Remind students to look for word clues that signal addition or subtraction.

▶ AFTER READING

Ask volunteers to review their Sequence Charts and to answer the purpose-setting question. Then have students complete the activities on pages 24–25.

Reading-Writing Connection

To find the facts they need to write word problems, suggest that students look up *fish, crustacean,* or *mollusk* in an encyclopedia and take notes on any number facts they find.

ESL/ELL Strategy

PERSONALIZING THE LESSON Have pairs of students write simple word problems based on people they know, objects they own, and distances in the classroom or at home. Partners can exchange papers and solve each other's problems.

Skill: Consonants (page 26)

OBJECTIVE:
▶ Recognize initial and final consonant sounds

Teaching the Skill

1. Remind students that the letters *a, e, i, o,* and *u* are vowels and that the remaining letters of the alphabet are consonants. Have students take turns naming the consonants in order and then saying the sound or sounds they associate with each.

2. Point to objects in the classroom, such as a book, a map, a pen, and a dictionary. Ask students to say the name of each object and to name the consonant sound that begins each word. Point to the same objects again. This time, have students note the consonant sound at the end of each word.

3. Direct students to the group of pictures in Exercise A on page 26. Call on individuals to say the name of each picture in the first row, emphasizing the beginning sound of each word. Then have them name the consonant that stands for each beginning sound.

4. Have students complete the remainder of the exercises on the page independently.

ESL/ELL Strategy

USING REALIA Distribute magazines to partners. Assign them five different consonant sounds. Ask them to cut out pictures of at least four objects that begin or end with each of their assigned consonant sounds. Students write the word for each picture and label the beginning or ending consonant sound for each one. If appropriate, students can tape the pictures onto sheets of construction paper to make a consonant minibook.

Extension Activity

Challenge students to write at least five nonsense sentences in which all the words begin or end with the same consonant sound. For example: *Father found five fantastic fossils for Fanny.*

Skill: Main Idea (page 27)

OBJECTIVE:
▶ Identify the main idea

Teaching the Skill

1. Stress that the main idea is the most important idea in a paragraph and that it is often stated directly as one sentence in a paragraph. Point out that the other sentences in a paragraph usually give details that tell more about the main idea.

2. Distribute the following as a handout:

   The typical beach has many different features. Often there are dunes, which are deep banks of sand. Part of the beach may be rocky, covered with boulders or pebbles. There may also be a marsh or a wetland on the beach.

   Have students underline the sentence they think states the main idea and circle the other sentences that give details supporting the main idea. Point out that the first sentence is the main idea because it is most important. The other sentences give more information about it or support it.

3. Read aloud the introductory paragraph and directions on page 27. Call on a volunteer to read paragraph 1. Ask students to decide which sentence in the paragraph states the main idea and to give reasons for their choices.

4. Have students complete the rest of the exercise independently.

ESL/ELL Strategy

ORGANIZING INFORMATION Hand out a copy of the Main Idea and Supporting Details Map on page T61 to partners. Have one partner read aloud one of the paragraphs from the lesson. Then have the other partner write the main idea in the correct place on the graphic organizer. Once they have identified the main idea, they can write the other sentences in the boxes labeled *Supporting Details.*

Extension Activity

Have students study the paragraphs from a chapter in one of their textbooks. Challenge students to find examples of paragraphs that have their main ideas stated in a sentence other than the first sentence.

Skill: Consonant Blends (page 28)

OBJECTIVE:
▶ Recognize consonant blends: *r* blends

Teaching the Skill

1. Ask students if they have ever used a blender to blend together fruit and ice cream or other foods. Explain that they will work with words that begin with two consonants that are "blended" together. List the following consonant blends on the chalkboard: *br, cr, dr, fr, gr, pr,* and *tr.* Explain that these are called "blends" because two letters come together in such a way that the consonant sound of each is heard.

2. Ask volunteers to name some words that begin with each blend and write them on the chalkboard below the correct blend. Emphasize the beginning sounds of each word. Some words are *bring, crumb, drink, fresh, grow, provide,* and *treat.*

3. Direct students to read the first paragraph on page 28. Explain that the blends in the box are called *r* blends because the consonant *r* is the second consonant in each of these blends.

4. Ask students to study the pictures in the first row and ask a volunteer to say the name of each picture, emphasizing the beginning sounds. Have students name the *r* blend.

5. Direct students to complete the rest of the exercise independently.

ESL/ELL Strategy

ORGANIZING INFORMATION Ask partners to draw seven columns on a sheet of paper. Have them write one of the *r* blends as a label at the top of each column and classify the words from the lesson by writing all the *br* words in one column, the *cr* words in the next, and so on. Partners take turns reading aloud each column of words.

Extension Activity

Challenge students to create tongue twisters that make use of one or more *r* blend. For example: *Crates of grapes and drapes are great.*

Skill: Consonant Blends (page 29)

OBJECTIVE:
▶ Recognize consonant blends: *l* blends

Teaching the Skill

1. Remind students that two consonants can be blended together such that you can hear the sounds of both consonants.

2. Say the following *l* blends as you list them on the chalkboard: *bl, cl, fl, gl, pl,* and *sl.* Ask volunteers to name words that begin with these blends. Write each example word next to the appropriate blend. Some words are *blue, clam, flap, glow, please,* and *slide.*

3. Ask a student to read aloud the definition of a consonant blend at the top of page 29. Then direct students to the first row of pictures. Ask individuals to say the name of each picture, emphasizing the beginning sounds of each word. Have students name the *l* blend.

4. Have students complete the remainder of the exercise independently.

ESL/ELL Strategy

USING RESOURCES Ask partners to use a dictionary to find additional, familiar words that begin with the blends *bl, cl, fl, gl, pl,* and *sl.* Have partners say each word, emphasizing the sound of the blend.

Extension Activity

Challenge students to write nonsense rhyming lines using the *r* blends and *l* blends they learned in Lessons 7 and 8. Suggest that the rhyming end-of-line words begin with the blends. As examples, you might share these rhymes: *How could she <u>trip</u> on a paper <u>clip</u>? The bride handed the <u>groom</u> a seven-foot <u>broom</u>. I've never seen <u>glue</u> that was colored bright <u>blue</u>.*

LESSON 9

Skill: Consonant Blends (page 30)

OBJECTIVE:
▶ Recognize consonant blends: *s* blends

Teaching the Skill

1. Review the definition of a consonant blend—two consonants that blend together so the sound each makes is heard.

2. List the following *s* blends on the chalkboard: *sc, sm, sn, sp, st, sw*. Have students say each *s* blend. Challenge students to name objects in the classroom that begin with these blends. (*students, spelling, scarf, snacks, sneakers, small, sweater,* and so on) Write each example next to the appropriate blend.

3. Have students read aloud the information about consonant blends on page 30. Then ask them to study the pictures in the first row and say the name of each object, emphasizing the beginning sound of each word. Have students name the *s* blend.

4. Have students complete the remainder of the exercise independently.

ESL/ELL Strategy

IDENTIFYING ESSENTIAL VOCABULARY Have students form small groups. Students take turns thinking of a word beginning with one of the *s* blends in the lesson. The first student gives one clue about the word. For example, for the word *stapler*, the student might say, "It is a tool." If no one guesses the word, more clues are offered until the riddle is solved.

Extension Activity

Have small groups of students choose one of the *s* blends. Each student in the group then says a word beginning with the blend and play proceeds around the circle. The winner is the student who remains after the other players can no longer think of words beginning with the blend.

LESSON 10

Skill: Long and Short Vowel Sounds (page 31)

OBJECTIVE:
▶ Recognize long and short vowel sounds

Teaching the Skill

1. Ask students to name the five vowels. (a, e, i, o, u) Review that each vowel can have a long sound or a short sound. The long sound is the name of the vowel itself.

2. Invite students to read the following list of words from the chalkboard: *ace, ease, ice, owe,* and *use*.

3. Ask what they notice about these words. (They each have two vowels. One is silent *e*.) Point out that these words have long vowel sounds. Pronounce the short vowel sound for each vowel, and ask students to name some words that have short vowel sounds, such as *at, elf, it, odd,* and *under*. List these as well. Ask what they notice about these words. (The words have one vowel, which is not at the end of the word.)

4. Have a volunteer read aloud the first paragraph on page 31. Then, have students complete the exercises and rules independently.

5. Explain that throughout this book, students will learn a series of rules to decide whether a vowel sound in a word is long or short. Review with students the two rules on page 31.

ESL/ELL Strategy

ORGANIZING INFORMATION Ask partners to draw two columns with the headings *Rule 1* and *Rule 2*. In each column, have students list five or more words that follow the rule.

Extension Activity

List the following on the chalkboard:

> *Rule 1: home, fire, make, race, tote;*
> *Rule 2: up, bag, run, truck, track.*

Ask students to combine words from Rule 1 and Rule 2 to make open and closed compound words. (*home run, firetruck, makeup, racetrack, tote bag*)

LESSON 11

Skill: Following Directions (pages 32–33)
OBJECTIVE:
▶ Follow directions

Teaching the Skill

1. Have students name everyday situations in which it is necessary to follow directions. (cooking a meal, building models, using a computer, playing a game or sport) Ask a volunteer to give directions to get from one place in the classroom to another and then ask another volunteer to follow them.

2. Ask students to describe a situation in which they made a mistake when following directions. Have them speculate on the reasons for the error. Were the directions hard to understand? Did they read the steps of the directions carefully and in order? Did they know the meaning of all the terms in the directions? List these reasons on the chalkboard. Discuss what happened when directions were not followed properly.

3. Have students read the first paragraph on page 32. If any students have seen flight attendants give these directions, have them recall their experiences. Then have students read the directions for putting on a life jacket and study the accompanying illustrations.

4. Direct students to complete the exercises, referring to the directions and illustrations when necessary.

ESL/ELL Strategy
SUMMARIZING Provide students with a simple recipe. Partners read and discuss the recipe, summarizing what should be done in each step of the process.

Extension Activity
Ask students to research and write directions for steps to take in various emergencies. Have them compile their sets of directions in a booklet titled "In Case of an Emergency."

LESSON 12

Skill: Long and Short Vowel Sounds (page 34)
OBJECTIVE:
▶ Recognize long and short vowel sounds

Teaching the Skill

1. Write the words *cut* and *cute* on the chalkboard. Ask a volunteer to pronounce the two words and tell which has a short vowel sound (*cut*) and which has a long vowel sound (*cute*). Place a macron over the *u* in *cute* (cūte), and explain that this mark is used to show a long vowel.

2. Remind students of the two rules they learned in Lesson 10 for long and short vowel sounds. Ask students which rule applies to *cut* (Rule 2) and which applies to *cute* (Rule 1). Then have them explain their answers.

3. Have students read the first paragraph on page 34 silently and complete Rules 1 and 2. Ask volunteers to read aloud the rules.

4. Complete items 1 and 2 of Exercise B with students. Write the word *make* on the chalkboard, and show students how to draw the macron over the letter a ($\bar{a}$) to indicate a long vowel sound.

5. Have students complete items 3–40 independently.

ESL/ELL Strategy
USING MANIPULATIVES Write the labels *long a, short a, long e, short e, long i, short i, long o, short o, long u,* and *short u* on separate index cards. Have partners place the cards in a bag. One partner draws out one card and names five words with the vowel sound indicated on the card. The other partner repeats the words aloud.

Extension Activity
Challenge students to write five sentences using as many of the words from the lesson as they can. Then have them exchange papers and identify all the Rule 1 and Rule 2 words in each other's sentences.

LESSON 13

> **Skill: Setting** (pages 35–40)
>
> **LITERATURE SELECTION: Angela's First Flight**
>
> **OBJECTIVES:**
> ▶ Identify the setting of a story
> ▶ Use comparisons as context clues
>
> **CONTEXT CLUE WORDS:** *trudged, glared, jolt*
>
> **ESL/ELL WORDS:** *catch the wind, clapped shut, nose*
>
> **GRAPHIC ORGANIZER:** Details About Setting Map, p. T56

SELECTION SUMMARY

"Angela's First Flight" is about a teenager who desperately wants to hang glide. After having an accident because of her lack of skills and poor judgment, Angela comes to the realization that she must not let her ambitions overrun her abilities.

▶ BEFORE READING

Read aloud the Background Information on page 35 about hang gliding. If any students have seen or ridden on hang gliders, ask them to share their experiences. Have students suggest some dangers of hang gliding.

Teaching Setting

1. Point out that all stories take place at a certain time in a certain place. This is called the story's setting.

2. Invite students to describe the settings of some stories they have read recently. List them on a chart on the chalkboard under the headings *Time* and *Place*.

3. Ask: *Would a movie about Robin Hood be believable if you could see telephone wires or cars in the background? Why not?* (The story of Robin Hood takes place hundreds of years ago, before telephones and cars were invented, so these details would not fit the setting.)

4. Have students complete the setting activity in the Skill Focus on page 35.

Teaching Context Clues

1. Explain that a comparison context clue helps define a new word by showing how it is like or different from something else.

2. Write the following on the chalkboard: *The hang glider soared through the sky like an eagle.* Have a volunteer identify the comparison (hang glider to eagle) and describe what a hang glider does. (soars through the sky)

3. Have students read the Context Clues section on page 35 and complete the activity.

4. Write the context clue words *trudged, glared,* and *jolt* on the chalkboard or word wall. Remind students to find comparisons for these words as they read the selection.

Previewing the Text

Have students preview, studying the illustrations. Ask volunteers what they learned about the setting and to predict what will happen in the story. Distribute copies of the Details About Setting Map, and have students fill in details as they read.

Purpose-Setting Question

Was Angela's first flight a success or a failure? Why?

▶ DURING READING

As students read, remind them to look for details about the setting that are important for the story. Also ask students to find comparisons that help explain the meanings of the underlined words.

▶ AFTER READING

Call on students to identify important details of the setting that they included on their Details About Setting Maps. Then invite volunteers to answer the purpose-setting question. Finally, have students complete the activities on pages 39–40.

Reading-Writing Connection

As prewriting for their descriptive paragraph on hang gliding over a beach, suggest that students brainstorm a list of things they might see at a beach. Then ask them to consider how the perspective of a hang glider—from above—might affect their view.

> **ESL/ELL Strategy**
>
> **ROLE-PLAYING** Have pairs of students role-play the scene between Paul and Angela after her crash. They should imagine how Angela might have responded after Paul's offer to help her.

Skill: Reading a Map (pages 41–45)

SOCIAL STUDIES SELECTION: Around the World in Twenty Days

OBJECTIVES:
- Read a world map
- Use definitions as context clues

CONTEXT CLUE WORDS: *meteorology, jet stream, stratosphere*

ESL/ELL WORDS: *make or break, air-traffic controllers, airspace*

GRAPHIC ORGANIZER: Sequence Chart, p. T53

SELECTION SUMMARY

"Around the World in Twenty Days" tells the true story of Bertrand Piccard and Brian Jones, the first balloonists to complete an around-the-world voyage in March 1999. The article describes their *Breitling Orbiter 3* balloon and focuses on the route of the voyage, with various references to the geographic areas the balloon flew over.

▶ BEFORE READING

Read aloud the Background Information on page 41 about hot-air ballooning. If any students have seen or ridden in balloons, ask them to share what they know about how the balloons float. Discuss books and movies students have seen about ballooning.

Teaching Reading a Map

1. Explain that a map can help them follow a voyage, including the balloon's route in this selection. Have students turn to the map on page 43 and read the map's title to determine its subject.

2. Ask students to find the compass rose on the map and discuss its purpose (to determine direction). Ask questions such as *Is North America east or west of Europe on the map?* (west) *What continents are south of the equator?* Discuss the map scale. Point out that a map scale helps determine distances between places.

3. Have students read the Skill Focus on page 41 and complete the activity based on the map.

Teaching Context Clues

1. Review that writers of nonfiction often define, or give the meanings of, new words.

2. Display the following sentences on an overhead projector: *The Chinese officials warned that the balloon must stay south of the 25th <u>parallel of latitude</u>.*

Parallels of latitude are imaginary lines that measure distance north and south of the equator.

3. Ask a volunteer which words are being defined and to explain *parallel of latitude* from reading the sentences.

4. Have students read the Context Clues section on page 41 and complete the activity.

5. Write the context clue words *meteorology, jet stream,* and *stratosphere* on the chalkboard or word wall. Remind students to look for definition clues for these words as they read the selection.

Previewing the Text

Have students preview, studying the section headings and map, to predict what they will learn about ballooning. Explain that the section titles give insight into sequence of events. Then distribute copies of the Sequence Chart. As they read, students list in order the places that the two balloonists passed over during their historic flight.

Purpose-Setting Question

What difficulties did Jones and Piccard face on their around-the-world balloon flight?

▶ DURING READING

As students read, remind them to list the balloon's route on their Sequence Charts and to find these places on the world map on page 43. Also remind them to look for definitions of the underlined words.

▶ AFTER READING

Have students use their Sequence Charts and the world map on page 43 to name, in order, the countries and oceans that the balloon passed over. Invite volunteers to answer the purpose-setting question. Ask students to complete the activities on pages 44–45.

Reading-Writing Connection

Have small groups use the world map on page 43 to plan their imaginary flights around the world. Encourage them to take different routes from the one taken by Jones and Piccard.

ESL/ELL Strategy

USING VISUALS Encourage partners to use their Sequence Charts and the world map to orally summarize the balloon voyage of Jones and Piccard.

Reading a Diagram (pages 46–49)

SCIENCE SELECTION: The International Space Station

OBJECTIVES:
▶ Read text with diagrams
▶ Use appositive phrases as context clues

CONTEXT CLUE WORDS: *orbiting, habitation, semiconductors*
ESL/ELL WORDS: *set a record, long-range, pave the way*
GRAPHIC ORGANIZER: KWL Chart, p. T57

SELECTION SUMMARY

"The International Space Station" is about the 16-nation cooperative effort to assemble the International Space Station (ISS). Along with information about earlier space stations, the selection describes how the ISS is being assembled and what life aboard the ISS will be like. It also describes the scientific experiments that will take place there once it is completed in 2010.

▶ BEFORE READING

Have students read the Background Information about the ISS on page 46. If possible, bring in recent magazine or newspaper stories that tell about the latest progress in building the ISS. Discuss whether it is important for people to live and explore in space.

Teaching Reading a Diagram

1. Bring in texts that contain diagrams, such as manuals for cars, directions for assembling items, and scientific magazine articles. Pass around the texts, and ask students why they think diagrams were included.

2. Have students read the Skill Focus on page 46, and call on volunteers to read aloud the four steps for reading diagrams. Ask a volunteer to summarize the steps.

3. Have students use the steps to study the diagram of the orbiting space station on page 46 and complete the Skill Focus activity.

Teaching Context Clues

1. Explain that an appositive phrase is one that follows a new word to explain its meaning. It is often set off by commas and starts with the word *or*.

2. Write the following sentence on the chalkboard: *People have wondered about stars since ancient, or _____,*

times. Ask students to fill in the blank. (long-ago) Explain that *long-ago* is an appositive for *ancient*.

3. Have students read the Context Clues section on page 46 and complete the activity.

4. Write the context clue words *orbiting, habitation,* and *semiconductors* on the chalkboard or word wall, and remind students to find appositive phrases that explain their meanings as they read the selection.

Previewing the Text

Have students preview, studying the section headings and diagrams to predict what the International Space Station is like. Then distribute copies of the KWL Chart and have students enter what they already know about the ISS in the first column and what they would like to find out about it in the second column. Direct students to fill in the third column as they read.

Purpose-Setting Question

Why are the nations of the world working together to build the ISS?

▶ DURING READING

As students read, remind them to use the diagrams to help them understand the process by which the ISS is being built. Also remind them to look for appositives that explain the meanings of the underlined words.

▶ AFTER READING

Invite students to discuss the final columns of their KWL Charts. Ask students to suggest answers to the purpose-setting question. Instruct students to complete the activities on page 49.

Reading-Writing Connection

Encourage students to visit one of the following Web sites on the Internet to find out more about the International Space Station before writing their paragraphs or drawing their diagrams: www.spaceflight.nasa.gov or www.heavens-above.com.

ESL/ELL Strategy

SUMMARIZING Have pairs of students study the diagrams in the selection and sum up in their own words what the diagrams show. Then ask them to share five facts about the ISS that they learned from the diagrams.

Reading Metric Terms (pages 50–53)

MATHEMATICS SELECTION: Metric Base Units and Prefixes

OBJECTIVES:
- Read and understand metric terms and abbreviations
- Use prefixes as word clues

ESL/ELL WORDS: *base units, volume, unlock the meaning*

GRAPHIC ORGANIZER: KWL Chart, p. T57

_____ SELECTION SUMMARY _____

"Metric Base Units and Prefixes" provides definitions of three metric base units: the meter, the gram, and the liter. It also introduces six metric prefixes—*kilo-, hecto-, deca-, deci-, centi-,* and *milli-*. Also discussed are the abbreviations used to denote each prefix and base unit.

▶ BEFORE READING

Have students read the Background Information on page 50. Ask them to recall when they have read or heard metric terms such as *liter, meter,* and *gram*. (*Liters* appear on soda bottles, *meters* are used to measure distances in races, and *grams* appear on snack bags.) Have students discuss whether they understood what the measurements meant.

Teaching Reading Metric Terms

1. Review that the metric system is based on the number 10. Draw a one-meter line on the chalkboard, and label it *1 meter*. Draw a second one-meter line, and divide it into ten equal parts. Label this line *10 decimeters*. Draw a third one-meter line, and suggest how it should be divided into 100 equal parts. If appropriate, invite volunteers to help mark the lines. Label this line *100 centimeters*.

2. Point out that each line is the same length, but that the second two lines are divided into smaller units. Ask students what happened to the measurements as the units got smaller. (The measurements increased, first by 10 times and then by 100 times.)

3. Have students turn to page 50 and complete the Skill Focus activity.

Teaching Word Clues

1. Remind students that a prefix is a word part added to the beginning of a base word to change its meaning. Give some examples of prefixes and base words, such as *un + happy = unhappy* and *re + consider = reconsider*.

2. List metric prefixes and the three metric base units in two columns on the chalkboard. Have students combine them to form metric units of measurement.

3. Have students read the Word Clues section on page 50 and complete the activity.

Previewing the Text

Have students preview, studying the section headings, the charts, and the photo with its caption. Based on these, ask students to predict what they will learn about metrics in this math selection. Have them record observations on KWL Charts.

Purpose-Setting Question

How can knowing the meaning of metric prefixes help someone better understand the metric system?

▶ DURING READING

As students read, encourage them to look at the lines on the chalkboard to remind them how metric measurements change as the metric units get smaller. Also urge them to study the charts that list the meaning of the metric prefixes and the abbreviations used to indicate metric terms.

▶ AFTER READING

Have students complete their KWL Charts. Ask students to answer the purpose-setting question and complete the activities on pages 52–53.

Reading-Writing Connection

To extend the metric measurement activity, have a meter stick (or smaller ruler with metric units indicated) and a gram scale available for students to actually measure the items they list.

ESL/ELL Strategy

USING MANIPULATIVES Have pairs of students write the metric prefix abbreviations *k, h, da, d, c,* and *m,* and the metric unit abbreviations *m, L,* and *g,* on separate index cards. Ask them to place the prefixes and the unit abbreviations in two separate envelopes. Then have students draw one index card from each envelope and say the metric term that is formed by combining the two abbreviations. They might also tell what each term means. For example: *cg = centigram = a weight one hundred times less than a gram.*

LESSON 17

Skill: Main Idea (page 54)

OBJECTIVE:
▶ Identify the main idea that appears at the beginning or end of a paragraph

Teaching the Skill

1. Remind students that the main idea is the most important idea in a paragraph and that it is often stated directly in one sentence in the paragraph. Review that the other sentences in the paragraph usually give details that tell more about the main idea. Ask students where the main idea sentence can appear in a paragraph. (at the beginning, in the middle, or at the end)

2. Present the following on an overhead projector slide:

   Salt was the first mineral mined from the sea. The sea also provides chemicals such as iodine and magnesium. In addition, a fortune in rare metals lies at the bottom of sea. These include nickel, cobalt, and copper. In many ways, the sea is a liquid mine.

3. Help students conclude that the last sentence expresses the main idea of the paragraph. It is the most important and general statement. The other sentences give details that tell about the main idea.

4. Read aloud the introductory paragraph and the exercise directions on page 54. Then have students complete the exercise independently.

ESL/ELL Strategy

ORGANIZING INFORMATION Have small groups read the paragraphs in the exercise aloud to each other. Then have the group members write a title for each paragraph that suggests its main idea. For example, a good title for Paragraph 1 might be "The Strange Appearance of the Sea Horse."

Extension Activity

Ask each student to write a main idea sentence about some aspect of school life. For example: *The school cafeteria is a noisy place.* Then have students exchange papers and write three or more detail sentences that support the main idea.

LESSON 18

Skill: Main Idea (page 55)

OBJECTIVE:
▶ Identify the main idea that appears at the beginning, in the middle, or at the end of a paragraph

Teaching the Skill

1. Review that the main idea is the most important idea in a paragraph and that it is often, but not always, found in the first or last sentence of a paragraph.

2. Distribute copies of the following paragraph, and have students underline the main idea sentence.

   Pheasants scratch for food and have rakelike toes. Eagles have large curved claws for snatching prey. The feet of birds are adapted to how they live and hunt. The webbed toes of ducks are ideal for swimming.

   Have a volunteer point out that the third sentence holds the main idea because it is the most important sentence in the paragraph. The other three support this statement.

3. Read the introductory paragraph and the directions on page 55 with students. Then have students complete the exercise independently.

ESL/ELL Strategy

ORGANIZING INFORMATION Give partners a copy of the Main Idea and Supporting Details Map on page T61, and assign each pair one paragraph to analyze. Have pairs read the paragraph aloud and then write the main idea and the supporting details in the correct boxes. Encourage students to add more boxes to the map, as needed.

Extension Activity

Ask students to write a paragraph about their favorite TV show, leaving out the main idea sentence. Partners then exchange paragraphs and write a main idea sentence. Encourage students to consider placing the main idea sentence in the middle of the paragraph.

LESSON 19

Skill: Consonant Blends (page 56)

OBJECTIVE:

▶ Recognize three-consonant blends: *scr, spl, spr, squ, str*

Teaching the Skill

1. Preview the consonant blends in Lessons 7, 8, and 9. Explain that in this lesson students will learn words that begin with the sounds of three consonants blended together.

2. List on the chalkboard: *scr, spl, spr, squ,* and *str.* Call on volunteers to name some words that begin with these blends. (scratch, splash, spring, squeak, string)

3. Ask students to silently read the introductory paragraph and the directions on page 56. Then direct students to say the names of pictures 1–4, emphasizing the beginning sounds of each word. Have students name the consonant blends.

4. Have students complete the remainder of the exercise independently.

ESL/ELL Strategy

USING RESOURCES Have partners draw five columns on a sheet of paper and label each with a three-letter blend taught in this lesson. Then ask them to use a dictionary to find three words that begin with each blend.

Extension Activity

Challenge students to use the words in the lesson and other words to create two-word rhyming pairs. Then have students write a definition for each pair of words and ask a partner to guess it. For example, students might write the definition "a yell from a small river" for the rhyming pair *stream scream,* or the definition "walking around while reading an ancient book" for a *scroll stroll.*

LESSON 20

Skill: Consonant Digraphs (page 57)

OBJECTIVE:

▶ Recognize initial and final consonant digraphs: *ch, ph, sh, th, wh*

Teaching the Skill

1. Review that in consonant blends all the letters can be heard, such as *bl* in *blue, sl* in *slipper, cr* in *crayon, and gr* in *grapes.* Explain that digraphs are two-consonant letter pairs that stand for one sound. List the digraphs *ch, ph, sh, th,* and *wh* in a column on the chalkboard.

2. Have students say the sound represented by each pair of consonants. Then ask students to name a word that begins with each digraph. (chat, phone, shout, thin, wheel) Write an example word next to each digraph. Then ask students to name a word that ends with each digraph. (peach, graph, cash, mouth) Write an example word next to each digraph.

3. Ask students to read the introductory paragraph on page 57. Then read aloud the directions for Exercise A. Ask individuals to say the names of the objects in pictures 1–4 of Exercise A, emphasizing the beginning sound of each word.

4. Have students complete the remainder of Exercises A and B independently.

ESL/ELL Strategy

PERSONALIZING THE LESSON Ask partners to look around the classroom and make a list of items whose names begin or end with a digraph. They might see a chair, a watch, a phone, a graph, a shopping bag, a paintbrush, a thumb, a tooth, and a wheel.

Extension Activity

Divide the class into small groups. Ask one student in each group to tell a true story. Ask the other members of the group to listen carefully, writing down any words they hear that begin or end with a digraph.

LESSON 21

Skill: Long Vowel Sounds (page 58)

OBJECTIVE:
▶ Recognize long vowel sounds

Teaching the Skill

1. Review the two rules for identifying long and short vowel sounds that students learned in Lessons 10 and 12. Explain that students are about to learn a new rule.

2. Write *boat, eat,* and *pail* on the chalkboard as you say each word. Ask students: *How many vowels do you see in each word?* (two) *Which vowel has the long sound? Circle it.* (o, e, a) *Which vowel is silent? Underline it.* (a, a, i)

3. Ask students to read the introductory paragraphs on page 58 and then complete Exercise A. Students should see that each word has two vowels, the first of which has a long vowel sound and the second of which is silent.

4. Have a volunteer read the rule aloud, complete it, and then direct students to complete Exercise C independently.

ESL/ELL Strategy

USING MANIPULATIVES Ask pairs of students to write the vowel pairs *ai, ea,* and *oa* each on separate slips of paper. One partner chooses a slip of paper, thinks of a word that contains the vowel pair, and then uses the word in a sentence. The other partner listens carefully to the sentence and identifies the word that has a long vowel sound represented by the letters *ai, ea,* or *oa.*

Extension Activity

Challenge teams of students to compile the longest list of rhyming words, using the same pair of vowels. For example, students could compile lists of rhymes ending in *-oad/-oam/-oan/-oat, -eat/-ean/-eal/-eap,* or *-aid/-ail/-ain/-ait.* (For example: toad, road/roam, foam/loan, roan/boat, float; heat, meat/bean, mean/seal, squeal/leap, reap; paid, maid/tail, wail/gain, main/wait, bait) The team with the most correctly spelled rhyming words wins.

LESSON 22

Skill: Long and Short Vowel Sounds (page 59)

OBJECTIVE:
▶ Recognize long and short vowel sounds

Teaching the Skill

1. Review the three rules for recognizing long and short vowel sounds on pages 34 and 58. Call on volunteers to give examples of words that fit each pattern. Explain that this lesson will review all three rules.

2. Direct students to read the opening paragraph on page 59 and then complete the three rules. Call on volunteers to read aloud the completed rules.

3. Work through exercise items 1–4 with the class. Have volunteers say each word, identify the vowel sound as long or short, and then identify the rule that applies to the word.

4. Direct students to complete the remaining items independently. Remind them to mark only the long vowels with a macron.

ESL/ELL Strategy

ORGANIZING INFORMATION Have partners draw three columns on a sheet of paper labeled Rule 1, Rule 2, and Rule 3. Then ask them to list five or more words that follow the pattern for each rule.

Extension Activity

Challenge students to write a three-sentence story that uses the patterns described in the three rules. The first sentence should contain words that follow the pattern of Rule 1. The second sentence should have words that follow Rule 2. The third sentence should use words that follow Rule 3. For example:

I wrote a note to tell Nate that I ate everything on my plate. Then I ran to the back of the hut to get the rest of my stuff. I put on my coat in the rain and took a boat to the East Coast.

Skill: Using a Train Schedule (pages 60–61)

OBJECTIVE:
▶ Use a train schedule

Teaching the Skill

1. Discuss the use of schedules or timetables in public transportation. If possible, display a copy of a train or bus schedule for a local line that runs in or near your community. If appropriate, have students discuss their experiences using public-transportation schedules.

2. Have students read the paragraph at the top of page 60. Then preview the sample train schedule together. Call their attention to the top row of headings on the schedule, and point out that it lists train numbers. Ask students to read down the first column of the schedule. Make sure they understand that these are stations where the trains stop. To check their understanding, ask: *When does Train 706 arrive in Windsor Gardens?* (6:59 A.M.) Direct students to the small type at the bottom of the schedule. Ask volunteers to read and explain the meanings of the symbols *L, O,* and *T* on the schedule. (*L:* train may leave ahead of schedule; *O:* ticket outlet at or near station; *T:* subway connection)

3. Work through the first few items in Exercise A with the class to make sure students are able to use the schedule. Then have them work independently to complete the rest of the exercises.

ESL/ELL Strategy

ROLE-PLAYING Have pairs of students role-play a traveler and a clerk at a railroad information desk. Using the train schedule on page 60, the traveler asks a specific question about the train schedule. The clerk then refers to the schedule to answer the question. Encourage students to switch roles.

Extension Activity

Ask students to suppose they were working for a new high-speed train line that runs between the major cities of their state or region. Have students create a timetable for the new train, showing the cities where it will stop and the times of these stops. Use a map for reference.

LESSON 24

Skill: Conflict and Resolution (pages 62–67)

LITERATURE SELECTION: Something to Cheer About

OBJECTIVES:

▸ Understand conflict and resolution

▸ Use synonym context clues

CONTEXT CLUE WORDS: *crisp, vendors, embarrassed*

ESL/ELL WORDS: *turned upside down, picked up, in-line skating*

GRAPHIC ORGANIZER: Prediction Chart, p. T58

_____ SELECTION SUMMARY _____

In "Something to Cheer About," Keema has moved from downtown Manhattan to uptown Harlem and misses her old friends. Maria Hernandez, a girl in her new school, tries to befriend Keema, but Keema is loyal to her old friends. At a basketball game between her old and new schools, Keema sees her old friends and is torn between conflicting loyalties. She decides, however, to cheer for her new school.

▸ BEFORE READING

Have students read the Background Information about Harlem on page 62. If any students have visited or read about Harlem, have them share their knowledge. You might suggest that a volunteer find and read aloud an encyclopedia entry for Harlem or the Harlem Renaissance.

Teaching Conflict and Resolution

1. Review that a conflict is a problem or struggle that a story character faces. The resolution is how the character resolves, or deals with, the problem. Conflicts are difficult for characters, but they make a story interesting or exciting. Point out that a conflict might be with another character, with an outside force such as nature, or within a person's own mind.

2. Invite students to suggest examples of each of the three types of conflict that people might have in everyday life. Have others suggest resolutions for these problems. List these ideas on the chalkboard under the headings *Conflict With Another Character, Conflict With an Outside Force,* and *Conflict With Self.*

3. Have students read the Skill Focus and complete the chart on page 62.

Teaching Context Clues

1. Review that synonyms are words with the same or similar meanings. Provide an example such as *eat/dine.*

2. Ask a volunteer to write a word on the chalkboard such as *cold.* Have students list as many synonyms as they can. (icy, freezing, frigid)

3. Have students read the Context Clues section on page 62 and complete the activity.

4. Write the context clue words *crisp, vendors,* and *embarrassed* on the chalkboard or word wall and remind students to find synonym clues for these words as they read the selection.

Previewing the Text

Have students preview the title and illustrations to predict what will happen to Keema. Distribute copies of the Prediction Chart and have students predict conflict and resolution as they read.

Purpose-Setting Question

What conflict does Keema face, and how does she resolve it?

▸ DURING READING

As students read, remind them to think about the conflict that Keema faces in her new neighborhood, and suggest that they make a prediction about how she might resolve it. Also have them look for synonym clues for the underlined words.

▸ AFTER READING

Ask volunteers to discuss their Prediction Charts and to answer the purpose-setting question. Then have students complete the activities on pages 66–67.

Reading-Writing Connection

Ask students to list reasons why they would cheer for Park East or Washington Irving High School. You might have students debate which choice would be best for Keema in the long run before they write their paragraphs.

ESL/ELL Strategy

ROLE-PLAYING Have partners act out key scenes, using the story dialogue. They might dramatize Keema's early conversations with Maria, her telephone call with Rita, or the final scene.

Skill: Comparing and Contrasting (pages 68–72)

SOCIAL STUDIES SELECTION: **The Rise of the American Suburbs**

OBJECTIVES:
- Compare and contrast information
- Use details as context clues

CONTEXT CLUE WORDS: *standardizing, urban, unsustainable*

ESL/ELL WORDS: *trolley cars, boom, bumper-to-bumper traffic*

GRAPHIC ORGANIZER: Comparison-and-Contrast Chart, p. T59

SELECTION SUMMARY

"The Rise of the American Suburbs" gives an overview of the growth of suburbs in the United States, starting with the first suburbs that appeared in the mid-nineteenth century. It speculates on the future of suburbs and describes the planned communities of the early twentieth century and the post-World War II suburban boom.

▶ BEFORE READING

Have students read the Background Information about suburbs on page 68. If students live in or have visited suburbs, have them tell what they like and dislike about these kinds of neighborhoods. Students can also contrast suburbs with other communities, such as big-city neighborhoods or small, rural towns.

Teaching Comparing and Contrasting

1. Review that when people compare, they point out what is the same or similar about two things. When they contrast, they point out what is different.

2. Have pairs of students compare and contrast an article of clothing they are wearing, such as their shoes. Suggest that they use words such as *like* or *both* to tell how the clothing is alike. Have them use words such as *unlike* or *but* to note differences. List ideas on a chart.

3. Have students read the Skill Focus section on page 68 and complete the activity.

Teaching Context Clues

1. Remind students that almost all reading passages will include some details that can help them figure out the meaning of new words.

2. Distribute the following on a handout: *The Suburban building boom continued through the 1950s. Many builders were busy. In 1950 alone, they built 1.4 million*

houses. In the 1950s, builders prepared about 3,000 acres of farmland per day for houses.

Ask volunteers to discuss what details in the passage explain *suburban building boom.* (built 1.4 million houses in one year; prepared 3,000 acres of land each day for building)

3. Have students read the Context Clues section on page 68 and complete the activity.

4. Write the context clue words *standardizing, urban,* and *unsustainable* on the chalkboard or word wall, and remind students to find detail clues for these words as they read the selection.

Previewing the Text

Have students preview the selection, studying the section headings, photos, and chart. Ask students to identify the three kinds of suburbs and predict what they will learn about them. Then distribute the Comparison-and-Contrast Charts. Have students list *first suburbs, garden suburbs,* and *postwar suburbs* on their charts under *Thing Being Compared.* As they read, students find similarities and differences between them.

Purpose-Setting Question

Why did so many people move to the suburbs after World War II?

▶ DURING READING

As students read, remind them to note the similarities and differences among the three types of suburbs. Also remind them to look for details to help them figure out the meaning of the underlined context clue words.

▶ AFTER READING

Ask students to share the details they have written on their Comparison-and-Contrast Charts. Invite volunteers to answer the purpose-setting question. Then have students complete the activities on pages 71–72.

Reading-Writing Connection

Before students conduct their interviews and complete their Comparison-and-Contrast Charts, have teams of students work together to write interview questions that explore what interviewees might like and dislike about their community.

ESL/ELL Strategy

USING VISUALS Have groups of students work together on a bulletin-board timeline showing important events in the growth of American suburbs from 1830 to the present.

Skill: Cause and Effect (pages 73–77)

SCIENCE SELECTION: Animals Among Us

OBJECTIVES

▶ Identify cause and effect

▶ Use synonyms as context clues

CONTEXT CLUE WORDS: *forsake, scavenge, voraciously*

ESL/ELL WORDS: *in the wild, in captivity, spot*

GRAPHIC ORGANIZER: Cause-and-Effect Charts, p. T54

_____ **SELECTION SUMMARY** _____

"Animals Among Us" explains why wild animals are becoming more common in suburban and urban settings. It looks at the rise in falcon and fox populations in downtown city areas and explores why Canada geese, black bears, and mountain lions have increasing numbers of contacts with people. It suggests how people can coexist with wildlife.

▶ BEFORE READING

Have students read the Background Information about wildlife on page 73. Then discuss different forms of wildlife seen in students' neighborhoods. Ask students to speculate on the causes for the animal's sudden appearance and to predict some problems that might arise as a result.

Teaching Cause and Effect

1. Review that a cause is what makes something happen and an effect is what happens as a result. Explain that in a cause-and-effect relationship, one event makes another event happen.

2. Ask a question about a recent local sporting event. For example: *Why did our basketball team lose last weekend?* Write the response on the chalkboard. For example: *Our basketball team lost because our best player was sick.* Underline the word *because*, and explain that it always signals a cause-and-effect relationship. Then ask students to identify the cause and the effect in the sentence. Draw a small Cause-and-Effect Chart like the one on page 73. Write the cause (Our best player was sick.) and the effect (Our basketball team lost.) in the correct boxes.

3. Have students read the Skill Focus on page 73 and complete the activity.

Teaching Context Clues

1. Point out that synonyms are words with similar meanings. Ask students to name some words that are synonyms, and list them on the chalkboard. For example: *good, wonderful, fantastic,* and *terrific*.

2. Explain that synonyms can help you figure out the meaning of new words and might appear before or after the unknown word. Write these sentences on the chalkboard: *He walked quietly. He tiptoed.* Ask students to circle the synonym for *tiptoed.* (walked quietly)

3. Have students read the Context Clues section on page 73 and complete the activity.

4. Write the context clue words *forsake, scavenge,* and *voraciously* on the chalkboard or word wall. Remind students to find synonyms for these words as they read.

Previewing the Text

Have students preview the section headings and photos to predict cause-and-effect relationships in the selection. Then distribute copies of the Cause-and-Effect Charts, and ask students to record causes and effects as they read.

Purpose-Setting Question

What are some of the reasons that wild animals are showing up in populated areas?

▶ DURING READING

As students read, remind them to identify cause-and-effect relationships. Also have them look for synonyms that explain the meanings of the underlined words.

▶ AFTER READING

Ask volunteers to share their Cause-and-Effect Charts and to answer the purpose-setting question. Then have students complete the activities on pages 76–77.

Reading-Writing Connection

Have students talk to local police officers, park rangers, animal control officers, or veterinarians to find out about wild animals in the community. Students prepare fact cards about each animal, listing details about its physical appearance, diet, habitat, and the precautions people should take in handling it.

ESL/ELL Strategy

PERSONALIZING THE LESSON Have partners write riddles about animals who live among us. For example: *I raid your garbage can before I take a long winter's nap. Who am I?* (a bear) Partners ask other pairs to answer their riddles.

> **Skill: Reading a Thermometer** (pages 78–81)
>
> **MATHEMATICS SELECTION: How We Measure Temperature**
>
> **OBJECTIVES:**
> - Read a thermometer
> - Interpret words and symbols related to temperature
>
> **ESL/ELL WORDS:** *symbol, degree lines, number systems*
>
> **GRAPHIC ORGANIZER:** Venn Diagram, p. T60

SELECTION SUMMARY

"How We Measure Temperature" provides step-by-step instructions for reading Fahrenheit and Celsius thermometers and for expressing temperatures in words and symbols. It also contrasts the Fahrenheit and Celsius scales.

▶ BEFORE READING

Have students read the Background Information on page 78 about thermometers. Ask students to recall some recent situations in which they have used thermometers. Discuss whether the thermometers measured degrees Fahrenheit or degrees Celsius.

Teaching Reading a Thermometer

1. Discuss what students know about the Celsius scale and how it compares with the Fahrenheit scale. (Students may have seen Fahrenheit and Celsius temperatures together on bank time-and-temperature readings or heard them on TV weather reports.)

2. Bring in both a Fahrenheit and a Celsius thermometer. Have students examine how numbers are marked on each thermometer. Ask them how many degrees each line stands for. Then have a student point to an unnumbered line and have another supply the number it represents. Encourage students to explain how they figured out the numbering system on the thermometer.

3. Have students read the Skill Focus on page 78 and complete the activity.

Teaching Word Clues

1. Write *F, C,* and ° on the chalkboard. Ask students if they know what these letters and symbols stand for. (Fahrenheit, Celsius, and degrees) Write the word next to its letter or symbol on the chalkboard.

2. Have students read the Word Clues section and complete the activity.

Previewing the Text

Have students preview the selection, studying the Fahrenheit and Celsius thermometers in Figures 1 and 2. Distribute copies of the Venn Diagram, and have students look for similarities and differences between the two temperature systems as they read.

Purpose-Setting Question

How are the Fahrenheit and Celsius scales different?

▶ DURING READING

As students read, encourage them to refer to the diagrams of the thermometers on page 79 often to make sure they understand how to interpret the temperatures shown on them. Explain that any two temperatures directly across from each other on the thermometers indicate the same amount of heat. For example, 68°F is the same as 20°C.

▶ AFTER READING

Discuss the similarities and differences students noted on their Venn Diagrams. Then have them answer the purpose-setting question and complete the activities on pages 80–81.

Reading-Writing Connection

Before writing their paragraphs about the weather during a previous picnic, point out that students can use the side-by-side thermometers on page 79 to find the Celsius equivalent of a Fahrenheit temperature.

> **ESL/ELL Strategy**
>
> **USING MANIPULATIVES** Have pairs of students make cardboard thermometers like those shown on page 79. Students should make sure that the scales of the thermometers line up exactly as they do in the diagrams. Suggest that students use a red strip of paper that can slide up and down each thermometer to show the temperature. Have one partner give a Fahrenheit temperature and the other say it in the Celsius scale.

LESSON 28

Skill: *r*-Controlled Vowel Sounds (page 82)

OBJECTIVE:
▶ Identify *r*-controlled vowel sounds

Teaching the Skill

1. Ask students to pronounce each pair of words as you write them on the chalkboard: *cat/cart, ten/tern, bid/bird, pot/port, bun/burn*. Invite volunteers to circle the *r* in each pair and note how the short vowel sound in the first word of each pair changes when it is followed by the letter *r*. Ask students to provide other word pairs, such as *pat/part, pet/pert, skit/skirt, spot/sport,* and *hut/hurt*.

2. Read the paragraph at the top of page 82. Then call on volunteers to read aloud each pair of words in boldface type. Answer items 1–3 in Exercise A with the class.

3. Write the words *car, her, sir, for,* and *fur* on the chalkboard and circle the *r* and the *r*-controlled vowel in each.

4. Direct students to complete Exercises B and C and the rules independently.

ESL/ELL Strategy

USING MANIPULATIVES Invite students to draw pictures that contain at least five objects whose names have an *r*-controlled vowel sound. Then have partners exchange papers and write the words with the *r*-controlled vowel sounds.

Extension Activity

Make a rhyming dictionary available to students. Ask them to find rhymes for the boldface words in Exercise C on page 82. Challenge them to write poems that use these rhymes at the end of lines.

LESSON 29

Skill: Prefixes, Suffixes, and Base Words (page 83)

OBJECTIVE:
▶ Recognize prefixes and suffixes

Teaching the Skill

1. Write the following words on the chalkboard: *tie, untie, retie*. Ask students to explain how the words differ in meaning. (*Untie* is the opposite of *tie. Retie* means "tie again.") Explain that *tie* is the base word for all three words. Then underline *un-* and *re-*, and point out that they are prefixes. Prefixes are word parts added to the beginning of a base word to change its meaning.

2. Write the words *kind, kindly,* and *kindness* on the chalkboard. Explain that *kind* is the base word for all three words. Underline the *-ly* and the *-ness*, and tell students that these are suffixes. Suffixes are word parts added to the end of a base word to change its meaning.

3. Write the words *quickly, unhappy, rebuild,* and *slowness* on the chalkboard. Ask volunteers to underline the suffix or prefix in each word. (*-ly, un-, re-, -ness*)

4. Have students read the opening paragraphs and list of prefixes and suffixes and their meanings on page 83.

5. Read the directions for Exercise A. Have volunteers complete items 1–3. Then have students complete the rest of the exercise independently. Do the same for Exercise B.

ESL/ELL Strategy

IDENTIFYING ESSENTIAL VOCABULARY Ask partners to write each of the prefixes and suffixes in this lesson on separate index cards. Have them choose an index card, say the prefix or suffix, and then suggest a base word to which the prefix or suffix could be added. Also have them tell the meaning of the word they have formed.

Extension Activity

Have students work in small groups to write a list of words that have both one of the prefixes and one of the suffixes taught in this lesson. For example, *unhappiness, preschooler, inconveniently,* and so on. Then have students explain the meaning of each word and use it in an original sentence.

LESSON 30

Skill: Syllables (page 84)

OBJECTIVE:
▶ Recognize syllables

Teaching the Skill

1. Say the word *pen*. Ask students how many vowels they hear. Have a volunteer write the word on the chalkboard and count the vowels. Explain that if one vowel sound is heard in the word, the word has one syllable. Have students offer other examples of one-syllable words.

2. Say the word *pencil*. Ask students how many vowels they hear. Call on a volunteer to write the word on the chalkboard and count the vowels. Ask how many syllables the word has. Explain that if two vowel sounds are heard in a word, the word has two syllables. Have students offer examples of two-syllable words.

3. Repeat with the word *game*. Have students note that even though the word has two vowels, there is only one vowel sound and therefore one syllable.

4. Have students read the definition of *syllable* and the directions for Exercise A on page 84. Have them say what each picture represents and list the number of syllables in each.

5. Have students complete the rest of the exercises independently. Then review the two rules.

ESL/ELL Strategy

PERSONALIZING THE LESSON Have partners write a list of ten objects in the classroom. Have them say the name for each object aloud, listen for the number of vowel sounds, and write the number of syllables in each word.

Extension Activity

Have partners list words with four, five, or six syllables. Have them pronounce each word, noting which of the vowels in each word are sounded and which are silent. If students have trouble with pronunciation, suggest that they refer to a dictionary.

LESSON 31

Skill: Syllables (page 85)

OBJECTIVE:
▶ Divide words into syllables

Teaching the Skill

1. Review that a syllable is each part of a word in which you can hear a vowel sound. Explain that students will be learning some rules to help them divide words into syllables. Read the opening paragraph on page 85.

2. Explain that the first rule will help them divide compound words into syllables. Review that a compound word is a word formed from two smaller words, such as *baseball* and *scoreboard*. Write *baseball* on the chalkboard, and draw a *slash* between the two words, *base* and *ball*. Say the word slowly and ask students how many syllables they hear in *baseball*. (two)

3. Have a volunteer read the Compound Words section on page 85. Have students complete Exercise A independently. Then review the rule together.

4. Explain that the second rule will help them divide words with double consonants. Write *summer* on the chalkboard, and as you say the word slowly, draw a slash between *mm*. Ask students how many syllables they hear in *summer*. (two)

5. Have a volunteer read the Words With Double Consonants section on page 85. Have students complete Exercise B independently. Then review the rule together.

ESL/ELL Strategy

USING VISUALS Have partners work independently to draw a picture that represents an object named by a compound word. Partners then exchange pictures, guess the pictured word, and divide it into syllables. Students can repeat the activity using words with double consonants.

Extension Activity

Working in small groups, students make a compound word chain by first writing any compound word. They then think of a second compound word that begins with the last part of the first compound word, and so on. For example: *sunlight—lighthouse—housework—workplace*, and so on. Challenge students to build the longest compound chain they can. Then have them divide each word into syllables.

LESSON 32

Skill: Comparing Food Labels (pages 86–87)

OBJECTIVE:
▶ Compare food labels

Teaching the Skill

1. Have students describe how they might go about deciding which brand of peanut butter or tuna fish to buy. Ask them to focus on the types of information they might find on the food labels and how this information might be helpful in making their decisions.

2. If possible, bring in several cans and boxes of food, and have students read the labels. Explain that paying attention to food labels can help people compare the prices, ingredients, and nutritional value of food.

3. Have students read the paragraphs at the top of page 86 silently. Then direct students' attention to the sample applesauce labels at the bottom of page 86. Have volunteers note what similarities and differences they see at first glance between the two brands. Draw a Venn Diagram on the chalkboard to record these observations.

4. Complete items 1–4 of Exercise A on page 87 together to be sure that students can read the labels. Then direct students to complete the remainder of the exercise independently.

ESL/ELL Strategy

USING REALIA Have pairs of students bring in a processed food. Ask each partner to study the labels and write five true/false questions based on the information. Then have the partners exchange their questions and use the labels to answer them.

Extension Activity

Have students use a copy of the Venn Diagram (page T60) to compare the information on the labels of two similar food items. Encourage students to use their findings to prepare a short oral report to present to the class.

LESSON 33

Skill: Theme (pages 88–93)

LITERATURE SELECTION: Hopping Mad!

OBJECTIVES:
▶ Infer the theme of a story
▶ Use details as context clues

CONTEXT CLUE WORDS: *eased, interrupt, barging*

ESL/ELL WORDS: *body, pumps, pickup*

GRAPHIC ORGANIZER: Prediction Chart, p. T58

_____ **SELECTION SUMMARY** _____

In "Hopping Mad!" Nancy Fuentes is restoring a 1969 car and converting it into a "low-rider" that she hopes to enter in a contest. The restoration work includes some difficult welding, which Fernando, a friend of Nancy's, offers to do for her. Nancy, however, is determined to do all the work herself.

▶ BEFORE READING

Have students read the Background Information on page 88 about restoring old cars. If any students have friends or relatives who have restored old cars, ask them to tell about it.

Teaching Theme

1. Explain that authors often have a message that they want to express to their readers. This message is called the story's theme. Oftentimes, a theme is the lesson that a character learns during the course of the story.

2. Have students recount a familiar fable, such as "The Tortoise and the Hare," and ask what lesson the fable teaches. (Slow and steady wins the race.) Ask how they knew what the theme was. (The hare takes a nap and forgets to get up on time. The tortoise walks slowly, but he keeps on going till he reaches the finish line.)

3. Direct students to read the Skill Focus on page 88 and complete the Idea Web.

Teaching Context Clues

1. Explain that reading carefully and picturing the details of a story in their minds can often help students figure out the meaning of new words.

2. Invite volunteers to write sentences on the chalkboard that contain a lot of details. Ask others to circle these words and phrases.

3. Have students complete the Context Clues activity on page 88.

4. Write the context clue words *eased, interrupt,* and *barging* on the chalkboard or word wall, and remind students to find detail clues for these words as they read the selection.

Previewing the Text

Have students preview, studying the story's title and illustrations to predict what might happen in the story. Distribute copies of the Prediction Chart, and have students add and revise their predictions as they read.

Purpose-Setting Question

Why does Nancy Fuentes get so angry?

▶ DURING READING

As students read, remind them to look for the theme that the author is expressing to readers. Also remind them to find details in the story that help them to figure out the meaning of the underlined words.

▶ AFTER READING

Ask students to discuss which predictions turned out to be correct and which they had to revise as they read. Then invite students to answer the purpose-setting question and complete the activities on pages 91–93.

Reading-Writing Connection

As prewriting for their paragraphs on wanting to finish a project on their own, have students create an Idea Web or use the one on page T55 to list details about their experiences.

ESL/ELL Strategy

ROLE-PLAYING Have students role-play the parts of Nancy, Fernando, and Mr. Fuentes. Have each student tell the events of the story from his or her character's point of view. Then the characters tell what lessons they learned from these events.

Skill: Reading a Table (pages 94–99)

SOCIAL STUDIES SELECTION: America on Wheels

OBJECTIVES:
▶ Read and interpret a table
▶ Use definitions as context clues

CONTEXT CLUE WORDS: *chassis, suspension, innovations*

ESL/ELL WORDS: *dashboard, Great Depression, standard features*

GRAPHIC ORGANIZER: Sequence Chart, p. T53

SELECTION SUMMARY

"America on Wheels" gives an overview of the development of the automobile in America, from the horseless carriages of the early 1900s to ethanol-burning prototypes of the early 2000s. It also looks at economic and social factors that have affected automobile design and use.

▶ BEFORE READING

Have students read the Background Information on page 94 about automobiles. If any students are familiar with classic or historic cars such as the Model T Ford or the Reo, have them share what they know about how these cars looked and operated.

Teaching Reading a Table

1. Review that tables show facts organized in columns and rows that are easy to read.

2. Distribute a handout of a table from a sports page or social studies book. Ask for specific pieces of information, and have volunteers read the tables to find the facts.

3. Have students read the Skill Focus on page 94 and complete the activity.

Teaching Context Clues

1. Review that textbooks often define new words in the text. The definitions can appear in the same or following sentences.

2. Write the following on the chalkboard. *Sports cars roared onto the scene in the 1920s. They were small cars with big engines.* Ask a volunteer to circle the definition of *sports cars*. (small cars with big engines)

3. Have students read the Context Clues section on page 94 and complete the activity.

4. Write the context clue words *chassis, suspension,* and *innovations* on the chalkboard or word wall. Remind students to look for definition clues for these words as they read the selection.

Previewing the Text

Have students preview, studying the section headings, photos, and tables to predict how cars have developed since the first automobiles. Then distribute copies of the Sequence Chart. As students read, have them fill in important developments in the history of cars and when they occurred. When finished, students should have a time-ordered summary of the history of cars.

Purpose-Setting Question

If people of the early 1900s could see today's cars, what might they find most surprising about them?

▶ DURING READING

Encourage students to pause during their reading to study the two tables. Also remind them to look for definitions of the underlined words.

▶ AFTER READING

Ask students to share the events and dates they listed on their Sequence Charts. Have volunteers answer the purpose-setting question. Finally, direct students to complete the activities on pages 98–99.

Reading-Writing Connection

To create their tables about future vehicles, have teams of students work together to research one type of future vehicle—electric cars, ethanol-powered cars, or hydrogen cars. Students can find many links to Web sites about cars of the future at www.automotive.com and at the Department of Energy's Web site, www.energy.gov.

ESL/ELL Strategy

PERSONALIZING THE LESSON Have pairs of students write their own questions based on the tables in this selection. Then have them exchange questions with another pair and answer each other's questions aloud.

LESSON 35

Skill: Reading a Diagram (pages 100–104)

SCIENCE SELECTION: What Makes a Car Run?

OBJECTIVES:
▶ Read text with diagrams
▶ Use diagrams as context clues

CONTEXT CLUE WORDS: *power stroke, exhaust stroke, flywheel*

ESL/ELL WORDS: *horseshoes, spark, antifreeze*

GRAPHIC ORGANIZER: KWL Chart, p. T57

SELECTION SUMMARY

"What Makes a Car Run?" provides an overview of how an automobile's engine, cylinders, and cooling system work. Diagrams are used to help explain the processes.

▶ BEFORE READING

Have students read the Background Information on page 100 about a car's engine, drivetrain, and cooling system. Have students share what they know about car maintenance and repair. Students might also compile a list of reasons that car owners should know the parts of a car and how they work.

Teaching Reading a Diagram

1. Explain that diagrams are especially important when people are trying to figure out how machines work.

2. Invite a volunteer to draw a simple diagram, such as a tape dispenser or a stapler, on the chalkboard. Ask others to help name the parts and draw lines from the names to the diagram. Students can include arrows, if appropriate. Ask a last volunteer to explain the diagram.

3. Have students read the Skill Focus on page 100 and complete the activity.

Teaching Context Clues

1. Review that diagram labels can often be used as context clues to help explain what each part is and how the parts go together.

2. Refer to the diagram drawn on the chalkboard. Have volunteers describe each part and its function based on the diagram.

3. Direct students to read the Context Clues section on page 100 and complete the activity.

4. Write the context clue words *power stroke, exhaust stroke,* and *flywheel* on the chalkboard or word wall. Remind students to look for these diagram labels as they read the selection.

Previewing the Text

Have students preview, studying the section headings and Figures 1–4 to predict what they will learn. Distribute copies of the KWL Charts. Have students write in the first column of the chart what they already know about what makes a car run. They list in the second column what they would like to know about how cars work. They fill in the third column as they read, noting important facts they learned.

Purpose-Setting Question

How is gasoline converted into power in a car's engine?

▶ DURING READING

As students read, remind them to study the diagrams to help them understand how a car works and to help them understand the meanings of the underlined words.

▶ AFTER READING

Have students share details from their KWL Charts and answer the purpose-setting question. Then direct students to complete the activities on pages 102–104.

Reading-Writing Connection

Before writing their explanatory paragraphs, have students make inferences based on their reading about why it is important to understand parts and systems of a car. Students can organize their thoughts on Inference Charts (page T62).

ESL/ELL Strategy

USING REALIA Have students look at photographs of cars from magazines or newspapers. Ask them to label as many parts of the car as they can—hood, trunk, headlights, bumpers, windshield, and so on. Have students discuss the purpose of each labeled part.

Skill: Reading Large Numbers (pages 105–108)

MATHEMATICS SELECTION: Place Value

OBJECTIVES:

▶ Use place values to read large numbers

▶ Use examples as word clues

ESL/ELL WORDS: *comma, odometer, signals*

GRAPHIC ORGANIZER: KWL Chart, p. T57

SELECTION SUMMARY

"Place Value" gives students practice with reading large numbers of up to six digits by introducing place-value charts, which assign each digit a value according to its place in a large number.

▶ BEFORE READING

Have students read the Background Information on page 105 about large numbers. Ask students to discuss situations in which they might have to read large numbers.

Teaching Reading Large Numbers

1. Ask students if they ever have trouble reading or understanding large numbers. Tell them that this lesson will help them read large numbers more easily.

2. Write the number 568 on the chalkboard. Ask students to say the number. Then ask: *What does the 5 in this number stand for?* (5 hundreds) *What does the 6 stand for?* (6 tens) *What does the 8 stand for?* (8 ones) Then draw a three-digit place-value chart on the chalkboard, like the one on page 105, and write the number 568 on the chart. Invite volunteers to write other numbers in the correct columns on the chart.

3. Have students read the Skill Focus on page 105 and complete the place-value chart.

Teaching Word Clues

1. Explain that by carefully studying examples of a word in a mathematics selection, students can learn the meaning of new terms.

2. Write the word *twenty-thousands* on the chalkboard. Below it write a sentence that explains this word, such as *The number 20,000 means two ten thousands, no thousands, no hundreds, no tens, and no ones.* Have a volunteer explain how this sentence helps them understand the meaning of the term *twenty-thousands*.

3. Have students read the Word Clues section on page 105 and complete the activity.

Previewing the Text

Have students preview the selection text. Ask them to make observations about the text structure. Hand them copies of the KWL Chart to record their observations.

Purpose-Setting Question

How will understanding place values help me read large numbers?

▶ DURING READING

Remind students to think about place value and to look for examples to help them read large numbers.

▶ AFTER READING

Ask a volunteer to answer the purpose-setting question. Have students complete their KWL Charts. Then have students complete the activities on pages 106–108.

Reading-Writing Connection

To help students write the large numbers from articles in words, suggest they first put the numbers in a place-value chart.

ESL/ELL Strategy

ORGANIZING INFORMATION Encourage students to create place-value charts that extend to six places. Then have them make up six-digit numbers, write them on their place-value charts, and say the numbers correctly.

LESSON 37

Skill: Accented Syllable and Schwa
(page 109)

OBJECTIVES:
▶ Recognize the accented syllable
▶ Recognize the schwa sound

Teaching the Skill

1. Ask students to listen carefully to the following questions as you stress the syllables in capital letters. *Do we buy things at the mar KET or at the MAR ket? Do children play with BAL loons or bal LOONS?* Lead students to see that one syllable in a word is usually accented, or said with more stress than the other syllable(s) in the word. Write *market* and *balloons* on the chalkboard, dividing the words into syllables, and use an accent mark (´) to show the accented syllables.

2. Have students read the introductory paragraph on page 109 and complete Exercise A independently.

3. Write the following words on the chalkboard: *about, police, depend.* Divide the words into syllables, and ask students to pronounce them. Ask which syllable is accented in each word. (the second) Then ask what vowel sound they hear in the unaccented syllable of each word. (a soft, short *u* sound) Explain that the short *u* sound is called the schwa sound. Underline the vowel that represents the schwa sound in each word, and tell students that the schwa sound can be represented by the vowels *a, e, i, o,* or *u.*

4. Call on students to read the text in the middle of page 109. Have individuals pronounce each of the example words and note the soft, short *u* sound. Show students the symbol that is used for the schwa sound. Have students complete Exercise B independently.

ESL/ELL Strategy

USING MANIPULATIVES Ask students to make labels for objects they see in the classroom, dividing the words into syllables and placing accent marks on the stressed syllables.

Extension Activity

Challenge students to name words that change their meaning depending on which syllable is accented. As an example, give them the word *record.* When the first syllable is accented, *record* is a noun, meaning "anything that is written and kept." When the second syllable is accented, *record* is a verb meaning "to put in some permanent form."

LESSON 38

Skill: Syllables (page 110)

OBJECTIVE:
▶ Divide words with prefixes or suffixes into syllables

Teaching the Skill

1. Explain that words can be divided into syllables at their prefixes and suffixes.

2. Write the words *reheat* and *faithful* on the chalkboard, and have a volunteer divide these words into syllables. Elicit that both the prefix *re-* and the suffix *-ful* have their own vowel sound and are separate syllables.

3. Have students read the paragraphs at the top of page 110 and then complete Exercise A independently. Then review the rule together.

4. Review the rules for dividing compound words and words with double consonants into syllables. Then have students complete Exercise C independently.

ESL/ELL Strategy

USING MANIPULATIVES Ask pairs of students to write five words from each exercise on page 110 on separate index cards. Have students take turns drawing cards, identifying whether Rule 1, Rule 2, or Rule 3 applies to the word, and then dividing the word into syllables.

Extension Activity

Give students a list of words that contain both prefixes and suffixes, and have them divide the words into syllables. Sample words include *unlikely, incorrectly, distasteful,* and *untruthful.*

LESSON 39

Skill: Fact and Opinion (page 111)

OBJECTIVE:
▶ Distinguish facts from opinions

Teaching the Skill

1. Read aloud a few brief ads from a magazine or newspaper. Stop after certain statements, and ask students whether they would be able to check if the information in them is true. Explain that a statement that can be checked and proven to be correct is called a *fact*, while a statement that cannot be checked and proven is called an *opinion*.

2. Say: *There are more than 100 million automobiles in the United States.* Ask students whether it is a fact or an opinion, and ask how they can check. (It is a fact. States register automobiles, so the total number of cars can be counted and checked.)

3. State: *Automobiles make our lives better.* Have students discuss whether this statement can be checked to see whether it is a fact. (It is an opinion. The word *better* signals a feeling or judgment that cannot be checked.)

4. Have students read the instructional paragraphs on page 111. Work through the first item in the exercise with the class. Then have students work independently on the remaining items.

ESL/ELL Strategy

PERSONALIZING THE LESSON Give pairs of students a list of topics such as *school, friends, clothes, cars,* and *music.* Have one partner state a fact about one of the topics. The other partner should then offer an opinion on the same topic. Have partners write their facts and opinions on five topics and then exchange lists with another pair. The pairs should distinguish the facts and opinions in each other's lists.

Extension Activity

Have groups of students read letters to the editor in a newspaper or magazine. Ask them to circle any facts and underline any opinions in the letters. Have the groups discuss how they might check the facts in the letters. Also ask them to evaluate whether each writer supported his or her opinion with enough facts.

LESSON 40

Skill: Main Idea and Supporting Details
(pages 112–113)

OBJECTIVE:
▶ Identify the main idea and supporting details of a paragraph

Teaching the Skill

1. Review that the main idea is the most important idea in a paragraph and the sentences that tell more about the main idea are called supporting details.

2. Display the following on an overhead transparency. *Steam-powered cars were very noisy. They frightened horses and people. Often they scattered hot coals, setting fire to fields and wooden bridges. Their black smoke dirtied the air in cities. All in all, early steam-powered vehicles had many problems.*

3. Distribute copies of the Main Idea and Supporting Details Map (page T61). Have students fill in the graphic organizer with the main idea and supporting details from the paragraph on the transparency.

4. Have students read the instructional paragraph and the sample paragraph about braking a car on page 112. Have them explain why the first sentence is the main idea. (It identifies the process that the rest of the paragraph explains in detail.) Then ask how each detail sentence supports the main idea. (Each detail explains part of the braking process.)

5. Have students complete the exercises on page 113 independently.

ESL/ELL Strategy

PERSONALIZING THE LESSON Have students work together to think of a sentence that states a main idea about their school or community. For example: *After 3:00, our school is still a busy place.* Then direct them to write three or more supporting details. For example: *Sports teams work out in the gym. Different clubs have meetings. Band members practice for a concert.*

Extension Activity

Have partners share recent writing assignments. Ask each partner to read the other's work, checking the paragraphs for main ideas and supporting details.

LESSON 41

Skill: Using a Table of Contents
(pages 114–115)

OBJECTIVE:
▶ Use a table of contents

Teaching the Skill

1. Review that a table of contents is found at the beginning of a book and that it lists chapter titles with pages that the chapters begin on. It may also list important topics.

2. Ask students to turn to the table of contents of this book on page 3. Ask: *In which lesson did we learn how to solve word problems?* (Lesson 4) *Which page would we turn to if we wanted to review that lesson?* (page 22) *In which unit did we learn about the International Space Station?* (Unit 2) *On what page does that selection begin?* (page 46) *What is the title of the literature selection we will read in Unit 5?* ("Test of Fire") Summarize by saying that a table of contents is a useful tool for quickly finding topics and page numbers.

3. Ask volunteers to read aloud the instructional paragraphs at the top of page 114. Then discuss the sample table of contents with students, summarizing what can be found in each chapter.

4. Work through item 1 on page 115 with the class. Then have students complete the remainder of the exercise independently.

ESL/ELL Strategy
USING REALIA Have pairs of students write five true/false questions based on the table of contents of this textbook. For example: *Lesson 45 is a science selection.* (true) *Lesson 35 teaches the skill of reading a map.* (false) Then have pairs exchange papers and answer each other's questions.

Extension Activity
Ask students to create a table of contents for a book they might like to write someday. Suggest that they choose a topic that interests them and with which they are familiar.

LESSON 42

Skill: Comparing Car Ads (pages 116–117)

OBJECTIVE:
▶ Compare and contrast ads for information

Teaching the Skill

1. Review that comparing is finding similarities between two things and that contrasting is finding differences.

2. Distribute handouts of two newspaper or magazine ads for two different types of cars. Ask students to note ways in which the cars are similar or different. Have them compare and contrast such features as size, design, cost, and special features.

3. Ask students to discuss how the ads might be useful if they were planning to buy a car. Point out that in addition to using persuasive techniques that appeal to emotions, ads often contain useful facts. Have students point out examples of facts in the ads.

4. Read the paragraph at the top of page 116. Then direct students to carefully read the ads for the Pashubi and Tilton cars. Direct students to complete the exercises on page 117.

ESL/ELL Strategy
USING REALIA Provide partners with car ads from a local newspaper or magazine. Ask students to circle facts and useful details about the cars with a red pencil. Suggest that they discuss what these facts mean and list them in chart form.

Extension Activity
Have small groups create their own car ads. Urge students to make their ads persuasive while including facts and details that would help a consumer learn more about the car. When groups are finished, have them display the ads on a bulletin board. Students can compare and contrast the ads for type of car, different facts and figures shown, type of persuasive language, and so on.

LESSON 43

Skill: Character (pages 118–122)

LITERATURE SELECTION: Test of Fire

OBJECTIVES:

▶ Analyze how a main character changes due to problems and goals

▶ Use synonyms as context clues

CONTEXT CLUE WORDS: *courageous, gear, crackling*

ESL/ELL WORDS: *medicine bag, parachute, flaming monster*

GRAPHIC ORGANIZER: Idea Web, p. T55

_____ **SELECTION SUMMARY** _____

In "Test of Fire," Tom Swift Eagle, a young American Indian smoke jumper, is fighting his first forest fire. Because many of the traditional rites of manhood have been lost by Tom's people, Tom sees fire fighting as a way to prove his courage.

▶ BEFORE READING

Have students read the Background Information on page 118 about American Indians long ago and the act of counting coup. Discuss some ways in which people today might try to prove their bravery.

Teaching Character

1. Explain that characters are the people in stories. They must often solve problems and overcome difficulties. As they do, readers learn what kind of people the characters are.

2. Have students name familiar characters from books or movies, identify the challenges they overcame, and suggest what their actions showed about them. List on the chalkboard characters and their qualities. Have students note which qualities appeared most often.

3. Direct students to read the Skill Focus on page 118 and complete the Idea Web about the characters.

Teaching Context Clues

1. Review that synonyms are words with the same or almost the same meanings. Ask students why authors often use synonyms in their writing. (to add variety to it) Point out that synonyms help explain new words in text.

2. Give this example. *I like baseball. I like football. I also like hockey.* Ask students to give synonyms for *like*. (enjoy, love)

3. Have students read the Context Clues section on page 118 and complete the activity.

4. Write the context clue words *courageous, gear,* and *crackling* on the chalkboard or word wall. Remind students to look for synonym clues for these words as they read the selection.

Previewing the Text

Have students preview the selection, studying the title and illustration to predict what will happen to Tom. Then distribute copies of the Idea Web. Have students write *Tom Swift Eagle* in the center and the following headings in the outer circles: *Tom's Goal, What Tom Is Like at First, How Tom Changes,* and *What Tom Learns.* As students read, they add details to the appropriate circles.

Purpose-Setting Question

How well does Tom do in his test of fire?

▶ DURING READING

As students read, remind them to look for details about Tom to add to their Idea Webs and use synonyms in the story to figure out the meanings of the underlined words.

▶ AFTER READING

Have volunteers discuss details they listed on their Idea Webs. Invite volunteers to sum up the story by answering the purpose-setting question. Then have students complete the activities on pages 121–122.

Reading-Writing Connection

As prewriting for a paragraph describing the bravest person students know, suggest that students use an Idea Web (page T55) to list details about the person, including his or her goals and the problems the person has overcome.

ESL/ELL Strategy

ROLE-PLAYING Have partners role-play the parts of Tom Swift Eagle and a newspaper reporter at the scene of the Pineville fire. The reporter interviews Tom about his experiences and tape-records his answers. The partners collaborate to write a short news story about the fire.

Skill: Using a Primary Source (pages 123–128)

SOCIAL STUDIES SELECTION: A Great and Honorable Leader

OBJECTIVES:
▶ Use a primary source
▶ Use details as context clues

CONTEXT CLUE WORDS: *retreat, pursuit, surrender*

ESL/ELL WORDS: *reservation, penned up, broken heart*

GRAPHIC ORGANIZER: Sequence Chart, p. T53

_____ **SELECTION SUMMARY** _____

"A Great and Honorable Leader" tells about Chief Joseph of the Nez Percé people. It describes his struggle to protect his people and save their land after gold was discovered there in 1860. An excerpt from Chief Joseph's memorable 1879 speech pleads his people's case in Washington, D.C.

▶ **BEFORE READING**

Have students read the Background Information on page 123 about the Nez Percé people. Then have students study the map of the Nez Percé region on page 124. Explain that the late 1800s was a sad and difficult time for most American Indians in the West. Have students share what they know about the problems American Indians faced then.

Teaching Using a Primary Source

1. Ask students if they have ever read a letter or diary written by someone long ago. Explain that such documents, called *primary sources*, can bring history to life by showing us what people in the past really thought and felt about the events they lived through.

2. Have students speculate on how a letter from a soldier describing a battle he had fought in might be different from an account of the same battle in a history book. (A soldier's letter might include personal feelings and observations; a history-book account would include facts, such as the causes and outcomes of the battle, the arms and strategies used, and the number of casualties.) List students' ideas on the chalkboard in two columns labeled *primary source* and *history book*.

3. Have students read the Skill Focus on page 123 and complete the chart on primary sources.

Teaching Context Clues

1. Remind students that details in the surrounding text can help explain a new word's meaning.

2. Distribute copies of the following: *The soldiers who fought Chief Joseph thought that he was a great and* <u>honorable</u> *man. The soldiers knew that the Nez Percé never killed without reason. The runaways could have burned and destroyed the property of many settlers, but they did not. Chief Joseph and his people fought only to defend themselves and their land.* Discuss details that help define *honorable*.

3. Have students read the Context Clues section on page 123 and complete the activity.

4. Write the words *retreat, pursuit,* and *surrender* on the chalkboard or word wall. Remind students to look for details that will help them understand these words.

Previewing the Text

Have students study the title, section headings, map, and photo. Based on this preview, ask students to predict what kinds of information they will learn. Distribute copies of the Sequence Chart. As students read, have them fill in important events in the lives of Chief Joseph and his people.

Purpose-Setting Question

Why did Chief Joseph deliver a speech to the U.S. government in 1879?

▶ **DURING READING**

As students read, have them carefully study the primary source, Chief Joseph's speech. Remind students to use details to figure out the meanings of the underlined words.

▶ **AFTER READING**

Ask students to share events listed on their Sequence Charts and use the details to answer the purpose-setting question. Have students complete the activities on pages 126–128.

Reading-Writing Connection

To help students write a speech from the point of view of a settler in the American West, provide primary sources for students, or ask a librarian to recommend books of letters and diaries written by settlers in the West in the 1800s.

ESL/ELL Strategy

SUMMARIZING Encourage partners to read the excerpt of Chief Joseph's speech aloud. Have students pause after every sentence or two to paraphrase.

Skill: Main Idea and Supporting Details
(pages 129–132)

SCIENCE SELECTION: Saving Parks and Wilderness Areas

OBJECTIVES:
▶ Identify main ideas and supporting details
▶ Use details as context clues

CONTEXT CLUE WORDS: *vandalism, defacement, extinct*

ESL/ELL WORDS: *fast-food restaurants, natural heritage, litter*

GRAPHIC ORGANIZER: Main Idea and Supporting Details Map, p. T61

SELECTION SUMMARY

"Saving Parks and Wilderness Areas" explores some of the threats facing many national parks and wilderness areas, such as overcrowding, litter, and vandalism. Threats are posed by ranchers, mining companies, and real-estate developers who want to exploit the resources of wilderness areas.

▶ BEFORE READING

Have students read the Background Information on page 129, and have them name some state or national parks that they have visited. Elicit whether the natural beauty and resources of the parks were being preserved and protected adequately or if problems existed.

Teaching Main Idea and Supporting Details

1. Remind students that the main idea is the most important idea in the paragraph, and supporting details tell more about that idea.

2. Invite a volunteer to state his or her feelings about a beautiful place. Write the statement on the chalkboard, and write *Main Idea* above it. For example, *Main Idea: A beautiful place makes me feel happy and content.* Ask other volunteers for statements that support the idea. List those, writing *Supporting Detail* next to each one. For example, *Supporting Detail: I find myself humming a song as I walk through a lovely meadow.*

3. Have students complete the Skill Focus activity on page 129.

Teaching Context Clues

1. Review that details in text often help explain the meaning of a new word.

2. Ask a volunteer to use a challenging word in a short sentence, and write it on the chalkboard. Invite other volunteers to write details on the chalkboard that help explain the word's meaning. For example: *I went spelunking.* Details: *I saw bats in the cave. I entered dark caverns. There was an underground lake.*

3. Have students read the Context Clues section on page 129 and complete the activity.

4. Write the context clue words *vandalism, defacement,* and *extinct* on the chalkboard or word wall. Remind students to find details to explain the words' meanings as they read the selection.

Previewing the Text

Have students preview, studying the photo and the numbered paragraphs. Ask what purpose the numbers might serve. (to label each paragraph for easy reference) Then distribute copies of the Main Idea and Supporting Details Map, and ask students to use the map to record the main idea and supporting details of each paragraph they read.

Purpose-Setting Question

What challenges do our country's national parks and wilderness areas face?

▶ DURING READING

As students read, remind them to identify the main idea and supporting details of each paragraph. Also have them look for details that reveal the meanings of the underlined words.

▶ AFTER READING

Ask students to state the main idea and supporting details of each paragraph. Have a volunteer answer the purpose-setting question. Then have students complete the activities on pages 131–132.

Reading-Writing Connection

Encourage small groups of students to debate the issue of whether more housing or more natural areas are needed in their community. Each group writes down the most persuasive arguments to use as main ideas and supporting details in their editorials.

ESL/ELL Strategy

USING VISUALS Encourage pairs of students to draw cartoons that illustrate threats to our national parks and wilderness areas. Partners then explain their cartoons to the class.

Skill: Reading a Table (pages 133–136)

MATHEMATICS SELECTION: A Growing Population

OBJECTIVES:

▶ Read a table

▶ Use synonyms as context clues

ESL/ELL WORDS: *New World, the West, records*

GRAPHIC ORGANIZER: KWL Chart, p. T57

SELECTION SUMMARY

"A Growing Population" presents information in text and mathematical tables about westward migration in the United States during the nineteenth century. It looks at changes in population in 11 states just west of the original 13 colonies between 1790 and 1830.

▶ BEFORE READING

Have students read the Background Information about tables on page 133. Discuss other real-life situations in which students might use tables to find information and where they might find these tables.

Teaching Reading a Table

1. Review that a table is a simple way to present number facts because it organizes facts in rows and columns. Have students look through their math, social studies, or science textbooks to find tables.

2. Using one of the tables students find, call on volunteers to name the title of the table and describe the labels for the rows and columns. Ask what information can be learned from them. Then ask students to state a few facts shown on the table.

3. Have students read the table on the Skills Focus on page 133 and complete the activity.

Teaching Word Clues

1. Review that synonyms are words with the same or similar meanings. They can help reveal new words in context.

2. Ask students to provide a synonym to help others understand the word *available* in this sentence. *No information was available, or _____, about the population of Ohio.* (handy, usable, accessible)

3. Have students read the Word Clues section on page 133 and complete the activity.

Previewing the Text

Have students preview the selection, studying the table on page 134. Ask them to predict what kinds of information they might learn about U.S. population. Have them fill in a KWL Chart with their ideas.

Purpose-Setting Question

How can using a table help me understand what I read?

▶ DURING READING

As students read, stress the importance of using the table on page 134 to help them understand the main idea of the selection. Also remind them to look for synonyms for the underlined words.

▶ AFTER READING

Have students think about what they learned from the table on page 134. *How did the number facts in the table support the main idea of the selection?* Based on this, have them answer the purpose-setting question. Then have students fill in their KWL Charts and complete the activities on pages 135–136.

Reading-Writing Connection

As research for their tables, students can find population data for their state at the U.S. Government's 2000 Census Web site: www.census.gov.

ESL/ELL Strategy

USING VISUALS Have pairs of students look at the tables on pages 134 and 136 and write four true/false questions based on the facts shown. Then have them exchange questions with another pair and answer each other's questions.

LESSON 47

Skill: Syllables (page 137)

OBJECTIVE:
▶ Divide two-syllable words with two consonants between two sounded vowels

Teaching the Skill

1. Review that a syllable is a part of a word in which you can hear a vowel sound. Words with more than one syllable can be separated according to the number of vowel sounds you hear. Ask students for a few examples of two-syllable words.

2. Write the words *winter* and *circus* on the chalkboard. Ask volunteers to name the vowels that are sounded in each word. Then ask a student to suggest how to divide these words into syllables. Explain that these words should be divided between the two consonants that come between the two sounded vowels. (win ter; cir cus)

3. Read the information at the top of page 137. Work through the first item in Exercise A with the class. Then have students complete the rest of Exercise A independently.

4. Have students fill in the rule and then read it aloud as a group.

5. Direct students to complete Exercise B independently.

ESL/ELL Strategy

USING MANIPULATIVES Ask students to write the words listed in Exercise B on a separate sheet of paper, one to a line. Direct them to hold an index card over the second syllable of each word and say the first syllable aloud. Then have them uncover the second syllable of the word and say it aloud. Finally, have students say the whole word, enunciating each syllable clearly.

Extension Activity

Invite students to use a dictionary to find at least ten words with three syllables. Each word should contain two consonants between two sounded vowels.

LESSON 48

Skill: Syllables (pages 138–139)

OBJECTIVE:
▶ Divide two-syllable words with one consonant between two sounded vowels

Teaching the Skill

1. Review the rule on page 137 for dividing words into syllables. Then explain that in this lesson they will learn three new rules for dividing words.

2. Write the words *spider* and *cabin* on the chalkboard. Have a volunteer identify the two sounded vowels in each word. Underline the vowels. Ask: *How many consonants come between each vowel?* (one) Circle the *d* in *spider* and the *b* in *cabin*. Then ask: *What vowel sound do you hear in the first syllable of* spider? (long *i*) *What vowel sound do you hear in the first syllable of* cabin? (short *a*). Write the words again, dividing them into syllables. (spi der, cab in) Tell students that they will learn new rules to help them divide words like these.

3. Turn to page 138 and read the instructional paragraph. Ask volunteers to answer the questions in Exercise A. Have students complete the rule and read it aloud. Then direct them to complete Exercise B independently.

4. For Exercise C, have students fill in the chart and then complete the rule.

5. Before beginning page 139, review the blends in Lessons 7, 8, 9, and 19. Call on volunteers to read the instructional paragraphs on page 139. Work through the first few items of Exercise D with the class. Then have students complete the remaining items independently and fill in the rule.

ESL/ELL Strategy

USING RESOURCES Give students the following list of words: *cradle, final, hotel, cycle, inflate, robin, fatal,* and *tonic.* Ask pairs of students to use the rules to decide how to divide the words into syllables. Suggest that students use a dictionary to check their answers.

Extension Activity

Have students write five sentences, using words from this lesson. Then have them exchange papers with a partner and divide the words in their partners' sentences into syllables.

LESSON 49

Skill: Making Inferences (page 140)

OBJECTIVE:
▶ Make inferences

Teaching the Skill

1. Ask students if they have ever heard the expression "to read between the lines." Discuss its possible meaning and determine that this idiom means "to fill in information that is not stated directly." Explain that authors cannot tell their readers everything when they write. They expect readers to fill in some information for themselves, using details in the text and what the readers already know from everyday life.

2. Read the following sentences. *Outside, Tip was barking, having cornered a small, furry black-and-white animal. Suddenly, a rank odor drifted toward the house. "Whew! What a smell!" said Mom, closing the window.* Ask: *Who is Tip and what is causing the awful smell?* When students state that Tip is the family dog and that he has cornered a skunk, ask if these details were stated directly in the paragraph (no), and how they knew the answer. (They inferred these ideas from details in the text and from what they already know about dogs and skunks.)

3. Read the instructional paragraph on page 140. Hand out copies of the Inference Chart (p. T62). Ask students to use this chart to make inferences as they read.

4. Have students use their Inference Charts to help them answer the questions on page 140.

ESL/ELL Strategy

ORGANIZING INFORMATION On their Inference Charts (p. T62) ask students to make two additional inferences about Ada Deer. Ask partners to discuss the new inferences.

Extension Activity

Have students find and read short articles about well-known national or local leaders. Have students write three inferences about the person, based on details in the text.

LESSON 50

Skill: Alphabetical Order (page 141)

OBJECTIVE:
▶ Arrange words in alphabetical order according to the first and second letter of the word

Teaching the Skill

1. With students, brainstorm a list of everyday situations in which alphabetical order is used to organize people, things, and information. (volumes of an encyclopedia, names in a telephone book, authors of books of fiction in the library, items in the index of a book, and so on)

2. Write the following words on the chalkboard: *spider, dragonfly, ant,* and *caterpillar.* Ask a volunteer to list the words in alphabetical order and to explain how they determined the order. (ant, caterpillar, dragonfly, spider; by the first letter of each word)

3. Then write these words on the chalkboard: *butterfly, beetle,* and *blackbird.* Ask students how they would put these words in alphabetical order. Lead students to see that if the first letters of the words are the same, they must look at the second letters. Underline the second letter in each word, and have students tell you the correct alphabetical order for the words. (beetle, blackbird, butterfly)

4. Have students read the instructional paragraph at the top of page 141 and alphabetize the words in Exercise A.

5. Have a student read aloud the instructional copy in the middle of page 141. Point out that all the words in Exercise B begin with *a,* so students will need to use the second letter of each word to alphabetize them. Have students complete Exercise B independently.

ESL/ELL Strategy

USING MANIPULATIVES Have pairs of students make flashcards using the words in Exercise A or B. They should shuffle the cards and then place them in alphabetical order.

Extension Activity

Ask students to create a list of ten or more words all beginning with the same two letters. Ask students to write the words in random order. Then have students exchange lists with partners and alphabetize the words.

LESSON 51

Skill: Using Guide Words (page 142)

OBJECTIVE:
▶ Use guide words to find entry words in a dictionary

Teaching the Skill

1. Give students a page number in a classroom dictionary, and ask them to find the guide words at the top of that page. Explain that guide words, like a guide, point you in the right direction when you are looking for a certain word in a dictionary. Point out that the guide words indicate the first and last words on a dictionary page, and all the other words on the page come between them in alphabetical order.

2. Give students the following two guide words: *drill* and *drone*. Ask: *Would the word* drape *appear on this page?* (no) *How do you know?* (*Dra* comes before *dri*.)

3. Have students read the instructional paragraph and the paragraph of directions on page 142. Work through items 1–3 of Exercise A together. Then allow them to work independently on the remainder of the exercises.

ESL/ELL Strategy

USING RESOURCES Have partners write down two actual guide words from a dictionary page. Then have them list ten words, some of which are on the page and some of which come before or after the page. Have partners exchange their list with another pair and complete each other's exercises.

Extension Activity

Have students turn to any dictionary page and read the guide words. Without looking further at the page, have them write at least five words that could appear on that page. Students could do this activity in teams, competing to see which team lists the most correct words in one minute.

LESSON 52

Skill: Reading a Dictionary Entry (page 143)

OBJECTIVE:
▶ Use a dictionary entry

Teaching the Skill

1. Provide a dictionary entry for a word such as *stock* or *stop*, which has many different meanings and parts of speech. Ask students to study the entry and tell you what they can learn from it. List students' responses on the chalkboard.

2. Ask questions such as *What do you think these letters in parentheses are for?* (pronunciation) *What do you think the letter* n *means?* (noun) *Why are there some sentences in wavy type?* (example of usage) *What are the words in heavy, or boldface, type at the end of the entry?* (other forms of the word)

3. Have volunteers read aloud the paragraphs on page 143. Stop after each paragraph to make sure that students can identify the appropriate information in the sample dictionary entry on the page. Then have students use the sample dictionary entry to complete the activity.

ESL/ELL Strategy

USING RESOURCES Give pairs of students three words to look up in a dictionary. For each entry word, have them locate the respelling, the part-of-speech labels, and the definitions. Then have them write an original sentence using each word and read it to their partners.

Extension Activity

Invite students to write a dictionary entry for a new word that they invent. Remind them to include the respelling, part-of-speech label, definition, and an example sentence using the word. If appropriate, students can add an illustration of their new word as part of the entry.

Skill: Using a Library Catalog (pages 144–145)

OBJECTIVE:

◗ Use a library catalog to find books

Teaching the Skill

1. Invite students to share the procedures they follow when trying to find books in the library. Ask: *How can you find a book when you know the title?* (title search) *How can you find a book when you only know the author's name?* (author search) *How can you find a book when you only know the subject you want to learn about?* (subject search)

2. Read aloud the information on page 144. If your school has an Internet connection or a computerized catalog, log on to your local library and have students follow the steps described as you read.

3. Draw students' attention to the screen from the computerized library catalog on page 144. Explain that the information on the screen tells about a book titled *Close Encounters: Exploring the Universe with the Hubble Space Telescope.* Ask students to speculate how you know that. Have students use this information to answer items 1–4 in Exercise A. Then go over the answers with the class.

4. Have students complete Exercises B and C independently.

ESL/ELL Strategy

USING RESOURCES Have pairs of students choose a topic they would like to know more about. Have them access the school or local library catalog to compile a list of five or more books related to their topic. Have them include the titles, authors' names, and call numbers.

Extension Activity

Ask students to interview a librarian to find out how nonfiction books are assigned a call number and arranged on the library shelves. Ask students to give a short oral report on the Dewey Decimal System and to bring in examples of the kinds of books students can find in different categories, from the 300s to the 900s of the Dewey Decimal system.

Skill: Using a Bus Route Map (pages 146–147)

OBJECTIVE:

◗ Use a bus route map

Teaching the Skill

1. If any students have used bus route maps, have them describe their experiences. If possible, bring in copies of local bus route maps for students to study.

2. Have students study the bus route map on page 146. Then ask what features this map has in common with world maps they have studied. Determine that both have a map key and a compass rose. Have students discuss how a map key and compass rose would be helpful when planning a trip by bus.

3. Ask students to point out specific landmarks on the map—such as City Hall, Baker Medical Center, and Memorial Library. Discuss how landmarks help in reading a bus route map. (Landmarks are things people can look for to find out where they are.)

4. Direct students to the opening paragraph and directions on page 146 and work through the first four items in Exercise A. Call on volunteers to explain how they figured out their answers. Then have students complete the remaining exercises independently.

ESL/ELL Strategy

ROLE-PLAYING Let pairs of students role-play a traveler and a bus driver. Using the map on page 146, the traveler asks a question about which bus or buses to take to reach a certain location. The driver then uses the map to suggest the best route to take. Then have students switch roles.

Extension Activity

Ask students to obtain bus route maps from their town or from a nearby city. You might want to have maps available in the classroom. Have students use the maps to plan a bus trip in which they stop at four or more sites.

LESSON 55

Skill: Setting and Dialogue (pages 148–154)

LITERATURE SELECTION: Talk

OBJECTIVES:
▶ Analyze setting and dialogue in a short story
▶ Use a dictionary to learn the meanings of new words

CONTEXT CLUE WORDS: *ford, wheezed, refrain*

ESL/ELL WORDS: *chewing her cud, what's the hurry, disturbing the peace*

GRAPHIC ORGANIZER: Prediction Chart, p. T58

SELECTION SUMMARY

This short story, "Talk," is a West African folktale in which some people are surprised by the things around them. A farmer, a fisherman, a weaver, and a bather are frightened when things begin to speak to them. They take their frightening story to the village chief. He calms them down, but then gets a surprise of his own.

▶ BEFORE READING

Have students read the Background Information on page 148 about the Asante people. The first Asante king was named Osei Tutu. He came to power in the 1600s. The symbol of his power was a golden stool. Ask students to look for a stool in "Talk" and find who uses it.

Teaching Setting and Dialogue

1. To teach setting, discuss a TV show that students know. Remind them that setting is time and place of a story.

2. Point out that many times, before a new scene, the camera uses an establishing shot. This brief shot of a building or other place shows what the setting is. TV shows also give clues about setting through props, sets, clothing, and the characters' ways of speaking. In a short story, students can look for similar details as clues to the story's setting.

3. To teach dialogue, ask students to think of lines from the TV show. Write the lines on the chalkboard next to the character's name. Use quotation marks, commas, and other proper punctuation for dialogue. Point out these elements to students.

4. Have students read the Skill Focus on page 148 and complete the activity.

Teaching Context Clues

1. Explain that when no context clue is nearby, students can use a dictionary to look up new words or new meanings of familiar words.

2. Write the following on the chalkboard: *"Now this is really a wild story,"* he said at last. Discuss the possible meanings of *wild*. Have a volunteer look up the word in a dictionary to find the meaning used in the sentence (going beyond normal or conventional bounds).

3. Have students read the Context Clues section on page 148 and complete the activity.

4. Write the context clue words *ford, wheezed,* and *refrain* on the chalkboard or word wall. Tell students to look up these words in a dictionary as they read the story.

Previewing the Text

Have students preview the story, including the illustrations. Ask them to think about the setting. Then distribute copies of the Prediction Chart and ask students to predict what might happen. Remind students to revise their predictions as they read the story.

Purpose-Setting Question

Why are so many of the characters frightened?

▶ DURING READING

As students read, encourage them to pay attention to the setting and dialogue. Have students use a dictionary to look up the unfamiliar words.

▶ AFTER READING

Ask students which predictions on their charts turned out to be accurate and which ones they had to revise. Then invite volunteers to answer the purpose-setting question. Have students complete the activities on pages 151–154.

Reading-Writing Connection

Before students write, remind them that quotation marks are used around dialogue. Explain that double quotation marks are for regular dialogue. Single quotation marks are for dialogue inside another character's speech.

ESL/ELL Strategy

MANIPULATIVES Have partners draw a map of Ghana. Ask them to indicate Accra and other major cities, as well as rivers, mountains, or other major geographical features.

Skill: Reading a Map (pages 155–160)

SOCIAL STUDIES SELECTION: The Great Rift Valley

OBJECTIVES:

▶ Reading political and physical maps

▶ Use appositives as context clues

CONTEXT CLUE WORDS: *dormant, craters, savannas*

ESL/ELL WORDS: *crust, branches, source*

GRAPHIC ORGANIZER: Idea Web, p. T55

_____ SELECTION SUMMARY _____

"The Great Rift Valley" gives an overview of the distinctive landforms of the Great Rift Valley of eastern Africa. After an account of the geologic forces that shaped the valley, the selection describes its volcanic mountains, salty lakes, and lush savannas. The piece also discusses some of the wildlife as well as the archaeological discoveries in the valley.

▶ **BEFORE READING**

Have students read the Background Information about the Great Rift Valley on page 155. On a world map, point out eastern Africa and the general region of the Great Rift Valley. Invite volunteers to share what they know about this region.

Teaching Reading a Map

1. Review the difference between physical and political maps. (A physical map shows the Earth's features. A political map shows countries, cities, and boundaries.)

2. Ask students to leaf through their social studies books or encyclopedias to find examples of each type of map. Have students jot down the kinds of information presented on physical and political maps. List these in two columns on the chalkboard.

3. Direct students to the map in the Skill Focus on page 155 and complete the activity.

Teaching Context Clues

1. Explain that an appositive is a word or phrase that comes after an unfamiliar word and is usually set off by commas. Point out that authors of textbooks often use appositives to define or explain words for readers.

2. Write the following on the chalkboard. *Lake Tanganyika fills a tremendous fault, or crack, in the Earth.* Ask: *What is the appositive?* (or crack) *What does the appositive define?* (fault)

3. Have students read the Context Clues section on page 155 and complete the activity.

4. Write the context clue words *dormant, craters,* and *savannas* on the chalkboard or word wall. Remind students to look for appositives for these words as they read the selection.

Previewing the Text

Have students preview the title, section headings, maps, and photo to predict what they will learn about the Great Rift Valley. Distribute two copies of the Idea Web to each student. Invite students to write *Physical Map* in one and *Political Map* in the other. Then ask them to fill in the web with examples of the features or items they would find on each type of map.

Purpose-Setting Question

What makes the Great Rift Valley a dramatic and rich natural environment?

▶ **DURING READING**

As students read, remind them to look at the political and physical maps. Also remind them to use appositives to figure out the meanings of the underlined words.

▶ **AFTER READING**

Ask students to share some of the features about physical and political maps that they have noted on their Idea Webs. Also invite volunteers to summarize what they have read by answering the purpose-setting question. Then have students complete the activities on pages 158–160.

Reading-Writing Connection

Before writing their paragraphs, have groups of students brainstorm lists of geographic features of their region. Discuss how they shape their communities and affect their experiences.

ESL/ELL Strategy

USING RESOURCES Have partners write five questions about each map on a sheet of paper. Then have pairs exchange papers and answer each other's questions.

SELECTION SUMMARY

"Antelopes" describes some of the features of these deerlike animals that live mainly in Africa. The article highlights a few of the 150 kinds of antelopes, including elands, gazelles, and impalas. The selection explains that antelopes are ruminants. It offers accounts of how antelopes process plants in their four-part stomachs.

▶ BEFORE READING

Have students read the Background Information about antelopes on page 161. Ask what students know about wild grazing animals in North America, such as deer, moose, caribou, and elk.

Teaching Making Inferences

1. Review with students that they can make inferences by combining the details they read with what they already know. Explain that making inferences is a way to figure out information that is not stated directly in the text.

2. Read the following sentence aloud. *A graceful, brown animal leaped over the fence in our suburban backyard and began eating our bushes.* Ask students what animal the sentence probably describes. (a deer) Ask students what they already knew that helped them figure this out. (Deer can jump; they are brown; they can live in suburbs; they eat bushes.)

3. Have students read the Skill Focus on page 161 and complete the Inference Chart.

Teaching Context Clues

1. Remind students that science texts often include definitions of important terms.

2. Write the following on the chalkboard: *A deer is _____.* Have volunteers complete the sentence with definitions. If you wish, have students use a dictionary.

3. Have students read the Context Clues section on page 161 and complete the activity.

4. Write the context clue words *permanent, chambers,* and *digestive* on the chalkboard or word wall. Remind students to look for definitions for these words as they read the selection.

Previewing the Text

Have students preview, studying the photos and the diagram. Then distribute copies of the Inference Chart. Ask students to combine details from the text and the photos with their own prior knowledge to make inferences as they read.

Purpose-Setting Question

How does an antelope's special stomach help it to digest grass and other plants?

▶ DURING READING

As students read, remind them to make inferences. Also have them look for definitions of the underlined words.

▶ AFTER READING

Invite students to share some of the inferences they made while reading. Ask students to provide an answer to the purpose-setting question and complete the activities on pages 163–165.

Reading-Writing Connection

Have students create a Venn Diagram or use the one on page T60 as a prewriting tool on which to list similarities and differences between an antelope and a deer. Students can compare and contrast the size, weight, diet, habitat, and appearance of the two animals.

ESL/ELL Strategy

USING VISUALS Have partners use the diagram of an antelope's stomach on page 163 to prepare a step-by-step oral report on how food moves through the different chambers of an antelope's stomach.

Skill: Reading Fractions (pages 166–169)

MATHEMATICS SELECTION: **How to Read Fractions**

OBJECTIVES:

▶ Read fractions

▶ Use definitions as word clues

ESL/ELL WORDS: *shaded, stand for, diagrams*

GRAPHIC ORGANIZER: Inference Chart, p. T62

SELECTION SUMMARY

"How to Read Fractions" uses figures to introduce the concept of fractions and to define the related mathematical terms. It also provides students with practice in identifying and reading fractions.

▶ BEFORE READING

Have students read the Background Information about fractions on page 166. Ask volunteers to suggest other everyday situations at home, at school, or at a store, in which fractions, or parts of a whole, are important.

Teaching Reading Fractions

1. Have students consider the following situation. *Eight friends are sharing a pizza that has been cut into eight equal slices. What part, or fraction, of the pizza will each person get?* Draw the pizza, cut into eighths, on the chalkboard, and ask a volunteer to shade the part each person would get. ($\frac{1}{8}$) Write the fraction $\frac{1}{8}$, and say the fraction's name, *one-eighth*. Explain to students that the bottom number tells how many equal parts of the pizza there are. The top number tells how many parts each person will get.

2. Have volunteers suggest other fractional examples and draw them on the chalkboard.

3. Have students read the Skill Focus on page 166 and complete the activity.

Teaching Word Clues

1. Explain that this selection defines two mathematical terms, *numerator* and *denominator*.

2. Refer to the fraction $\frac{1}{8}$ on the chalkboard. Write *numerator* next to the top number and *denominator* next to the bottom number. Ask students if they can guess what these words mean.

3. Have students read the Word Clues section on page 166.

4. Remind students to look for the definitions of *numerator* and *denominator* as they read to determine if their guesses of the definitions were accurate.

Previewing the Text

Have students preview the selection text, paying attention to the underlined words and the many figures shown. Provide students with copies of the Inference Chart, and ask them to complete the Charts based on their observations.

Purpose-Setting Question

How will being able to read fractions help me in math and in everyday life?

▶ DURING READING

Remind students to think of fractions as parts of a whole and to look for the definitions of *numerator* and *denominator*.

▶ AFTER READING

Ask students to answer the purpose-setting question and to give definitions of the terms *numerator* and *denominator*. Allow them to use their completed Inference Charts to respond to the questions. Then have students complete the activities on pages 168–169.

Reading-Writing Connection

Invite pairs of students to brainstorm situations in which they recently used fractions. Have them choose two of the ideas for their paragraphs.

ESL/ELL Strategy

USING MANIPULATIVES Give groups a cut-out square, rectangle, and circle. Ask them to divide each shape into enough equal parts so that each member of the group will receive an equal share of the whole. Then have them write and name the fraction that represents each individual's share.

LESSON 59

Skill: Multiple-Meaning Words (page 170)
OBJECTIVE:
▶ Recognize multiple meanings of words

Teaching the Skill

1. Read the following sentences aloud to the group. *The prisoner was in his cell. A solar cell powered the calculator.* Ask what the word *cell* means in the first sentence. (a small room in a jail) Ask what it means in the second sentence. (a small battery) Point out that many words have more than one meaning.

2. Explain that words with multiple meanings often have an everyday meaning and a special meaning when used in science, mathematics, or social studies. For example, a *line* in everyday life is a group of people standing and waiting their turn; in mathematics, however, a *line* is an endless number of points that go on forever in two directions.

3. Have students read the paragraph at the top of page 170. Call on volunteers to read aloud the list of words with multiple meanings, and ask students to explain some different meanings for each word.

4. Work with students to complete the first item of the exercise. Then have students work independently on the remaining items.

ESL/ELL Strategy

USING VISUALS Ask partners to choose five of the multiple-meaning words from page 170. Have them divide a sheet of paper into two columns and draw pictures or cartoons that illustrate the two meanings of each word. Then have them write a caption for each picture, giving the word and its definition.

Extension Activity

Have students use a dictionary to find words with many different meanings. Some possibilities include *cover, block, court, set,* and *run.* Students write sentences using at least three meanings of each word.

LESSON 60

Skill: Prefixes (page 171)
OBJECTIVES:
▶ Add prefixes to change the meanings of words
▶ Use prefixes as clues to the meanings of words

Teaching the Skill

1. Review that a prefix is a word part added to the beginning of a word to change its meaning. Explain that prefixes can be used to figure out words' meanings.

2. Write the words *heated, preheated,* and *reheated* on the chalkboard and ask a volunteer to circle the prefixes. Explain that the prefix *pre-* means "before" or "in advance." The prefix *re-* means "again" or "back." Ask students for the meaning of *preheat* (to heat before) and *reheat* (to heat again).

3. Have a student read aloud the opening paragraph on page 171 and the list of prefixes with their meanings. Then have students complete Exercises A and B independently.

ESL/ELL Strategy

USING MANIPULATIVES Ask small groups to write each of the prefixes in this lesson on a separate index card. Students take turns drawing a card, saying the prefix, and suggesting a base word to which it could be added. Another student from the group defines the word and uses it in an original sentence.

Extension Activity

Ask students to read magazine or newspaper articles to find 10 words with prefixes. First have them write each word they find and figure out its meaning. Then they can write a brief story using as many of the words as they can.

LESSON 61

Good ideas — apply to comprehension too

Skill: Suffixes (page 172)

OBJECTIVES:
▶ Add suffixes to change the meanings of words
▶ Use suffixes as clues to the meanings of words

Teaching the Skill

1. Review that a suffix is a word part added to the end of a word to change its meaning. Explain that suffixes can be used as clues to figure out words' meanings.

2. Write the words *shy, shyly,* and *shyness* on the chalkboard. Ask a volunteer to underline the base word *shy* in all three words, and explain that the words are all related but have slightly different meanings. Circle the suffixes *-ly* and *-ness*, and explain that the suffix *-ly* means "like in appearance or certain manner," and the suffix *-ness* means "the quality or state of." Have students explain the meanings of *shyly* (in a shy manner) and *shyness* (the state of being shy).

3. Have students read the opening paragraph and the list of suffixes and their meanings on page 172. Then have students complete Exercises A and B independently.

ESL/ELL Strategy

IDENTIFYING ESSENTIAL VOCABULARY Encourage pairs of students to write a word for each of these suffixes: *-er, -en, -ful, -ly,* and *-ness.* Then have them write a sentence using each word. Have partners take turns reading their sentences to each other, using a base word and a suffix definition instead of the word. For example: *My uncle is a person who sings.* Students can replace the base word and definition with a suffixed word: *My uncle is a singer.*

Extension Activity

Challenge students to think of words that contain two or more suffixes. As examples, give them the words *strengthener, powerfully,* and *joyfulness.* Invite students to write an original sentence using each of the two-suffix words.

LESSON 62

Skill: Using an Encyclopedia (page 173)

OBJECTIVE:
▶ Use an encyclopedia

Teaching the Skill

1. Explain that encyclopedia articles are arranged in alphabetical order and that each volume covers topics beginning with different letters of the alphabet. Ask students which volumes they would need in order to look up articles on the Great Rift Valley and antelopes. (G and A)

2. If possible, bring in several volumes and distribute them to groups of students. Ask each group to list five interesting topics in alphabetical order in its volume.

3. Have students read the instructional paragraphs at the top of page 173 and study the illustration of a set of encyclopedias. Ask: *How many volumes does this set of encyclopedias have?* (16) *What letters are covered in Volume 7?* (G and H) *Which volume covers topics that begin with T?* (Volume 14) *Which volume would you need to find out more about antelopes?* (Volume 1)

4. Have students complete the exercise on page 173.

ESL/ELL Strategy

USING RESOURCES Ask pairs of students to think of a topic they would like to know more about. Students brainstorm five questions they would like to answer about the topic and use encyclopedias in the library to find answers to the questions.

Extension Activity

Have students write reports on a topic that interests them. Have students use online encyclopedias to research information before they write. Explain to students that online encyclopedias are set up the same way as printed encyclopedias.

Skill: Using a Mall Floor Plan (pages 174–175)

OBJECTIVE:
▶ Use a mall floor plan

Teaching the Skill

1. Invite volunteers to tell about some of the larger malls in which they have shopped and whether they ever had trouble finding specific stores or other services. Point out that most large malls have floor plans posted in central locations of the mall.

2. If possible, obtain copies of the floor plan for a large mall in your area, and distribute them to students. Otherwise, draw a simple floor plan on the chalkboard. Include stores, service areas, and landmarks. Call on volunteers to ask questions about the stores or services in the mall, and have other volunteers answer them.

3. Direct students to page 174, and have volunteers read the paragraphs at the top of the page. Make sure students can find the arrow that indicates where they would be standing if they were reading the floor plan in the mall. Make sure they can identify specific locations, using the numbers shown on the key and on the floor plan. Have students identify the symbols in the key used to show benches, telephones, and restrooms. Ask a volunteer to point out the location of the mall parking lots and the roads that lead to the mall.

4. Have students complete the exercises on page 175.

ESL/ELL Strategy

USING MANIPULATIVES Ask partners to draw a rough floor plan of their school. Have them create a key that lists the classrooms, other areas in the school, and symbols they've included in their floor plan.

Extension Activity

Suppose that the Randolph Road Shopping Mall underwent an expansion that doubled its size and number of stores. Have students create a floor plan for the new mall, showing the types of stores and other features that they would like to add. Remind students to include the new features in a revised key.

BE A BETTER READER

READER

EIGHTH EDITION

NILA BANTON SMITH

PEARSON

Pronunciation Key

Symbol	Key Word	Respelling		Symbol	Key Word	Respelling
a	act	(akt)		u	book	(buk)
ah	star	(stahr)			put	(put)
ai	dare	(dair)		uh	cup	(kuhp)
aw	also	(AWL soh)				
ay	flavor	(FLAY vər)		ə	a *as in*	
					along	(ə LAWNG)
e	end	(end)			e *as in*	
ee	eat	(eet)			moment	(MOH mənt)
er	learn	(lern)			i *as in*	
	sir	(ser)			modify	(MAHD ə fy)
	fur	(fer)			o *as in*	
					protect	(prə TEKT)
i	hit	(hit)			u *as in*	
eye	idea	(eye DEE ə)			circus	(SER kəs)
y	like	(lyk)				
ir	deer	(dir)		ch	chill	(chil)
	fear	(fir)		g	go	(goh)
				j	joke	(johk)
oh	open	(OH pen)			bridge	(brij)
oi	foil	(foil)		k	kite	(kyt)
	boy	(boi)			cart	(kahrt)
or	horn	(horn)		ng	bring	(bring)
ou	out	(out)		s	sum	(suhm)
	flower	(FLOU ər)			cent	(sent)
oo	hoot	(hoot)		sh	sharp	(shahrp)
	rule	(rool)		th	thin	(thin)
				th	then	(*then*)
yoo	few	(fyoo)		z	zebra	(ZEE brə)
	use	(yooz)			pose	(pohz)
				zh	treasure	(TREZH ər)

Acknowledgments: Grateful acknowledgment is made to the following for copyrighted material: **Henry Holt and Company, LLC:** "Talk" by Harold Courlander and George Herzog from *The Cow-Tail Switch and Other West African Stories.* Copyright © 1947, 1974 by Harold Courlander. Reprinted by permission of Henry Holt and Company, LLC. **John Wiley & Sons, Inc.:** "Wear" from *Webster's New World Dictionary, Basic School Edition.* Copyright © 1989 by John Wiley & Sons, Inc. Reprinted by permission of John Wiley & Sons, Inc. Note: Every effort has been made to locate the copyright owner of material reproduced in this component. Omissions brought to our attention will be corrected in subsequent editions.

Photo Credits: Cover images, clockwise from top left: © Getty Images, © Steffen Foerster Photography/Shutterstock, © Juicedrops, Charmaine Whitman/Pearson, © PhotoSky 4t com/Shutterstock, © hfng/Shutterstock, © Art Explosion, © Juice Drops, © Kirill Roslyakov/Shutterstock, © Brand X Pictures; Cover background: © Juicedrops; Lesson and unit opener: © Stockbyte; p. 8: © AP Images; p. 18: © Geoff Dann/DK Images; p. 19 (left): © T.W./Shutterstock; p. 19 (right): © Robert Taylor/Shutterstock; p. 51: © Mike Liu/Shutterstock; p. 63: © Jochen Tack/Das Fotoarchiv/Black Star/Alamy; p. 64: © PhotoAlto/Jupiter Images; p. 69: © Gary Blakeley/Shutterstock; p. 70: © Thierry Maffeis/Shutterstock; p. 74: © Jim Rider/AP Images; p. 75: © Kim D. French/Shutterstock; p. 89: © Birgid Allig/zefa/Corbis; p. 91: © Simon Eldon/PYMCA/Jupiter Images; p. 95: © SuperStock, Inc./SuperStock; p. 96: © Hemera Technologies/Jupiter Images; p. 97: © Michael Shake/Shutterstock; p. 125: © Bettmann/CORBIS; p. 130: © Diana Jo Currier/Shutterstock; p. 140: © MPI/Getty Images; p. 149 (all illustrations): © Art Explosion; p. 149–151 (border): © Juice Drops; p. 150 (bottom): © North Wind Picture Archives/Alamy; p. 157: © Photodisc/Getty Images; p. 162 (clockwise from top left): © EcoPrint/Shutterstock, © Sebastien Burel/Shutterstock, © Steffen Foerster Photography/Shutterstock, © Steffen Foerster Photography/Shutterstock.

Staff Credits: Joshua Adams, Melania Benzinger, Karen Blonigen, Laura Chadwick, Andreea Cimoca, Katie Colón, Nancy Condon, Barbara Drewlo, Kerry Dunn, Marti Erding, Sara Freund, Daren Hastings, Ruby Hogen-Chin, Mariann Johanneck, Julie Johnston, Mary Kaye Kuzma, Mary Lukkonen, Carol Nelson, Carrie O'Connor, Marie Schaefle, Julie Theisen, Chris Tures, Mike Vineski, Charmaine Whitman, Sue Will

ISBN-13: 978-0-7854-6656-7

ISBN-10: 0-7854-6656-8

1 2 3 4 5 6 7 8 9 10   12 11 10 09 08

Contents

Contents
continued

How to Use *Be A Better Reader*

For more than thirty years, **Be A Better Reader** has helped students improve their reading skills. **Be A Better Reader** teaches the comprehension and study skills that you need to read and enjoy all types of materials—from library books to the different textbooks that you will encounter in school.

To get the most from **Be A Better Reader**, you should know how the lessons are organized. As you read the following explanations, it will be helpful to look at some of the lessons.

In each of the first four lessons of a unit, you will apply an important skill to a reading selection in literature, social studies, science, or mathematics. Each of these lessons includes the following nine sections.

▶ BACKGROUND INFORMATION

This section gives you interesting information about the selection you are about to read. It will help you understand the ideas that you need in order to learn new skills.

▶ SKILL FOCUS

This section teaches you a specific skill. You should read the Skill Focus carefully, paying special attention to words that are printed in boldface type. The Skill Focus tells you about a skill that you will use when you read the selection.

▶ CONTEXT CLUES OR WORD CLUES

This section teaches you how to recognize and use different types of context and word clues. These clues will help you with the meanings of the underlined words in the selection.

▶ STRATEGY TIP

This section gives you suggestions about what to look for as you read. The suggestions will help you understand the selection.

▶ SELECTIONS

There are four kinds of selections in **Be A Better Reader**. A selection in a literature lesson is similar to a selection in a literature anthology, library book, newspaper, or magazine. A social studies selection is like a chapter in a social studies textbook or an encyclopedia. It often includes maps or tables. A science selection, like a science textbook, includes special words and sometimes diagrams. A mathematics selection will help you acquire skill in reading mathematics textbooks.

▶ COMPREHENSION QUESTIONS

Answers to the questions in this section can be found in the selection itself. You will sometimes have to reread parts of the selection to complete this activity.

▶ CRITICAL THINKING ACTIVITY

The critical thinking activity includes questions whose answers are not directly stated in the selection. For these questions, you must combine the information in the selection with what you already know in order to infer the answers.

▶ SKILL FOCUS ACTIVITY

In this activity, you will use the skill that you learned in the Skill Focus section at the beginning of the lesson to answer questions about the selection. If you have difficulty completing this activity, reread the Skill Focus section.

▶ READING-WRITING CONNECTION

In this writing activity, you will have a chance to use the information in the selection you read about, by writing about it. Here is your chance to share your ideas about the selection.

Additional Lessons

The remaining lessons in each unit give you practice with such skills as using a dictionary, an encyclopedia, and other reference materials; using phonics and syllabication in recognizing new words; locating and organizing information; and adjusting your reading rate. Other reading skills that are necessary in everyday life, such as reading a bus schedule, are also covered.

Each time you learn a new skill in **Be A Better Reader**, look for opportunities to use the skill in your other reading at school and at home. Your reading ability will improve the more you practice reading!

unit one

For ESL/ELL support, see highlighted words, page T68, and pages T28–T30.

The Ocean

For theme support, see page T26.

LESSON 1

Skill: Sequence of Events

For lesson support, see page T68.

BACKGROUND INFORMATION

"Broken Voyage" is the true story of one family's attempt to sail around the world. By sailing west from England, they sailed across the Atlantic Ocean and then into the Pacific Ocean through the Panama Canal. The Panama Canal was completed in 1914. Before that, ships crossing from the Atlantic to the Pacific had to sail to the tip of South America and around it.

SKILL FOCUS: Sequence of Events

A **sequence of events** is the order in which things happen. The sequence of events forms the plot of a story. Most plots have a **beginning**, a **middle**, and an **end**. Use questions like the ones below to identify events in each story part.

Beginning

- What are the characters doing as the story begins?
- What problems do the characters have at first?

Middle

- What is the most exciting event of the story?
- What happens as a result of this event?

End

- How do the characters solve their problems?

▶ Think of a familiar story, such as "Cinderella." On the chart in the next column, list an event from each part of the story.

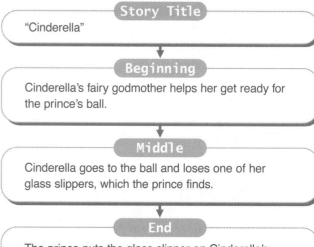

Story Title

"Cinderella"

Beginning

Cinderella's fairy godmother helps her get ready for the prince's ball.

Middle

Cinderella goes to the ball and loses one of her glass slippers, which the prince finds.

End

The prince puts the glass slipper on Cinderella's foot, and Cinderella marries the prince.

CONTEXT CLUES: Synonyms

Context clues are words near an unknown word that help show its meaning. Some context clues are synonyms. **Synonyms** are words with the same, or nearly the same, meaning.

What synonym shows the meaning of the word *galley* in these sentences?

> It was 13-year-old Neil's turn to wash dishes and clean the **galley** after breakfast. The boat's kitchen was very small, but it had everything they needed.

If you don't know the meaning of *galley*, the synonym *kitchen* can help you. A galley is a ship's kitchen.

▶ Circle the synonym that shows the meaning of the word *abandon* in the sentences below.

> Get ready to **abandon** ship!" shouted Mr. Robertson. "We must (leave) as quickly as possible."

As you read the story, look for synonyms for the underlined words *course, charts,* and *flare.*

Strategy Tip

As you read, think about events in the beginning, middle, and end of the story.

Broken Voyage

The first two days of sailing on the Pacific had been stormy. On the third day, the Robertson family was happy to see the sun rise through the clouds. They had bravely battled the waves of the Pacific Ocean in their small sailboat, and they needed a rest.

Their 43-foot (13-meter) sailboat was named the *Lucette*. It had carried the Robertsons from their home in England across the Atlantic and into the Pacific on their journey around the world. They had just left the Galapagos Islands off the northwest coast of South America.

During the last six months, they had sailed the *Lucette* through many storms, but they agreed that the last two days were the worst they had seen. As the Robertsons ate breakfast, they talked happily about the day of quiet sailing ahead.

"Now we have work to do," said Mr. Robertson.

It was 13-year-old Neil's turn to wash dishes and clean the galley after breakfast. The boat's kitchen was very small, but it had everything they needed. Neil's twin sister, Sandy, gathered the broken fishing gear to repair it. Douglas, their older brother, was already at the wheel in the cockpit, keeping the *Lucette* on course. It was his responsibility to make sure that they were going in the right direction.

On deck, Mrs. Robertson picked up the rubbish left by the storm. Below, Mr. Robertson checked the *Lucette*'s course by reading the charts. According to the maps, the Robertsons were 3,000 miles (4,830 kilometers) from the islands where they planned to stop next.

In the galley, Neil washed and dried the last pan. He had finished his work for the morning, and now he planned to read a book. As he headed for the cabin, he could hear the water gently slapping against the sides of the boat. It was a comfortable sound. Neil, who had lived all his live on a farm in England, now called this sailboat his home.

He climbed into his bunk and leaned back to enjoy his book. He had just started to read when something hit the side of the boat. Neil was thrown across the cabin and against the far wall. The *Lucette* was rolling wildly. Neil was on the floor. His ears were ringing and his shoulder hurt.

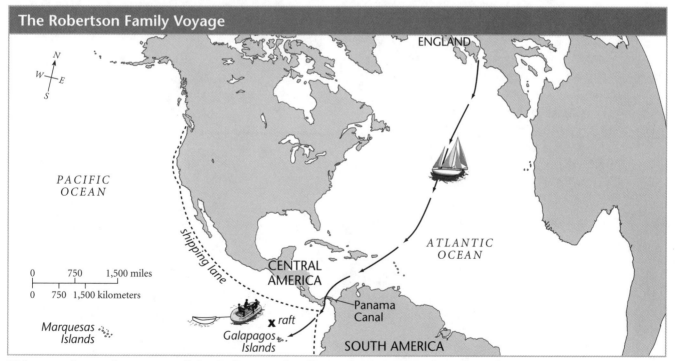

The Robertson Family Voyage

This map shows the course of the Robertson family on the *Lucette* and on the raft.

As he tried to stand up, Neil heard his family shouting outside. Then he heard his mother yell, "Whales!" A moment later, she ran into the cabin. "Neil, put on your life jacket and get on deck."

The whales had punched a huge hole in the *Lucette*'s side, and water was rushing in. As Neil left the cabin, the water already covered the floorboards. He heard his brother Douglas call, "Are we sinking, Dad?"

"Yes! Get ready to abandon ship!" shouted Mr. Robertson. He picked up a knife as he dashed out of the galley. He then cut the ropes to free the small rowboat tied to the mast. "Get the raft ready. We'll need that, too," he cried.

The boys pulled down the raft. Douglas pressed the button to fill it with air. Then he and Neil turned to help their father free the rowboat. The sea was nearly up to the *Lucette*'s deck. She was sinking fast. The rubber life raft swiftly filled with air. Douglas looked at his father. "When do we lower the raft, Dad?"

"Now! Tie the rowboat to the raft!" Mr. Robertson shouted as he ran into the galley.

Water was rolling over the sailboat's decks as Mr. Robertson returned with a bag of food. He had thrown bread, biscuits, sugar, and other food into the bag. He gave it to Neil. "Put this into the raft and tell everyone to get in. Hurry! She's going under."

Mr. Robertson made one last trip into the galley. He returned with two bags of oranges, lemons, and onions. He tossed them into the rowboat, now tied to the raft. Then he took a last look around. His family waited in the raft. Behind it, the sea stretched as far as he could see. The killer whales were nowhere in sight. The Robertsons were alone. Mr. Robertson jumped into the water and began swimming to the raft. A moment later, the *Lucette* began sinking into the deep, dark heart of the Pacific.

That afternoon, Neil wrote on a piece of sail: *June 15. Neil's log in the lifeboat.* Lucette *sunk by killer whales. Very sad. She went down in 2 minutes.*

The Robertsons were lucky to be alive. As the sun went down, they wondered about their chances of staying alive. They had no radio. They were hundreds of miles away from a shipping lane and 3,000 miles (4,830 kilometers) from their next port. They would not be missed for at least five weeks.

That night, each person had a piece of biscuit and a sip of water. They divided one orange among them.

The Roberston family is pictured aboard the tuna boat that rescued them.

A week passed on the lonely Pacific. The rubber life raft had tiny pinholes in the sides. It had to be blown up every hour. High waves forced the Robertsons to bail the raft regularly. After almost three weeks, the family knew that the raft would soon sink. They moved to the tiny rowboat.

The five members of the family crowded together in the little boat. Everyone knew that a sudden movement might cause the boat to tip over. No one moved without warning the others.

Their two greatest problems were thirst and hunger. Their mouths always felt like cotton. Because most of the food from the *Lucette* was gone, they were always hungry. Also their skin was raw from the burning sun and the stinging salt water.

For as long as the rowboat could carry them, they could stay alive on the dangerous sea. During storms, they caught rainwater with a rubber sheet. They filled all the cans they had with water. Yet each person drank only a little water each day. They did not know when another rain might come. By the time their food was gone, they had learned to catch fish with hooks of wire. Sometimes big turtles poked their heads up next to the boat. Douglas and his father pulled them aboard and quickly slit them open with a knife. The turtle meat would keep them all alive for another day.

The tiny rowboat crept along the course the Robertsons had set for South America. Five weeks had passed since they had abandoned the *Lucette*. "With luck, we should make the coast in about three weeks," said Mr. Robertson, "but I'm afraid the wind's changing. So we may have to start rowing. . . ."

Suddenly he stopped talking and stared straight ahead. The others looked at him. "A ship," he said. "There's a ship!"

"Where?" they asked, and everyone turned to look.

"Keep still!" shouted Mr. Robertson. "We don't want to tip over now. I must signal the ship. Neil, hand me a <u>flare</u> from that box."

Carefully standing up, he lit the flare and held the emergency signal light high overhead until it burned his fingers. Then he threw it into the air.

The family watched him, hardly breathing. Mr. Robertson stood frozen, eyes fixed on the distant ship. Moments passed. Then he looked at his family and quietly said, "She's seen us. She's changed course. We're saved."

A passing Japanese tuna boat picked up the Robertsons on July 22. Mr. Robertson was the last to climb on board. He was surprised to see that his family was lying down on the deck. Suddenly he realized why. Living for 38 days on a raft and in a rowboat had weakened his legs, too. Four days later, the Robertson family was back on land.

COMPREHENSION

Recalling details
1. How many members are in the the Robertson family?

   There are five members: two parents and three

   children, two boys and a girl.

Recalling details
2. What course did the Robertsons sail?

   The Robertsons sailed from England, across the

   Atlantic Ocean, and into the Pacific Ocean.

Recalling details
3. At what point in the Robertsons' journey does this story begin?

   The Robertsons had just left the Galapagos Islands off

   the northwest coast of South America.

Recalling details
4. Tell what work each member of the family had to do after breakfast.

   Mrs. Robertson picked up rubbish on the deck.

   Mr. Robertson read the charts to make sure that

   they were on course.

   Sandy repaired fishing gear.

   Neil washed dishes and cleaned the galley.

   Douglas was at the wheel in the cockpit.

Recalling details
5. What did Neil do after he finished cleaning the galley?

   Neil went to his cabin and started to read.

Identifying cause and effect
6. What caused the *Lucette* to sink?

Killer whales punched a huge hole in the side of the

boat.

Recalling details
7. What were the two most serious problems that the Robertsons faced at sea?

The two most serious problems were thirst and hunger.

Recalling details
8. How did the Robertsons get fresh drinking water?

During storms, they used a rubber sheet to catch rain.

Recalling details
9. How did they get food?

They caught fish with hooks of wire and killed turtles

with a knife.

Recalling details
10. Why did Mr. Robertson tell the family to keep still when he saw a ship?

He was afraid the rowboat would tip over.

Identifying cause and effect
11. What effect did living at sea for 38 days have on the Robertsons?

Their legs were so weak that when they were rescued,

they could not stand up right away.

Using context clues
12. Write the letter of the correct meaning in front of each word.

_b_ course   **a.** maps used by sailors

_a_ charts   **b.** the direction taken by a ship

_c_ flare   **c.** a bright light used to signal for help.

CRITICAL THINKING

Making inferences
1. Give details to explain what time of day the *Lucette* sank.

The *Lucette* sank in the morning. Neil had just finished cleaning the galley after breakfast;

in the afternoon he wrote about the *Lucette*'s sinking.

Making inferences
2. Explain why the Robertsons took the rowboat with them.

In case something happened to the raft, they could use the other boat.

Making inferences
3. Explain why the Robertsons used the raft instead of the rowboat.

The raft was larger and more comfortable.

Making inferences
4. Put a ✔ before the three words that best describe the Robertson family.

_____ playful   _✔_ helpful   _✔_ cooperative

_✔_ responsible   _____ lazy   _____ nervous

Drawing conclusions
5. Discuss the meaning of the title "Broken Voyage."

The Robertsons had to end their trip around the world because killer whales destroyed their boat.

Below are some of the events in "Broken Voyage." Which events happened at the beginning of the story? in the middle? at the end? On the numbered lines, write the events in the sequence in which they took place. Then on the blank lines, fill in another incident that occurred during each part of the story.

a. Killer whales hit the *Lucette*.

b. The Robertsons are alone with little food and water.

c. The Robertsons get into the rubber raft and watch the *Lucette* sink.

d. A passing ship rescues the Robertsons.

e. The Robertsons hit storms in the Pacific.

f. The Robertsons look forward to a quiet day of sailing.

Beginning

1. e. The Robertsons hit storms in the Pacific.

2. f. The Robertsons look forward to a quiet day of sailing.

Answers will vary. The Robertsons do chores after breakfast.

Middle

3. a. Killer whales hit the *Lucette*.

4. c. The Robertsons get into the rubber raft and watch the *Lucette* sink.

Answers will vary. Because of holes in their raft, the Robertsons crowd into a tiny rowboat.

End

5. b. The Robertsons are alone with little food and water.

6. d. A passing ship rescues the Robertsons.

Answers will vary. Four days later, the Robertsons are back on land.

Reading-Writing Connection

Suppose that you were on board the *Lucette* as it started to sink. On a separate sheet of paper, write a list of at least five items you might grab to take with you on the life raft. Explain why you would take each item.

LESSON 2

Skill: Cause and Effect

For lesson support, see page T69.

BACKGROUND INFORMATION

The next selection is about the changes in the whaling industry. For centuries, whales were a valuable source of food and oil. Today, due to widespread hunting, many types of whales no longer exist. Other types of whales are in danger of disappearing from the Earth, too. To keep this from happening, the United States and many other countries have banned the hunting of many kinds of whales.

SKILL FOCUS: Cause and Effect

When one event causes another event to happen, the process is called **cause and effect**. A **cause** is an event that makes something happen. An **effect** is what happens. Everyday life is full of causes and effects. Figuring out causes and effects also helps you understand history and science.

What is the cause and what is the effect in the following sentence?

Because people needed food and oil, they hunted whales.

This chart shows the cause and the effect.

Cause	Effect
People needed food and oil.	They hunted whales.

▶ Find the cause and the effect in the sentence below. Write them in the boxes.

Whales were put on the endangered list because they were in danger of dying out.

Cause	Effect
Whales were in danger of dying out.	They were put on the endangered list.

CONTEXT CLUES: Definitions

In a social studies textbook, a writer will often give a **definition** of an important new word. The writer will tell you the word's meaning in the same sentence or a nearby sentence. Look for these definitions as you read.

Read the sentences below. Look for a definition that explains the meaning of the underlined word.

By 1700, right whales had become important for their __blubber__, whalebone, and meat. Blubber is the fat under the skin of the whale.

If you don't know the meaning of *blubber,* read on. The second sentence defines, or states, its meaning. Blubber is the fat under the skin of a whale.

▶ Read the following sentences. Underline the words that tell the meaning of the word *baleen.*

Baleen whales have __baleen__ in their mouths instead of teeth. Baleen is the name for the 400 thin plates through which the whales filter sea water.

In "The Whaling Industry," use definition context clues to find the meaning of the underlined words *harpoons*, *spermaceti*, and *ambergris*.

Strategy Tip

Before you read "The Whaling Industry," look at the headings in heavy type. Look at the pictures and read their captions. As you read the article, remember to look for the important events and what caused them.

The Whaling Industry

People have hunted whales for food and oil since early times. Even before there were whaling voyages, people killed whales that washed up on beaches. Later, people used boats to hunt whales. They killed whales with harpoons. A harpoon is a spear with a line attached to it. Today many countries are against whaling.

The Early Days of Whaling

The people of France and Spain hunted whales during the 1200s. They made the first whaling voyages using large ships. At first, they hunted close to shore, in a part of the Atlantic Ocean called the Bay of Biscay. When whales no longer came close to shore, the whalers went farther out to sea. During the 1500s, they hunted whales across the Atlantic Ocean as far as Newfoundland.

In the 1600s, Dutch and English sailors found many whales in the Arctic waters. Soon a group of islands north of Norway became the center of Arctic whaling.

At the same time, American Indians were also hunting whales. They hunted whales in much the same way as the first whalers. When the American colonists arrived in the 1600s, they hunted whales off the Atlantic coast. They built lookout towers in many New England towns along the coast. When someone in the towers saw whales, the whalers launched their boats.

The "Right" Whale to Hunt

There are two main groups of whales: those with teeth and those without teeth. Before the 1700s, whalers hunted only whales without teeth. These are called **baleen** (bə LEEN) **whales.**

Baleen whales have baleen in their mouths instead of teeth. Baleen is the name for the 400 thin plates through which the whales filter seawater. The plates are also known as whalebone. They strain out the small fish whales feed on.

There are many kinds of baleen whales. The whalers hunted for the kind that swam slowly and floated when it was dead. This type provided a great deal of oil and whalebone. Because this whale was the right kind to hunt, whalers called it the "right" whale. Today the whale is still called by that name.

By 1700, right whales had become very important for their blubber, whalebone, and meat. Blubber is the fat under the skin of the whale. People melted this blubber to make whale oil. They used the whale oil for cooking and lighting lamps. They used whalebone for fishing rods, buggy whips, and umbrellas. They cooked and ate the whale meat.

Discovery of the Sperm Whale

In 1712, an American whaling ship got lost in a storm at sea. The whalers came upon a school of whales. They killed one and brought it back to shore. To the whalers' surprise, the whale had teeth.

Whales with teeth are called **toothed** (TOOTHd) **whales.** The New England whalers had discovered the largest of the toothed whales, the sperm whale. The sperm whale was larger and stronger than the right whale. This discovery started the American whaling industry.

The Golden Age of American Whaling

✔ The discovery of the sperm whale helped the American whaling industry to grow quickly. By 1800, Americans were hunting sperm whales throughout the Atlantic Ocean. The town of New Bedford, Massachusetts, became the whaling capital of the world. Nantucket, Salem, and other New England cities also became whaling centers. By 1835, Americans were whaling in the Pacific Ocean. San Francisco became an important whaling center.

✔ Whalers got three valuable things from sperm whales. The first was sperm oil, which people used for lamps. It was better than the oil of the right whale. As a result, sperm oil soon became the chief source of lamp fuel. Another very valuable substance was spermaceti (sperm ə SET ee). Spermaceti is a pure wax found in the sperm whale's head. It was used in making candles. A third

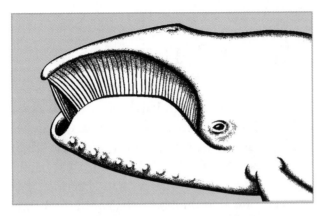

Baleen hangs from the upper jaw of baleen whales.

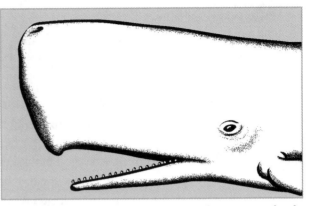

Teeth grow from the lower jaw of most toothed whales.

valuable substance was <u>ambergris</u> (am bər GREES). Ambergris is a waxy substance found in the belly of the sperm whale. It was used in making perfumes. The high value of sperm oil, spermaceti, and ambergris more than made up for the lack of whalebone in the sperm whale.

The Decline of the Whaling Industry

The American sperm-whaling industry grew until 1848. In that year, people discovered gold in California. Many whalers decided to leave their ships to search for gold. During the Civil War, many navy whaling ships were sunk. With fewer whalers and ships, whaling began to suffer. The discovery of oil in the ground hurt whaling most of all. It led to the start of a new industry. Soon it was cheaper to use this oil for lamps than to use sperm oil.

Whaling in the Twentieth Century

During the first half of the 1900s, whaling fleets killed large numbers of whales. As a result, they reduced the world's whale population and endangered many kinds of whales. Today people still use whale oil and sperm oil to make soap. They still use ambergris in making perfumes. People in Japan and Norway still eat the meat of baleen whales.

To protect whales, several nations met in 1946 and formed the International Whaling Commission. This group decides how many whales may be killed each year. They do not allow the killing of certain whales. Because the whale population continued to decline, the group then banned commercial whaling in 1986. Twenty-five nations agreed to the ban. Other groups have since tried to ban whaling completely.

Recalling details
1. Who were the first whalers?

The people of France and Spain were the first whalers.

Recalling details
2. What is baleen?

Baleen is the name for the thin plates of whalebone that

some whales have instead of teeth. They use the baleen

to filter seawater for food.

Recalling details
3. Why did the early whalers hunt for the right whale?

They hunted for the right whale because it swam slowly,

floated when it was dead, and provided lots of oil and

whalebone.

Recalling details
4. Identify the two main groups of whales.

The two main groups are those with teeth (toothed

whales) and those without teeth (baleen whales).

Identifying cause and effect
5. What discovery caused the beginning of the whaling industry in America?

The discovery of the sperm whale caused the beginning

of the American whaling industry.

Comparing and contrasting
6. Name one difference between right whales and sperm whales.

Right whales have no teeth; sperm whales have teeth.

Recalling details
7. What three parts of the right whale were valuable?

The meat, blubber, and whalebone of the right whale

were valuable.

Recalling details
8. What three parts of the sperm whale were valuable?

The sperm oil, spermaceti, and ambergris of the sperm

whale were valuable.

Identifying cause and effect
9. Name the three events that caused the decline of whaling in America.

The discoveries of gold and ground oil as well as the

Civil War, contributed to the decline of whaling in

America.

Recognizing sequence of events
10. Number the following events in the order in which they happened.

___2___ The islands north of Norway became the center of Arctic whaling.

___4___ The discovery of ground oil hurt the whaling industry.

___1___ Whalers from France and Spain began hunting whales in the Atlantic Ocean.

___3___ New Bedford, Massachusetts, became the whaling capital of the world.

___5___ Twenty-five nations supported a ban on commercial whaling.

Identifying the main idea
11. Two paragraphs have a ✔ next to them. Reread both paragraphs. Then underline the sentence that tells what each paragraph is about.

Using context clues
12. Write the letter of the correct meaning in front of each word.

___b___ harpoons

a. a pure wax found in the head of sperm whales

___a___ spermaceti

b. spears used to kill whales

___c___ ambergris

c. a waxy substance found in sperm whales that is used in making perfume

Inferring comparisons and contrasts

1. Explain why the sperm whale was more valuable than the right whale.

Sperm oil was better for lighting lamps than oil from right whales. The sperm whale also provided wax for making

candles and ambergris for perfumes. This was more valuable than the right whale's meat, blubber, and whalebone.

Inferring cause and effect

2. Discuss why the discovery of ground oil was one of the major causes of the decline of whaling in America.

Ground oil was cheaper and more in demand than whale oil. That meant that whalers could no longer

earn a big profit from hunting whales.

Making inferences

3. Identify ways in which the American whaling industry provided jobs for many people, besides the whalers themselves.

Answers may vary. Shipbuilders were needed to build whaling ships. People were needed to remove the sperm oil,

ambergris, and spermaceti from the whales. Candle makers and perfume makers could find more jobs.

SKILL FOCUS: CAUSE AND EFFECT

Match each cause with its effect. You may need to reread the selection.

Cause

1. _e_ Because whales no longer came close to shore,

2. _g_ Because the Dutch and English found Arctic waters filled with whales,

3. _a_ Because whale meat, blubber, and whalebone were valuable,

4. _b_ Because American whalers were able to get valuable sperm oil, spermaceti, and ambergris from sperm whales,

5. _d_ Because there was an abundance of sperm oil,

6. _f_ As a result of the California Gold Rush, the Civil War, and the discovery of ground oil,

7. _h_ As a result of whaling fleets' killing large numbers of whales in the early 1900s,

8. _c_ Because the population of many whales has declined,

Effect

a. right whales became very important.

b. the American whaling industry grew quickly.

c. a ban was placed on commercial whaling.

d. sperm oil became the chief source of lamp fuel.

e. the first whalers went farther out to sea.

f. the whaling industry in the United States rapidly declined.

g. the islands north of Norway became the center of Arctic whaling.

h. there is a smaller whale population today.

Reading-Writing Connection

Do you think that whaling should be outlawed in all parts of the world? On a separate sheet of paper, write your opinion. Use facts, examples, and reasons to support your opinion.

For ESL/ELL support, see highlighted words, page T70, and pages T28–T30.

Skill: Classifying

For lesson support, see page T70.

BACKGROUND INFORMATION

The next selection is about three different groups of water animals found in the world's oceans. There are thousands of different kinds of living things in the ocean. To keep track of them all, scientists divide them into different groups. Each time they find a new life-form, scientists study it. Then they decide which group of living things it belongs to.

SKILL FOCUS: Classifying

One good way to organize information is to group similar things together. This type of organization is called **classifying**. You classify things every day. If you were describing a new TV show, for example, you might start by classifying the show as a game show, a comedy, a drama, or a news program.

When scientists classify living things, they break large groups into smaller ones. The members of each smaller group are similar in some way. Goldfish and sharks, for example, are similar in some ways. They are both classified in the group called fish. Lobsters and crabs are water animals too, but they are not fish. Scientists put lobsters and crabs in a different group.

When reading about different groups of animals, ask yourself the following questions.

- What is similar about the animals that scientists put in the same group?
- How are the animals in one group different from the animals in another group?

▶ Use what you already know to list on the chart some ways in which a shark is similar to a goldfish.

Shark	Goldfish
have fins	have fins
breathe through gills	breathe through gills
have scales	have scales

Use what you know to list some ways that a fish is different from a crab or a lobster.

Fish	Crab or Lobster
have bones	don't have bones
don't have a hard shell	have a hard shell

CONTEXT CLUES: Photographs

The photographs in a science article are not just decorations. They give important information. You can use these **photos** to help you figure out the meaning of new words or to learn more about the animals the words name. Look at Figure 1 on page 18. The photo helps you understand the meaning of the word *haddock*.

▶ Look again at Figure 1. Write a brief description of a haddock, based on the photograph.

<u>Answers will vary. A haddock is a kind of fish with several</u>

<u>large spots on its side and three fins on its back. It is</u>

<u>covered with scales.</u>

Use the photos in this selection to help you learn more about the underlined words *scallops* and *lobsters*.

> ### Strategy Tip
>
> When reading a science selection, look at the words that are printed in heavy, or boldface, type. These are the most important words in the selection. Also look at the three headings in the selection to help you classify information.

Three Groups of Water Animals

The Group Called Fish

Haddock, codfish, and mackerel are all fish. The body of a fish has a backbone and a skeleton. Animals that have backbones are known as **vertebrates** (VER tə brates). The bodies of most fish are covered with flat scales, like shingles on a roof. Fish can breathe underwater through gills. Most fish also have air bladders inside their bodies. These air bladders are filled with gases. By changing the amount of gas in its air bladder, a fish can move up or down through the water.

A fish uses its tail to push itself through the water. The shape of its body helps it move through the water easily. Most fish have fins that they use for balancing, steering, and braking.

Sharks are fish, but they do not have true backbones or air bladders. Some sharks are dangerous to people. The great white shark can be 7.6 meters (25 feet) long. White sharks have attacked swimmers as far north as Cape Cod, Massachusetts, on the Atlantic coast. Other dangerous sharks are the hammerhead shark and the tiger shark.

Fish are a very important food for people. Hundreds of millions of dollars' worth of fish are sold every year. Scientists are helping to feed the people of the world by finding new ways to raise fish.

The Group Called Mollusks

Oysters, scallops, clams, snails, squids, and octopuses are all **mollusks** (MAH lusks). The word *mollusk* means "soft-bodied." All mollusks have soft

FIGURE 1. The mackerel, above, along with codfish and haddock, belongs to the group called fish.

bodies. Many have tough, hard shells outside for protection. Clams, oysters, and scallops have two-piece shells that are connected by a hinge of muscle. Their soft, fleshy bodies are used as food by many people.

Mollusks have no backbones, but they do have gills. Mollusks are sometimes called shellfish, but they are not really fish.

For protection, the squid depends not on a heavy shell, but on its ability to swim quickly. The octopus does not have a shell either. It can also move quickly. The octopus has eight arms, and the squid has ten arms.

You may have heard the term "sea monster" used in stories of giant squids and octopuses. However, most squids and octopuses are not giants. They swim away when they see a large creature. They can also squirt a black fluid that forms a dark cloud in the water. This makes it more difficult for their enemies to find them.

Scallops move through the water in an interesting way. These mollusks "clap" their two shells together. The large muscle that closes the scallop shell is enjoyed as a food by many people. The rest of the body is thrown away.

Oysters are a very good food. Some oysters also grow pearls inside their shells. In Japan, people make oysters grow pearls by placing single grains of sand inside the oysters' shells. The pearls grow around these grains of sand. After several years, the oysters produce a very valuable crop of pearls.

The Group Called Crustaceans

Another group of animals that live mostly in saltwater is called **crustaceans** (krus TAY shənz). Crustaceans are covered with a heavy crust or hard shell. They have gills for breathing underwater. Their bodies have many joints and sections but no backbones. Most of them move by crawling. Lobsters, crabs, and shrimp are all crustaceans.

Lobsters are caught in wooden or metal traps called lobster pots. When alive, lobsters are a greenish-blue color. When they are cooked, their shells turn a bright red.

Many kinds of crabs are found along the seashore. Among these are the blue crab, the rock crab, the hermit crab, and the fiddler crab. Crabs that have shed their hard shells are called soft-shelled crabs. The soft-shelled blue crab is used for food.

Shrimps found in saltwater have narrower bodies than crabs. Like lobsters and crabs, shrimps are valued as a food. Every year, large numbers of shrimps and other crustaceans are sold fresh, frozen, or canned.

FIGURE 2. **Inside this shell is a scallop. Scallops belong to the group called mollusks.**

FIGURE 3. **Lobsters belong to the group called crustaceans.**

COMPREHENSION

Recalling details
1. Name three kinds of fish.

Codfish, mackerel, and haddock are all fish.

Recalling details
2. How does a fish use its tail?

A fish uses its tail to push itself through the water.

Recalling details
3. How does the shape of a fish help it?

The shape of a fish's body helps it move through water

easily.

Recalling details
4. Name three ways in which a fish uses its fins.

A fish uses its fins to balance, to steer, and to brake.

Identifying cause and effect
5. What is one way a fish moves up through the water?

It changes the amount of gas in its air bladder.

Identifying cause and effect
6. Octopuses can squirt a black fluid. What effect does the fluid have on their enemies?

It makes it more difficult for their enemies to find them.

7. Describe what clams and oysters have that protect them from their enemies.

Their shells protect them.

8. Do mollusks have backbones?

No, mollusks do not have backbones.

9. How do people make oysters grow pearls?

They place a single grain of sand inside the shell of an

oyster.

10. What is the body of a crustacean covered with?

A crustacean's body is covered with a heavy crust or

hard shell.

11. Do crustaceans have backbones?

No, crustaceans do not have backbones.

12. Name four kinds of crabs.

The blue crab, rock crab, hermit crab, and fiddler crab

are four kinds of crabs.

13. How is a soft-shelled crab different from a hard-shelled crab?

A soft-shelled crab is a crab that has shed its hard

shell.

14. How do the following creatures move?

a. fish Fish push themselves through the water with

their tails.

b. scallops Scallops clap their two shells together.

c. most crustaceans Most crustaceans crawl.

15. What does the squid rely on to protect itself?

The squid relies on its ability to swim quickly for

protection. It can also squirt a black fluid.

16. Write the letter of the correct definition on the line in front of each word.

____b____ lobsters

____a____ scallops

a. animals covered by two shells that they can clap together

b. animals with two large claws and many legs

CRITICAL THINKING

Circle the letter of the best answer.

1. What would be the effect of more gas in a fish's air bladder?

a. The fish would move up.

b. The fish would move down.

c. The fish would stay in the same place.

d. The fish would move from side to side.

2. Why would an oyster form a pearl around a grain of sand?

a. The sand chills it.

b. The sand irritates it.

c. The sand makes it hungry.

d. The sand heats it up.

After reading this selection, you should be able to classify three groups of water animals. Complete the following exercises to show the differences among the three groups.

1. Write answers to the questions in the following table. The first one is done for you.

Sea creatures	What are their bodies like?	What covers their bodies?
Fish	*Fish have backbones and skeletons.*	Flat scales cover their bodies.
Mollusks	Mollusks have soft, fleshy bodies.	Tough, hard shells cover their bodies.
Crustaceans	Crustaceans have many joints and sections.	Heavy crusts or hard shells cover their bodies.

2. Oysters, snails, crabs, codfish, clams, lobsters, mackerel, haddock, and shrimps are all water animals. Write the name of each animal under the heading where it belongs.

Fish	Mollusks	Crustaceans
codfish	oysters	crabs
mackerel	snails	lobsters
haddock	clams	shrimps

Reading-Writing Connection

Work with a partner to research the following question: Why are fish an important food source for the world? On a separate sheet of paper, write a short report that gives reasons, facts, and examples about the importance of fish as food.

For ESL/ELL support, see highlighted words, page T71, and pages T28–T30.

Skill: Word Problems

For lesson support, see page T71.

BACKGROUND INFORMATION

The next selection teaches you the steps to solve word problems. This can often help you in everyday life. For example, suppose you go to the grocery store with only $5. You need to buy a quart of milk for $.89, a dozen eggs for $1.09, and a pint of ice cream for $3.19. Will you have enough money? If you can do word problems, you'll know *before* you reach the cash register!

SKILL FOCUS: Word Problems

Follow these five steps to solve a word problem.

1. **Read the problem.** Be sure that you know all the words, especially the labels, that are used with each number. For example, *meters*, *dollars*, and *hours* are some commonly used labels. Think about what the problem is asking. Try to picture the information. Read the problem again to be sure that you understand it.

2. **Decide how to find the answer.** It may be helpful to draw a picture of the information that is given. Decide whether you should add, subtract, multiply, or divide. Look for key words in the last sentence to help you figure out what to do.

3. **Estimate the answer.** Use rounded numbers to quickly figure out a number that is close to the correct answer.

4. **Carry out the plan.** Do the arithmetic that will give you the answer.

5. **Reread the problem.** Does the answer make sense? How close is it to your estimate? Be sure your answer includes the correct labels.

▶ If you have read a word problem and have decided how to find the answer, what is your next step in solving the problem?

The next step is to estimate the answer.

WORD CLUES

Certain words in math can give you a clue about how to solve a word problem. The words *in all*, *total*, *together*, and *sum*, for example, usually signal that you have to add. They are called key words. The words *difference*, *more*, *less*, *shorter*, *longer*, *left*, *change*, and *part* often signal that you have to subtract to find the answer. Look for these word clues in the last sentence of a problem.

▶ Underline the key words in the last sentence of this problem that show that you have to add.

During a whale watch, one ship spotted 17 whales. Another spotted 19 whales. How many whales were spotted in all?

Strategy Tip

Scientists use numbers in word problems to learn about ocean animals and rocks. In "Solving Word Problems," you will learn how to use the five steps in solving such word problems.

Look at the headings for these steps as you read. Look for key words, too.

Solving Word Problems

Knowing how to work with different number facts can help you answer questions. Suppose these two number facts about whales are known.

1. A humpback whale is 18 meters long.
2. A blue whale is 31 meters long.

One question that can be asked is "What is the difference in length between the blue whale and the humpback whale?" How can the facts be used to answer this question? Follow the five steps below.

Step 1: Read the Problem

A humpback whale is 18 meters long. A blue whale is 31 meters long. What is the difference in length between the blue whale and the humpback whale?

Read the problem again. Be sure you know the label of measurement used with each number fact. Are there any words you don't know? If so, look them up in a dictionary. What question does the problem ask? Often the question is asked in the last sentence: *What is the difference in length between the blue whale and the humpback whale?*

Step 2: Decide How to Find the Answer

It can be helpful to make a drawing or diagram that shows the facts in a problem.

31 meters
blue whale

18 meters
humpback whale

Should the numbers be added, subtracted, multiplied, or divided to answer the question? They should be subtracted because you are comparing lengths. The key word *difference* tells you that you need to subtract.

Step 3: Estimate the Answer

Use rounded numbers to make an **estimate**, or judgment, of about how much the difference should be. Round to the nearest ten. Then subtract.

$$30 - 20 = 10$$

Your estimate is 10.

Step 4: Carry Out the Plan

Do the arithmetic. $31 - 18 = 13$

Step 5: Reread the Problem

After rereading the problem, write the complete answer.

The blue whale is 13 meters longer than the humpback whale.

Does the answer make sense? How close is your answer to your estimate? If the answer is not close to your estimate, you should start all over.

These five steps can be used to solve word problems.

1. Read the problem.
2. Decide how to find the answer.
3. Estimate the answer.
4. Carry out the plan.
5. Reread the problem.

Read: *Mt. Pico is 6,100 meters from the ocean bottom to sea level. Then it rises 2,300 meters above the sea. What is the total height of Mt. Pico?*

Decide:

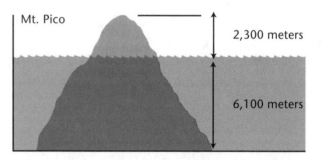

To find the answer to this problem, you need to combine the two number facts. The key word *total* is a clue to use addition. Add the numbers to put the two measurements together.

Estimate: Round each number to the nearest thousand and add.

$$2,000 + 6,000 = 8,000$$

Carry Out: $2,300 + 6,100 = 8,400$

Reread: After reading the problem, write the complete answer. *Mt. Pico is 8,400 meters tall.* Does this answer make sense? How close is this answer to your estimate?

Recalling details
1. What number label is used in the first example problem on page 23?

The label *meters* is used in the problem.

Recognizing sequence of events
2. Write the five steps for solving word problems.

a. Read the problem.

b. Decide how to find the answer.

c. Estimate the answer.

d. Carry out the plan.

e. Reread the problem.

Recalling details
3. Explain what to do if your answer is quite different from your estimate.

Check your work and go through the five steps again.

Using context clues
4. What are two key words that tell you how to answer a word problem? Give one for addition and one for subtraction.

The word *difference* is a key that you need for

subtraction. *Total* is a key word for addition.

CRITICAL THINKING

Making inferences
1. Explain why making an estimate is important in problem solving.

It will help you find out whether your answer is correct.

Making inferences
2. If your estimate is 100 and your answer is 104, why might your answer be correct?

The answer might be correct because it is close to the estimate.

Making inferences
3. If your estimate is 40 and your answer is 86, why might your answer be incorrect?

The answer might be incorrect because it is more than double the estimate.

SKILL FOCUS: WORD PROBLEMS

Use the five steps to solve these word problems. The first one is started for you. If necessary, draw pictures or diagrams on another sheet of paper to help you with the second step.

1. **Read:** In May, a tuna weighs 181 kilograms. By September, it has gained 136 kilograms. What is the tuna's total weight in September?

Decide: Add to put the two weights together.

Estimate: $180 + 140 = 320$

Carry Out: $181 + 136 = 317$

Reread: The tuna weighs 317 kilograms in September.

2. **Read:** Most deep-sea divers can go only 40 meters under water. Some divers can go 21 meters deeper. How deep can the best divers go?

Decide: Add to find the total depth.

Estimate: 40 + 20 = 60

Carry Out: 40 + 21 = 61

Reread: The best divers can dive 61 meters deep.

3. **Read:** A blue marlin swims 48 kilometers per hour. A dolphin swims 40 kilometers per hour. What is the difference between the two speeds?

Decide: Subtract to compare the two speeds.

Estimate: 50 − 40 = 10

Carry Out: 48 − 40 = 8

Reread: There is a difference in speed of 8 kilometers per hour.

4. **Read:** The highest ocean mountain is 9,693 meters tall. The highest land mountain is 8,840 meters. How much lower is the land mountain?

Decide: Subtract to compare the two heights.

Estimate: 10,000 − 9,000 = 1,000

Carry Out: 9,693 − 8,840 = 853

Reread: The land mountain is 853 meters lower.

5. **Read:** The Pacific Ocean covers 166,000,000 square kilometers, the Atlantic Ocean covers 87,000,000 square kilometers, and the Indian Ocean covers 73,000,000 square kilometers. What is their area all together?

Decide: Add to find the total area.

Estimate: 170,000,000 + 90,000,000 + 70,000,000 = 330,000,000

Carry Out: 166,000,000 + 87,000,000 + 73,000,000 = 326,000,000

Reread: The total area is 326,000,000 square kilometers.

6. **Read:** The Java Trench is 7,125 meters deep. The Mariana Trench is 10,924 meters deep. How much deeper is the Mariana Trench?

Decide: Subtract to compare the two depths.

Estimate: 11,000 − 7,000 = 4,000

Carry Out: 10,924 − 7,125 = 3,799

Reread: The Mariana Trench is 3,799 meters deeper.

Reading-Writing Connection

Look up more facts about sea animals. On a separate sheet of paper, write two of your own word problems using the facts. Use addition in one problem and subtraction in the other.

Skill: Consonants

For lesson support, see page T72.

A. Say each picture name. Listen to the beginning sound. It is a **consonant** sound. On the line, write the letter that stands for this consonant sound. The first one is done for you.

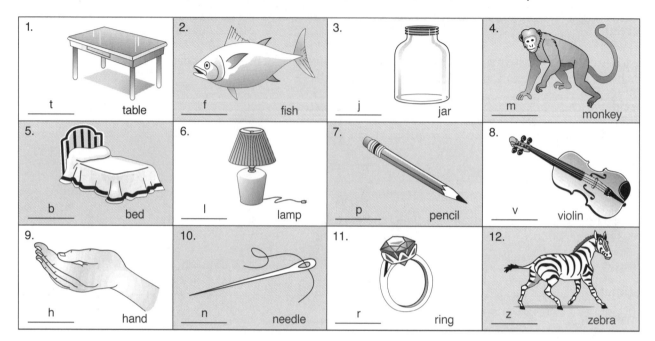

1. __t__ table	2. __f__ fish	3. __j__ jar	4. __m__ monkey
5. __b__ bed	6. __l__ lamp	7. __p__ pencil	8. __v__ violin
9. __h__ hand	10. __n__ needle	11. __r__ ring	12. __z__ zebra

B. Say each picture name. Listen to the ending sound. It is a consonant sound. On the line, write the letter that stands for this consonant sound. The first one is done for you.

1. __b__ crab	2. __r__ door	3. __d__ bed	4. __l__ nail
5. __k__ book	6. __n__ train	7. __p__ soap	8. __m__ drum
9. __t__ foot	10. horse __s__	11. __g__ dog	12. __n__ sun

Skill: Main Idea

For lesson support, see page T72.

In many of the paragraphs that you read, one sentence is more important than the others. This sentence states the **main idea** of the paragraph. The main idea is the idea that is most important in the paragraph. It tells what the paragraph is about.

Read the following paragraphs. Below each one are four sentences from the paragraph. Underline the sentence that is the main idea of the paragraph.

Oysters

1. The largest supply of oysters in the world is found in Atlantic waters. Oysters live in quiet, shallow waters. They like bays and river mouths. The Atlantic coast has quiet bays. This is why so many more oysters are found along this coast than in any other waters.
   a. Oysters live in quiet, shallow waters.
   b. The Atlantic coast has quiet bays.
   c. The largest supply of oysters in the world is found in Atlantic waters.
   d. They like bays and river mouths.

2. Oysters like warm waters. They grow best in temperatures between 66 and 70 degrees Fahrenheit. In southern waters, they grow to full size in two to three years. In the north, growth takes about four years.
   a. Oysters like warm waters.
   b. In southern waters, they grow to full size in two to three years.
   c. In the north, growth takes about four years.
   d. They grow best in temperatures between 66 and 70 degrees Fahrenheit.

3. Oysters are grown as a crop. People who make oyster farms set up the beds on hard mud. They clean the rubbish from the beds. Then they place seed oysters in the beds. They feed and care for the oysters until the crop is ready to harvest.
   a. They clean the rubbish from the beds.
   b. People who make oyster farms set up the beds on hard mud.
   c. Then they place seed oysters in the beds.
   d. Oysters are grown as a crop.

4. Fine pearls come from "pearl oysters." Once in a while, a pearl is found in an edible oyster. However, it is a low-grade pearl. Pearl oysters grow in the warm waters of southern seas.
   a. Once in a while, a pearl is found in an edible oyster.
   b. However, it is a low-grade pearl.
   c. Pearl oysters grow in the warm waters of southern seas.
   d. Fine pearls come from "pearl oysters."

5. Oysters have many enemies. Boring snails bore a hole through the oysters' shells and eat them. Crabs kill small and weak oysters. Fish with sharp teeth crush and eat young oysters.
   a. Crabs kill small and weak oysters.
   b. Oysters have many enemies.
   c. Fish with sharp teeth crush and eat young oysters.
   d. Boring snails bore a hole through the oysters' shells and eat them.

6. Oysters have been valuable to people for hundreds of years. Early people prized beautiful pearls for jewelry. Oysters were a good source of food. They considered oysters to be important.
   a. Early people prized beautiful pearls for jewelry.
   b. Oysters have been valuable to people for hundreds of years.
   c. They considered oysters to be important.
   d. Oysters were a good source of food.

Skill: Consonant Blends

For lesson support, see page T73.

Many words begin with the sound of just one consonant. Some words have two consonants at the beginning. If you can hear the consonant sounds that both letters stand for, the two letters are called a **consonant blend**. The consonant blends below are called *r* blends.

| br cr dr fr gr pr tr |

Say each picture name. Listen to the beginning sounds. On the line, write the blend from the list above that stands for the consonant sounds that you hear at the beginning of the picture name.

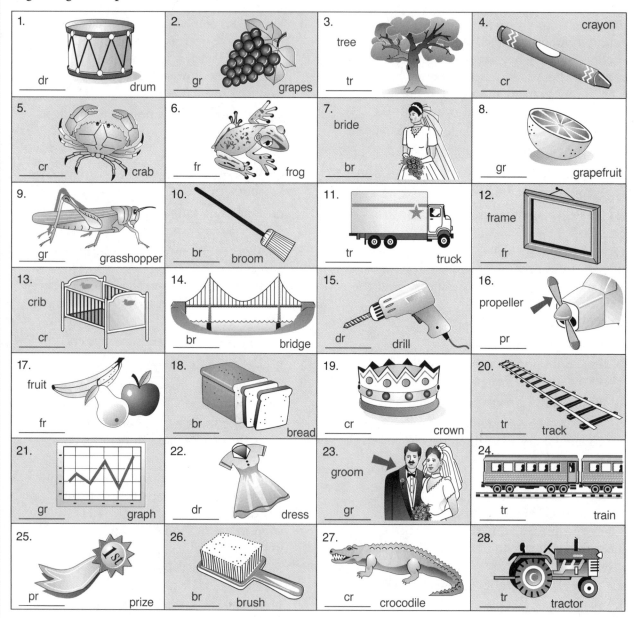

1. __dr__ drum
2. __gr__ grapes
3. tree __tr__
4. crayon __cr__
5. __cr__ crab
6. __fr__ frog
7. bride __br__
8. __gr__ grapefruit
9. __gr__ grasshopper
10. __br__ broom
11. __tr__ truck
12. frame __fr__
13. crib __cr__
14. __br__ bridge
15. __dr__ drill
16. propeller __pr__
17. fruit __fr__
18. __br__ bread
19. __cr__ crown
20. __tr__ track
21. __gr__ graph
22. __dr__ dress
23. groom __gr__
24. __tr__ train
25. __pr__ prize
26. __br__ brush
27. __cr__ crocodile
28. __tr__ tractor

Skill: Consonant Blends

For lesson support, see page T73.

A **consonant blend** is two or more consonant letters that blend together in such a way that you can hear the consonant sound each letter stands for. The consonant blends below are called *l* blends.

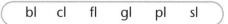

> bl   cl   fl   gl   pl   sl

Say each picture name. Listen to the beginning sounds. On the line, write the blend from the list above that stands for the consonant sounds that you hear at the beginning of the picture name.

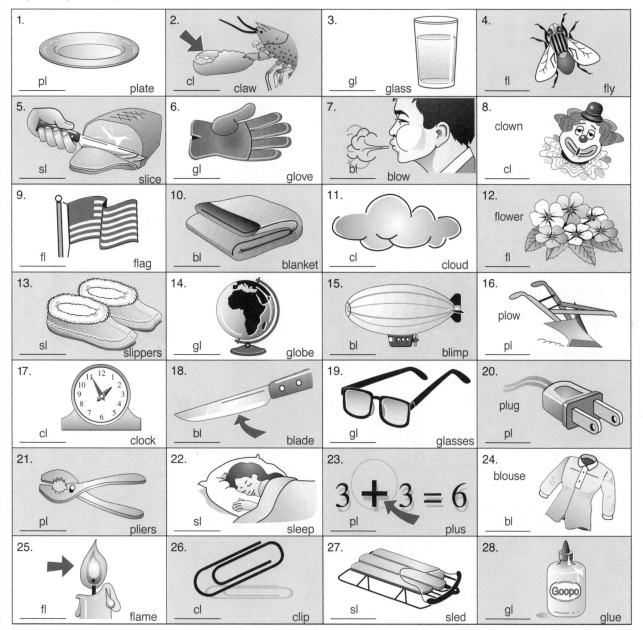

1. ___pl___ plate

2. ___cl___ claw

3. ___gl___ glass

4. ___fl___ fly

5. ___sl___ slice

6. ___gl___ glove

7. ___bl___ blow

8. clown ___cl___

9. ___fl___ flag

10. ___bl___ blanket

11. ___cl___ cloud

12. flower ___fl___

13. ___sl___ slippers

14. ___gl___ globe

15. ___bl___ blimp

16. plow ___pl___

17. ___cl___ clock

18. ___bl___ blade

19. ___gl___ glasses

20. plug ___pl___

21. ___pl___ pliers

22. ___sl___ sleep

23. ___pl___ plus

24. blouse ___bl___

25. ___fl___ flame

26. ___cl___ clip

27. ___sl___ sled

28. ___gl___ glue

For ESL/ELL support, see page T74.

Skill: Consonant Blends

For lesson support, see page T74.

Some words have two consonants at the beginning of them. If you hear the sounds that both of these letters stand for, the two letters are called a **consonant blend**. Here are some *s* blends.

> sc   sm   sn   sp   st   sw

Say each picture name. Listen to the beginning sounds. On the line, write the blend from the list above that stands for the consonant sounds that you hear at the beginning of the picture name.

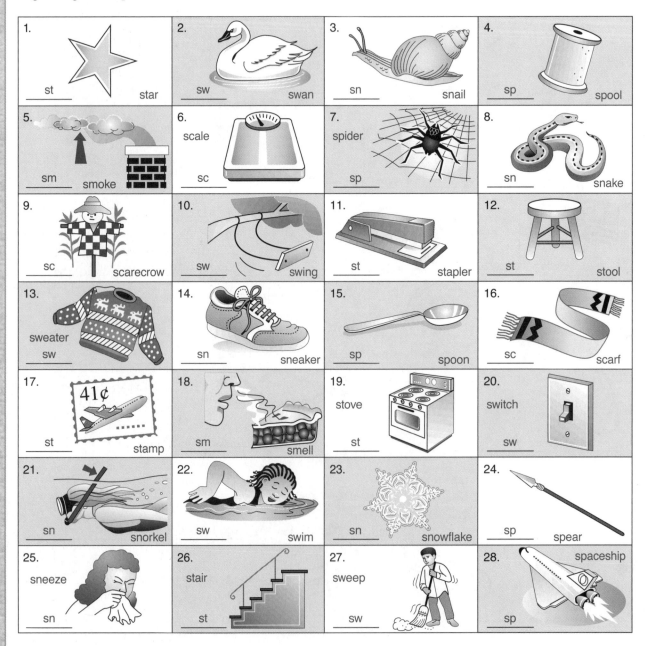

1. __st__   star
2. __sw__   swan
3. __sn__   snail
4. __sp__   spool
5. __sm__   smoke
6. scale   __sc__
7. spider   __sp__
8. __sn__   snake
9. __sc__   scarecrow
10. __sw__   swing
11. __st__   stapler
12. __st__   stool
13. sweater   __sw__
14. __sn__   sneaker
15. __sp__   spoon
16. __sc__   scarf
17. __st__   stamp
18. __sm__   smell
19. stove   __st__
20. switch   __sw__
21. __sn__   snorkel
22. __sw__   swim
23. __sn__   snowflake
24. __sp__   spear
25. sneeze   __sn__
26. stair   __st__
27. sweep   __sw__
28. spaceship   __sp__

Skill: Long and Short Vowel Sounds

For lesson support, see page T74.

Say the word *apple*. Listen to its beginning sound. This sound is called the short sound of *a*. Other **short vowel sounds** are *e* as in *egg*, *i* as in *it*, *o* as in *on*, and *u* as in *umbrella*. Most dictionaries do not mark short vowel sounds.

Long vowel sounds give the name of the vowel, as *a* in *age*, *e* in *eagle*, *i* in *ice*, *o* in *open*, and *u* in *unit*. Most dictionaries mark long vowel sounds with a macron (¯). A macron is found above the vowel letter. For example: āge.

Words Ending in the Letter *e*

A. Look at each picture. Read the words. Write the word that names the picture.

pin or pine?

_____pine_____

rob or robe?

_____robe_____

cub or cube?

_____cube_____

can or cane?

_____cane_____

B. Fill in the chart below. Then complete Rule 1.

Words Ending in the Letter *e*			
Word	Is the first vowel sound long or short?	Does the word end in the letter *e*?	Is the *e* silent or sounded?
1. page	long	yes	silent
2. ice	long	yes	silent
3. globe	long	yes	silent

RULE 1: When a word contains two vowels, one of which is final _____e_____, the first vowel is usually _____long_____, and the final e is _____silent_____.

Words That Do Not End in the Letter *e*

C. Fill in the chart below. Then complete Rule 2.

Words That Do Not End in the Letter *e*		
Word	Is the vowel sound long or short?	Is there a vowel at the end of the word?
1. sand	short	no
2. bend	short	no
3. rock	short	no

RULE 2: When a word contains only one vowel, and that vowel is not at the end of the word, the _____vowel_____ is usually _____short_____.

Skill: Following Directions

For lesson support, see page T75.

Flight attendants on airplanes show passengers how to use safety and emergency devices, such as seat belts and oxygen masks. If the plane is flying over an ocean or other large body of water, the flight attendants also show passengers how to use life jackets. Cards with **directions** and drawings for using life jackets are in the seat pockets for passengers to read.

Below and on the next page are the steps for using a life jacket. Each step is numbered and illustrated. These directions are given in English and Spanish. Study the directions and the illustrations carefully so that you will understand how a life jacket works.

2 Pull Tab and Remove Jacket From Package
Tire de la Cinta y
Remueva el Chaleco

4 Hook Back of Jacket to Front
Una la Parte de Atras del
Chaleco a la Parte Delantera

3 Put Jacket Over Head
Ponga el Chaleco
Sobre la Cabeza

1 Take Life Jackets From Under Seats
Chalecos Salvavidas
Baja el Asiento

A. The steps to follow when using a life jacket are listed in the wrong order below. Write *1* in front of the step to follow first, *2* in front of the step to follow next, and so on.

__3__ Put the life jacket on over your head, keeping the tabs in front.

__5__ Tighten the belt around your waist by pulling the ends of the belt.

__7__ If the life jacket does not fill up with air, blow into the tubes to inflate it.

__1__ Get the package containing the life jacket from under your seat.

__6__ After leaving the plane, pull down on the tabs to inflate the life jacket.

__4__ Buckle both ends of the belt to the center ring on the front of the life jacket.

__8__ If it is dark outside, pull down on the center tab for light.

__2__ Pull the tab to open the package and remove the life jacket.

B. Choose one of the topics listed below, and write directions for it. Make sure that your directions are clear enough for other students to follow them.

1. how to play your favorite game

2. how to make your favorite sandwich or dessert

3. how to build a model car, airplane, or boat

4. how to use your personal computer

Answers will vary. Students' directions should show a clear and logical sequence of steps.

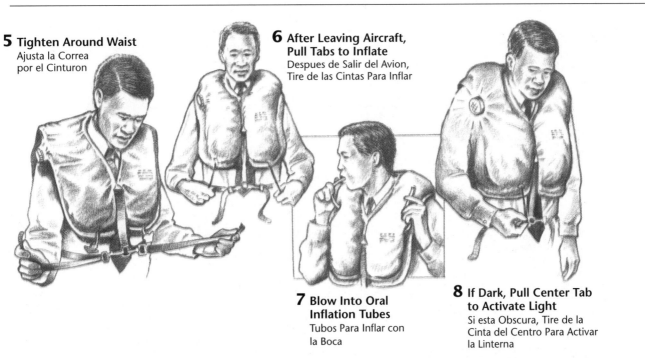

5 Tighten Around Waist
Ajusta la Correa
por el Cinturon

6 After Leaving Aircraft, Pull Tabs to Inflate
Despues de Salir del Avion,
Tire de las Cintas Para Inflar

7 Blow Into Oral Inflation Tubes
Tubos Para Inflar con
la Boca

8 If Dark, Pull Center Tab to Activate Light
Si esta Obscura, Tire de la
Cinta del Centro Para Activar
la Linterna

Skill: Long and Short Vowel Sounds

For lesson support, see page T75.

A. The vowel sound in a one-syllable word is either long or short. You have learned two rules that will help you decide which vowel sound is correct. These rules are given below, but each rule has a missing word. Write a word on the line to complete each rule.

RULE 1: When a word contains two vowels, one of which is final e, the first vowel is usually _____long_____, and the final e is silent.

RULE 2: When a word contains only one vowel, and that vowel is not at the end of the word, the vowel is usually _____short_____.

B. Decide how to pronounce each word below. On the line, write the number of the rule that you used to make your decision. Mark each long vowel with a macron (ˉ). Do not mark the short vowels.

	Rule Number		Rule Number		Rule Number
1. māke	1	15. shīne	1	29. gāme	1
2. leg	2	16. clam	2	30. man	2
3. smīle	1	17. plāce	1	31. bīte	1
4. grin	2	18. mīle	1	32. lock	2
5. hot	2	19. hit	2	33. flāme	1
6. mūle	1	20. rāke	1	34. slip	2
7. land	2	21. mīce	1	35. grand	2
8. deck	2	22. pot	2	36. lāte	1
9. ship	2	23. cūbe	1	37. stōve	1
10. hill	2	24. thēse	1	38. set	2
11. tīme	1	25. brīde	1	39. rūle	1
12. hōse	1	26. sun	2	40. crab	2
13. flag	2	27. rōpe	1		
14. shut	2	28. bed	2		

unit two

For ESL/ELL support, see highlighted words, page T76, and pages T28–T30.

Flight

LESSON 13

For theme support, see page T26.

Skill: Setting

For lesson support, see page T76.

BACKGROUND INFORMATION

In "Angela's First Flight," Angela Holland is eager to go hang gliding before she is ready. Hang gliding became a popular sport in the United States in the early 1970s. Most hang gliders are about 18-feet wide. They have a large sail attached to an aluminum frame. The pilot hangs from a harness and steers with a metal bar. In order to become a pilot, a hang glider needs to take lessons.

SKILL FOCUS: Setting

The **setting** is the **time** and the **place** in which a story takes place. For example, a story might be set in the 1850s in a Western mine, in the year 2300 on the moon, or early this morning in your own backyard.

Often an author tells you exactly when and where a story takes place. In some stories, though, you have to figure out the setting from details in the text. As you read, look for words or phrases that tell about the setting.

The place where a story is set can affect the events in the story. For example, characters lost in a desert will face different problems than characters lost in a jungle. The time of the setting is important, too. If a story is set long ago, for example, characters cannot use a telephone to call for help when they are in trouble.

To understand the setting of a story, ask yourself these questions as you read.

- Where does the story take place?
- When does the story take place?
- How does the setting fit the events in the story?

▶ Think of a story you have read or a movie you have seen. On the web in the next column, write its title. Then write where and when the story takes place.

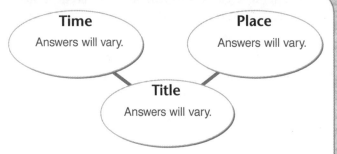

Time — Answers will vary.

Place — Answers will vary.

Title — Answers will vary.

CONTEXT CLUES: Comparisons

If you don't know the meaning of a word, look for the word *like* or *as* nearby. These words introduce a **comparison** that can help you understand a new word. Notice the comparison that helps you picture the word *dunes* in the following sentence.

*The road ended in sandy, white **dunes** that looked like snowdrifts above the beach.*

The comparison *like snowdrifts* helps you picture the dunes as piles of white sand that look like snowdrifts.

▶ Read the following sentence. Circle the comparison that helps you understand the meaning of *glide*.

*Once you catch the wind, you **glide** along on waves of air just like a bird.*

Use comparison context clues to figure out the meaning of the underlined words *trudged*, *glared*, and *jolt* in the story.

Strategy Tip

As you read "Angela's First Flight," think about the setting of the story. Where and when do the events take place? Then ask yourself what features of this setting are necessary for successful hang gliding.

Angela's First Flight

Angela Holland slammed the screen door. "That Paul Daniel!" she shouted. "I can't stand him!"

Her mother stood by the kitchen counter. She was slicing bread for lunch. She glanced at Angela.

"Now what happened?" she asked.

Angela flopped down on a kitchen chair.

"He won't let me try his hang glider." Angela rolled her eyes. "I'm 18 years old, and you'd think I never had a hang gliding lesson."

"Angela, you've only had two lessons. You've never flown more than a few feet off the ground."

"But I have my own helmet and gloves. Besides, Paul could teach me. He's been hang gliding for a long time now. He's had plenty of lessons."

Her mother set the bread and a jar of peanut butter on the table. As Angela sliced a banana for her peanut butter sandwich, her mother listened to her and shook her head.

"Hang gliding is really great, Mom! Once you catch the wind, you glide along on waves of air just like a bird." Angela took a big bite of her sandwich.

When Angela finished her sandwich, she jumped up from the chair, grabbed her helmet and gloves, and headed for the door.

"Thanks for lunch, Mom," she said.

"Where are you going?" her mother asked. "I want you back here by four o'clock to help weed the garden."

"Okay, I'll be back to help." Angela opened the screen door. "I'm going to ride down to the beach."

"Don't do anything foolish, Angela."

As the screen door clapped shut behind her, Angela thought, "There must be some way to get a ride on that glider."

Angela climbed on her bicycle and rode for ten minutes to the beach. All the way, she tried to think of ways to get Paul to let her use his glider.

The road ended in sandy, white dunes that looked like snowdrifts above the beach. With her equipment in hand, Angela walked to the edge of the dunes. The land dropped off in a steep slope to the beach below. On most days, the wind came in off the ocean. Blowing across the beach, it hit the sandy cliff and rose higher. The rising air was just right for hang gliding.

"Oh, no! Are you back?" said Paul. He was standing a little way down the slope.

Angela said nothing as she put on her helmet and gloves. She crossed her legs and sank down on the sand.

The bright blue-and-green glider lay on the sand next to Paul. He put on his safety helmet. Paul then put on his harness and fastened it to the frame of the glider. Once securely hooked to the glider, Paul lifted it so that the harness straps were tight and tugging at his body. He was now attached to the glider. When the glider took off, he would hang in the air just behind the guide bar.

Paul grabbed the bar and then swung the big wing up over his head and pointed it down the slope. As fast as he could go, Paul ran down the slope, trying all the while to maintain his balance. He was building speed and taking longer and longer strides.

Angela held her breath. The sail filled with air. Within seconds, Paul's feet were off the ground. He was lifted higher as the wind caught the hang glider.

He sailed along the slope, keeping the glider pointed into the wind and the control bar in the flying position.

Angela cheered and said to herself, "I just have to do it."

Suddenly the nose of the sail pointed up. The back dipped low. The glider had "stalled." Paul and the glider dropped down, bouncing on the sand. He unhooked his harness and took off his helmet. Pulling the glider behind him, Paul <u>trudged</u> up the slope like a tired pack mule.

"What happened?" Angela called out, grinning. "Haven't you learned to fly yet?"

The sun was beating down. Paul was hot, and he was tired from so much gliding. He didn't like people watching him. He had had good flights while Angela was away at lunch.

Like an angry lion, Paul <u>glared</u> at Angela. "I bet you couldn't even lift it."

"What!" Angela ground her teeth.

Paul dragged himself up the steep slope. The glider came to a stop. Paul took off his harness and sat down in the sand.

"Bet I can!" Angela yelled, jumping up. She grabbed the harness and slipped it on. Then she ran down to the glider and hooked the harness to the frame as her instructor had showed her. She lifted the glider off the ground. With the control bar in the flying position, Angela began running down the slope.

Paul shouted, but Angela didn't hear what he said. The glider wasn't heavy, but it tipped to one side. She lost her footing and tumbled to the ground. The glider dug into the sand and tipped over.

Angela's mouth was full of sand. Sand was in her eyes and hair, too. She heard Paul laughing from up the slope. He cupped his hands and shouted, "How does it taste?"

Angela jumped up, brushing the sand from her face. She grabbed the glider's bar.

"Hey, you had a chance! Beat it!" shouted Paul. Angela had the glider over her head and was running down the slope again. The wind rushed past her face. The ocean roared in her ears. She remembered what her instructor had said, "Don't think about flying. Think about running to the bottom of the hill."

Paul's voice came after her. "Tear that sail and you'll pay for it!"

Angela raced down the slope. She was going fast. Each step got longer and longer. Her legs could barely keep up. She started to stumble again. Then she felt a strong tug on the handle. Her feet came off the ground. She was in the air!

The world seemed to fall away. Angela floated slowly along the face of the cliff. The ocean's roar seemed far off. A seagull drifted by right next to her.

Angela leaned toward the ocean side. The wing tipped that way and began a slow, silent turn over the beach.

Angela could hardly breathe. Her heart pounded with excitement. She loved this feeling of freedom. Flying was so easy.

The glider turned back toward the cliff. Suddenly Angela was afraid. She had never landed from such a height. Her instructor had warned her about wind currents. Angela felt her fear turning into panic.

The glider was heading straight for the sandy cliff. Angela tried to remember how to land—but it was too late. The wing tip dug into the sand with a jolt as sudden as a flash of lightning. Angela hit the sand hard before coming to a stop.

Angela shook her head and opened her eyes. Slowly, she looked around. She saw Paul running down the slope toward her and his glider. He glared at Angela and then turned to check the sail.

"You're lucky, Angela," said Paul. "Everything was fine until you landed. You need more lessons. Maybe I can give you some tips."

Paul started to explain to Angela what she did wrong. "You must remember these rules: If you try to keep the hang glider on the ground as you run down the hill, you will have a better takeoff. If you try to keep the hang glider in the air as you land, you will have a good landing."

Angela listened to Paul attentively. He was absolutely right about takeoffs and landings. She knew that once she finished her lessons, Paul would give her another try. She realized now how foolish she had been to take Paul's glider. She was lucky that she hadn't been seriously hurt. Next time, though, her landing would be perfect.

Recalling details
1. What is a hang glider?

A hang glider is a large sail with a metal bar

connected to it.

Recalling details
2. How does a hang glider fly?

The wind lifts the sail into the air, and the bar drops down.

By holding on to the bar, a person can fly the hang glider.

Recalling details
3. How many hang gliding lessons has Angela had?

She has had only two lessons.

Recalling details
4. What equipment must a hang glider pilot have?

A helmet, gloves, and harness are all items that a

hang glider pilot must have.

Recalling details
5. What drifts right by Angela on her flight?

A seagull flies past Angela during her flight.

Comparing and contrasting
6. Was Angela's second attempt to hang glide more or less successful than her first? Explain.

Her second attempt was more successful. The glider

took off, but Angela crashed.

Recalling details
7. What must Angela do before Paul will let her have another ride on his glider?

Angela must finish taking her flying lessons.

Using context clues
8. Complete each sentence with the correct word from below.

glared   jolt   trudged

a. Robert had trouble pulling the sled as he

_____trudged_____ through the snow.

b. The _____jolt_____ of the car hitting a tree threw the driver forward in his seat.

c. Lisa _____glared_____ at her brother when he used her computer without permission.

CRITICAL THINKING

Making inferences
1. Describe how Mrs. Holland feels about Angela's wanting to hang glide.

She worries because she knows that Angela hasn't finished her flying lessons.

Drawing conclusions
2. Do you think Paul is a selfish person? Explain.

Answers will vary. Yes. He won't share his glider with anyone. *or* No. He's cautious and concerned

about friends using his glider when they don't know how to control it.

Making inferences
3. Describe how Angela feels about her first flight with a hang glider.

She loved the feeling of freedom it gave her; she can't wait to try it again. She realizes, though, that

she was foolish to try hang gliding before she was ready to control the glider.

Drawing conclusions
4. Explain why hang gliding could be dangerous.

It could be dangerous if the person flying isn't trained or if he or she doesn't have the right equipment.

Drawing conclusions
5. Do you think that Angela would try other new sports if she discovered them? Explain why or why not.

Yes. Angela seems adventurous and willing to try almost anything.

Inferring cause and effect
6. Why is the beach a good place for hang gliding?

At the beach, the air blows in off the ocean, hits the steep cliffs, and rises. When the glider

catches the wind, it quickly lifts off the ground and "glides."

Drawing conclusions
7. Discuss whether Angela could have gone hang gliding if she lived in an inland city? Explain why or why not.

No. Hang gliding needs high, open places where someone can run until the wind lifts the sail.

It also needs a large, open area to sail over.

SKILL FOCUS: SETTING

1. Where does the story take place?

The story takes place near and at the beach.

2. When does it take place?

The story probably takes place during the summer, in

the afternoon, and in the present.

3. Does the setting fit the events in the story?

Yes, the setting fits the events in the story.

4. In what way does the setting fit?

To hang glide, one needs a high, open place, such as

the beach's cliffs. Setting the story in the present fits

because hang gliding is currently popular.

5. Could you hang glide where you live? Why or why not?

Answers will vary. Students should consider wind and

high, open places as essential to hang gliding.

Reading-Writing Connection

Suppose you are flying a hang glider over a beach. On a separate sheet of paper, write a paragraph to describe what you see as you are flying. Use vivid details to help readers visualize your flight.

LESSON 14

For ESL/ELL support, see highlighted words, page T77, and pages T28–T30.

Skill: Reading a Map

For lesson support, see page T77.

BACKGROUND INFORMATION

"Around the World in Twenty Days" is about the fascinating sport of hot-air ballooning. For years, balloonists have dreamed of flying a hot-air balloon around the world. Between 1982 and 1999, almost 20 balloonists had tried to make this challenging flight. Storms, breakdowns, or lack of fuel cut short their flights. Then in 1999, two balloonists from Europe once again tried to float around the world.

SKILL FOCUS: Reading a Map

When reading about different parts of the world, you can use a globe to locate places. When a globe is not handy, a **map** can show you the same places. A map can show the whole world at once or only part of the world.

Maps have many features to help you find places. The **title** or the **caption** tells what the map shows. The **compass rose** shows the directions north, south, east, and west. A world map will also show the **equator**. This imaginary line divides the world into the Northern Hemisphere and the Southern Hemisphere.

Maps contain a great deal of information. You can find the names of cities, countries, bodies of water, and so on. Reading a map along with the text will give you more information than either one can provide alone.

▶ Use the map on this page to answer the questions below.

Is Australia in the Northern Hemisphere or Southern Hemisphere? How do you know?

It is in the Southern Hemisphere. You can tell

because it is below the equator on the map.

CONTEXT CLUES: Definitions

Writers of social studies articles often define important terms for you. Look for these **definitions** as you read. In the sentence below, the writer explains the meaning of the underlined word.

Brian and Bertrand stood in the balloon's **capsule***. This would be their living quarters and command center for the next three weeks.*

If you don't know the meaning of *capsule* in the first sentence, read the next sentence. The words *living quarters* and *command center* explain the meaning of *capsule*.

▶ Read the following sentence. Circle the words that explain the meaning of the underlined word.

The men's goal was not to touch down until they had **circumnavigated** *the globe.* Flying 25,000 miles (40,250 kilometers) around the world *would not be easy.*

Use definition context clues to find the meaning of the underlined words *meteorology*, *jet stream*, and *stratosphere* in the selection.

Strategy Tip

As you read "Around the World in Twenty Days," remember to study the maps. Look for places mentioned in the text. Use the title, compass, and place names on the map to help you follow the balloonists' path.

Africa, Asia, Australia, and Antarctica

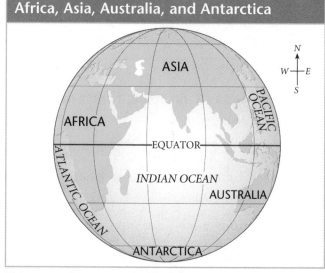

This map shows one half of the world.

Around the World in Twenty Days

Taking Off

The date was March 1, 1999. The place was the Swiss Alps, the tallest mountains in Europe. Bertrand Piccard of Switzerland and Brian Jones of England checked their balloon one last time. Then with gas burners roaring, their balloon rose into the sky. Before long, mountain winds grabbed it. Up and away it went.

As the mountains disappeared below them, Brian and Bertrand stood in the balloon's capsule. This would be their living quarters and command center for the next three weeks. The men's goal was not to touch down until they had circumnavigated the globe. Flying 25,000 miles (40,250 kilometers) around the world would not be easy. So far, no one had been able to do it. Bertrand himself had already tried twice before.

Their balloon was named the *Breitling* (BREYT ling) *Orbiter 3*. It was 180 feet high (55 meters) and cost $3 million. The balloon used both **helium** (HEE lee əm) gas and hot air. To go up, the pilots turned on burners that heated the helium and air. To go down, they turned down the heat.

Balloons don't have steering wheels. They move in the same direction as the wind. The winds carried Brian and Bertrand's balloon south at first. After one day, the men were over Spain. Then the balloon reached Egypt in North Africa after four days.

Catching the Jet Stream

Meteorology (MEE tee ə RAL ə jee) plays a key role in ballooning. Balloonists need to study the weather because storms and winds can make or break a flight. Before their flight, Bertrand and Brian had studied weather maps and charts. They had also brought along radios, telephones, a computer, and a fax machine.

During their long flight, Brian and Bertrand used these machines to keep in touch with meteorologists in Switzerland. When they learned of storms, they changed course to miss them. In case of an emergency, the balloon carried parachutes and rafts. Luckily the men did not need them.

The balloonists knew that a jet stream was in place over North Africa. This high, fast wind was blowing from west to east. To catch the jet stream, they turned up the gas over Egypt. The balloon rose to 30,000 feet (9,000 meters) and entered the jet stream. They sailed east at about 85 miles per hour (mph).

Like a bubble in the sky, the *Breitling Orbiter 3* floated east across the Sahara Desert, which covers much of North Africa. Inside the capsule, the balloon seemed as if it weren't moving. The smooth ride wasn't very comfortable, though. Brian and Bertrand ate mainly dried food and slept in tiny spaces. The air temperature at 30,000 feet was −58° Fahrenheit. The small heater in the capsule didn't always keep the men warm.

However, ballooning seemed to come naturally to Bertrand Piccard. His grandfather, Auguste Piccard, was the first person to reach the Earth's stratosphere in a balloon. That layer of the atmosphere is 50,000 feet (15,250 meters) up!

Crossing the Middle East and Asia

After flying over North Africa, the balloon crossed into the Middle East. Brian and Bertrand had gotten permission to pass over the countries below them—Saudi Arabia, Yemen, and Oman. Swiss air-traffic controllers kept each country aware of the balloon's location. The controllers also stayed in touch with the balloon.

Soon, the balloon cut across India and Bangladesh. Then it reached the mountains of Yunnan on China's border. China had refused earlier balloonists the right to cross its airspace. However, it gave Bertrand and Brian permission.

The Chinese officials warned, however, that the balloon must stay south of the 25th **parallel of latitude** (PAIR ə lel uhv LAT ə tood). Parallels of latitude are imaginary lines that measure distance north and south of the equator.

Flight of the *Breitling Orbiter 3* Balloon

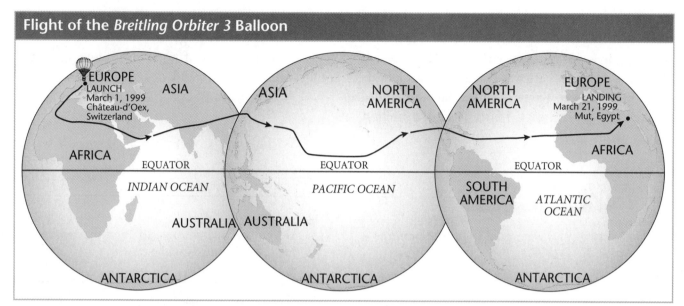

This map shows the *Breitling Orbiter 3*'s trip around the world.

At one point, the *Breitling Orbiter 3* drifted too far north toward the **restricted** (ri STRIKT əd), or forbidden, zone. The Chinese ordered the balloonists to make an emergency landing. For a while, it seemed as if the flight might end in China.

Then at the last minute, a wind pushed the balloon south. The voyage continued. For 1,300 miles (2,100 kilometers), *Breitling Orbiter 3* followed a straight line across China. After 15 hours, the balloon had crossed the continent of Asia.

Floating Over the Ocean

With Asia behind them, the balloonists faced a new challenge—the Pacific Ocean. Ten thousand miles of open sea lay between them and North America. Storms over the ocean had forced down many other balloons in the past. The balloonists studied weather maps and satellite photographs. They tried to decide whether to take a northern or southern route across the Pacific.

Meanwhile a new jet stream was forming high over the equator to the south. The balloonists hoped to find it. They let the winds blow them slowly south. No one had ever flown a balloon so far south across the Pacific before. Brian and Bertrand did not know what to expect.

For six days, it was slow going. The speed of the *Breitling Orbiter 3* dropped to 25 mph. Bertrand and Brian grew worried. They were burning gas steadily just to keep their balloon in the air. At that rate, they

risked using up their fuel before they reached their goal. At last, *Breitling Orbiter 3* found the jet stream over the equator. The balloon sped up to 115 mph. Brian and Bertrand were back in the race.

The Final Leg of the Journey

Over Mexico, a new problem developed. The balloon popped out of the jet stream and lost speed. Then it headed south—the wrong direction. Bertrand and Brian believed the jet stream was still somewhere above them. To find it, they decided to take the balloon as high as it would go. Slowly the balloon rose—32,000, 33,000, 34,000 feet.

At 35,000 feet (10,500 meters), *Breitling Orbiter 3* found the jet stream again. The big balloon veered slowly east and picked up speed. By the time the balloonists crossed the island of Jamaica, they were back on course and traveling at 105 mph.

As they moved out over the Atlantic Ocean, the balloonists worried about fuel. They had taken off with 32 tanks of fuel. Now only four were left. Luckily, the Atlantic crossing went smoothly. After just two days, the balloon again reached the continent of Africa.

At sunrise on March 20, Brian and Bertrand studied their maps. After flying 26,050 miles (41,940 kilometers), they had once again reached the Sahara Desert. That was the point where they had first headed east!

SOCIAL STUDIES

LESSON 14 Reading a Map **43**

Bertrand Piccard and Brian Jones had reached their goal. The date was March 21, 1999. Their flight around the world had taken 19 days, 21 hours, and 47 minutes. Since there was still a little fuel left, the balloonists flew to Egypt the next day and landed. There they got a hero's welcome and a million-dollar prize!

"Mother Nature carried us around the world," said Brian, "and set us gently back down."

"May the winds of hope keep blowing around the world," said Bertrand.

COMPREHENSION

Recalling details
1. What two gases were used to lift the *Breitling Orbiter 3*?

   The balloon used helium and hot air.

Recalling details
2. How far did the balloon travel in its flight around the world?

   It traveled more than 26,000 miles.

Recalling details
3. How did the balloonists keep track of the weather?

   They used radios, telephones, a computer, and a fax

   machine to keep in touch with meteorologists on the ground.

Recalling details
4. What prize did the balloonists receive for their achievement?

   They got a $1 million prize.

Identifying cause and effect
5. Why was the *Breitling Orbiter 3* almost forced to land in China?

   The balloon had drifted too close to a restricted zone.

Identifying cause and effect
6. Why was slowing down to 25 mph a problem for the balloonists while crossing the Pacific?

   Unless they went faster, they would run out of fuel

   before completing their trip.

Recognizing sequence of events
7. After crossing Asia, what was the next challenge the balloonists had to overcome?

   They had to cross the Pacific Ocean.

Recalling details
8. About how high did the balloon have to fly to take advantage of the jet stream?

   The balloon had to fly 35,000 feet.

Using context clues
9. Write the letter of the correct meaning on the line next to each word.

   _b_ stratosphere   a. the science of weather

   _c_ jet stream   b. the layer of the atmosphere 50,000 feet above the Earth

   _a_ meteorology   c. a high, fast wind

CRITICAL THINKING

Making inferences
1. Describe personal qualities that Bertrand Piccard and Brian Jones needed to complete their journey.

   Answers will vary. They needed to be adventurous, brave, skilled, smart, quick-thinking,

   and determined to succeed.

Making inferences

2. Explain how advances in weather forecasting and communications helped Brian and Bertrand achieve their goal.

The balloonists had radios, telephones, a computer, and a fax machine, so they could communicate with people on the

ground. Advances in weather forecasting helped the men to find the jet streams and avoid bad storms.

Drawing conclusions

3. List some ways in which Bertrand and Brian prepared for their voyage.

Answers will vary. They had to load their balloon with supplies and communications equipment. They had to practice flying

the balloon and using the equipment. They had to get permission to cross the airspace of many countries.

SKILL FOCUS: READING A MAP

1. Find the point on the map on page 43 where the balloon began its journey. Name the country.

The balloon began its journey in Switzerland.

2. On which continent is Switzerland located?

Switzerland is located in Europe.

3. In what direction did the balloon travel around the world?

It traveled eastward.

4. How many views of Earth are shown on this map?

The map shows three views of Earth.

5. Find the equator. Which continents lie completely south of it?

Australia and Antarctica

6. Which continents lie both north and south of the equator?

Africa, South America, and Asia lie both north and

south of the equator.

7. Tell, in order, the continents that the balloon passed over in its flight around the world.

The balloon passed over Europe, Africa, Asia, North

America, and then Africa again.

8. Which continents were not along the route of the balloon?

South America, Australia, and Antarctica were not along

the balloon's route.

9. Find the point on the map where the balloon landed. Name the country and continent.

The balloon landed in Egypt, in Africa.

10. Did the balloon travel farther over the Pacific Ocean or the Atlantic Ocean? How can you tell?

It traveled farther over the Pacific Ocean. The length of

the lines over the oceans shows this.

Reading-Writing Connection

Use the map to plan an imaginary balloon flight around the world. On a separate sheet of paper, describe the countries, continents, and bodies of water you would pass over. Tell about the challenges you might face during the flight.

For ESL/ELL support, see highlighted words, page T78, and pages T28–T30.

Skill: Reading a Diagram

For lesson support, see page T78.

BACKGROUND INFORMATION

"The International Space Station" is about an enormous new space venture. For more than 40 years, the United States has been exploring space. Russia and other countries also have space programs. In the 1990s, 16 nations began working together to build the International Space Station (ISS). When it is finished, the ISS will allow scientists from around the world to do experiments in space. It may also help us reach the planet Mars someday.

SKILL FOCUS: Reading a Diagram

Writers often use drawings, or **diagrams**, to help them explain a science topic. Diagrams, also called **figures**, usually appear after the text they illustrate. **Labels** name the parts of a diagram. There may also be a **caption** under a diagram to provide more information.

When reading a selection with diagrams, follow these steps.

1. First, read the text that appears before a diagram. Then study the diagram that goes with it. Read all the labels and the caption.

2. As you continue reading, look back at the diagram whenever you need help in understanding the text.

3. Picture the details in the text and the diagram together. That way, you will understand the topic better.

4. When you finish reading, look at the diagram again. Try to explain, in your own words, what the diagram shows.

▶ Look at the diagram. How far from Earth is the International Space Station?

_____220 miles_____

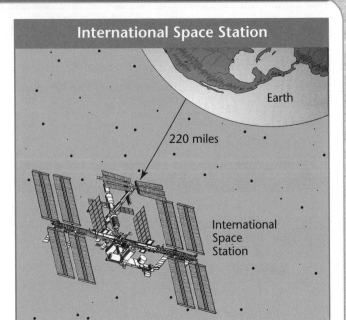

International Space Station

Earth

220 miles

International Space Station

This diagram shows the distance from Earth to the International Space Station.

CONTEXT CLUES: Appositive Phrases

An **appositive phrase** is a group of words that explains the meaning of a word coming right before it. An appositive phrase is usually set off from the word it explains by commas and the word *or*.

Read the sentence below. What appositive phrase explains the meaning of the underlined word?

*First, workers on Earth put together **modules**, or self-contained sections, of the space station.*

In case you don't know the meaning of *modules*, the appositive phrase *self-contained sections* tells you.

▶ Circle the appositive phrase that explains the meaning of *solar power* in the sentence below.

*The space station will rely on **solar power**, or* (energy from sunlight.)

As you read the selection, use appositive phrases to help you figure out the meaning of the underlined words *orbiting*, *habitation*, and *semiconductors*.

Strategy Tip

When reading this selection, study the diagrams, their labels, and their captions, to understand what a space station is like.

The International Space Station

If you look up at the sky tonight, you might see the International Space Station. The ISS is <u>orbiting</u>, or circling the Earth, at 220 miles (355 kilometers). It is traveling at 17,000 miles per hour, about 5 miles a second. It circles the Earth every 92 minutes.

When it is done, the International Space Station will be the size of two football fields. It will weigh more than a million pounds. We could never launch something that big into space. So astronauts are building the ISS in outer space.

First, workers on Earth put together modules, or self-contained sections, of the space station. Then space shuttles carry these modules into orbit. It will take more than 40 shuttle flights total to transport all the modules. The flights began in 1998. They will continue until 2010. Astronauts will take more than 150 space walks to bolt all the modules together.

When it is done, the International Space Station will look like a collection of steel boxes, soda cans, and winglike panels. The station will measure 290 feet (88 meters) long and 143 feet (44 meters) high. It will be 356 feet (109 meters) wide. That's as wide as a 16-story building is tall. Inside, there will be 46,000 cubic feet of living and working space. That's as much space as there is inside two large passenger jets.

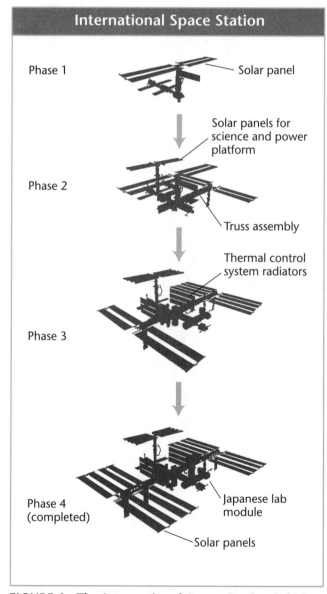

FIGURE 1. The International Space Station is being built in stages. It should be completed in 2010.

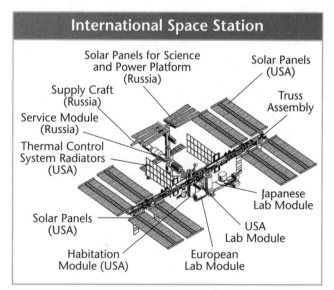

FIGURE 2. More than 100,000 people have contributed to the building of the ISS.

The space station will rely on solar power, or energy from sunlight. Eight huge solar panels will jut out from the sides of the station to collect sunlight. Together their surface area will be about an acre. We will be able to see these golden panels from Earth. In fact, after the moon and Venus, the space station will be the brightest object in the night sky.

Earlier Space Stations

The International Space Station is by far the largest space station ever built. It is not the first one, though. Back in 1973, the United States launched a space station called *Skylab*. Astronauts entered *Skylab* during 1973 and 1974. They did some experiments there. Then, the United States stopped using *Skylab*. It fell to Earth safely over the Pacific Ocean in 1979.

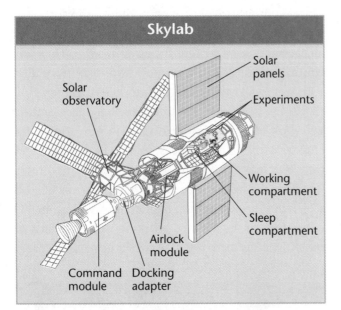

Skylab

- Solar observatory
- Solar panels
- Experiments
- Working compartment
- Sleep compartment
- Airlock module
- Command module
- Docking adapter

FIGURE 3. *Skylab*, the first American space station, was much smaller than later space stations.

Russia's space station, *Mir*, set a record for years in orbit. First launched in 1986, it finally fell to Earth in 2001 over the Pacific Ocean. Dozens of Russian **cosmonauts** (KAHZ mə nahts) had lived and worked on *Mir*. American astronauts had also visited the station.

Life Aboard the International Space Station

A few astronauts will live aboard the ISS while it is being built. Others will come up for visits. They will travel aboard the space shuttles that bring the modules. In 2007, astronauts attached the *Harmony* module, or Node 2. This module connects the research labs to the habitation areas, or living quarters. Each crew will stay aboard the space station for three to six months. Then a new crew will take its place.

✔ Earth's **gravity** (GRAV ə tee) is barely felt aboard the ISS. This "weightlessness" will affect life aboard the ISS in many ways. To cook, astronauts will squirt water into bags filled with dried food. Regular cooking would cause food crumbs to clog the space station's air filters. Normal showers will also be impossible. Weightless water would just float around the bathroom. To sleep, astronauts will strap special sleeping bags to the wall.

Astronauts from many nations will make up the crew of the ISS. Some crew members will control the flight of the space station. Others will do experiments in the space station's six laboratories.

The Benefits of ISS

One long-range space goal is to travel to Mars. There is much we must learn before astronauts can travel there. Knowledge gained on the ISS may pave the way for a flight to Mars. In the meantime, scientists will do many experiments aboard the ISS. Several labs will be set up. For example, astronauts who live in space for several weeks begin losing some of their bone density and muscle. These changes are like what happens during aging. By studying these changes in the astronauts, scientists may learn to slow down the aging process on Earth.

Biologists (bi AHL ə jists) are scientists who study living things. They plan to study cell growth in space. Body cells grow differently in very low gravity. These studies may lead to new treatments for cancer. Scientists may also be able to make better medicines in low gravity.

Physicists (FIZ ə sists) are scientists who study different kinds of energy. Aboard the ISS, they hope to make new semiconductors, the materials used in computer chips. These new semiconductors could make computers run much faster.

Scientists who study the Earth also have plans for the ISS. As it flies over the Earth's surface, the station is a "window on the world." Scientists on board will have a constant view of the Earth. Using new tools, they will be able to measure weather and climate changes. They will also note plant growth and the size and health of bodies of water.

One Final Benefit

One benefit of the space station has nothing to do with science. Sixteen nations are working together to build this great structure. Scientists and governments around the world are sharing ideas, money, and materials. To build the International Space Station, nations have put aside their differences. They have come together for a peaceful purpose in space. As a result, they may get along better on Earth.

COMPREHENSION

Recalling details
1. How much will the finished International Space Station weigh?

   It will weigh more than a million pounds.

Identifying cause and effect
2. Why is the ISS being built in sections by astronauts in space?

   The completed space station would be too large and

   heavy to launch into space.

Finding the main idea
3. Find the paragraph that has a ✔ next to it. Then underline the sentence that tells the main idea.

Using context clues
4. Write the meaning of each word on the line.

   a. habitation _____living_____

   b. orbiting _____circling the Earth_____

   c. semiconductors _____materials used in computer chips_____

CRITICAL THINKING

Inferring cause and effect
1. Describe how the astronauts' experiences on the ISS might prepare them for a trip to Mars.

   Answers will vary. A flight to Mars would take a long time. Aboard the ISS, astronauts

   can learn to cope with the effects that being in space for a long time has on their bodies and minds.

Drawing conclusions
2. Discuss the importance of different nations of the world studying space together.

   Answers will vary. Working together in space will draw nations together. We will make more progress in space if people

   from different parts of the world can share their talents.

SKILL FOCUS: READING A DIAGRAM

1. Look at Figure 1. What changes will occur in the ISS's solar panels between Phase 3 and Phase 4?
   More solar panels will be added during those years.

2. Look at Figure 2. How many lab modules are shown for the complete ISS?
   There are three lab modules shown.

3. Look at Figure 3. Describe where the astronauts lived while on *Skylab*.
   They lived in a tightly packed sleep compartment within the same module where they slept and did experiments.

Reading-Writing Connection

Find out more about the International Space Station. On a separate sheet of paper, write a paragraph about a part of the project that interests you the most. Draw a diagram.

Skill: Reading Metric Terms

For lesson support, see page T79.

BACKGROUND INFORMATION

"Metric Base Units and Prefixes" explains the metric system. Our English system of measurement—using inches, feet, yards, and miles—dates back to England in the 1200s. The problem with this system is that it follows no pattern. Unless a person is very familiar with the system, it is difficult to follow.

A group of French scientists created the metric system in the 1790s. Until that time, each country had its own system of measurement. That was especially confusing for scientists from different countries who wanted to share their ideas. Having one shared system of measurement made it much easier to compare their work.

During the last two centuries, the countries of the world have gradually changed over to the metric system. Great Britain and Canada were among the last nations to do so. Once they did, the United States decided to shift gradually to the metric system, too.

SKILL FOCUS: Reading Metric Terms

The **metric system** is simple to use. It is based on the number 10. To change a measurement from one unit in the metric system to the next larger unit, divide the measurement by 10. To change a measurement from one unit to the next smaller unit, multiply the measurement by 10.

▶ Answer the following question:
One weekend Jay bicycled 60 kilometers. The next smallest metric unit of distance is hectometers. How many hectometers did Jay bike?

600 hectometers

WORD CLUES

When working with metric measurements, you will often see the base words *meter*, *gram*, and *liter*. A meter is a measure of length. A gram is a measure of weight. A liter is a measure of volume of a liquid.

Prefixes are added to these three base words to change their meaning. Some common metric prefixes are listed in the chart below.

You will learn more about the meaning of these prefixes and how to use them in the next selection.

Prefixes
kilo-
hecto-
deca-
deci-
centi-
milli-

▶ On the lines below, write two metric terms for things that you have seen. Circle the term's prefix, if it has one. Then tell what each term is used to measure.

Answers will vary. *Liter* is used to measure amounts of juice. *Kilo*meter is used to measure the length of a race.

Strategy Tip

You know many English terms of measurement, including miles, feet, pounds, and gallons. The next selection describes the words and prefixes used to form terms of metric measurement. Try to become as familiar with these metric terms as you are with the English system.

Metric Base Units and Prefixes

Base Units

There are seven base units in the metric system. You can do most everyday measurements with only three of these units.

- To measure length, use the **meter**. A meter is about the length of a baseball bat.

- To measure weight, use the **gram**. A gram is about the weight of a dollar bill.

- To measure volume, use the **liter**. A liter of milk is about as much as a quart of milk.

Metric Prefixes

To name larger and smaller units in the metric system, you add prefixes to the base units. You know that a prefix can change the meaning of a base word. In the metric system, you can add several prefixes to the units meter, gram, and liter to change their meanings. Following are six prefixes for you to learn. Knowing these prefixes can help you unlock the meaning of most words in the metric system.

kilo-	1,000 times larger
hecto-	100 times larger
deca-	10 times larger
deci-	10 times smaller
centi-	100 times smaller
milli-	1,000 times smaller

A **hectometer** (HEK tə mee tər) is 100 times longer than a meter. That means that a hectometer is about the length of 100 baseball bats put end to end. A hectometer is a little longer than a football field.

A **milliliter** (MIL ə lee tər) is 1,000 times smaller than a liter. A milliliter of water is only a few drops.

A **kilogram** (KIL ə gram) is 1,000 times heavier than a gram. A brick weighs about 1 kilogram.

Abbreviations

There are abbreviations that stand for the metric units and their prefixes. This means that the whole word does not have to be written each time. Notice that the abbreviations do not have periods after them. Also notice that only the abbreviation for liter is capitalized.

Prefixes				Units	
kilo-	k	deci-	d	meter	m
hecto-	h	centi-	c	liter	L
deca-	da	milli-	m	gram	g

The abbreviations for the prefixes and units can be combined. The abbreviation for kilogram is *kg*, the abbreviation for **decaliter** (DEK ə lee tər) is *daL*, and so on.

As you learn to use the metric system, these units will be easier for you to recognize. For now, the most important thing is to remember what each unit measures and to get a feeling for the size of the measurements.

A hectometer is a little longer than a football field.

COMPREHENSION

Recalling details
1. How many base units are in the metric system?

   There are seven base units in the metric system.

Recalling details
2. How many base units are commonly used for measurements?

   Three base units are commonly used for measurements.

Recalling details
3. Name the three most commonly used base units in the metric system.

   They are meter, gram, and liter.

Recalling details
4. Explain how to name larger or smaller metric units.

   Adding a prefix makes the base unit's meaning larger or smaller.

Recalling details
5. Put a ✔ next to the words that complete each of the following sentences.

   a. When the prefixes *kilo-*, *hecto-*, and *deca-* are added to a base unit, the unit of measurement is

      _____ the same as the base unit.

      ✔ larger than the base unit.

      _____ smaller than the base unit.

   b. When the prefixes *deci-*, *centi-*, and *milli-* are added to a base unit, the unit of measurement is

      _____ the same as the base unit.

      _____ larger than the base unit.

      ✔ smaller than the base unit.

CRITICAL THINKING

Drawing conclusions
1. All the prefixes that make the base unit smaller end in what letter? i

Drawing conclusions
2. All the prefixes that make the base unit larger end in what letters? a, o

Drawing conclusions
3. Explain how knowing the meaning of the prefix *kilo-* helps you understand the word *kilometer*?

   If you know *kilo-* means "1,000," you can figure out that *kilometer* means "1,000 meters."

Making inferences
4. Evaluate what might happen if a country chose not to use the metric system.

   Scientists in that country might have difficulty sharing information with other countries.

   Producers of goods might have trouble selling their products in other countries.

SKILL FOCUS: READING METRIC TERMS

A. Complete each sentence with the correct word. Choose from *meters, liters,* and *grams.*

   1. In 1903, the first airplane flew a short distance. It flew about 37 ____meters____.

   2. The Lockheed C-5A *Galaxy* can carry 110,000 kilo ____grams____ of cargo.

   3. The *Hindenburg* was about the length of 30 buses, about 245 ____meters____.

   4. The steward served 200 milli____liters____ of coffee to each passenger.

   5. The fuel gauge showed the pilot that she had 47 ____liters____ of fuel left.

B. Write the abbreviation for the following measurement on the lines provided. Remember that only the abbreviation L is capitalized. You may look back at the selection to find an answer.

1. kilometer _____km_____
2. milligram _____mg_____
3. deciliter _____dL_____

4. decagram _____dag_____
5. centimeter _____cm_____
6. hectoliter _____hL_____

7. milliliter _____mL_____
8. kilogram _____kg_____
9. decameter _____dam_____

C. Write the word for each abbreviation on the lines provided.

1. mm _____millimeter_____
2. cg _____centigram_____
3. kL _____kiloliter_____

4. daL _____decaliter_____
5. hm _____hectometer_____
6. dg _____decigram_____

7. cL _____centiliter_____
8. hg _____hectogram_____
9. dm _____decimeter_____

D. Circle the unit in each box that you would use to measure the thing pictured.

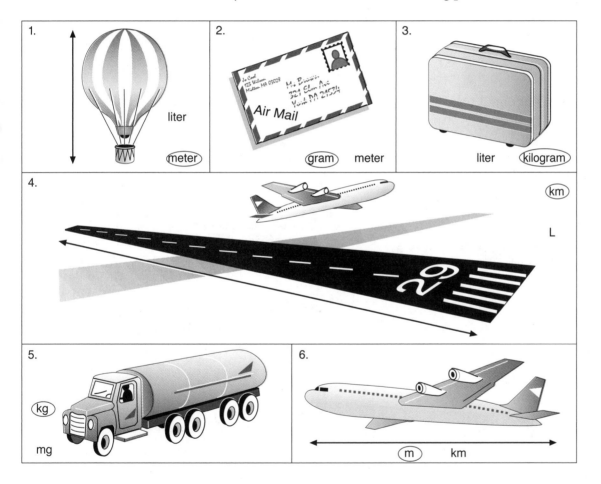

1. liter / (meter)
2. (gram) / meter
3. liter / (kilogram)
4. (km) / L
5. (kg) / mg
6. (m) / km

Reading-Writing Connection

On a separate sheet of paper, write down the names of three objects you see in your classroom. Next to each name, write the unit you would use to measure it.

Skill: Main Idea

For ESL/ELL support, see page T80.

For lesson support, see page T80.

The **main idea** of a paragraph is often found in the first sentence. However, it can sometimes be found in the last sentence of the paragraph.

Read the following paragraphs. Below each one are four sentences from the paragraph. Circle the letter of the sentence that is the main idea of the paragraph.

1. The sea horse isn't like most fish. Its head looks like that of a pony. The sea horse has hard, spiny skin. Its tail looks like that of a monkey. It has one fin that isn't much help in swimming. Sea horses drift upright in the water.

   a. The sea horse has hard, spiny skin.

   b. Its tail looks like that of a monkey.

   c. Sea horses drift upright in the water.

   d. The sea horse isn't like most fish.

2. The father sea horse has a pocket somewhat like a kangaroo's pouch. He carries the mother's eggs around in this pouch. He even carries the baby sea horses around for some time after they have hatched. The father sea horse takes very good care of his young.

   a. The father sea horse has a pocket somewhat like a kangaroo's pouch.

   b. He carries the mother's eggs around in this pouch.

   c. The father sea horse takes very good care of his young.

   d. He even carries the baby sea horses around for some time after they have hatched.

3. The giant clam is an interesting sea creature. The giant clam is the largest of all clams. It sometimes weighs as much as 500 pounds. Its shell may measure four feet across. This clam is not found in American waters. It lives in the warm waters of the Indian and Pacific Oceans.

   a. This clam is not found in American waters.

   b. The giant clam is an interesting sea creature.

   c. It sometimes weighs as much as 500 pounds.

   d. It lives in the warm waters of the Indian and Pacific Oceans.

4. The octopus has a soft, pouchlike body. It has a head with eyes that look like human eyes. Instead of having fins like a fish, it has eight long arms coming out from its body. Some octopuses have arms nine or ten feet long. Each arm is lined with cuplike suckers. Like the sea horse, the octopus's shape is different from that of most fish.

   a. It has a head with eyes that look like human eyes.

   b. Like the sea horse, the octopus's shape is different from that of most fish.

   c. Some octopuses have arms nine or ten feet long.

   d. The octopus has a soft, pouchlike body.

5. The octopus uses its arms to get food. It moves along the ocean floor looking for something to eat. When it finds a crab or fish, it wraps its arms around the victim. The suckers on its arms hold the animal as the arms draw the food to the mouth.

   a. When it finds a crab or fish, it wraps its arms around the victim.

   b. It moves along the ocean floor looking for something to eat.

   c. The suckers on its arms hold the animal as the arms draw the food to the mouth.

   d. The octopus uses its arms to get food.

Skill: Main Idea

For lesson support, see page T80.

> In many paragraphs you read, the **main idea** is in the first or last sentence.
> However, the main idea can sometimes be found in a sentence in between.

Read the following paragraphs. Below each one are four sentences from the paragraph. Circle the letter of the sentence that is the main idea of the paragraph.

1. Birds are alike in many ways. All of them have backbones. All birds have two legs and two wings. All birds have feathers and lungs. Birds are warm-blooded. *Warm-blooded* means "their bodies are warm even when the weather is cold."

   a. All birds have feathers and lungs.

   b. Birds are alike in many ways.

   c. Birds are warm-blooded.

   d. All birds have two legs and two wings.

2. Some birds, like the ostrich, are taller and heavier than a person. Some are very small, like the hummingbird. Many birds are good flyers. Other birds cannot fly at all. There are many different kinds of birds.

   a. Some birds, like the ostrich, are taller and heavier than a person.

   b. Many birds are good flyers.

   c. There are many different kinds of birds.

   d. Other birds cannot fly at all.

3. The outer feathers of birds form a smooth covering for their bodies. The down feathers next to their bodies keep in body heat. Wing feathers are used for flying. Tail feathers help birds in balancing or steering. Not only does each feather type have a purpose, but the feathers can be replaced. Birds usually shed their old, worn-out feathers in the fall and grow a new set. Shedding of feathers is known as molting.

   a. Tail feathers help birds in balancing or steering.

   b. Shedding of feathers is known as molting.

   c. Wing feathers are used for flying.

   d. Not only does each feather type have a purpose, but the feathers can be replaced.

4. Birds weigh very little because their bones are thin-walled and hollow. Their feathers are also very light. Flying birds have powerful muscles attached to the breastbone. The bodies of most birds are built for flying.

   a. Birds weigh very little because their bones are thin-walled and hollow.

   b. Their feathers are also very light.

   c. The bodies of most birds are built for flying.

   d. Flying birds have powerful muscles attached to the breastbone.

5. Birds' eggs must be kept warm. The baby bird grows inside the egg, eating up the food stored in the egg. By the time the food is used up, the bird fills the whole egg. Then it hatches. All birds develop in eggs. Large birds, such as ostriches, lay eggs that are often as large as six inches long. Tiny birds, such as hummingbirds, lay eggs that are only a quarter of an inch long.

   a. Then it hatches.

   b. Birds' eggs must be kept warm.

   c. Tiny birds, such as hummingbirds, lay eggs that are only a quarter of an inch long.

   d. All birds develop in eggs.

For ESL/ELL support, see page T81.

Skill: Consonant Blends

For lesson support, see page T81.

Some **consonant blends** have three letters. Three consonants are blended together in such a way that the consonant sound each stands for is heard.

> scr   spl   spr   squ   str

Say each picture name. Listen to the beginning sounds. On the line, write the blend from the list above that stands for the consonant sounds that you hear at the beginning of the picture name. The first one is done for you.

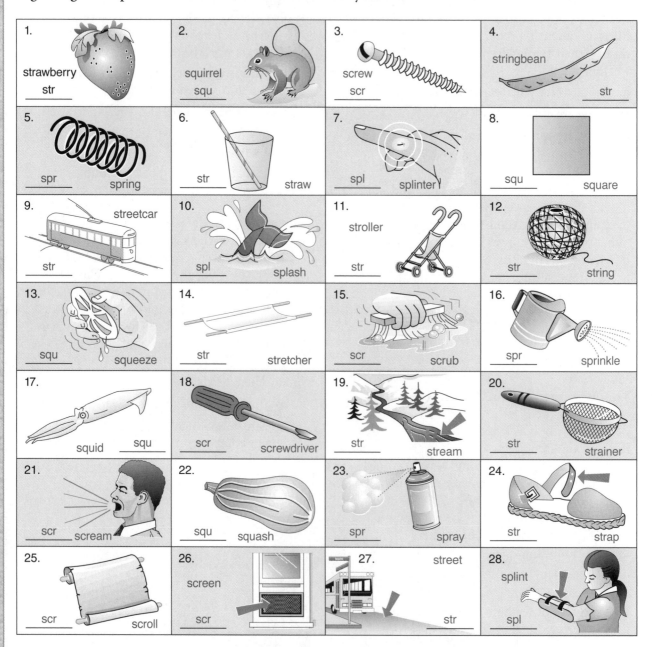

1. strawberry
   str

2. squirrel
   squ

3. screw
   scr

4. stringbean
   str

5. _spr_ spring

6. _str_ straw

7. _spl_ splinter

8. _squ_ square

9. streetcar
   str

10. _spl_ splash

11. stroller
    str

12. _str_ string

13. _squ_ squeeze

14. _str_ stretcher

15. _scr_ scrub

16. _spr_ sprinkle

17. squid _squ_

18. _scr_ screwdriver

19. _str_ stream

20. _str_ strainer

21. _scr_ scream

22. _squ_ squash

23. _spr_ spray

24. _str_ strap

25. _scr_ scroll

26. screen
    scr

27. street
    str

28. splint
    spl

Skill: Consonant Digraphs

For lesson support, see page T81.

Say the word *shadow* and listen to its beginning sounds. You hear only one sound at the beginning of the word. When two letters stand for one sound, as in *sh*, the two letters are called a **consonant digraph**. Look at the consonant digraphs below.

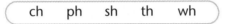

ch   ph   sh   th   wh

A. Say each picture name. Listen to the beginning sound. On the line, write the digraph from the list above that stands for the sound that you hear.

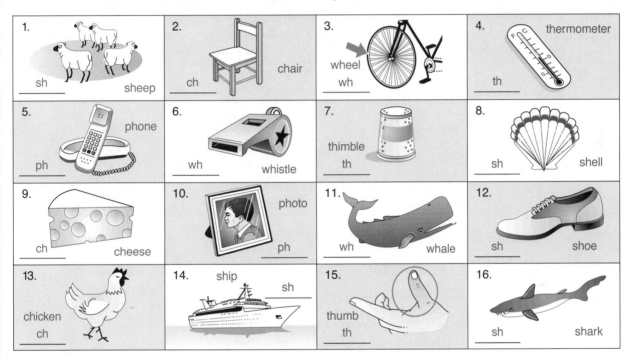

1. sh sheep	2. ch chair	3. wheel wh	4. thermometer th
5. phone ph	6. wh whistle	7. thimble th	8. sh shell
9. ch cheese	10. photo ph	11. wh whale	12. sh shoe
13. chicken ch	14. ship sh	15. thumb th	16. sh shark

B. Say each picture name. Listen to the ending sound. On the line, write the digraph from the box that stands for the sound that you hear.

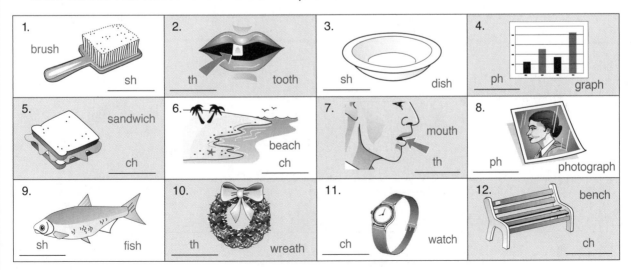

1. brush sh	2. th tooth	3. sh dish	4. ph graph
5. sandwich ch	6. beach ch	7. mouth th	8. ph photograph
9. sh fish	10. th wreath	11. ch watch	12. bench ch

Skill: Long Vowel Sounds

For lesson support, see page T82.

You have had practice in working with one-syllable words with and without a final *e*. You have learned two rules to use in deciding whether the first vowel sound in such words is long or short.

There is another rule that you can use to decide if a **vowel** is **long**. See if you can discover this guide for yourself.

A. Complete the chart below. The first is done for you.

Words With Two Vowels Together			
Word	How many vowels are there?	Which vowel has a long sound?	Which vowel is silent?
1. boat	two	first	second
2. real	two	first	second
3. wait	two	first	second
4. heal	two	first	second
5. roast	two	first	second
6. pain	two	first	second

B. Fill in the words necessary to complete the following rule.

RULE 3: When two ___vowels___ come together in a word, the first ___vowel___ is usually ___long___, and the second is usually ___silent___.

C. Read each sentence below. Look for a word in each sentence that has two vowels together. Say this word softly. Circle the vowel that has a long sound.

1. Tom went to M(a)ine to spend the summer months.

2. He liked the s(e)a.

3. He can swim and he can fl(o)at.

4. His father has a b(o)at.

5. They often went for a s(a)il.

6. One day, Tom invited Lisa and Dom to the b(e)ach.

7. It started to r(a)in but stopped by lunchtime.

8. They had a corn r(o)ast.

9. Afterward, they had fresh p(e)aches.

10. Finally, they had nonfat ice cr(e)am.

For ESL/ELL support, see page T82.

Skill: Long and Short Vowel Sounds

For lesson support, see page T82.

The three rules that you have learned to help you decide whether the **vowel sound** in a one-syllable word is **short** or **long** are given below. However, there are one or more words missing in each one. Write the missing words on the lines.

RULE 1: When a word contains two vowels, one of which is a final *e*, the first vowel is usually _____long_____, and the final *e* is silent.

RULE 2: When a word contains only one vowel, and that vowel is not at the end of the word, the vowel is usually _____short_____.

RULE 3: When two vowels come together in a word, the first vowel is usually _____long_____, and the second vowel is usually _____silent_____.

Decide how to pronounce each word below. On the line, write the number of the rule that you used in making your decision. Mark each long vowel with a macron (¯). Do not mark the short vowels.

	Rule Number			Rule Number
1. wāge	1	19.	tank	2
2. drōve	1	20.	tīme	1
3. truck	2	21.	shed	2
4. bēan	3	22.	job	2
5. grāpe	1	23.	mēal	3
6. pēa	3	24.	lāte	1
7. man	2	25.	rīde	1
8. thēse	1	26.	hōme	1
9. ēach	3	27.	lōad	3
10. īce	1	28.	whīle	1
11. fresh	2	29.	gāin	3
12. tēam	3	30.	trim	2
13. grāin	3	31.	fēast	3
14. rōad	3	32.	sāme	1
15. rush	2	33.	rēap	3
16. tāke	1	34.	still	2
17. ēat	3	35.	lāke	1
18. rāin	3	36.	flōat	3

For ESL/ELL support, see page T83.

Skill: Using a Train Schedule

For lesson support, see page T83.

Many people travel to work every day on commuter trains. Most trains follow a **schedule,** a printed timetable of arrivals and departures. People who commute every day at the same time do not need to think much about train schedules. However, shoppers, visitors, and workers without work times often look at a train schedule so that they can plan their travel.

TRAIN SCHEDULE

INBOUND *Read Down*	Train Number	700 A.M.	702 A.M.	704 A.M.	706 A.M.	708* A.M.	752 A.M.
Departs: **Forge Park**	O	5:15	5:45	6:15	6:33	7:06	
Franklin	O	5:22	5:52	6:22	6:42	7:13	
Norfolk		5:29	5:59	6:29	6:49	7:20	
Walpole	O	5:35	6:05	6:35	6:55	7:27	
Windsor Gardens		5:39	6:09	6:39	6:59	7:31	
Norwood Central	O	5:43	6:13	6:43	7:05	7:36	7:58
Norwood Depot		5:46	6:16		7:08		8:01
Islington		5:49	6:19		7:11		8:04
Dedham Corporate Ctr.		5:52	6:22	6:48	7:14	7:42	8:07
Endicott		5:55	6:26		7:18		8:11
Readville		6:00	6:29		7:21		8:15
Ruggles	T			7:00	7:32	7:56	
Back Bay	T,O		L 6:43	L 7:04	L 7:36	L 8:00	
Arrives: **South Station, Boston**	T,O	6:20	6:48	7:09	7:41	8:05	8:35

SYMBOLS

L: Regular stop to discharge or pick up passengers but train may leave ahead of schedule.

O: Ticket outlet is located at or near station

T: Subway connection

Handicapped accessibility at Forge Park, Norfolk, Norwood Central, Norwood Depot, Dedham Corporate Ctr., Ruggles, Back Bay and South Station.

Train 706 stops at Plimptonville at 6:38 A.M.

* Train does not operate on Martin Luther King, Jr. Day, Columbus Day, and Veterans Day

A. Write the answer to each question on the line.

1. What is the number of the earliest train you can take from Forge Park? _____ 700 _____

2. At which stations can you connect with the subway system? _____ Ruggles, Back Bay, and South Station _____

3. At which station does Train 752 begin? _____ Norwood Central _____

4. What is the number of the train that stops at Plimptonville? _____ 706 _____

5. What time does Train 704 leave Walpole? _____ 6:35 A.M. _____

6. What is the number of the train that leaves Endicott at 7:18 A.M.? _____ 706 _____

7. Which train can't you take on Veterans Day? _____ 708 _____

8. At which station could a train leave early? _____ Back Bay _____

9. Where can you connect with the subway but not buy tickets? _____ Ruggles _____

10. Which train makes the fewest stops? _____ 752 _____

11. By what time do you have to leave Franklin to get to South Station before 7:00 A.M.? _____ 5:52 A.M.

12. If you leave Norfolk at 6:49 A.M., what time will you arrive at South Station? _____ 7:41 A.M.

B. Circle the letter of the correct answer to each question.

1. How long does it take to get from Franklin to Norfolk?
   a. 7 minutes   **b.** 3 minutes   **c.** 6 minutes   **d.** 9 minutes

2. How many trains stop at all stations?
   a. 2   **b.** 5   **c.** 1   **d.** 3

3. At which of these stations can you *not* buy train tickets?
   a. Franklin   **b.** Back Bay   **c.** Norwood Central   **d.** Islington

4. Which of these stations should you avoid if you are in a wheelchair?
   a. Norwood Central   **b.** Endicott   **c.** Ruggles   **d.** Back Bay

5. You have an important breakfast meeting near South Station at 7:45 A.M. It takes about ten minutes to walk from the station to your meeting. What is the latest you could leave Walpole to be at your meeting on time?
   a. 6:05 A.M.   **b.** 6:35 A.M.   **c.** 6:55 A.M.   **d.** 5:35 A.M.

6. How long does it take to go from Forge Park to South Station on Train 700?
   a. 65 minutes   **b.** 55 minutes   **c.** one hour   **d.** 45 minutes

7. Which town do you think is closest to Walpole?
   a. Franklin   **b.** Norfolk   **c.** Forge Park   **d.** Windsor Gardens

8. If you miss the first train out of Readville, how long will you have to wait for the next train?
   a. 29 minutes   **b.** 20 minutes   **c.** 5 minutes   **d.** 21 minutes

9. How many trains stop at Norwood Depot?
   a. 4   **b.** 3   **c.** 6   **d.** 5

10. Which train takes the least time to make the entire trip?
    a. 702   **b.** 704   **c.** 706   **d.** 708

11. Which stations have the most trains leaving from them?
    a. Norwood Central and Dedham Corporate Ctr.   **c.** Forge Park and Norwood Central
    b. Walpole and Dedham Corporate Ctr.   **d.** Norwood Depot and Ruggles

12. How often do the first three trains of the day leave from Forge Park?
    a. every hour   **b.** every 15 minutes   **c.** every 10 minutes   **d.** every half hour

unit three

For ESL/ELL support, see highlighted words, page T84, and pages T28–T30.

City Life, Country Life

For theme support, see page T26.

LESSON 24

Skill: Conflict and Resolution

For lesson support, see page T84.

BACKGROUND INFORMATION

The selection you will read, "Something to Cheer About," is the story of a 16-year-old girl who moves to a new neighborhood. It is in Harlem, a section of New York City at the northern tip of Manhattan. For a century, Harlem has been one of the largest African American communities in the United States. During the 1920s, many African American writers, artists, and musicians gathered there.

SKILL FOCUS: Conflict and Resolution

In most stories, the main character faces a problem. The struggle to solve this problem is called the **conflict.** Conflicts add energy and interest to a story.

There are three main types of conflicts. A character might have a conflict with his or her self. That means, he or she is struggling with inner feelings. Or a character might have a conflict with another character. Two characters might dislike each other, for example, or be enemies. In some stories, there is a conflict with nature. A character might face a storm, fire, or other powerful force of nature. As a story unfolds, characters try to solve their problems. The solution to a conflict is called the **resolution.** The resolution comes near the end of the story.

▶ Think about each conflict on the chart below. Decide how the character might solve it. Write a possible resolution on the chart.

CONTEXT CLUES: Synonyms

If you don't know the meaning of a word, look for a synonym context clue nearby to help explain it. **Synonyms** are words that have the same, or nearly the same, meanings.

Read the sentences below. Circle a synonym context clue that explains the underlined word.

> The crowd **roared** as the basketball players took their places on the court. Keema and Jamal (cheered) too.

If you don't know the meaning of *roared,* the word *cheered* will help. *Roared* and *cheered* are synonyms. They are words with similar meanings.

▶ Circle the synonym context clue that helps you figure out *bustle* in this sentence.

> Keema loved the **bustle** of this busy street. Everywhere she looked, the street was bursting with (activity.)

In the story, look for synonym context clues that help you figure out the meanings of the underlined words *crisp, vendors,* and *embarrassed.*

Strategy Tip

As you read the story, think about Keema's problem. What type of conflict does she face? What is the resolution of this conflict?

Type of Conflict	Example	Resolution
Conflict with self	Jan has to make a speech but is nervous about speaking in public.	Answers will vary. Jan realizes that her fears are unfounded.
Conflict with another character	Joe bullies Ramón in the school cafeteria.	Answers will vary. Joe and Ramón become friends.
Conflict with nature	Terry is hiking alone when a snowstorm hits.	Answers will vary. Terry trudges home through the snow.

Something to Cheer About

Nothing was going the way that 16-year-old Keema Watkins thought it would. After her family moved to Harlem in August, her life changed completely. "It's like my whole world turned upside down," Keema thought to herself. "One day I'm walking around my old neighborhood talking to my best friend, Lisa. The next day, here I am with a new house, a new school, and no best friend."

Early one afternoon, Keema was walking down Amsterdam Avenue with her younger brother, Jamal. It was a crisp October day. The cool, sharp air felt good after the hot, rainy summer. As much as she missed her old neighborhood, Keema loved the bustle of this busy street. Everywhere she looked, the street was bursting with activity. Skaters on in-line skates whizzed by them. Shoppers crowded the busy stores. Music blared at Keema and Jamal from a dozen radios. Street vendors sold everything from hot dogs to CDs. One of these street sellers held out a steaming hot dog to Jamal. "The best in New York," he said, grinning. "There's no charge for the mustard, either."

However Jamal and Keema didn't have time to stop. They were looking for a hardware store so that they could buy house paint for their mother. This weekend, the whole family was going to paint the living room of their new house. The house was another thing that Keema couldn't quite get used to. It was great having a room to herself. In her old apartment, Keema had shared a bedroom with her mother. But fixing up an old house took a lot of time and work. Sometimes Keema wished that she could just shut her eyes and wake up in her old apartment again. More than anything, she missed her old life.

Jamal looked up at Keema. "Hey, stop daydreaming. If we don't find that hardware store, we are going to be in serious trouble. You know how important painting the house is to Mom," Jamal said, grinning.

Keema sighed and shook her head. "Tell me about it," she said. "Look, there's the hardware store.

It's right next to the subway." As they crossed the street, a girl waved to Keema and called her name.

"Who's that?" Jamal asked, as they entered the hardware store.

"Maria Hernandez," Keema answered. "She's in some of my classes."

Ten minutes later, Keema paid for the paint, while Jamal loaded it into their shopping cart.

"You two must be new to the neighborhood," the store manager said. "I've worked here almost forty years. I must know everyone in the area. Where do you live?"

"On West 13th Street—right near Sixth Avenue," Keema said without thinking.

The store manager looked surprised. "Then you sure are a long way from home," he said. "That's at the other end of the city."

Suddenly Keema felt embarrassed. "I mean, we live on Hamilton Place," she said, looking uncomfortable. "We just picked up and moved here two months ago."

"Well, stop by again," the manager said as Keema and Jamal left the store. "Welcome to the neighborhood," he called after them.

"Hey, big sister," Jamal said, grinning. "I know you're not too happy about moving and everything, but you can at least learn our new address. I think it's kind of a cool place to live."

Before Keema could answer, Maria Hernandez walked up to them. "I thought I saw you go into the hardware store," she said to Keema. "A couple of us are going in-line skating in the park this afternoon. Why don't you come along?"

Keema shook her head. "Thanks, but I promised my mom that I'd help her around the house today. Maybe some other time."

"Okay," Maria said. "See you in school on Monday."

As Maria walked away, Jamal turned to Keema. "She seems nice," he said.

Keema walked on without answering.

"Hey," Jamal yelled, as he tried to catch up with her. "What's wrong with you? At least help me with this shopping cart. This paint is heavy."

When Keema and Jamal carried the cans of paint into the living room, their mother was waiting for them. "Just in time," she said with a grin. "I've plastered every crack in this room. Now I can't wait to get my hands on a paint brush. Who's going to help me stir this paint?"

"Mom, I'm going to change into my old jeans," Keema said. "I'll be down in a minute." As Keema ran upstairs, Jamal looked at his mother and shrugged his shoulders.

The walls of Keema's bedroom were covered with pictures of her friends from her old high school. A banner that said "Washington Irving High School" hung above her bed. Keema looked at a photograph from last year's class party. She and Lisa grinned at the camera surrounded by all their friends. "It just isn't the same without you guys," Keema said to herself.

Keema was still thinking about her old friends on her way to school Monday morning. As she got off the crowded subway car and hurried down the street, she remembered what her mother had said to her at breakfast. "Honey, you have to give your new school a fair chance. You'll make new friends. Once you do, you'll like your new home as much as Jamal does. You'll see."

"Face it, Keema," she said to herself. "Mom's right. So you had to move because of her great new job. What's the big deal? Lots of people move every day of the year. This job is important to Mom. So is owning a home. You really haven't given Park East a chance. Today is going to be different."

Yet when Keema walked into Park East High School, she didn't feel any different. All around her, groups of students were talking and laughing. Keema waved to a few students she knew on her way to the locker room. She didn't stop to talk to any of them. She was putting away her jacket when she saw Maria Hernandez.

"I'm glad I ran into you," Maria said. "I'm having a party this Friday night, and I'd love for you to come. A lot of the kids from school will be there."

Keema wanted to say yes, but the thought of going to a party with a bunch of kids she didn't know really scared her.

"Thanks for asking me, Maria," she said, "but this Friday, I'm seeing some friends from my old school. It's kind of a class party. They invited me weeks ago." Keema was trying so hard to sound natural that her words came out in a rush. It was all a lie and Maria knew it. Keema could tell by her look that Maria didn't believe her. The strange thing was that Keema felt bad about lying to Maria.

On her way to her math class, Keema saw Maria walking down the hall ahead of her. For a second, Keema felt like telling her how she really felt. She wanted to tell Maria how she was the only one in her family who didn't like moving to a new neighborhood, and how weird it was to walk to class without anyone to talk to or laugh with, and how she didn't really feel like herself anymore. "Forget it, Keema," she thought to herself. "Maria won't know what you're talking about."

That night, Keema and Jamal were washing the dinner dishes when the phone rang. It was Lisa.

As soon as she heard her friend's voice, Keema felt better. "Let's go to a movie this Friday," she said. "Maybe hang out with Lee and Josh afterward."

"I can't," Lisa said. "Don't you remember? We're going on a class trip this weekend. We won't be back until Sunday night."

Keema tried to hide the disappointment in her voice. "Oh, sure," she said, "I forgot that it was this weekend. We went on a class trip the same time last year."

"This one won't be the same without you. We really miss you," Lisa said.

Keema smiled, but she felt like crying, too, and she wasn't sure why. "Let's do something when you guys get back," she said.

"Don't forget. We'll be seeing you in two weeks," Lisa said. "Our basketball team plays Park East at the end of this month. I'll save a seat for you on our side of the court."

For the next two weeks, Keema kept thinking about what her "side of the court" really was. She missed Lisa and her friends from her old high school. Still, Keema was starting to feel more at home in her new school.

The day before the big basketball game, Keema walked to English class with Maria. They were laughing about a really bad movie that they both had seen. "You're the only person who likes bad movies as much as I do," Keema said.

"I really got into them when I transferred to Park East last spring," Maria said.

"I thought that you had been here since ninth grade," Keema said.

Maria shook her head. "Nope. I'm a newcomer, just like you. So I know what it's like leaving your old friends behind," she said. Then she and Keema walked into English class together.

That Friday night, the gym was filled with students from Park East and Washington Irving. When Keema and Jamal walked into the gym, she heard Lisa call her name. The two friends hugged.

"I have so much to tell you," Keema said. "I don't know where to begin."

Lisa pointed to an empty seat beside her. "Come sit with us."

Keema looked across the court. She could see Maria and her new friends waving to her. Then she turned back to Lisa. "You know how much you all mean to me, but tonight I want to cheer for Park East. It's where I belong now." Then she and Jamal sat down next to Maria.

The crowd roared as the basketball players took their places on the court. Keema and Jamal cheered too. For the first time in a long time, Keema had something to cheer about.

Comparing and contrasting
1. How do Keema and Jamal feel about moving to their new neighborhood?

    Keema doesn't like moving there, but Jamal enjoys the

    new neighborhood.

Recognizing sequence of events
2. What happens after Maria sees Keema and Jamal come out of the hardware store?

    Maria invites Keema to go in-line skating with a group

    of friends.

Recognizing cause and effect
3. Why did Keema and Jamal move to Harlem?

    Their mother moved there because she started a new

    job.

Recalling details
4. How does Keema react when she arrives at school on Monday?

    Although she wants to behave differently, she still doesn't

    talk to any of the students she sees in the hallway.

Recognizing cause and effect
5. Why doesn't Keema accept Maria's invitation to her party?

    The thought of going to a party with people she doesn't

    know scares her.

Recalling details
6. Why can't Lisa go to the movies with Keema?

    Lisa is going on a class trip.

Comparing and contrasting
7. In what ways are Keema and Maria alike?

    They both transferred to Park East. They both enjoy bad

    movies.

Recalling details
8. At the basketball game, which team does Keema cheer for?

    Keema cheers for Park East.

Using context clues
9. Decide if each statement below is true or false. Write *T* or *F* on the line.

    __T__   a. When the air feels <u>crisp</u>, the temperature is cool and dry.

    __F__   b. <u>Vendors</u> are people who sing and dance.

    __F__   c. If a person feels <u>embarrassed</u>, he or she is very self-confident.

Inferring details
1. Why do you think Keema gives the wrong address when the store manager asks her where she lives?

    Answers will vary. She still thinks of West 13th Street as her home, so she automatically gives that address.

Drawing conclusions
2. Explain why Keema walks away from Jamal after he says that Maria Hernandez seems nice.

    Answers will vary. She misses her old friends and isn't ready to be friends with Maria yet.

Inferring comparison and contrast
3. Explain why Keema and her brother react so differently to the move to a new neighborhood.

    Answers will vary. Keema is older and has already started high school. She can't adjust as easily as her younger brother.

Drawing conclusions
4. Explain why Keema feels bad about lying to Maria.

    Answers will vary. Keema knows Maria is trying to be nice to her.

Drawing conclusions

5. Why do you think Keema feels like crying when she talks to Lisa on the phone?

Answers will vary. She is sad because she realizes that her old friends are doing things without her.

Making inferences

6. How do you think Maria feels when Keema turns down her invitation to go in-line skating?

Answers will vary. She's sorry that Keema doesn't want to meet her friends, but understands how Keema feels about starting a new school.

SKILL FOCUS: CONFLICT AND RESOLUTION

Think about the conflict that Keema faces and how she solves it. Write your answers below.

1. Reread the three kinds of conflict described on page 62. What kind of conflict does Keema face?

She faces conflict with herself.

2. What causes this conflict?

Keema and her family move to Harlem because her mother is starting a new job. Keema has to

transfer to a new school and make new friends.

3. How does Keema feel about this conflict?

After her mother talks to her, she tries to act differently. However, she still feels shy and turns down

Maria's party invitation.

4. How is this conflict resolved?

Keema begins to feel more at home at her new school and becomes friends with Maria. When the basketball teams

from Washington Irving and Park East play against each other, Keema cheers for the Park East team.

5. What does Keema learn from her experience?

She realizes that she's a part of Park East now and is beginning to make friends with the students there.

6. How do you think Keema will change as a result of this experience?

She will probably be more open and accepting of change in the future. She will be more willing to give

new people and new places a chance.

Reading-Writing Connection

Put yourself in Keema's place. Which side would you sit on at the basketball game?
On a separate sheet of paper, write a paragraph describing what you would do. Tell why.

For ESL/ELL support, see highlighted words, page T85, and pages T28–T30.

Skill: Comparing and Contrasting

For lesson support, see page T85.

BACKGROUND INFORMATION

In "The Rise of the American Suburbs," you will read about a big change in American life. For much of our history, most Americans lived on farms or in big cities like Boston, Massachusetts, and Philadelphia, Pennsylvania. Today, however, most Americans live in suburbs, which are like villages or towns near big cities.

SKILL FOCUS: Comparing and Contrasting

When you notice how things are alike, you are **comparing**. When you notice how things are different, you are **contrasting**. Comparing and contrasting are ways to understand information.

Special words signal that two things are alike. The words *similar*, *same*, *like*, and *both*, for example, show comparisons. Other words signal contrasts. These words, such as *unlike*, *however*, *but*, *different*, and *on the contrary*, show that things are different. Looking for signal words will help you find comparisons and contrasts.

You can often use a chart to keep track of similarities and differences. For example, a comparison-and-contrast chart for city living and country living might look like this.

Comparing City Living and Country Living

Place	Transportation	Shopping
city	subway, bus, taxi	mostly individual stores
country	private cars	many shopping malls

▶ Study the chart. How are city living and country living alike or different? Write a sentence on the lines that tells about their similarities or differences.

Answers will vary. The city is crowded, but space in the

country is more open.

CONTEXT CLUES: Details

You can often figure out the meaning of a new word from **details** in the surrounding sentences. These details can offer important clues. Look for details that explain the meaning of the underlined word in these sentences.

*That is when more than 10 million **veterans** of World War II returned home. After fighting the war, they wanted to start families.*

The details in the second sentence explain the meaning of *veterans*. Veterans are people who have fought in a war.

▶ Underline the details in the following sentences that help you figure out the meaning of the underlined word.

*The people living in these communities had their own parks, schools, and shopping areas. The **residents** could walk everywhere.*

As you read "The Rise of the American Suburbs," use details in the text to figure out the meaning of the underlined words *standardizing*, *urban*, and *unsustainable*.

Strategy Tip

As you read "The Rise of the American Suburbs," look for clue words that signal comparisons and contrasts. Look for similarities and differences between different types of suburbs. Also note the differences between city and suburban life.

The Rise of the American Suburbs

The First Suburbs

The first American suburbs appeared during the 1830s and 1840s. At that time, New York City, Boston, Philadelphia, and Washington, D.C. became quite crowded. Many people were eager to leave these cities. They looked at the farmland near the cities. Farmers were leaving this worn-out soil for better land in the West. Why not build houses on it? At that time, the United States was also building railroads. Families could now live in the "country" because fathers could now ride trains to their jobs in the city. (Very few mothers worked at this time.)

The first **suburbanites** (sə BER bən eyets) were proud of their lifestyle. They thought that living in the suburbs was more natural and healthier than city life. To avoid city crowding, they built houses on acres of rolling lawns. They planted trees, flowers, and gardens. The houses in the first suburbs were quite expensive. Each house was different. Builders designed each one especially for the family that lived there.

Garden Suburbs

By the 1920s, a new type of suburb had appeared. People called them garden suburbs because they were built on curved streets that offered pretty views, like those in a garden. Garden suburbs were planned communities that were close to cities. Some were even within a city. Land was scarce there. So the houses were on small lots. More people could afford them. The houses were well designed, but they looked similar.

Builders planned the garden suburbs carefully. The people living in these communities had their own parks, schools, and shopping areas. The residents could walk everywhere. Sadly, the Great Depression ended the building of garden suburbs. There was no money to build anything in the 1930s.

The Post-War Suburban Boom

Suburbs really began growing after 1945, when more than 10 million American veterans of World War II returned home. After fighting the war, they wanted to start families. There was no housing for them, however. In 1947, six million American families had to live with relatives or friends. Half a million more lived in temporary houses. Some even lived in military storage buildings, old trolley cars, and grain bins.

Millions of people needed cheap housing. Builders knew that they could make money by providing that housing. City land was too expensive, though. So builders looked outside the cities. They looked beyond the older suburbs, as well. They decided to buy farmland. This land might be 30 miles or more from a city's downtown.

The need to build houses quickly after World War II led to the **post-war** suburban boom. The most famous post-war suburb was Levittown, New York. In 1948, Abraham Levitt began building houses on New York's Long Island. He built the houses on farmland 30 miles east of New York City.

Levitt used **mass production** (MAS prə DUK shən) to build his houses. That means he found a way to make millions of houses very quickly. Every house was built exactly the same. Every lot was exactly 60 × 100 feet. Along the roads, he planted trees exactly every 28 feet. Standardizing the houses in this way cut costs and building time. Therefore Levitt could sell the houses very cheaply.

The first houses in Levittown sold for less than $8,000. Many families could now afford a home for the first time. People lined up to buy the houses.

By standardizing houses, Abraham Levitt created homes millions of Americans could afford.

SOCIAL STUDIES

Soon Levittown had a population of 10,000 people. A second Levittown, outside Philadelphia, housed 17,000 families. New Jersey also had a Levittown.

✘ The suburban building boom continued through the 1950s. In 1950 alone, 1.4 million houses were built. Most of these houses were in new suburbs. That same year, the world's first regional shopping center opened. In the 1950s, builders prepared about 3,000 acres of farmland *per day* for houses.

Life in the New Suburbs

The post-war suburbs were different from earlier suburbs. Unlike garden suburbs, the new suburbs were not well planned. There was no center

The Suburban Boom in the 1950s		
Number of:	1950	1960
U.S. homeowners	23.6 million	32.8 million
Children 5–14 years	24.3 million	35.5 million
Lawn mowers sold	1.0 million	3.8 million
Lawn furniture sales	$153.0 million	$145.0 million
Commuter railroads	46.0 million	30.0 million
Commuter rides	277.0 million	203.0 million

of public life. There were no schools or stores close to the houses. People could no longer walk to these places. They had to drive everywhere.

People could not take a train to many new suburbs either. So workers had to drive to their jobs in the city. The "two-car family" became common. Fathers used one car for driving to work. Mothers used the other car for shopping and family activities.

Driving long hours to a city job was one drawback of suburban life. There were others. Former city dwellers were not used to mowing lawns or repairing houses. Taxes rose often so that towns could build schools.

The cities had museums, concerts, and plays. Most new suburbs did not. In old city neighborhoods, grandparents, aunts, and uncles often lived nearby. Now family members generally lived in different suburbs. They didn't see each other as often. Despite the drawbacks, most suburbanites liked their new lives. In 1956, 90 percent of the homeowners in

Levittown said they would recommend their way of life to others.

The post-war housing shortage soon ended. The suburbs, however, continued to grow. People left the cities in great numbers. Many said they were looking for cleaner air and more space. Others hoped suburban schools might be better than city schools. In general, people hoped to escape <u>urban</u> problems simply by moving away from the cities.

Suburbs grew even faster during the 1960s and 1970s. Suburban malls took shoppers away from the downtowns of many cities. During the 1980s, millions of jobs also moved from cities to suburban office parks. Today, about half of all Americans live in suburbs. Only about one-quarter of Americans live in central cities.

What About the Future?

Today, people complain that suburbs are growing too fast. We call this problem **suburban sprawl**. Row upon row of similar houses line the streets. Bumper-to-bumper traffic clogs the suburban roads. Gas stations, strip malls, and fast-food restaurants pop up everywhere.

The suburbs cannot keep up with this growth; critics say it is <u>unsustainable</u>. The air and water quality in some suburbs is getting worse. Open land has just about disappeared and there is no more room for suburbs to keep growing. Suburban sprawl also hurts cities. Older cities lose people to the suburbs. In some cities, whole neighborhoods are now empty. Cities grow weaker as they continue losing jobs and taxpayers to the suburbs.

Mayors and city council members are trying to solve these problems by making new rules to control sprawl. They want to bring old city neighborhoods back to life and encourage public transportation. The right mix of solutions will make our suburbs—and cities—better places to live.

Suburban sprawl uses up open land.

Recalling details
1. Near what cities were some of the first suburbs located?

The first suburbs were built near Boston, New York City,

Philadelphia, and Washington, D.C.

Recalling details
2. When did garden suburbs begin to appear in the United States?

Garden suburbs began in the 1920s.

Identifying cause and effect
3. What stopped the building of garden suburbs?

There was no money to build anything during the Great

Depression of the 1930s.

Recalling details
4. Where were most of the new post-war suburbs built?

They were built on farmland 30 miles or more from the

cities.

Comparing and contrasting
5. Look at the chart on page 70. How did the number of homeowners change between 1950 and 1960?

The number of homeowners increased by a little more

than 9 million.

Identifying cause and effect
6. Did railroads play a key role in the growth of post-war suburbs? Explain your answer.

No. Many of these suburbs did not have train stops.

Identifying cause and effect
7. Why were the houses in Levittown so affordable?

The builder used mass production to cut costs and

building time. All of the houses were exactly alike.

Recalling details
8. Circle the letter next to the statement that is most true of the garden suburbs.

   a. They were set on rolling acres of lawn.

   b. They were far from cities.

   c. The houses were all very different.

   d. They were carefully planned communities.

Identifying the main idea
9. Find the paragraph in the selection that has an **✗** next to it. Underline the sentence in the paragraph that states its main idea.

Using context clues   Wording of definitions will vary.
10. Write a definition for each word.

   a. standardizing making things exactly the same

   b. urban having to do with cities

   c. unsustainable not able to continue for very long

Making inferences
1. Look at the chart on page 70. Explain the increase in sales of lawn mowers and lawn furniture between 1950 and 1960.

Suburbs grew rapidly during this decade. Everyone who bought a house for the first time had to buy

lawn furniture and a lawn mower.

2. Do you think that post-war suburbs are easier places for living than garden suburbs? Explain your answer.

Answers will vary. Post-war suburbs are less convenient because you need to have a car to get everywhere.

In garden suburbs, people could walk to schools, stores, and parks.

3. On the lines below, write three details that support this main idea. *The growth of suburbs is unsustainable.*

Answers will vary. We are running out of space to build new houses in the suburbs; suburban sprawl

is causing air and water pollution; traffic jams are making suburbs less pleasant places to live.

4. Look at the chart on page 70. Contrast the number of commuter railroads in 1950 and 1960. Also contrast the number of commuter rides. What do these numbers tell you about how people were getting to their jobs in the cities?

The number of commuter railroads fell from 46 to 30 million. Riders fell from 277 million to 203 million.

These numbers suggest that more and more people were driving their cars to work after 1950.

SKILL FOCUS: COMPARING AND CONTRASTING

Use details from the selection to complete this comparison-and-contrast chart about the three different kinds of American suburbs described in the selection.

Three Kinds of American Suburbs				
Kind of Suburb	**Location**	**Size of Lot**	**Type of Houses**	**Cost**
First suburbs	near the city	large	each was different	expensive
Garden suburbs	near the city	small	similar in appearance	affordable
Post-war suburbs	far from city: 30 miles (48 km) or more	60 feet × 100 feet	all exactly the same	less than $8,000

Reading-Writing Connection

Interview two people you know—one who lives in the suburbs and one who lives in the city. Ask them what they like or dislike about where they live. On a separate sheet of paper, create a comparison-and-contrast chart that summarizes what you have learned.

LESSON 26

For ESL/ELL support, see highlighted words, page T86, and pages T28–T30.

Skill: Cause and Effect

For lesson support, see page T86.

BACKGROUND INFORMATION

"Animals Among Us" is about wild animals moving into our communities. In recent years, many wild animals that were once endangered have become more common. The numbers of deer, falcons, foxes, coyotes, and other species are steadily increasing. These animals are now a common sight in suburbs and even in cities. Wildlife delight many people. At the same time, problems can arise when people and wild animals get too close for comfort.

SKILL FOCUS: Cause and Effect

When one event makes another event happen, the process is called **cause and effect**. A **cause** is an event that makes something happen. An **effect** is what happens as a result. In a cause-and-effect relationship, either the cause or the effect can be stated first.

Look for the cause and the effect in these sentences. Then look at the chart that follows.

Hunting and trapping are forbidden in cities. So these foxes are safe from human predators.

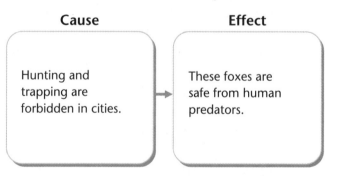

Cause

Hunting and trapping are forbidden in cities.

Effect

These foxes are safe from human predators.

Certain words and phrases can signal a cause-and-effect relationship. These signal words include *so*, *because*, *as a result*, *due to*, and *that is why*. Looking for these signal words will help you find causes and effects.

▶ Circle the cause-and-effect signal words in the sentences below. Then write the cause and the effect on the chart at the top of the next column.

Coyote attacks on humans and pets are very rare. However, coyotes have been rapidly extending their range.... (As a result,) *coyote attacks on pets and young children are increasing.*

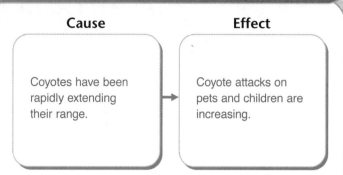

Cause

Coyotes have been rapidly extending their range.

Effect

Coyote attacks on pets and children are increasing.

CONTEXT CLUES: Synonyms

Some context clues are **synonyms**. Synonyms are words with the same or similar meanings.

Read the following sentences. What synonym explains the meanings of the underlined word?

Foxes are <u>wily</u>. These clever creatures can usually avoid people.

If you don't know the meaning of *wily*, the word *clever* in the next sentence will help you. The words *wily* and *clever* are synonyms.

▶ Read the following sentences. Circle the synonym that shows the meaning of the underlined word.

The last 50 years have been a time of suburban <u>expansion</u>. This (growth) *has cut into the foxes' natural habitat.*

While you read the next selection, look for synonym context clues. Use the synonyms to figure out the meanings of the underlined words *forsake*, *scavenge*, and *voraciously*.

Strategy Tip

As you read "Animals Among Us," look for words that signal cause-and-effect relationships. Recognizing causes and effects will help you understand the ideas in the selection.

Animals Among Us

Falcons swoop down from New York City skyscrapers. Red foxes dig dens under porches in Washington, D.C. Black bears wander onto golf courses. Canada geese take over New Jersey soccer fields. All over the country, wild animals are moving from the countryside into our towns. Why is this happening? Let's look at some of the reasons.

Urban Falcons

Peregrine (PAIR ə grin) falcons are the fastest birds in the world. They can travel the length of a football field in a single second. Normally these birds live in rugged mountain areas. Why, then, are peregrine falcons nesting in skyscrapers? At least 12 breeding pairs and their chicks were living in New York City in 2001.

In some ways, tall city buildings are an ideal habitat for peregrine falcons. Skyscrapers offer the birds a high perch for hunting. There is also a steady supply of animals to hunt, including city birds such as sparrows, starlings, and pigeons. The city also allows peregrine falcons to escape their own **predators** (PRED ə tərz). In the wild, raccoons and owls feed on falcon eggs and chicks.

Ledges on skyscrapers provide good nesting spots and hunting perches for falcons.

The increase in urban falcons has another cause, too. Nearly 40 years ago, the birds were in danger of dying out. That is because too many farmers were using a chemical called DDT. DDT killed insects and it also kept falcon eggs from hatching. So the U.S. government banned DDT, and scientists began raising peregrine falcons in captivity. When the scientists released these birds, many settled in and around cities.

The Foxes Go to Town

Foxes are wily. These clever creatures can usually avoid people. In addition, foxes hunt mainly at night. As a result, no one has ever been able to count how many foxes there are in U.S. cities. We do know that people are seeing foxes more often, however. Golfers in Minneapolis, Minnesota, recently watched some fox cubs dash onto the green and steal a golf ball. In Toronto, Canada, officials say there are at least 40 fox dens in that city.

Why would foxes <u>forsake</u> the open meadows? Why would they abandon their meadows in the country for the crowded city? One reason is that there are not as many open meadows as there used to be. The last 50 years have been a time of suburban expansion. This growth has cut into the foxes' natural habitat. Many foxes have been forced to find new homes.

Moving to the city was a practical move for some foxes. Foxes are **territorial** (TAIR ə TOR ee əl) animals. Each fox marks its own area and fights off other foxes. Because most city neighborhoods have not been claimed by foxes yet, it is easy for foxes to find "open territory" there.

Also, cities make a good habitat for foxes. Empty city lots are full of moles and mice, a fox's favorite foods. Hunting and trapping are not allowed in cities, so these foxes are safe from human predators. ✗ <u>In the city, foxes are good citizens.</u> They go about their business silently, usually unseen. Weighing only about 12 pounds, foxes do not attack cats or dogs. They run away from young children. Foxes don't <u>scavenge</u> for garbage, either, unlike raccoons or dogs.

Instead of searching for a free meal, they hunt, getting rid of pests such as mice and rats.

The Bear Raiders

The voters in Cross City, Michigan, got a big surprise one recent Election Day. A 400-pound black bear kept them from leaving the building where they were voting. That same fall, more than a dozen bears entered Colorado homes. Most of the bears headed straight for the kitchen.

In autumn, bears prepare to sleep away the winter. To survive the coming winter, they eat <u>voraciously</u>. They hungrily gobble up wild fruits and nuts. If the summer has been very dry, there will not be enough fruits and nuts for them all.

When bears cannot find enough food in the forest, they turn to dumpsters, landfills, garbage cans, and bird feeders in cities and suburbs. As a result, people often see bears in the autumn.

If food is scarce in forests in the fall, bears might raid garbage cans to fatten up for the winter.

Bear attacks on humans are very rare. Still, these powerful animals can be dangerous to city residents. So wildlife managers in cities trap bears and release them in the wild. They may also try to scare the bears away by shooting them with stinging rubber bullets. However, some bears return time after time, hoping to find an easy meal.

The Geese Mess

In the 1800s, many people hunted Canada geese for their meat. By 1900, the geese were very rare. Then in the 1960s, scientists found a group of Canada geese in Minnesota. The excited scientists took pairs of the birds to many different areas around the country.

They hoped the geese would start new flocks. The Canada geese loved their new homes. They were protected from hunters. They had plenty of grass, their favorite food. People also fed them bread. In fact, there was so much food that the geese no longer needed to migrate in winter. Because the geese had plenty of food and no predators, their numbers increased.

The goose population on golf courses, playgrounds, and parks began to skyrocket. Geese live for 20 years or more. A pair of geese can produce 100 new birds in just five years. At certain times of the year, more than 500 geese might gather in one place.

Goose droppings can make parks unsafe. They **pollute** (pə LOOT) ponds and drinking water, and cleaning up the mess is expensive. To limit the number of geese, some cities and parks now use herding dogs to keep the geese from nesting. Officials also discourage the feeding of geese. Even so, the solution to the goose problem has not been found.

Problems and Solutions

As the human population increases, people will have more encounters, or run-ins, with wild animals. Some encounters are more frightening than others. Coyote attacks on humans and pets are very rare. However, coyotes have been rapidly extending their range. They have spread from the central United States to all of the lower 48 states, Alaska, and Canada. As a result, coyote attacks on pets and young children are increasing.

In the West, people have begun building houses in remote areas where mountain lions live. People are beginning to spot the big cats in and around parks and other public places. Attacks by mountain lions are very rare. Still, getting too close to these powerful creatures could be deadly.

Can people live in peace with wildlife? Most wildlife experts urge us to try. Some towns are setting aside special paths and areas for wild animals. Others use special fences and chemical sprays to keep wildlife away.

Experts urge people to enjoy wild animals only from a distance. Approaching or feeding them can be dangerous or can cause wild animals to become pests. Experts say that it is always better to keep the "wild" in wildlife.

Recalling details
1. Why are cities a good habitat for peregrine falcons?

Skyscrapers make good perches for hunting. There are

lots of other birds in the city for the falcons to hunt. There

are fewer of the falcon's own predators in the city.

Recalling details
2. What are some of the predators that attack falcon eggs and chicks in the wild?

Raccoons and owls feed on falcon chicks and eggs in

the wild.

Identifying cause and effect
3. Why is it difficult to count all the foxes that are living in cities?

The foxes are clever and can usually avoid people.

They also come out mainly at night.

Recalling details
4. How do wildlife managers in cities deal with bears?

They trap them and release them into the wild or try to

scare them away by shooting them with rubber bullets.

Comparing and contrasting
5. How has the size of the Canada goose population changed from the early 1960s to today?

In the 1960s, scientists found one small group of

Canada geese. Today, the population has skyrocketed.

Identifying cause and effect
6. What is the effect of using herding dogs in parks?

Herding dogs can reduce the number of Canada geese

in the parks. The dogs prevent the geese from nesting.

Identifying main idea
7. Find the paragraph on page 74 that is marked with an ✗. Underline the sentence in that paragraph that states the main idea.

Identifying cause and effect
8. Why have people in the West begun seeing more mountain lions recently?

People have begun building houses in remote areas

where mountain lions live.

Identifying cause and effect
9. Which of the following is *not* a reason why foxes are good citizens in cities? Circle the letter next to the correct answer.

   a. They are quiet and rarely seen.

   b. They help get rid of mice.

   c. They eat garbage.

   d. They do not attack pets.

Using context clues
10. Write the letter of the correct synonym next to each word.

   _b_ voraciously   a. abandon

   _a_ forsake   b. hungrily

   _c_ scavenge   c. search

Inferring cause and effect
1. What effect might an increase in the falcon population have on a city's pigeon population?

An increase in falcons might lead to a decline in the pigeon population because falcons hunt pigeons.

Inferring cause and effect
2. Tell what might happen to a bear that keeps returning to a town, even after being trapped or being shot at with rubber bullets.

Answers will vary. The bear might be killed by town officials.

Comparing and contrasting

3. Which would you rather have living in your neighborhood, foxes or coyotes? Use details from the selection to support your answer.

Answers will vary. Foxes would make better neighbors because they do not attack children or pets,

while coyotes occasionally do.

Inferring cause and effect

4. Explain how the growth of suburbs has led to more contacts between people and wild animals.

As suburbs fill up, people have begun building houses in remote areas that were once wild. As people take over the habitats

of wild animals, the animals are forced to live closer to people and to invade their yards and houses in search of food.

SKILL FOCUS: CAUSE AND EFFECT

Answers will vary.

1. Write one or more possible causes for each of the following effects.

   a. The population of geese in a local park increases rapidly each year.

   The geese have no predators in the park and can find plenty of food there. People like to feed bread to the geese.

   b. More and more red foxes are digging dens in city areas.

   The cities may be the only territory open to the foxes. The cities have mice to hunt.

Answers will vary.

2. Write one or more possible effects of each of the following causes.

   a. Hunting and trapping is forbidden in city neighborhoods.

   Without hunters and trappers, foxes have an easier time surviving.

   b. Wildlife managers shoot stinging rubber bullets at bears in city neighborhoods.

   Bears find the bullets so unpleasant that they leave the area and return to the woods.

3. In the following sentences, underline the *cause* once. Underline the *effect* twice. Then circle the signal word or phrase that shows a cause-and-effect relationship.

   a. Bears often enter cities in the fall (because) they cannot find enough food in the forest to fatten themselves up for winter.

   b. Herding dogs disturb the nesting of Canada geese in a park. (As a result,) the geese leave the park.

Reading-Writing Connection

Research a wild animal that lives in or near your community. Find out more facts about its habitat and diet. On a separate sheet of paper, write a short report about the animal, based on your findings.

LESSON 27

Skill: Reading a Thermometer

For lesson support, see page T87.

BACKGROUND INFORMATION

In "How We Measure Temperature," you will learn about the two ways temperature is measured. You can use the Fahrenheit (FAIR ən hyt) thermometer, or you can use the Celsius (SEL see əs) thermometer. A thermometer measures temperature, which is the amount of heat in a substance. We use thermometers to measure the air temperature, both indoors and out. In stoves, thermometers measure the cooking temperatures of food. We also use thermometers to measure our body temperatures. For example, if your body temperature is 101°F (101 degrees Fahrenheit) or 38°C (38 degrees Celsius), you have a fever and should probably see a doctor.

SKILL FOCUS: Reading a Thermometer

Today people use two different systems for measuring temperature in everyday life. People in the United States generally use the **Fahrenheit** thermometer. Most of the rest of the world uses the **Celsius** thermometer.

The Fahrenheit and Celsius systems use different scales to measure heat. So their readings sound quite different. For example, on a hot summer day, a Fahrenheit thermometer might read 90°F. On a Celsius thermometer, the temperature would read 32°C.

Look carefully at how the lines are numbered in each thermometer above. On the Fahrenheit thermometer, lines are marked 5 degrees apart. However, on the Celsius thermometer, the lines are marked 2 degrees apart. You can tell it is 32° on the Celsius thermometer because the purple color showing the liquid is at one line above the numbered line 30 (30 + 2 = 32). It is easy to read the Fahrenheit thermometer because the liquid is at a numbered line, 90.

▶ The TV weather forecaster says that today's temperature is 100°F. In the diagram below, draw a line to show where the liquid will rise on the Fahrenheit thermometer.

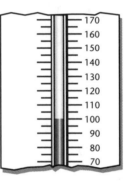

Fahrenheit

What is 100°F on the Celsius scale?

about 38°C

WORD CLUES

When reading the next selection, look for these important words and symbols: *Fahrenheit (F), Celsius (C),* and *degrees (°).* They will help you understand more about temperature and thermometers.

▶ A newspaper reports that the temperature is 74°F. What does the *F* stand for?

Fahrenheit

Another newspaper reports that the temperature is 25°C. What does the *C* stand for?

Celsius

Strategy Tip

When you read "How We Measure Temperature," pay attention to the figures. They will help you understand how temperature is measured.

How We Measure Temperature

Look at the thermometer in Figure 1 below. Notice that the colored liquid is at the line marked 68. The symbol ° stands for the word *degrees*. The letter *F* stands for the word *Fahrenheit*. The temperature shown on the Fahrenheit thermometer in Figure 1 is 68°F.

As the air gets warmer, the liquid in the thermometer goes up. This shows that the temperature is rising.

As the air becomes cooler, the liquid goes down. This shows that the temperature is dropping.

Notice that there are degree lines above zero and below zero. The numbers below zero have a minus sign. When the liquid is at the line marked −10°, we say it is minus 10 degrees Fahrenheit, or 10 degrees below zero on the Fahrenheit scale.

✔ The Celsius thermometer works in the same way as the Fahrenheit thermometer, but it uses different numbers to show the same degree of heat. On the Celsius scale, 0° shows the temperature at which water freezes. On the Fahrenheit scale, 32° shows the temperature at which water freezes. On the Celsius

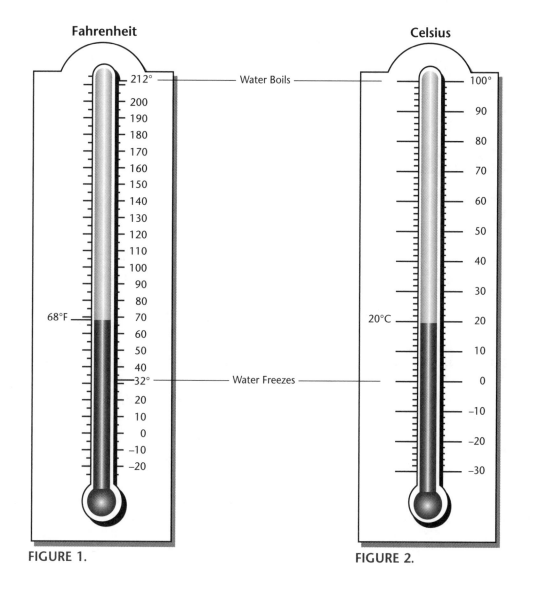

FIGURE 1.

FIGURE 2.

scale, 100° shows the temperature at which water boils. On the Fahrenheit scale, 212° shows the temperature at which water boils.

Look at Figure 2 on page 79. It shows a Celsius thermometer. The letter *C* stands for *Celsius*. Notice that 0°C is the same as 32°F.

Compare the thermometers in Figure 1 and Figure 2. Notice that the lines showing degrees are marked off in different ways. On the Fahrenheit thermometer, each of the small lines stand for 5 degrees. On the Celsius thermometer, each stands for 2 degrees. If the liquid goes up one line above 70° in the Fahrenheit thermometer, you know that it is 75°F. If the liquid goes up one line above 30° on the Celsius thermometer, you know that it is 32°. Thermometers can have different number systems so it is important to figure out how many degrees each line stands for.

COMPREHENSION

Fill in the missing words for sentences 1–3.

Recalling details
1. Most thermometers have numbers above zero

   and _____below_____ zero.

Recalling details
2. The liquid in both Fahrenheit and Celsius

   thermometers _____goes up_____

   when the air gets warmer.

Recalling details
3. The liquid _____goes down_____

   when the air gets cooler.

Identifying the main idea
4. Reread the paragraph in "How We Measure Temperature" that has a ✔ next to it. Underline the sentence that tells the main idea.

CRITICAL THINKING

Making inferences
1. Explain in your own words why the liquid in a thermometer goes up when it gets warmer.

   As the air gets warmer, the liquid expands and needs

   more room. That is why it moves up the glass tube.

Making inferences
2. Explain in your own words why the liquid in a thermometer goes down when it gets cooler.

   As the air gets colder, the liquid contracts and needs

   less room. That is why it moves down the glass tube.

SKILL FOCUS: READING A THERMOMETER

1. Thermometer 1 on page 81 shows the temperature that is close to the usual temperature of our bodies. What is our usual body temperature?

   0°F

2. What is the temperature shown on Thermometer 3 on page 81?

   98°F

3. If the temperature dropped to 20°F below zero, would this be colder or warmer than 10°F above zero?

   colder

4. Thermometer 2 on page 81 shows 212°F, the boiling point of water. How many Fahrenheit degrees above the freezing point of water is its boiling point?

   180°F

5. If the temperature of the water at the beach in the summer is 67°F, how much cooler is the water than a person's body?

31°F cooler

6. Thermometer 3 below shows your normal body temperature on a Fahrenheit scale. Thermometer 4 shows it on the Celsius scale. What is the normal body temperature in Celsius degrees?

about 37°C

7. Look at the two thermometers on page 79. Which is colder, 10°F or 10°C?

10°F

8. Look at the two thermometers on page 79. Which is colder, −20°F or 10°C?

−20°F

9. What is the freezing point of water on the Celsius scale?

0°C

10. What is the boiling point of water on the Celsius scale?

100°C

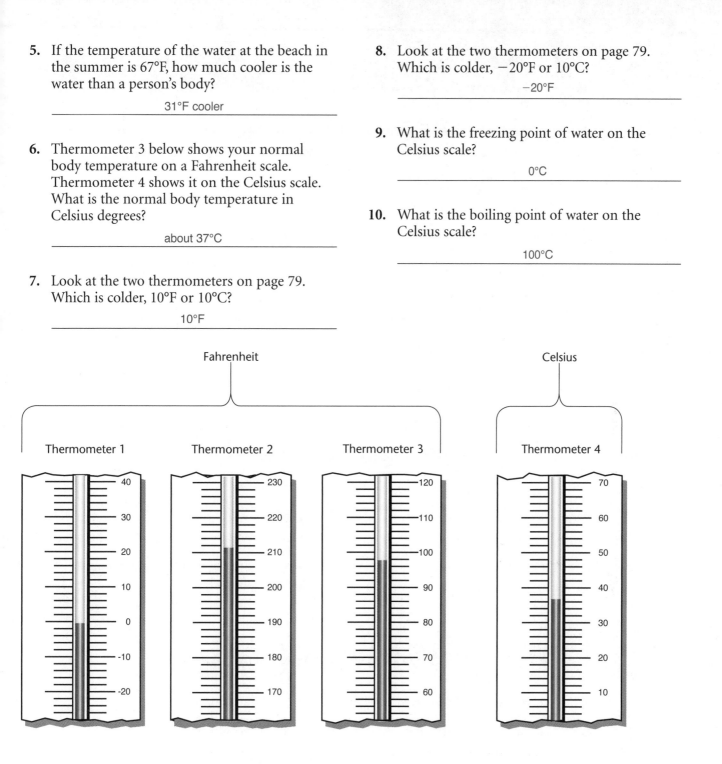

Fahrenheit

Celsius

Thermometer 1   Thermometer 2   Thermometer 3   Thermometer 4

Reading-Writing Connection

What was the weather like the last time you went on a picnic or hike? On a separate sheet of paper, write a paragraph about your day, stating the day's temperature both in the Fahrenheit scale and Celsius scale.

Skill: *r*–Controlled Vowel Sounds

For lesson support, see page T88.

> Vowels can have other sounds in addition to their long and short sounds. If the letter *r* comes after a vowel, the *r* controls the sound of the vowel. The sounds of *ar*, *er*, *ir*, *or*, and *ur* are called **r-controlled vowel sounds.**

A. Say the word pairs below, listening to each vowel sound. Then answer the questions that follow.

| cap | hem | sit | fog | fun |
| car | her | sir | for | fur |

1. Is the sound of the vowel in the top word of each pair long or short? _____short_____

2. Does the vowel in the bottom word of each pair have a different sound? _____yes_____

3. What letter follows the vowel in the bottom word of each pair? _____r_____

B. Say the three words in the list that follows each number below. Listen to the vowel sound in each word. Answer each question with *yes* or *no*. Then complete the rule below.

1. bar   Does the *a* in these words have
   star   a sound that is different from
   farm either long *a* or short *a*? __yes__

2. herd Does the *e* in these words
   term have a sound that is different
   tern   from either long *e* or short *e*? __yes__

3. shirt Does the *i* in these words have
   bird   a sound that is different from
   third either long *i* or short *i*? __yes__

4. for   Does the *o* in these words have
   born a sound that is different from
   storm either long *o* or short *o*? __yes__

5. burn Does the *u* in these words have
   hurt a sound that is different from
   curve either long *u* or short *u*? __yes__

RULE: When the vowel in a one-vowel word is followed by __r__, the sound of

the vowel is usually changed by the __r__, and the sound of the vowel

is neither short nor long.

C. Listen to the sound of *e*, *i*, and *u* in the following words. Then complete the rule below.

| jerk | term | dirt | mirth | fur | curl |
| perk | her | fir | shirk | burn | urn |

RULE: When the vowels *e*, *i*, and *u* are followed by __r__, all three vowels usually have the

__same__ sound.

Skill: Prefixes, Suffixes, and Base Words

For lesson support, see page T88.

A **prefix** is a word part that is added to the beginning of a **base word**. A **suffix** is a word part that is added to the end of a **base word**. Both prefixes and suffixes change the meaning of a base word.

Some common prefixes and suffixes with their meanings are listed below. Study them before doing the exercises that follow.

Prefix	Meaning
in-	in, toward
pre-	before
re-	again, or do over
un-	not, or the opposite of

Suffix	Meaning
-en	made of, to become
-er	one who does
-ful	full of
-ly	like in appearance or manner
-ness	quality or state of

A. Choose one of the prefixes in the box to add to the beginning of each base word below. Write the prefix on the line next to it. Make the new word mean the same thing as the phrase that follows it.

1. _____re_____ do   do again
2. _____pre_____ pay   pay before
3. _____un_____ happy   not happy
4. _____pre_____ game   before the game
5. _____re_____ paint   paint again
6. _____un_____ lucky   not lucky

7. _____re_____ wrap   wrap again
8. _____un_____ lock   opposite of lock
9. _____re_____ start   start again
10. _____pre_____ war   before the war
11. _____re_____ make   make again
12. _____pre_____ cook   cook before

B. Choose one of the suffixes in the box to add to the end of each base word below. Write the suffix on the line next to it. Make the new word mean the same thing as the phrase that follows it.

1. teach _____er_____ one who teaches
2. kind _____ly_____ in a kind way
3. truth _____ful_____ full of truth
4. loud _____ness_____ state of being loud
5. polite _____ness_____ quality of being polite
6. hope _____ful_____ full of hope

7. build _____er_____ one who builds
8. dark _____en_____ to become dark
9. slow _____ly_____ in a slow way
10. paint _____er_____ one who paints
11. read _____er_____ one who reads
12. joy _____ful_____ full of joy

Skill: Syllables

For lesson support, see page T89.

> A **syllable** is a word or part of a word. Each part of a word in which you can hear a vowel sound is a syllable.

A. Look at the following pictures and say their names. Listen for the number of vowel sounds that you hear in each one. Write *1* or *2* on the line after each picture to show the number of vowel sounds in its name.

dog ___1___

monkey ___2___

shark ___1___

camel ___2___

giraffe ___2___

tiger ___2___

B. Write the number of vowel letters that you see in each word below.
Then read each word and write the number of vowel sounds that you hear.

	Vowel Letters	Vowel Sounds		Vowel Letters	Vowel Sounds
skin	1	1	darkness	2	2
jacket	2	2	pencil	2	2
felt	1	1	trap	1	1

Write the correct word in the sentence below.

The number of vowel sounds that you hear tells you the number of ___syllables___ a word has.

You have learned that *e* is usually silent when it comes at the end of a word that has only one other vowel, such as *mile* or *same*. A final silent *e* is not counted as a vowel sound in deciding how many syllables are in a word.

What about a word in which two vowels are together, such as *boat* or *reach*? Would you count each one of these vowels as a vowel sound?

C. Write the correct numbers on the lines.

	Vowel Letters	Vowel Sounds	Silent Vowels	Syllables		Vowel Letters	Vowel Sounds	Silent Vowels	Syllables
race	2	1	1	1	wait	2	1	1	1
trade	2	1	1	1	coast	2	1	1	1
wise	2	1	1	1	team	2	1	1	1

Write the correct word in the sentence below.

The only vowel that affects the number of syllables is the one that is ___sounded___.

For ESL/ELL support, see page T89.

Skill: Syllables

For lesson support, see page T89.

There are several ways of deciding how a word should be divided into **syllables**. To help you pronounce compound words, divide the words into smaller words. To help you pronounce words with double consonants, divide the words between those consonants.

Compound Words

Most compound words are made up of two words. Each of these must have at least two syllables. Always divide a compound word into syllables by separating it between the smaller words first.

rowboat   row boat

A. Read each of the following compound words. Divide the word into syllables by writing each of the two smaller words separately on the line next to it.

1. snowflake   snow flake
2. sunlight   sun light
3. daytime   day time
4. snowshoe   snow shoe
5. flashlight   flash light
6. cupboard   cup board

7. sandstorm   sand storm
8. classroom   class room
9. campfire   camp fire
10. fishhook   fish hook
11. popcorn   pop corn
12. spearhead   spear head

Fill in the words necessary to complete the following rule.

RULE: A compound word is divided into _____ syllables _____ between the _____ smaller _____ words.

Words With Double Consonants

In words with double consonants, divide the word into syllables between the two consonants.

hammer   ham mer

B. Underline the double consonants in each of the following two-syllable words. Then divide each word into syllables between the double consonants. Write each syllable separately on the line next to it.

1. ga<u>ll</u>on   gal lon
2. ma<u>mm</u>al   mam mal
3. ha<u>pp</u>en   hap pen
4. vi<u>ll</u>age   vil lage

5. le<u>tt</u>er   let ter
6. su<u>mm</u>er   sum mer
7. su<u>pp</u>ose   sup pose
8. a<u>pp</u>ear   ap pear

9. le<u>tt</u>uce   let tuce
10. flu<u>tt</u>er   flut ter
11. bo<u>tt</u>om   bot tom
12. pu<u>pp</u>y   pup py

Fill in the words necessary to complete the following rule.

RULE: A word that has _____ double _____ consonants is divided into syllables between the _____ two _____ consonants.

Skill: Comparing Food Labels

For lesson support, see page T90.

When shopping at a supermarket for a product, such as applesauce, you will notice that several brands are available. How do you know which kind to buy? The best thing to do is to compare the **labels** on the jars.

The information on food labels tells you about the products. Every food label tells the weight of the product in ounces or quarts and in grams or liters. Federal law also requires food companies to list ingredients on every food label. The ingredients show exactly what the product is made of. They are listed in order from the largest amount to the smallest amount. A food label also tells how many servings are in the container and the number of calories per serving. The percent daily value (%DV) is also listed for nutrients most closely related to health, based on a 2,000-calorie diet. Food labels give facts about weight, ingredients, and nutrition. However, there is usually other information provided on a label to try to convince you to buy the product. Such information represents the opinion of the company that sells the product and may or may not be true.

Study the labels below on the jars of Mighty Apple Applesauce and Uncle Mort's Applesauce.

A. Use the information on the labels to complete each sentence below.

1. The applesauce made in Iowa is __Uncle Mort's Applesauce__.

2. Each jar of Uncle Mort's Applesauce contains ____200____ calories.

3. The jar with the greater amount of applesauce is __Mighty Apple Applesauce__.

4. Corn syrup and ____sugar____ are added to Mighty Apple Applesauce to make it sweeter.

5. The two ingredients found in both brands of applesauce are ____apples and water____.

6. The applesauce that adds Vitamin C is ____Uncle Mort's____.

7. The ingredient used in the highest amount in both kinds of applesauce is ____apples____.

8. The ingredient used in the least amount in Uncle Mort's Applesauce is ____Vitamin C____.

9. The ingredient used in the least amount in Mighty Apple Applesauce is ____water____.

10. The nutrient in Uncle Mort's Applesauce with the highest percent daily value is ____carbohydrates____.

11. Someone on a diet would be better off eating ____Uncle Mort's____ Applesauce because ____it contains fewer calories____.

12. There are ____2____ servings in a ____7½____-ounce jar of Uncle Mort's Applesauce.

13. There are ____4____ servings in a ____15____-ounce jar of Mighty Apple Applesauce.

14. The applesauce that offers a money-back guarantee is __Mighty Apple Applesauce__.

15. The money-back guarantee means that if you are not satisfied with the product, ____Right Off the Tree Foods____ will return the money you paid for the applesauce.

16. The company that makes Uncle Mort's Applesauce is ____Mort Corp.____.

17. The metric weight of Mighty Apple Applesauce is ____425 grams____.

18. What is the percent daily value of protein in one serving of Uncle Mort's Applesauce? ____0%____

B. Write the answer to each question below.

1. Why do you think the company created the name "Uncle Mort's Applesauce"?
   It may have been created to make the buyer think that someone's uncle makes the applesauce.

2. If you were going to purchase one of these two brands of applesauce, which would you buy?
   Answers will vary.

unit four

For ESL/ELL support, see highlighted words, page T91, and pages T28–T30.

Cars—Old and New

For theme support, see page T26.

LESSON 33

Skill: Theme

For lesson support, see page T91.

BACKGROUND INFORMATION

In "Hopping Mad!" the main character, Nancy Fuentes, likes to restore old cars. Old cars often have rusty frames and springs that can be repaired by welding. A welder heats two pieces of metal to the melting point. That way, they flow together to form one piece. Some owners try to make their old cars look almost new. Then they get together for car shows and competitions.

SKILL FOCUS: Theme

Theme is the meaning or message in a story. It is the main idea that the author wants you to get from the story. Often the theme is a general statement about life or people. "People should cooperate to get things done" is an example of a theme.

Sometimes an author states the theme of a story directly. A character, for example, might say the theme. Usually, however, the theme is not stated. Instead the reader has to infer, or figure out, the theme. You can figure out the theme by paying attention to what the characters do and say. A story's title may also be a clue to its theme.

The following questions will help you infer the theme of a story.

- What does the title of the story mean?
- What do the main characters discover about themselves in the story?
- What do the characters learn about life in the story?
- What message is the author giving to readers?

▶ Think about a short story or novel you have read recently. Think about the meaning of its title. Recall what the main characters said and did in the story. Then use the questions above to figure out the theme of that story. Fill in the Idea Web in the next column.

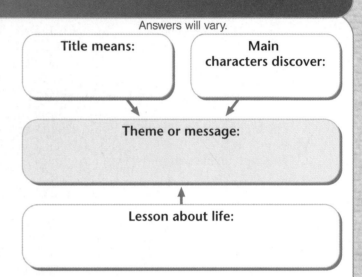

Answers will vary.

Title means:

Main characters discover:

Theme or message:

Lesson about life:

CONTEXT CLUES: Details

Details help show the meaning of a new word. In the sentences below, look for details that help you understand the meaning of the underlined word.

The figure stood up, stretching out its legs. It moved almost in slow motion, like an old man who had been <u>crouching</u> in one position too long.

If you don't know the meaning of *crouching*, the details will help you figure it out. Details describe how the figure came out of a crouching position by standing, moving slowly, and stretching its legs. Crouching means stooping low, with bent legs.

▶ Read the following sentences. Underline the details that help you figure out the meaning of *grime*.

*He had obviously had time to <u>clean up</u> before coming to visit Nancy. Only the <u>ground-in</u> <u>**grime**</u> on his hands marked him as a fellow mechanic.*

As you read the story, use details to figure out the meaning of the words *eased*, *interrupt*, and *barging*.

Strategy Tip

As you read "Hopping Mad!" think about the message the author wants you to understand.

HOPPING MAD!

Fwwwp! The welding torch went out. Nancy Fuentes rocked back onto her heels. She <u>eased</u> the tight-fitting welding mask off her head and wiped the sweat off her face with the back of her glove. The car was taking shape, but her welding was terrible. It was the only thing her dad hadn't taught her at the garage. Maybe the car wouldn't be finished in time for the contest.

There was a sudden, tiny grinding sound in back of her, and Nancy leaped to her feet. Her heart was pounding as she spun around.

"Fernando, don't you ever sneak up on me like that!" she shouted, almost dropping the welding torch.

Fernando grinned. The expression on his face was playful. "Sorry, Nan," he said. "I didn't want to <u>interrupt</u> your welding. When you stopped, you just stood there. I shifted my weight, and my boot rolled over a pebble. That's what scared you." Fernando had on a clean white T-shirt and clean jeans. He worked in his uncle's garage a few blocks away, but he had obviously had time to clean up before coming to visit Nancy. Only the ground-in grime on his hands marked him as a fellow mechanic.

He looked at the car. It was a 1969 four-door that Nancy had bought a year ago. It was in really bad shape, but Nancy had been working hard to restore it. Now it was running fine, but the body needed a lot of work. In fact, it needed more work than usual because she was converting it into a "low rider."

A low rider is created when the springs are cut to lower the body about four inches. Low riders usually have special paint, body work, and inside decorations. Sometimes special lifting parts are put in so that the car can be raised or lowered on its wheels. The lifters are sometimes powerful enough to make the car hop off the ground. There are low-rider clubs that have contests and award prizes to the best-looking or most unusual cars.

Nancy really wanted to win first prize in the Low-Rider Club's yearly contest. For one thing, she had already worked very hard. For another, no woman had ever won first prize. Finally, she could use the money. Her car had cost a lot to rebuild, and her savings were almost gone.

"You know, you've got some really tricky curves on those fenders. If I were you, I'd simplify the design." Fernando pointed to the welding that troubled Nancy. "Either that, or I could do the welding for you."

"No way," Nancy answered. She swallowed hard. She knew Fernando was one of the best welders in town. "I know that you can do it, but then I'd never find out if I could do it. I'll try again tomorrow."

"The deadline is getting close," Fernando reminded her. "Do you even have a color picked out—or a name?"

"I can't worry about colors or names now," Nancy replied. She walked away. "I have to close up the garage. Dad went home early to fix dinner."

Fernando started to say something more about the contest, but suddenly he had no one to talk to. Nancy had rolled the big door down between them. It didn't lock. The lock had been broken for years, but Fernando didn't try to open it. He just smiled and walked away.

The next morning, Nancy got to the garage just before her dad. She unlocked the pumps, got the cash drawer out of the safe, and opened the big door next to her car.

"Oh, no!" she yelled. "What happened?" Nancy started yelling and stomping around. She pounded the car with her fists. "No, no, no, no!" she yelled. Her father ran over to see what the problem was.

Nancy whirled around and stuck her face in front of his. "Did you do this?" she demanded.

"Do what?" said her father.

"This! This!" Nancy shouted, pointing to her car's fenders. The welding had been done, tricky curves and all.

Nancy saw that her father was looking confused. She backed off and patted him on the shoulder.

"Sorry, Dad," she said. "I just yelled at the first person I saw. Fernando did this. We were talking about it last night. When I get my hands on him...." Her voice started to rise again.

"Whoa, slow down," Mr. Fuentes said. "Look, you're hopping mad. You need a day away from this car, and I need parts from the city. Get the list from the office and take the pickup—some of the parts are heavy."

Nancy looked over her shoulder at the car. "It'll be here when you get back," her father said. "It's not going anywhere. A day off will do you good."

Reluctantly, Nancy got the list and drove off in the pickup.

The parts hadn't been ready when Nancy got to the city, and she had to wait for her order. When she got back to the garage, it was nearly dark. As she turned off the highway onto her street, she could see a bright light flickering in the garage. Someone was welding! Nancy gritted her teeth. Fernando was really going to get it now!

She parked the truck and ran toward the garage. A figure was bending over the right front fender. She could see sparks flying. "Fernando, you get away from that car!" she shouted as loud as she could.

The figure stood up, gradually stretching out its legs. It moved almost in slow motion, like an old man who had been crouching in one position too long. In the middle of her yelling, Nancy noticed how familiar the motion was, and her voice trailed off into silence, as if someone were turning the volume down on a stereo. The figure was her dad.

"You, too?" Nancy said. "Won't anyone let me finish this car by myself?"

Mr. Fuentes put down the welding torch. "Have a look," he said.

Nancy brushed past him. There was the car, looking just as though Fernando had never touched it. "Wow!" she said, understanding at last. She turned and looked at him and then lowered her eyes a little. "Dad, how did you do that?" she asked quietly.

"I just undid everything Fernando did," her father replied. "I want this car to be all yours, too. Maybe I shouldn't have helped you either, but ...."

Nancy threw her arms around him. "You did just the right thing," she said. "I got mad at you before I had all the facts. I should have known you wouldn't mess up my car."

Her father said, "You know, even Fernando was just trying to help. That doesn't excuse his barging in like that, I know."

"Yes, I shouldn't have pushed myself in when you didn't want me to." Fernando had walked into the garage and stood next to Nancy's father. "Your dad told me all about it—how angry you were and everything. I guess I wanted to show off what a great welder I am instead of just being a good friend. What I did wasn't any help at all. I came over to apologize."

"I accept. Anyway, you did help in one way," laughed Nancy.

"How's that?" Fernando asked.

"I'm going to get stronger lifters, paint the car bright red, and call it Hopping Mad."

COMPREHENSION

Recalling details
1. Who are the characters in the story?

    Nancy Fuentes, Mr. Fuentes, and Fernando are the

    characters in the story.

Recalling details
2. Who is Fernando?

    Fernando is Nancy's friend.

Recalling details
3. What kind of car is Nancy restoring?

    She is restoring a 1969 four-door.

Recalling details
4. What is special about a low rider?

    The springs are cut to lower the car; the inside is decorated;

    special lifters allow the car to be raised or lowered.

Recalling details
5. What part of Nancy's work is she having trouble with?

    She is having trouble with the welding.

Recalling details
6. Where does Fernando work?

    Fernando works at his uncle's garage.

Recalling details
7. What does Fernando offer to do for Nancy?

    He offers to weld the fender on her car.

Recalling details
8. Why does Nancy refuse the offer?

    She wants to do all the work herself. She wants to prove

    to herself that she can do it.

Recalling details
9. What does Fernando do that night?

    He sneaks into the garage and does the welding for

    Nancy.

Identifying cause and effect
10. How does Nancy feel about what Fernando did?

    She is very angry.

Recalling details
11. What does Nancy's father do while she is gone?

    He returns the car to the way it was before Fernando

    helped.

Using context clues
12. Complete each sentence with the correct word from below.

    eased   interrupt   barging

    a. A rainstorm could _____interrupt_____ the baseball game.

    b. My little brother is always _____barging_____ into my room uninvited.

    c. The child _____eased_____ the last puzzle piece into place.

LESSON 33 Theme **91**

Drawing conclusions

1. Discuss why Nancy is so nervous at the beginning of the story.

Answers will vary. She is very nervous about getting the car finished in time for the contest,

and she isn't doing well with the welding.

Drawing conclusions

2. Explain how Fernando gets into the garage to do the welding.

The lock on the door is broken.

Making inferences

3. Describe what sort of person Nancy is.

Answers will vary. Nancy is determined, proud, a skilled mechanic, and hot-tempered.

Making inferences

4. Analyze the sort of person that Fernando is.

Answers will vary. Fernando is friendly, willing to help, pushy, and one of the

best welders in town.

Drawing conclusions

5. Discuss three reasons Mr. Fuentes has for sending Nancy to the city. Which is the real reason?

He wants her to cool off from being angry with Fernando. He needs parts from the city. The real reason

is that he wants to work on the car.

Drawing conclusions

6. Describe how Nancy feels after she sees what her father has done.

Answers will vary. She is ashamed of herself for yelling at him. *or* She is grateful to him for understanding her feelings.

Making inferences

7. Predict what happens after the story ends. Write a few sentences telling your ideas.

Answers will vary. Nancy does the welding herself and wins the contest.

There she explains why the car is called "Hopping Mad."

The following questions will help you figure out the theme of "Hopping Mad!" Thinking about the title of the story and the people in the story will help you find the message behind the story.

Title of the Story

1. What is the title of the story? The title of the story is "Hopping Mad!"

2. Who becomes very angry in the story? Nancy becomes very angry.

3. What two events make this character so angry? Fernando tries to help Nancy by doing the welding for her. Nancy thinks that her father has also helped with the car.

4. How does this person's anger cause trouble?

Nancy's anger causes her to accuse her father of something that he didn't do.

5. Why is the title a good one for this story?

Answers will vary. Nancy's getting "hopping mad" gives her the idea for the name for her car.

People in the Story

1. What does Nancy learn about herself in the story?

Answers will vary. She learns that she should get the facts before jumping to conclusions.

2. What does Fernando learn about himself in the story?

Answers will vary. He learns that being helpful is not always the best action for the other person.

Theme of the Story

What is the author's message to the reader?

Answers will vary. Being a good friend sometimes requires people to step back and let the other person do something for himself or herself.

Reading-Writing Connection

Have you ever been upset with someone who finished a project of yours that you wanted to finish? On a separate sheet of paper, write a few paragraphs describing what happened, how you felt, and why you felt the way you did.

For ESL/ELL support, see highlighted words, page T92, and pages T28–T30.

Skill: Reading a Table

For lesson support, see page T92.

BACKGROUND INFORMATION

In "America on Wheels," you will read about the history of cars in the United States and about some of the influences and developments that have shaped the cars people love to drive. In the 1890s, automobiles were so new and exciting that they were shown in circuses. By 1920, there were more than 8 million cars on our nation's roads. In 2004, American cars numbered over 135 million.

SKILL FOCUS: Reading a Table

When you want to find a fact quickly, you might read a **table**, or chart. Tables organize facts in columns and rows. Football cards and newspaper sports pages often have tables with facts about different players. Social studies books often have tables that show facts about the way people live.

To find information on a table, read the **title** first. That will tell you the kind of information the table shows. Then read the **labels** for the columns and rows. They will show you how the table is organized. Finally read down the columns and

across the rows to find the information you need. You can use your finger to follow a column or row.

▶ Read the title and the labels in the table in the first column. Then use the table to answer the questions.

How many cars were registered in the United States in 1920? _____8,131,500_____

How many cars were registered in Canada in 1950? _____1,913,400_____

CONTEXT CLUES: Definitions

Textbooks often include **definitions** of important new words. A definition usually appears in the sentence after the new word.

Look for the definition of the underlined word in the sentences below.

The rich didn't drive these cars themselves. They hired **chauffeurs.** *These professional drivers also repaired the cars.*

If you don't know the meaning of *chauffeurs*, the definition in the next sentence tells you. Chauffeurs are "professional drivers."

▶ Read this sentence from the selection. Underline the definition of the word *chrome*.

Chrome *was another important feature of cars in the 1950s and 1960s. This heavy, shiny metal seemed to reflect the American dream.*

As you read "America on Wheels," look for context clues that are definitions. Use the definitions to understand the underlined words *chassis*, *suspension*, and *innovations*.

Number of Cars Registered in the United States and Canada		
Year	United States	Canada
1900	8,000	———
1910	458,400	5,900
1920	8,131,500	251,900
1930	23,034,800	1,061,500
1940	27,465,800	1,236,500
1950	40,339,100	1,913,400
1960	61,671,400	4,104,400
1970	89,243,600	6,701,300
1980	121,600,800	10,256,000
1990	133,700,500	12,622,000
1995	128,386,800	13,192,300
2000	133,621,400	10,460,000
2005	136,568,083	10,327,400

Strategy Tip

Before you read "America on Wheels," preview the tables in the selection. They will help you understand what you read better. They will also give you extra information that is not in the text.

America on Wheels

Horseless Carriages

People called the first automobiles "horseless carriages." That is because the first carmakers simply mounted engines into carriages that used to be pulled by horses. These early cars had large wheels and boat-shaped bodies. Inside, each had a high driver's seat and a dashboard. The dashboard kept mud from splashing into the open carriage.

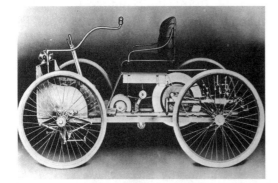

The first cars were "horseless carriages." They simply had engines instead of being pulled by horses.

Riding in early automobiles was an adventure. The cars had no tops and no windshields. Each driver wore goggles and a special hat for protection. Still, drivers often came home soaking wet or covered with dust. There were no heaters in the cars, so people could not drive in winter.

The first cars were not very reliable either. They were likely to break down at any time. When they did, the drivers had to fix them. There were no repair shops yet.

Driving a car back then took skill, strength, and courage. To start the car, the driver had to crank the engine by hand. It was like winding up a clock, only much harder. Drivers also had to operate the brakes by hand. This took a lot of strength. Instead of a steering wheel, the cars had control levers. Roads were bumpy, and tires wore out easily, so these cars were not easy to control.

Mass Production

In 1900, more than 100 American companies made cars. Workers built the cars by hand, one by one. As a result, cars were expensive. Only the rich could afford them.

Henry Ford's dream was to build a car that ordinary people could afford. With his Model T, the dream came true. In 1908, fewer than 200,000 Americans owned cars. Five years later, more than 250,000 owned Model T's.

Mass production was the key to Ford's success. As cars were being made, they were pulled past each worker on an **assembly line** (ə SEM blee lyn). That way, each worker could do one small job over and over for each car on the line. In this way, workers could make cars faster. The cost of making a car fell. Ford could sell his cars for about $500. The more cars Ford sold, the cheaper they became. Other carmakers soon copied him.

Model T's were cheap, but they lacked style and power. Rich people wanted fancier cars. Carmakers were happy to make them. In the early 1900s, sleek luxury cars rolled through wealthy neighborhoods. Inside, these cars had velvet, fine leather, and thick carpets. The engines were powerful and ran smoothly. The rich didn't drive these cars themselves. They hired chauffeurs (SHO fərz). These professional drivers also repaired the cars.

Production of Ford Automobiles: 1908–1927			
Year	No. of Cars Made	Year	No. of Cars Made
1908	6,398	1918	642,750
1909	10,607	1919	521,600
1910	18,664	1920	945,850
1911	34,528	1921	989,785
1912	78,440	1922	1,216,792
1913	168,220	1923	2,055,309
1914	248,307	1924	1,991,518
1915	308,213	1925	1,966,099
1916	533,921	1926	1,629,184
1917	751,287	1927	380,741

SOCIAL STUDIES

The Roaring Twenties

The 1920s were an exciting time. The business of selling cars was booming. As a result, gas stations and car repair shops popped up everywhere. Paved roads became more common. People opened motels and restaurants to serve motorists. America was on wheels.

Driving became popular with young people. They loved the freedom of the open road. Cars were a way for people to escape their homes and towns. The movies of this era glorified cars. Top actors posed with their luxury cars. "The bigger the star, the bigger the car," people said.

Sports cars also roared onto the scene in the 1920s. These were small cars with huge engines. People bought them to discover the joy of driving fast. Many Americans bought sports cars in the 1920s. Some competed in the new sport of car racing. Others just liked to speed around the countryside. There were few speed limits at that time.

✔ By the 1920s, cars no longer looked like horseless carriages. <u>Carmakers had made many improvements</u>. By 1925, most car bodies were enclosed, not open. The car <u>chassis</u> (CHAS ee) was lower to the ground. A chassis is the frame of a car. It also had a new <u>suspension</u> (sə SPEN shən) system. A suspension system uses springs and shock absorbers to cushion the car's ride. Cars now had balloon tires and four-wheel brakes. They had shatterproof glass windows, radios, and heaters.

The first cars had all been black. By the 1920s, red, yellow, and green were popular car colors. The star of the 1924 auto shows was a baby-blue sedan.

To keep up with demand, car production increased rapidly in the 1920s. The number of carmakers, however, decreased. Large companies cut their prices to increase sales. Only companies that could make and sell many cars stayed in business. In 1923, the United States had 108 carmakers. By 1927, the number had dropped to 44.

The Great Depression and World War II

The Great Depression began late in 1929. People had little money to spend, and most people stopped buying cars. In 1931, companies sold 2.5 million fewer cars than in 1929. In 1932, they sold only 1.1 million cars.

By the mid-1930s, car sales began to rise again. Many families spent what little extra money they had on a new car. They wanted practical cars, so cars of the 1930s were not as luxurious as those of the 1920s.

In the 1940s, the United States entered World War II. Automobile manufacturers had to make tanks, not cars, so most Americans could not buy new cars. By 1945, more than half of the cars in the United States were over ten years old. When the war finally ended, everyone wanted a new car.

The American Dream

By the 1950s and 1960s, Americans felt wealthy and confident. In the 1950s alone, auto dealers sold more than 58 million cars. The cars of those decades were large and flashy.

Today, cars usually change little from year to year. Changes in design are just too expensive to make. During the 1950s and 1960s, however, companies created new car designs, or models, each year. People knew at a glance when you were driving that year's model. To display their wealth, some Americans bought a new car every year.

You can still spot these flashy, old cars by their fins. Designers first added fins to cars in 1955. They got the idea by copying the wings of World War II aircraft. The fins got bigger and bigger over the years. By the early 1970s, however, the fins were gone.

Chrome was another important feature of cars in the 1950s and 1960s. This heavy, shiny metal seemed to reflect the American dream. Chrome also added to a car's weight, which meant that the car used more gasoline. As a result, many cars of that time averaged less than 10 miles (6 kilometers) to a gallon of gasoline.

In this period, carmakers loved to add new gadgets to vehicles. Some <u>innovations</u>, such as power steering and power brakes, were needed for heavy cars. These new advances soon became standard features in most cars.

In the 1950s and 1960s, Americans loved big, flashy cars with fins and lots of chrome.

New Challenges for Carmakers

Gasoline had always been cheap in the United States. So Americans were free to drive "gas guzzlers." These were large cars that used a lot of fuel. In Germany and Japan, however, gas was expensive. Therefore, those countries built smaller cars.

In 1973, some countries stopped selling oil to the United States. A huge gas shortage developed. The price of gasoline skyrocketed. Driving a large car became very expensive. In 1975, the U.S. Congress passed a law. It said that cars must use gas more efficiently. American carmakers hurried to design smaller and lighter cars.

The Japanese, however, had a head start. They had already been making small, efficient cars for a long time. For this reason, many Americans began buying Japanese cars. Between 1975 and 1980, the United States **imported** (im PORT əd) more than 16 million foreign cars. By 1980, a Japanese company was the leading seller of cars in the United States.

Gradually, U.S. carmakers caught up with the Japanese. They learned to make small, efficient cars, too. By the early 1990s, imports leveled off. Today American companies make about 65 percent of the automobiles sold in the United States.

New challenges then faced the automobile industry. One was safety. During the 1970s, more than 4 million people were injured in car crashes every year. More than 50,000 people died.

Congress passed laws to make cars safer. Since 1984, carmakers have put seatbelts into new cars. Seatbelts save more than 12,000 lives a year. Airbags, another safety device, also appeared in the 1980s.

Pollution is another challenge. To meet clean-air standards, carmakers designed cleaner-burning engines. Still, cars remain the leading cause of air pollution today. As concerns about pollution grow, people are looking for cleaner ways to power cars.

One possible fuel for cars is **ethanol** (ETH ə nahl). Ethanol comes from plants, such as corn. Another possible fuel is hydrogen gas. U.S. space shuttles use hydrogen fuel cells for their power. Cars can, too. Yet another possibility is electric cars. Some people feel that they are our best hope for the future.

In little more than a century, cars have come a long, long way. However, there are still many challenges ahead. The United States will remain a nation on wheels. We just need to find new ways to make our cars cleaner, smarter, less expensive, and safer.

In the future, electric cars like this may help Americans save fuel and clean up air pollution.

Leading Automobile-Producing Nations				
Year	United States	Japan	Germany	Canada
1965	9,340,000	696,000	2,440,000	707,000
1970	6,550,000	3,180,000	3,130,000	823,000
1975	6,720,000	4,570,000	2,690,000	1,030,000
1980	6,380,000	7,040,000	3,240,000	820,000
1985	8,180,000	7,850,000	3,860,000	1,080,000
1990	6,080,000	9,950,000	4,810,000	1,050,000
1995	6,350,000	7,610,000	4,360,000	1,340,000
2000	5,542,000	8,359,000	5,132,000	1,550,000
2005	4,321,000	9,017,000	5,350,000	1,356,000

Recalling details

1. Why were the first cars called "horseless carriages"?

   They were simply open carriages with engines mounted

   into them.

Identifying cause and effect

2. Why was Henry Ford able to sell cars so cheaply?

   He cut the cost of making cars by using an assembly

   line to make cars more quickly.

Identifying cause and effect

3. How did World War II affect car sales?

   Carmakers had to make tanks instead of cars, so car

   sales fell.

Identifying cause and effect

4. What effects did the use of chrome have on cars in the 1950s?

   It made the cars heavier and lowered their gas mileage.

Comparing and contrasting

5. How did yearly model changes in the 1950s differ from yearly changes in cars today?

   In the 1950s, car companies made big changes in their

   designs each year. Today, car designs change little.

Identifying the main idea

6. Read the paragraph on page 96 that has a ✔ next to it. Underline the sentence that states the main idea of that paragraph.

Recalling details

7. Circle the letter next to the detail that does *not* describe cars of the 1950s.

   a. Many of these cars had large fins.

   b. Cars were smaller than earlier cars.

   c. Chrome was very popular.

   d. Cars had many new gadgets.

Using context clues

8. Write the definition of each word.

   a. chassis   the frame of a car

   b. innovations   new advances

   c. suspension   the springs and shock absorbers that

   cushion a car's ride

Distinguishing fact from opinion

1. Write *F* if each sentence below is a fact. Write *O* if it is an opinion.

   O   Riding in early automobiles was an adventure.

   F   Henry Ford could sell his cars for about $500.

   O   The movies of the 1920s glorified cars.

   F   In 1923, the United States had 108 carmakers.

   F   In the 1950s alone, automobile dealers sold more than 58 million cars.

Inferring the main idea

2. Circle the letter next to the sentence that best describes automobile sales during the Great Depression.

   a. Car sales fell sharply in the early 1930s but began rising again in the mid-1930s.

   b. Car sales remained steady throughout the 1930s.

   c. Car sales fell every year from 1929 to 1939.

   d. Car sales remained strong until the mid-1930s and then fell off sharply.

Identifying cause and effect

3. Explain how the fuel shortages of the 1970s affected car sales and designs.

As the cost of gas rose, many people wanted smaller, lighter cars that used less fuel. Because Japan made

some of the best small cars, the number of imported cars rose, while the sales of large American cars fell.

SKILL FOCUS: READING A TABLE

A. Use the table on page 95 to answer these questions.

1. What is the title of the table? Production of Ford Automobiles: 1908–1927

2. How many cars did Ford produce in 1912? 78,440

3. In what year shown on the table were the most cars produced? 1923

4. What was the first year in which Ford produced more than 1 million cars? 1922

5. What happened to production at Ford between 1925 and 1926? The number of cars produced fell by

about 337,000.

B. Use the table on page 97 to answer these questions.

1. What is the title of the table? Leading Automobile-Producing Nations

2. What are the labels of the columns of this table? Year, United States, Japan, Germany, Canada

3 Look at the dates in the column labeled *Year*. How many years apart are the dates shown?
The table shows information at five-year intervals.

4. How many cars did Germany produce in 1995? 4,360,000

5. In which year did Japan first produce more cars than the United States? 1980

Reading-Writing Connection

Use a library or the Internet to research at least three cars of the future. Find out the make and model of each car and what kind of fuel each car might use. Then, on a separate sheet of paper, create a table that lists the information you found.

LESSON 35

For ESL/ELL support, see highlighted words, page T93, and pages T28–T30.

Skill: Reading a Diagram

For lesson support, see page T93.

BACKGROUND INFORMATION

In "What Makes a Car Run?" you will learn about parts and systems that work together to make cars run. A car is made of groups of parts, or systems, that work together. One system is the engine. It contains the parts that power the car. Another system is the drive train. It sends power to the wheels. The cooling system keeps the engine from overheating.

SKILL FOCUS: Reading a Diagram

To understand how something works, it helps to look at **diagrams**. A diagram is a drawing that shows the arrangement of things and the relationship of things to each other. When reading a text with diagrams, study each diagram carefully. If a diagram has a caption, read that first. The **caption** is like a title. It tells what the diagram is about.

Many diagrams also have labels. **Labels** name the parts of the objects shown in the diagram.

Follow these steps when using diagrams to help you understand what you read.

1. Read the paragraphs that come just before and after each diagram. Study the diagram closely.

2. Look back at the diagrams when you need help understanding the information you have read.

3. Use the diagrams and the text together to sum up in your own words what you have read.

▶ Look at the diagram below of the Suspension System. On the lines, list its three parts.

shock absorbers, coil springs, frame

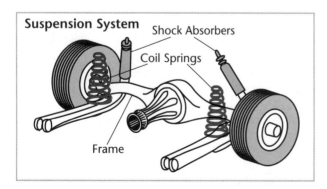

CONTEXT CLUES: Diagram Pictures and Labels

Diagrams can be used like context clues. The **pictures** and **labels** let you see things that are described in the text. You can figure out what a new word means by finding that word in the diagram. You can look at arrows and other symbols, too.

The diagram below shows the cylinder of a car engine. From the diagram, you can figure out that the *intake stroke* occurs when the piston moves down. This lets air and gasoline into the cylinder.

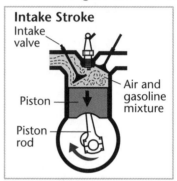

▶ Use the diagram below to figure out the meaning of the term *compression stroke*. Write what happens during the compression stroke.

The piston moves up. The gas and air are pressed against

the top of the cylinder.

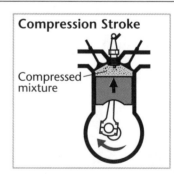

As you read, use the diagrams to understand the meanings of the underlined words *power stroke*, *exhaust stroke*, and *flywheel*.

Strategy Tip

As you read the selection, look back and forth between the text and the diagrams to better understand the main ideas in the selection.

What Makes a Car Run?

The heart of the automobile is the engine. The first successful American gasoline engine was invented in 1893 by Frank and Henry Duryea. The gas engine became successful very quickly. Blacksmith shops that made horseshoes soon changed into service stations and garages. The engine mixes gasoline and air and then burns the mixture at a high temperature. The following paragraphs explain how and where the mixture burns.

How a Gasoline Engine Works

All the parts of a car engine work together. An important part of the engine is a hollow metal tube called a **cylinder** (SIL ən dər). Tightly fitted inside the cylinder is a solid piece of metal called a **piston** (PIS tən). It is here, in the cylinder, that the air and gasoline mixture burns. The mixture burns so fast and at such a high temperature that it produces hot gases. When the air and gasoline mixture burns, the valves are closed and the cylinder is tightly sealed. The gases are under great pressure. This rapid burning makes an **explosion** (ek SPLOH zhən). The spark that causes the explosion is made by a spark plug. An automobile engine gets its power from hundreds of small but powerful explosions. The earliest gasoline engines had only one cylinder. Today's gasoline engines have four, six, eight, or more cylinders.

How the Cylinders Work

✔ Look at the diagrams in Figure 1. Each diagram shows one of the four steps that occur in a cylinder. Each step is called a stroke. Step 1 is the intake stroke. In this step, the piston moves down. At the same time, the air and gasoline mixture moves into the cylinder through the intake valve. Step 2 is the compression stroke. In this step, the piston moves upward. This motion compresses, or squeezes, the air and gasoline into a smaller space. Step 3 is the power stroke. In this step, the spark plug makes a spark. The spark explodes the air and gasoline mixture. The pressure of the explosion then forces the piston down. Step 4 is the exhaust stroke. In this step, the gases produced by the explosion are forced out of the cylinder through the exhaust valve.

How the Power Is Sent to the Wheels

The up-and-down motion of the pistons produces power. However, to move the car, the up-and-down motion has to be changed to a turning or spinning motion. Piston connecting rods connect the pistons to the backbone of the engine, the **crankshaft** (KRANK shaft). As the pistons move up and down, they move the connecting rods. The connecting rods then turn the crankshaft. The crankshaft changes the up-and-down motion to a spinning motion. As the crankshaft turns, it spins the flywheel. The spinning power turns the drive wheels that move the car. Look at Figure 2 on the next page.

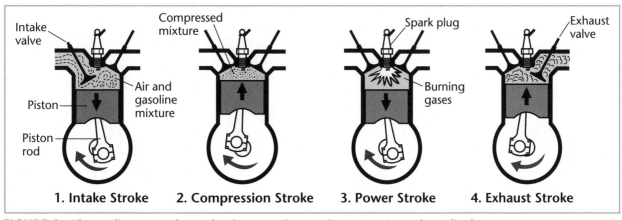

1. Intake Stroke   2. Compression Stroke   3. Power Stroke   4. Exhaust Stroke

FIGURE 1. These diagrams show the four strokes in the operation of a cylinder.

How the Engine Is Cooled

When the air and gasoline mixture burns in the cylinders, the temperature can reach 4,500 degrees Fahrenheit (2,481 degrees Celsius). This much heat can melt iron and speed up rusting. That is why a gasoline engine needs a cooling system. The cooling system removes heat from the metal parts. Water stored in the **radiator** (RAY dee ayt ər) does the job.

A pump moves the water through the engine and cools the cylinders. In doing this, the water also gets very hot. It has to be cooled. This is the job of air blowing through the radiator by the fan. Look at Figure 3. In very cold weather, antifreeze is added to the water. The antifreeze helps keep the water from freezing.

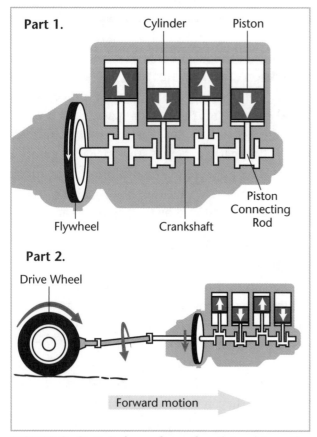

FIGURE 2. **Part 1 shows how the pistons turn the crankshaft and the crankshaft turns the flywheel. Part 2 shows how power is carried to the wheels.**

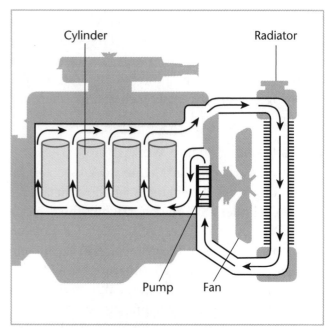

FIGURE 3. **The engine is cooled by water. The water is cooled by air that is blown by the fan.**

COMPREHENSION

Recognizing sequence of events

1. Write the following steps in the order in which they occur in a cylinder: *compression stroke, intake stroke, exhaust stroke, power stroke.*

    a. intake stroke

    b. compression stroke

    c. power stroke

    d. exhaust stroke

Recalling details

2. Who invented the first successful American gasoline automobile engine?

    Frank and Henry Duryea invented the first successful

    automobile engine.

Recalling details

3. In what part of the engine is the air and gasoline mixture burned?

    The air and gasoline mixture is burned in the cylinders.

4. What provides the spark that causes the gases to explode?

The spark plug provides the spark that causes the

gases to explode.

_____

Recognizing cause and effect
5. What moves up and down, causing the piston rods to move?

The piston moves up and down, causing the piston

rods to move.

_____

Recalling details
6. What cools the water in the engine?

Air from a fan cools the water in the engine.

_____

_____

Identifying the main idea
7. Reread the paragraph from the selection that has a ✔ next to it. Underline the sentence that has the main idea.

Using context clues
8. Use Figure 1 on page 101 and Figures 2 and 3 on page 102 to answer the following questions.

a. Does the piston move up or down during the power stroke?

The piston moves down during the power stroke.

_____

b. What do the burning gases go through during the exhaust stroke?

The burning gases go through the exhaust valve.

_____

c. What causes the flywheel to spin?

The piston rods turn the crankshaft, and the turning

crankshaft spins the flywheel.

CRITICAL THINKING

For questions 1–3, circle the letter next to the word that best completes each sentence.

Making inferences
1. An engine with eight cylinders would probably be _____ powerful than an engine with four cylinders.

   a. less

   b. three times more

   c. more

   d. no more

Making inferences
2. When a car is moving along a highway, the pistons move up and down _____.

   a. very quickly

   b. and from side to side

   c. very slowly

   d. twice then stop

Making inferences
3. In cars with front-wheel drive, the power is carried to the_____ wheels.

   a. rear

   b. front and rear

   c. side

   d. front

4. What causes the water in an engine's cooling system to get hot?

The water picks up heat from the hot engine.

5. Why is the engine referred to as the heart of the automobile?

The engine is what makes a car run in the same way that the heart makes our bodies run.

SKILL FOCUS: READING A DIAGRAM

1. In Figure 1, what causes the power stroke? A spark from the spark plug causes an explosion.
The pressure of the explosion forces the piston down.

2. In Figure 2, what turns the flywheel? The crankshaft turns the flywheel.

3. In Figure 3, what moves the water through the engine? A pump moves the water.

4. Explain in your own words the four-stroke operation of a cylinder, as shown in Figure 1.

Answers will vary. In the intake stroke, the piston moves down, and the air and gasoline mixture moves into the cylinder.

In the compression stroke, the piston moves up, and the mixture is squeezed into a tight space. In the power stroke, a

spark causes the mixture to explode, and the piston is forced down. In the exhaust stroke, the piston moves up, and the

burned gases are forced out of the cylinder.

Reading-Writing Connection

Why is it important to understand parts and systems of a car? On a separate sheet of paper, write a paragraph that explains what might happen if you didn't know.

For ESL/ELL support, see highlighted words, page T94, and pages T28–T30.

Skill: Reading Large Numbers

For lesson support, see page T94.

BACKGROUND INFORMATION

After you read "Place Value," you will have a better understanding of how to read large numbers. When you see a number like 1,334,768,765, you may have trouble making sense of it. Even so, large numbers are part of our everyday life. For example, an odometer might show a large number. Also, large cities and states have populations that number in the millions. State governments spend billions of dollars every year, and the federal budget is in the trillions. Fortunately, with practice, you can read and understand large numbers.

SKILL FOCUS: Reading Large Numbers

The value of a **digit**, or numeral, in a number depends on the position, or place, of the digit. This position is called its **place value**. You can use the digits 0, 1, 2, 3, 4, 5, 6, 7, 8, and 9 to write any number. Of course, it is important to put each digit in the correct place.

The chart below shows place value. For example, the number *39* means 3 tens and 9 ones. The number *93* means 9 tens and 3 ones. The number *933* means 9 hundreds, 3 tens, and 3 ones.

Number:	hundreds	tens	ones
39 =		3	9
93 =		9	3
933 =	9	3	3

You can make a place-value chart to understand larger numbers, too. The chart would have the same number of columns shown above in addition to columns labeled *thousands, ten-thousands, hundred-thousands, millions,* and so on. In the next selection, you will see examples of such charts.

Learning to look for commas in large numbers will also help you read them. As you read "Place Value," you will see how commas are used in large numbers. It also includes some new words that will help you read large numbers.

▶ On the place-value chart below, write the value of each digit in these numbers: 37, 73, 737.

Number:	hundreds	tens	ones
37 =		3	7
73 =		7	3
737 =	7	3	7

WORD CLUES: Examples

In math selections, **examples** often help you figure out the meaning of new words. These examples are often numbers that demonstrate something explained in the text.

As you read "Place Value," pay careful attention to the examples. These examples will help you figure out the meanings of *digits, place value,* and *place holder.*

▶ On the lines below, give an example that illustrates the word *thousands.*

Answers will vary. The number 7,052 means seven

thousands, no hundreds, five tens, and two ones.

Strategy Tip

Thinking about the place value of each digit in a numeral can help you understand large numbers. Learning how commas are used in large numbers can also help you read them.

Place Value

When a number has four, five, or six <u>digits</u>, we use a comma to separate the three digits, or numbers, at the right from the others. The digits to the left of the comma are *thousands*. You first read the digits to the left of the comma. Then add the word *thousands*.

For example, if the odometer in a car reads 125,216 the number is read as "one hundred twenty-five thousand, two hundred sixteen."

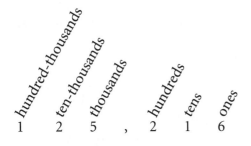

The <u>place value</u> of each digit is shown above it.

The 1 means 1 hundred-thousands, or ⟶ 100,000
The 2 means 2 ten-thousands, or ⟶ 20,000
The 5 means 5 thousands, or ⟶ 5,000
The 2 means 2 hundreds, or ⟶ 200
The 1 means 1 ten, or ⟶ 10
The 6 means 6 ones, or ⟶ 6
125,216

The number 325,007 is read as "three hundred twenty-five thousand, seven."

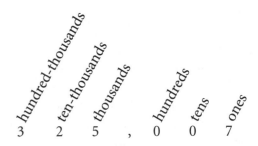

When reading large numbers that have one comma, the comma signals you to say the word *thousand*.

Do not use the word *and* to connect parts of the number. For example:

5,611   five thousand, six hundred eleven

The word *and* is used only when reading numbers like dollars and cents. The *and* is used between the dollars and cents.

$8,684.54 eight thousand, six hundred eighty-four dollars *and* fifty-four cents

✔ Zero is used as a <u>place holder</u>. In the number 589,068, the zero holds the place for hundreds. It tells you that there are no hundreds in the number. The number is read as "five hundred eighty-nine thousand, sixty-eight."

COMPREHENSION

For items 1–3, fill in the blank with the correct word.

Recalling details
1. When there are more than three digits in a number, a comma is used to separate the ___three___ digits at the right from the other digits.

Recalling details
2. The value of the place to the left of hundreds is ___thousands___.

Recalling details
3. The value of the place to the left of ten-thousands is ___hundred-thousands___.

Identifying the main idea
4. Reread the paragraph with a ✔ next to it. Draw a line under the sentence that states the main idea.

Using context clues

5. Write the meaning for each word below.

digits: numbers from zero through nine as 0, 1, 2, 3, 4, 5, 6, 7, 8, 9

place value: the value of a digit in a number based on its position

place holder: zero when it is used to show there is no value for a particular place in a number

CRITICAL THINKING

Circle the letter of the word that completes each sentence.

Drawing conclusions

1. The value of the digit in the place that is on the far _____ affects the total value of a number most.

   a. left   **b.** right

Inferring cause and effect

2. In the number 4,932, raising the value of the digit 9 would cause the place to the left of it

   to _____.

   a. increase   **b.** decrease

Drawing conclusions

3. Zero _____ affect the value of a number if it is in the first place on the far left of the number.

   a. does   **b.** does not

Drawing conclusions

4. In a five-digit number, there would be _____ digits to the left of the comma.

   a. two   **b.** three

SKILL FOCUS: READING LARGE NUMBERS

A. Read the number words below. Then rewrite them using numbers. Remember to put in commas and zeros where they are needed.

1. six thousand, two hundred fifteen _____6,215_____

2. ten thousand, seven hundred eighty-eight _____10,788_____

3. nine thousand, four _____9,004_____

4. seven hundred sixty-four thousand, two hundred ninety _____764,290_____

5. four hundred forty thousand, two hundred six _____440,206_____

6. three hundred thousand, five hundred twenty _____300,520_____

7. nine hundred forty thousand, five hundred two _____940,502_____

8. eighty-six thousand, fifty _____86,050_____

9. five hundred twenty-eight thousand, four hundred seventy-nine _____528,479_____

10. sixty-three thousand, four hundred seventeen _____63,417_____

B. Rewrite each of the following numbers in words. Include commas where they are needed.

1. 2,008 _two thousand, eight_

2. $348.22 _three hundred forty-eight dollars and twenty-two cents_

3. 240,000 _two hundred forty thousand_

4. 4,682 _four thousand, six hundred eighty-two_

5. 75,343 _seventy-five thousand, three hundred forty-three_

6. 279,600 _two hundred seventy-nine thousand, six hundred_

7. $3,001.18 _three thousand, one dollars and eighteen cents_

8. $243,078 _two hundred forty-three thousand, seventy-eight dollars_

9. $89,266.16 _eighty-nine thousand, two hundred sixty-six dollars and sixteen cents_

C. Rewrite each group of number words as numbers on the lines at the right. Add up the three numbers and write the sum as a number. Then, on the line at the left, write the sum in words.

1. One hundred twenty-seven thousand, four hundred twenty.

   Sixty thousand, four hundred twenty-eight.

   Thirty-two.

   one hundred eighty-seven thousand, eight hundred eighty

	127,420
	60,428
+	32
	187,880

2. Six hundred thirty-six thousand, forty.

   Three.

   Five hundred fifteen.

   six hundred thirty-six thousand, five hundred fifty-eight

	636,040
	3
+	515
	636,558

Reading-Writing Connection

Look through some newspapers and magazines. On a separate sheet of paper, jot down a list of five large numbers that have four or more digits. Then exchange papers with a partner, and write the numbers in words.

Skill: Accented Syllable and Schwa

For lesson support, see page T95.

> When words contain two syllables, one of the syllables is stressed, or accented, more than the other. In dictionaries, the **accent mark** (') is placed at the end of the syllable that is said with more stress. For example, the first syllable in *funny* is said with more stress than the second syllable (fun' ny).

A. Say each of the following words to yourself. Write an accent mark after the syllable that is accented.

mar' ket	sur prise'	plas'tic	be fore'	pic' nic
or'chard	bas'ket	won'der	no'tice	al low'
ho tel'	de pend'	proc'ess	rad'ish	friend' ly
farm'er	poul'try	or'der	pro tect'	a mount'
mo'vie	prod'uct	spark'ling	chick'en	

Sometimes the vowels *a, e, i, o,* and *u* all have the same sound. This is a soft sound like a short *u* pronounced very lightly.

Pronounce *balloon.* Did the *a* sound like a soft, short *u*?
Pronounce *children.* Did the *e* sound like a soft, short *u*?
Pronounce *easily.* Did the *i* sound like a soft, short *u*?
Pronounce *confuse.* Did the *o* sound like a soft, short *u*?
Pronounce *support.* Did the *u* sound like a soft, short *u*?

When any one of the five vowels has this sound, it is called the **schwa** sound.

B. Place an accent mark where it belongs in each of the words below. Then underline the letter that stands for the schwa sound in each word. The first word is marked for you.

<u>a</u> bout'	o'p<u>e</u>n	jew'<u>e</u>l	<u>a</u> loud'	wool'<u>e</u>n
cab'<u>i</u>n	cen'tr<u>a</u>l	s<u>u</u>c cess'	sof't<u>e</u>n	par'<u>e</u>nt
pi'l<u>o</u>t	A'pr<u>i</u>l	meth'<u>o</u>d	kitch'<u>e</u>n	so'd<u>a</u>
wal'r<u>u</u>s	s<u>u</u>p pose'	post'<u>e</u>r	p<u>o</u> lice'	cir'c<u>u</u>s
prob'l<u>e</u>m	pur'p<u>o</u>se	sev'<u>e</u>n	wag'<u>o</u>n	

C. Look back at the words in the list above. Does the schwa sound come in the accented syllable or the unaccented syllable? Write the correct word in the sentence below.

The schwa sound always falls in an _____unaccented_____ syllable of a word.

In most dictionaries, the schwa sound is shown by the symbol ə. When you see this symbol in a dictionary respelling, you now know that it stands for the schwa sound and that it is pronounced like a soft, short *u*.

Skill: Syllables

For lesson support, see page T95.

WORDS WITH A PREFIX OR SUFFIX

A **prefix** is a word part that is added to the beginning of a base word to change its meaning. The prefixes *re-* and *un-* have one vowel sound. When added to a word, they form their own syllable.

unwrap   un wrap

A **suffix** is a word part that is added to the end of a base word. The suffixes *-er* and *-ness* have one vowel sound. When added to a word, they form their own syllable.

painter   paint er

When a two-syllable word has a prefix or suffix, you divide it into syllables between the prefix or suffix and the base word.

A. Divide each word below into two syllables by writing each syllable separately on the line next to it.

Dividing Words With Prefixes

1. unsafe	un safe	4. preview	pre view	7. exchange	ex change
2. refill	re fill	5. dislike	dis like	8. untrue	un true
3. subway	sub way	6. refund	re fund	9. disband	dis band

Dividing Words With Suffixes

10. farmer	farm er	12. useful	use ful	14. careful	care ful
11. rarely	rare ly	13. darkness	dark ness	15. treeless	tree less

B. Fill in the words necessary to complete the following rule.

RULE: A word that has a prefix or _____ suffix _____ is divided into syllables

between the prefix or suffix and the _____ base _____ word.

C. Divide each compound word below by writing each of the two smaller words separately on the line.

Dividing Compound Words

1. sidewalk	side walk	4. wishbone	wish bone	7. snapshot	snap shot
2. barefoot	bare foot	5. football	foot ball	8. sundown	sun down
3. rainfall	rain fall	6. textbook	text book	9. spaceship	space ship

Dividing Words With Double Consonants

10. trapper	trap per	12. cabbage	cab bage	14. ladder	lad der
11. correct	cor rect	13. button	but ton	15. barren	bar ren

For ESL/ELL support, see page T96.

Skill: Fact and Opinion

For lesson support, see page T96.

How many advertisements do you hear or read each day? You hear them on radio and television, and you read them in magazines and newspapers.

Most advertisements contain both **facts** and **opinions**. The writer of the ad hopes that the reader or listener will believe the whole ad. A good reader is able to sort out facts and opinions and decide how much to believe.

How do you tell the difference between a fact and an opinion? Look at these two statements.

    a. Flakies are good for you.

    b. A cup of Flakies gives you 60 grams of protein, all the protein needed in a day.

Which sentence states a fact and which states an opinion? A **fact** can always be checked. You can find out if it's true or not. Therefore *b* is a statement of fact. An **opinion** is a statement of someone's feelings or beliefs. You cannot prove it true or false. Therefore statement *a* is an opinion. What does "good for you" mean? Perhaps you agree with the opinion, but you cannot check it. When you see words such as *good, better, terrible, pretty, everyone,* or *always,* you are reading someone's opinion. There is nothing wrong with opinions, but a careful listener or reader should be able to tell the difference between opinions and facts.

The following statements might be found in an ad. If the statement contains a fact, fill in the circle before the word *fact.* If the statement contains an opinion, fill in the circle before the word *opinion.*

1. Everyone thinks that the Zippy is the car of the future.
   ○ fact   ● opinion

2. Road tests show that the Zippy gets 45 miles per gallon in highway driving.
   ● fact   ○ opinion

3. The Zippy carries a warranty on 50,000 miles or 12 months, whichever comes first.
   ● fact   ○ opinion

4. Famous race car driver Hotrod Harry says, "Buy a Zippy! It's the best car on the road."
   ○ fact   ● opinion

5. The Zippy has an air-cooled engine.
   ● fact   ○ opinion

6. All the Zippy dealers are good people.
   ○ fact   ● opinion

7. We offer more attractive rates for longer leases.
   ○ fact   ● opinion

8. All Zippy cars come with air conditioning.
   ● fact   ○ opinion

9. Zippy dealers go wild on convertible prices.
   ○ fact   ● opinion

10. Pound for pound, dollar for dollar, the Zippy is the best car in the world.
    ○ fact   ● opinion

11. Now through April 1, all new Zippy cars have a $300 rebate.
    ● fact   ○ opinion

12. The Zippy model T14 comes with a CD player at no extra charge.
    ● fact   ○ opinion

Skill: Main Idea and Supporting Details

For lesson support, see page T96.

Many times in reading, you will look for the **main idea** and **supporting details.**
Details give more information about the main idea. They are called supporting details
because they support the main idea.

**Below is a paragraph about how the brakes work in a car. After the paragraph, its
main idea and the supporting details are listed.**

Braking a car is a process that involves several steps. In most cars, a liquid called brake fluid begins the steps that stop the moving automobile. When the brakes are not being used, the fluid rests in the master cylinder and the brake tubes. When the driver steps on the brake pedal, the fluid is pushed toward the brake shoe. The brake shoe presses against the brake drum, stopping the wheel. Each wheel has its own braking system.

Main Idea: Braking a car is a process that involves several steps.
Supporting Details:

  a. In most cars, a liquid called brake fluid begins the steps that stop the moving automobile.
  b. When the brakes are not being used, the fluid rests in the master cylinder and the brake tubes.
  c. When the driver steps on the brake pedal, the fluid is pushed toward the brake shoe.
  d. The brake shoe presses against the brake drum, stopping the wheel.
  e. Each wheel has its own braking system.

On the next page, write the main idea and three supporting details for each paragraph.

1. In the United States, almost everyone's life is linked to the auto industry. Most people depend on a car, bus, or truck for transportation. More than 12 million people earn their living in some part of the car industry by building, shipping, servicing, or selling cars, buses, or trucks. These people account for about one tenth of the labor force. In fact, there are 500,000 automobile-related businesses in the United States.

2. Several steps go into designing a new car model. Automobile designers create hundreds of sketches on computers. Final ideas for the new model come from these sketches. Then a full-sized clay model is made. Further improvements are made in the design. A fiberglass model is made. Finally, when every part has been approved, blueprints of the car are drawn so that the car can be cut out of steel and built.

3. Most of the early automobile builders were mechanics or knew about machines before they built cars. Ransom E. Olds made gasoline engines for farm equipment. Henry Ford was an engineer in a power house. Alexander Winton repaired bicycles. Elwood Haynes was in charge of a gas company.

4. When cars were first made, most drivers did not go past the city limits in case the "horseless buggy" broke down. Drivers had to wear goggles because there were no windshields to keep dust and dirt from their eyes. Women had to tie their hats on their heads with scarves to keep the hats from blowing off. Everyone wore linen dusters to protect clothes against the clouds of dust from the dirt roads. The early days of cars were an adventure.

5. Today the manufacturing of cars is aided by technology. Computer-aided manufacturing (CAM) directs computers to make car parts. It also directs robots in performing assembly tasks. To ensure quality in all stages of the assembly, cars are inspected by lasers.

Paragraph 1

Main Idea: In the United States, almost everyone's life is linked to the auto industry.

Supporting Details: Answers will vary.

a. Most people depend on a car, bus, or truck for transportation.

b. More than 12 million people earn their living in the car industry by building, shipping, servicing, or selling cars, buses, or trucks.

c. In fact, there are 500,000 automobile-related businesses in the United States.

Paragraph 2

Main Idea: Several steps go into designing a new car model.

Supporting Details: Answers will vary.

a. Automobile designers create hundreds of sketches on computers.

b. Then a full-sized clay model is made.

c. Finally, when every part has been approved, blueprints are drawn so that the car can be cut out of steel and built.

Paragraph 3

Main Idea: Most of the early automobile builders were mechanics or knew about machines before they built cars.

Supporting Details: Answers will vary.

a. Ransom E. Olds made gasoline engines for farm equipment.

b. Henry Ford was an engineer in a power house.

c. Alexander Winton repaired bicycles.

Paragraph 4

Main Idea: The early days of cars were an adventure.

Supporting Details: Answers will vary.

a. When cars were first made, most drivers did not go past the city limits in case the "horseless buggy" broke down.

b. Drivers had to wear goggles because there were no windshields to keep dust and dirt from their eyes.

c. Women had to tie their hats on their heads with scarves to keep the hats from blowing off.

Paragraph 5

Main Idea: Today the manufacturing of cars is aided by technology.

Supporting Details: Answers will vary.

a. Computer-aided manufacturing (CAM) directs computers to make car parts.

b. It also directs robots in performing assembly tasks.

c. To ensure quality in all stages of the assembly, cars are inspected by lasers.

Skill: Using a Table of Contents

For lesson support, see page T97.

Sometimes you may need to find information about a certain subject in a book. To locate the information that you need, you should use the **table of contents** in the book.

The table of contents is found at the beginning of a book. It lists the titles of the chapters and gives the page on which each chapter begins. Sometimes a table of contents also lists the most important topics included in each chapter. It may also tell the page on which each topic begins.

To use a table of contents, glance through the titles and topics until you find one that has to do with your subject. Then turn to the page number given next to the chapter title or topic, and read until you find the information you need. In this way, you don't have to "leaf through" the whole book. You can quickly locate the information that you want.

Below is a table of contents from a book about automobiles. To answer the questions on page 115, use two steps.

1. Look at the chapter titles to find out in which chapter you might find the information asked for.

2. Read through the topics under that title to find out on which page the topic begins.

CONTENTS

1. Suppose you wish to find information about the auto industry at the present time.

   a. Under which chapter title would you look? <u>The Automobile Today</u>

   b. On which page would you start to read? <u>104</u>

2. Suppose you wish to find information about the drive train in a car.

   a. Under which chapter title would you look? <u>Major Systems of an Automobile</u>

   b. On which page would you start to read? <u>160</u>

3. Suppose you wish to find information about different kinds of early cars.

   a. Under which chapter title would you look? <u>The First Automobiles</u>

   b. On which page would you start to read? <u>2</u>

4. Suppose you wish to find out the kinds of materials used in building a car.

   a. Under which chapter title would you look? <u>Building an Automobile</u>

   b. On which page would you start to read? <u>207</u>

5. Suppose you wish to find information about the problems of pollution and auto safety.

   a. Under which chapter title would you look? <u>The Automobile Today</u>

   b. On which page would you start to read? <u>115</u>

6. Suppose you wish to find information about a career as an auto salesperson.

   a. Under which chapter title would you look? <u>Careers in the Auto Industry</u>

   b. On which page would you start to read? <u>232</u>

7. Suppose you wish to find information about research and testing of cars.

   a. Under which chapter title would you look? <u>Building an Automobile</u>

   b. On which page would you start to read? <u>192</u>

8. Suppose you wish to find information about car production in Japan.

   a. Under which chapter title would you look? <u>Growth of the Auto Industry</u>

   b. On which page would you start to read? <u>81</u>

9. Suppose you wish to find information about the brake system.

   a. Under which chapter title would you look? <u>Major Systems of an Automobile</u>

   b. On which page would you start to read? <u>175</u>

For ESL/ELL support, see page T97.

Skill: Comparing Car Ads

For lesson support, see page T97.

If you are interested in buying a new car, reading **ads** in newspapers and magazines should start you in the right direction. The details in ads can help you decide what kind of car will meet your needs and your budget. Then you can shop around for the best price.

Carefully read the following ads to compare the two cars.

PASHUBI: WE DESIGNED OUR CAR FOR YOU, THE DRIVER

At Pashubi, we think you are very important. So we have created the 630-X, a fully equipped luxury sports car. The 630-X surrounds the driver with more window than other sports cars. The 630-X has an anti-glare coating on the inside rearview mirror.

The roomy bucket seats can be easily moved and can tilt back as far as you like. The large storage area in back lifts up to become two additional seats.

There are 30 standard equipment features, including air-conditioning, keyless entry, electrically heated outside rearview mirrors, a CD player with MP3/WMA playback capability, and fully programmable settings.

At $33,025, the 630-X offers more than other imported cars. You'll save on gas. You'll get an exceptional **43 EST MPG, 25 EST MPG.** Use MPG for comparison. Mileage may differ depending on conditions. Highway mileage may be lower.

The 630-X. By Pashubi. It's not for everyone, but it is for you.

TILTON
The American way to get more for your money!

You get more for your money with our cars. Take the Star, for example. This compact car uses 3,000 computer-assisted robot welds—more than any other car, which will give you more for your money for years to come.

The Star gives you more for your money because it is sensibly priced. It starts as low as $20,999*. The Star gives you more for your money with front-wheel drive. With the engine pulling in front, plus rack-and-pinion steering, you get the real feel of the road. The six-passenger Star also gives you more for your money with spacious comfort. The Star gives you more for your money when you study the mileage figures:

41 EST HWY MPG, 26 EST MPG.[+]

The Star's standard equipment includes air-conditioning, a CD player, and 5-speed transmission (3-speed automatic is extra). Among the other extras are two-tone paint, luggage rack, leather steering wheel, keyless entry, and more.

Last year's Star was the best-selling compact car. See the Star today—and learn how to get more for your money the American way.

* $23,698 as shown
+ Use EST MPG for comparison. Mileage may vary depending on speed, trip length, and weather. Actual highway mileage may be lower.

A. Circle the letter in front of the phrase that best completes each sentence.

1. The Pashubi ad stresses that
   a. the gas mileage of the 630-X is comparable to that of other cars.
   b. the 630-X is designed with the driver in mind.
   c. you get more for your money when you buy the Pashubi.
   d. The 630-X is a fully equipped compact car.

2. The Tilton ad stresses that
   a. much of the Star's standard equipment is considered extra on other cars.
   b. the Star uses fewer robot welds than any other compact car.
   c. you get more for your money when you buy a Star.
   d. the Star is not easy to maintain.

3. All car ads must state the estimated miles per gallon (EST MPG) of gas that a car needs for highway (HWY) and for city driving. So a car boasting 43 EST HWY MPG, 28 EST MPG means that
   a. its estimated mileage is 43 miles per gallon for highway driving and 28 for city driving.
   b. its estimated mileage is 28 miles per gallon for highway driving and 43 for city driving.
   c. its actual mileage is 43 miles per gallon for highway driving and 28 for city driving.
   d. its actual mileage is 25 miles per gallon for highway driving and 43 for city driving.

4. Both ads advise that the gas mileage may vary from the estimates because
   a. the gas mileage the cars get probably has never been tested.
   b. the cars probably get much better mileage than the ad states.
   c. the cars may not get lower gas mileage than the ad states.
   d. the cars may get lower gas mileage than the ad states.

5. The ad states that the Star is sold for as low as $20,999, but the car pictured in the ad costs $23,698. The price of the car in the picture is probably higher because
   a. it has many of the extra features, such as two-tone paint and a luggage rack.
   b. it is not really a Star but another kind of car made by Tilton.
   c. $20,999 is the sale price.
   d. it has better mileage.

6. The standard equipment common to both the 630-X and the Star includes
   a. a leather-covered steering wheel and two-tone paint.
   b. air-conditioning and a CD player.
   c. an electrically heated outside rearview mirror and keyless entry.
   d. a luggage rack and bucket seats.

B. Complete the chart comparing the 630-X and the Star. If no information is given for a particular item, write *NI*.

Comparing Cars		
Car Features	630-X	STAR
Price	$33,025	$20,999
Number of passengers	4	6
City gas mileage	25 EST MPG	26 EST MPG
Number of standard equipment features	30	3
Country where the car is made	NI	U.S.

unit five

For ESL/ELL support, see highlighted words, page T98, and pages T28–T30.

Close to the Earth

For theme support, see page T26.

LESSON 43

Skill: Character

For lesson support, see page T98.

BACKGROUND INFORMATION

"Test of Fire" is about a young American Indian who tests his bravery. Proving one's bravery is important in many cultures. Long ago, some young American Indians showed bravery in battle by counting coup (koo). To count coup, a warrior would approach an enemy and touch him with a stick. He would not hurt or kill the enemy, though. Warriors won respect by this act of great bravery.

SKILL FOCUS: Character

Characters are the people in a story. Some stories have many characters. Others have only a few. Usually, there is one main character. The others are not as important. The main character usually wants to reach a goal or solve a problem. The character's goals, actions, and words show what kind of person he or she is.

As you read, keep in mind the questions below.

- Who is the main character?
- What kind of person is he or she at the beginning of the story?
- What goal or problem does the main character have? Why is it important for the character to reach the goal or solve the problem?
- How does the main character change by the end of the story?
- What has the main character learned by the end of the story?

▶ Think about a story you know well. Recall who is the main character of the story. Then fill in the Idea Web on this page about the character.

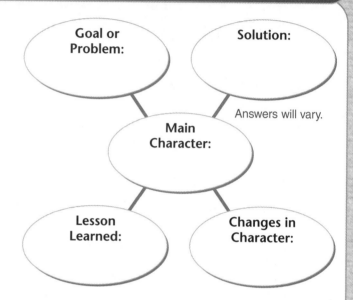

Answers will vary.

CONTEXT CLUES: Synonyms

Some context clues are **synonyms**—words with the same or similar meanings. In the sentences below, look for a synonym for the underlined word.

> *Some of the American Indians Tom grew up with no longer followed the old __traditions__. In Tom's family, however, the old customs were not forgotten.*

If you don't know the meaning of *traditions*, the word *customs* in the second sentence will help you. *Customs* is a synonym for *traditions*.

▶ Read the sentence below. Circle the synonym that helps you figure out the meaning of *examination*.

The ⟨test⟩ that Tom faced today was far more important than any __examination__ at school.

In "Test of Fire," use synonym context clues to figure out the meanings of the underlined words *courageous*, *gear*, and *crackling*.

Strategy Tip

As you read, consider what the main character's words, actions, and goal tell you about him.

TEST OF FIRE

Excitement ran through Tom Swift Eagle as he looked out the plane window. This would be his training unit's first jump with other firefighters.

These firefighters belonged to a special group called smoke jumpers. They were trained to jump from planes to fight fires in parts of a forest that could not be reached by firefighters on the ground. Tom thought smoke jumpers were the bravest men alive. Today he would have the chance to use all of the skills that John Dull Knife had taught him. He would show himself to be as underlined{courageous} as the brave smoke jumpers.

Long ago, every Lakota boy learned how to become a warrior. He learned the arts of shooting arrows, throwing spears, tracking animals, and fighting enemies. To become a man, a boy had to go through several sacred ceremonies. Once he became a man and received his adult name, he was expected to prove his bravery by counting coup and going on his first buffalo hunt.

Those days are gone now. Many American Indians, like Tom and his family, live in cities. Some of the American Indians Tom grew up with no longer followed the old traditions. In Tom's family, however, the old customs were not forgotten.

But Tom lived in the twenty-first century. He couldn't prove his bravery as his ancestors had done in the past. Instead of proving himself with a bow and arrow, he would show his bravery by fighting a forest fire.

Tom pressed his face to the plane window and watched the green woods below him. Then he saw it. Great clouds of thick, black smoke were foaming up into the sky. His heart beat faster and faster.

Others in the plane had fought fierce fires like this one many times before. They were talking together as they got their underlined{gear} ready. Their equipment included hard hats, gloves, shovels, and axes.

"This fire is a bad one," Rita Connelly said gravely.

Bill Williams nodded. "Soon Pineville will be nothing but ashes unless we can stop the fire," he said.

The test that Tom faced today was far more important than any examination at school. He had to pass this test. It was a test of life or death.

Tom wanted nothing more than the respect of these brave firefighters. He reached inside his shirt to be sure that he was wearing his sacred medicine bag. The medicine bag contained sacred objects that would protect him. It was important to Tom to have his sacred medicine with him when he made his first jump.

It was almost time. Jumping at the right instant was important. Smoke jumpers have to land near the fire without falling into the hungry flames.

At John's signal, Tom leaped out of the plane. He slowly dropped through the smoky air—down, down, toward the raging fire. He guided his parachute to an open spot between the trees. He had learned how to keep his parachute from getting hung up in tree branches.

As Tom hit the ground, the sharp smell of burning wood surrounded him. He heard the great fire roaring in the distance like a huge waterfall.

The firefighters quickly put on their hard hats and protective gloves. Armed with shovels and axes, they set to work making a firebreak, which is a strip of cleared land used to stop the spread of a fire. They cut down trees and cleared away brush on a wide strip of land in front of the racing flames. Then they scraped away some of the soil until bare ground showed. When the fire reached this bare ground, it would have nothing to feed on and would stop.

If they could finish in time.

The fire was moving fast, pushed by the wind and by its own heat. The air was full of flying sparks, ash, and falling branches.

Tom swung his ax as fast as he could. He could hardly breathe the hot, smoke-filled air. He had never felt anything like this heat. The thick smoke stung his eyes and burned his throat.

A underlined{crackling} sound was all around them. The popping noises from dry, burning wood grew louder. Worst of all were the echoing booms as trees

crashed down. Tom worked as he had never worked before.

Over the roar of the fire, Tom heard John shout, "Hurry! The fire is almost on us!"

Tom's arms were sore and tired, but he swung his ax even faster. He didn't even stop to wipe the tears from his stinging eyes. The greedy fire kept coming. The more the fire destroyed, the more it wanted. Tom worked shoulder to shoulder with the other smoke jumpers. His only thought was to stop the flaming monster that was raging through the forest.

At last, the smoke jumpers finished the firebreak. If the fire was powerful enough, it would jump over the firebreak that they had worked so hard to make. Then they would have to start all over again.

Tom stood motionless, his face black with ash, his shirt wet with sweat. He was too exhausted to move. He had given all of himself to fighting the fire. He turned his head and noticed John watching him. John nodded.

Suddenly all that John had taught Tom about proving his bravery was clear. A man was not brave if he did something just to prove his courage. He was brave only when he forgot about himself. Today Tom had showed that he cared very much about the others with whom he was working. Like John, Bill, Rita, and the others, he wanted most of all to stop the fire.

"Look!" Rita yelled.

The fire was burning down. It was not going to jump the firebreak.

"Pineville is saved!" Tom cried. He felt more tired than he ever had in his life. Yet a feeling of joy rose in Tom. He had proved that, like the other brave smoke jumpers, he could make a contribution. He had helped his friends save Pineville.

John put his hand on Tom's shoulder, as the others looked on. "Good work, Tom," he said. "Glad you're with us." Tom knew that he had passed his test and proven his bravery.

Recalling details

1. Why do the firefighters jump from planes instead of going to the fire in trucks?

The fire cannot be reached by land.

Recalling details

2. Why is it important that the firefighters jump at just the right time?

Timing is important because the firefighters need to

land near the fire but not fall into the flames.

Recalling details

3. What is in danger if the fire isn't stopped?

The forest and the town of Pineville are in danger.

Identifying setting

4. a. Where does Tom live?

Tom lives in a city.

b. Where does Tom fight the fire?

He fights the fire in a forest.

Recalling details

5. Who has prepared Tom for his "test of fire"?

John Dull Knife prepared him.

Recalling details

6. What special item does Tom wear on his first jump?

He wears his sacred medicine bag.

Identifying cause and effect

7. Why does the fire stop when it reaches the firebreak?

Because the ground is bare and the fire has nothing

to feed on, it stops.

Recalling details

8. What do the smoke jumpers do after they finish the firebreak?

They wait to see if the firebreak will stop the fire.

Using context clues

9. Draw a line to match each word to its correct meaning.

gear — brave
crackling — equipment
courageous — popping

Making inferences

1. Explain why at the beginning of the story, the "test of fire" means more to Tom than any test at school.

The test of fire was more important to Tom because it would prove that he was brave; no school test could prove that.

Inferring sequence of events

2. Determine what the firefighters would have to do if the fire jumped over the firebreak.

They would have to start all over again and make another firebreak.

Drawing conclusions

3. Discuss whether or not Swift Eagle is a good name for Tom.

Answers will vary. Students should show an awareness that the eagle's powerful wings and sharp vision make it strong,

fierce, and brave. These qualities are important to an American Indian boy wishing to prove that he is brave. Also the eagle

is a bird and flies. Tom Swift Eagle is part of a special group of firefighters who are dropped from planes to fight fires.

4. Explain how Tom Swift Eagle passes his "test of fire."

Tom passes his test by working with brave people and being as brave as they are.

Like them, he thinks only about stopping the fire, not about himself.

5. Discuss why John says to Tom, "Glad you're with us."

By working so hard and being so brave, Tom has shown that he will be a valuable

member of the smoke jumpers' team.

6. There is a message about life in "Test of Fire." Discuss what the author is trying to tell you.

Answers will vary. The author's message is that true bravery means forgetting about yourself

and working for the good of other people.

SKILL FOCUS: CHARACTER

1. Who is the main character in this story?

Tom Swift Eagle is the main character.

2. a. What goal does he want to reach?

Tom's goal is to become a smoke jumper.

b. Why is it important for him to reach this goal?

Reaching this goal is important because it will prove that he is brave.

3. What kind of person is Tom at the beginning of the story?

Tom is someone who is determined to prove himself by demonstrating his courage.

4. How has Tom changed by the end of the story?

Tom has become more concerned about others than about himself. Stopping the fire is more

important to him than proving his bravery.

5. What has Tom learned by the end of the story?

Tom has learned that a person is brave only when he or she forgets about himself or herself

and works instead for the good of others.

Reading-Writing Connection

Who is the bravest person you know? On a separate sheet of paper, write a paragraph describing how this person shows his or her courage.

LESSON 44

For ESL/ELL support, see highlighted words, page T99, and pages T28–T30.

Skill: Using a Primary Source

For lesson support, see page T99.

BACKGROUND INFORMATION

In "A Great and Honorable Leader," you will read about Chief Joseph, a leader of the Nez Percé (nez pers). The Nez Percé are an American Indian people. They once lived where the states of Washington, Oregon, and Idaho meet. French-Canadian fur trappers gave the Nez Percé their name. It means "pierced nose." Their original name for themselves was *Nee Me Poo*, which means "the Real People." Chief Joseph (1840–1904) was leader of the Nez Percé at a sad time in their history.

SKILL FOCUS: Using a Primary Source

There are many ways to find out about the past. The best way is to use **primary sources**. Primary sources are documents that were written at the time that an event occurred. The writer was someone who actually took part in the event or witnessed it. Letters, diaries, newspaper articles, and speeches are a few kinds of primary sources.

Sometimes textbooks, encyclopedias, or magazine articles contain excerpts, or pieces, of primary sources. These are usually set apart in some way from the rest of the text.

When you read a primary source, use these steps.

1. Find out all you can about the source.

   - What type of document is it? Is it a letter, a diary entry, a newspaper article, a speech?
   - Who wrote it? Was the author part of the event or a witness?
   - When was it written?

2. Study the source to learn about the past.

   - Separate facts from opinions. A fact can be proven. An opinion cannot be proven. It is a judgment that a person makes based on feelings or beliefs.
   - What facts can I learn from this document?
   - What was the author's opinion of the events?

▶ Write the correct label for each column of the chart on this page. Choose either *Primary Source* or *Other Source*. Then add one more item to each column.

Other Source	Primary Source
1. Encyclopedia article about the Civil War	1. Letter from a soldier in the Civil War
2. Story set in the Civil War by a modern author	2. Speech by a Civil War general
3. Answers will vary. Internet entry for Civil War	3. Answers will vary. News article by a reporter on the battlefield

CONTEXT CLUES: Details

Some context clues are **details**. These details help show the meaning of a new word. In the sentences below, look for details that explain the meaning of the underlined word.

By 1871, thousands of white __settlers__ had moved onto Nez Percé land. The settlers had left their homes to find new land. They wanted land for farming and for raising cattle.

If you don't know the meaning of *settlers*, the next two sentences give details that tell you what the settlers did and wanted. Details such as *left their homes*, *find new land*, and *wanted land for farming and for raising cattle* show the meaning of *settlers*.

▶ Underline the details in the following sentences that help you figure out what *illegally* means.

However, in 1860, white miners __illegally__ entered Nez Percé lands and found gold…. They ignored an earlier treaty, or signed agreement, between the Nez Percé and the U.S. government.

In "A Great and Honorable Leader," use detail context clues to figure out the meanings of the underlined words *retreat*, *pursuit*, and *surrender*.

Strategy Tip

As you read this selection, look for excerpts from primary sources. When you find them, ask yourself what you can learn about the document, its author, and past events.

A GREAT AND HONORABLE LEADER

The Gold Rush

The Nez Percé are an American Indian people. For hundreds of years, they lived peacefully in their homeland. Their lands lay where the states of Washington, Oregon, and Idaho now meet.

The Nez Percé had long been friends with white trappers and explorers. However, in 1860, white miners illegally entered Nez Percé lands and found gold. Soon thousands of miners settled on Nez Percé lands. They ignored an earlier **treaty**, or signed agreement, between the Nez Percé and the U.S. government. For the first time, trouble grew between whites and the Nez Percé.

In 1863, the U.S. government demanded that the Nez Percé give up about 6 million acres of land. The land was on the Nez Percé **reservation** (REZ ər VAY shən). This was the land the U.S. government had set aside for them earlier. The Nez Percé refused. Then a government agent bribed several chiefs, who sold the land and signed the treaty. The agent said that he had bought the lands "at a cost not more than 8 cents per acre."

After the land sale, the Nez Percé split into "treaty" and "nontreaty" bands. A Nez Percé leader called Old Joseph was angry about the land sale. By 1871, thousands of white settlers had moved onto Nez Percé land. Near his death, Old Joseph spoke to his son, Young Joseph, about their homeland:

My son, my body is returning to my mother earth, and my spirit is going very soon to see the Great Spirit Chief. When I am gone, think of your country. You are the chief of these people. They look to you to guide them. Always remember that your father never sold his country. You must stop your ears whenever you are asked to sign a treaty selling your home.

…My son, never forget my dying words. This country holds your father's body. Never sell the bones of your father and your mother.

Chief of Peace

Upon his father's death, Joseph became the peace chief of his father's band. Chief Joseph held many **councils** (KOUN səlz), or meetings, with leaders from the U.S. government. In 1873, Joseph

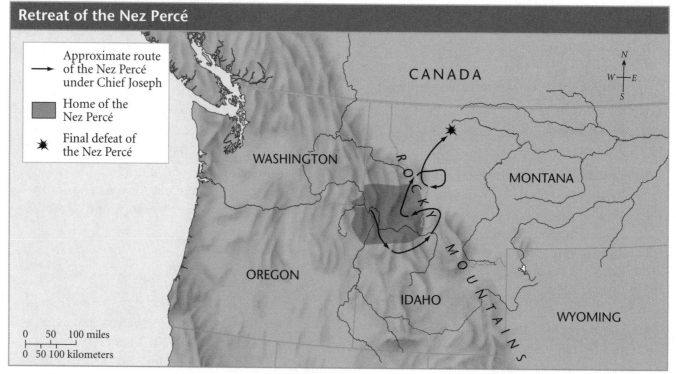

Retreat of the Nez Percé

Approximate route of the Nez Percé under Chief Joseph

Home of the Nez Percé

Final defeat of the Nez Percé

CANADA

WASHINGTON

MONTANA

ROCKY MOUNTAINS

OREGON

IDAHO

WYOMING

0 50 100 miles
0 50 100 kilometers

This map shows the retreat of the Nez Percé in 1877.

convinced the government that it did not buy the reservation lands legally. The government ordered the whites to move out of the territory. However, the government then changed its mind under pressure from Oregon settlers.

For several years, Joseph continued to work for a peaceful solution to the land problem. However, in 1877, General Oliver O. Howard decided to force all the Nez Percé off their land and onto a reservation in Washington.

Many of the "nontreaty" Nez Percé wanted to fight for their land. Chief Joseph didn't want to fight. He knew that fighting would only bring death and sadness to his people. Joseph believed that he had no other choice but to lead his people to the reservation. So in the spring of 1877, Chief Joseph agreed to the demands of the U.S. government. Several other nontreaty bands joined Joseph's band for one last gathering on their land. While they were there, however, several Nez Percé men decided to take revenge on the white settlers. They killed four of the settlers.

Knowing that General Howard would send U.S. troops after them, the bands withdrew to White Bird Canyon. Thus began a remarkable <u>retreat</u>. As the Nez Percé were running away to avoid death or capture, they fought, hid from, or outwitted one military force after another for four months. With about 750 people, including the sick, the elderly, women, and children, the Nez Percé circled over a thousand miles trying to reach safety in Canada.

The soldiers who fought Chief Joseph thought that he was a great and honorable man. The soldiers knew that the Nez Percé never killed without reason. The runaways could have burned and destroyed the property of many settlers, but they did not. Chief Joseph and his people fought only to defend themselves and their land. The white soldiers were also impressed with the runaways' ability to avoid capture for so many months and over so many miles.

"I Will Fight No More, Forever"

The end finally came. The Nez Percé were not aware that the U.S. army, under Colonel Nelson A. Miles, was in close <u>pursuit</u>. The army was following right behind them, ready to capture them. The Nez Percé camped less than 40 miles south of the Canadian border. After a five-day battle, Chief Joseph decided to <u>surrender</u> on October 5, 1877. He rode into the army camp alone and handed his rifle to the soldiers. He said:

I am tired of fighting. My people ask me for food and I have none to give. It is cold and we have no blankets, no wood. My people are starving.... Hear me, my chiefs. I have fought, but from where the sun now stands, Joseph will fight no more, forever.

After Chief Joseph's surrender, the U.S. government ordered the Nez Percé onto a reservation in Kansas, then to a reservation in Oklahoma. Many of the Nez Percé died from diseases they caught while on these reservations.

Chief Joseph pleaded on behalf of his people to return to a reservation in the Northwest. In 1879, Chief Joseph traveled to Washington, D.C., to plead his case to President Rutherford B. Hayes. There, he delivered the following speech.

Chief Joseph's Speech

If the white man wants to live in peace with the Indian, he can live in peace. There need be no trouble. Treat all men alike. Give them the same laws. Give them all an even chance to live and grow.

All men are made by the same Great Spirit Chief.

Chief Joseph of the Nez Percé Indians

They are all brothers. The earth is the mother of all people, and all people should have equal rights upon it. You might as well expect all rivers to run backward as that any man born a free man should be contented penned up and denied liberty to go where he pleases. If you tie a horse to a stake, do you expect he will grow fat? If you pen an Indian up on a small spot of earth and compel him to stay there, he will not be contented, nor will he grow and prosper.

I have asked some of the Great White Chiefs where they get their authority to say to the Indian that he shall stay in one place, while he sees white men going where they please. They cannot tell me.

I only ask of the government to be treated as all other men are treated. If I cannot go to my own home, let me have a home in a country where my people will not die so fast. I would like to go to Bitterroot Valley. There my people would be healthy; where they are now, they are dying…. Three have died since I left my camp to come to Washington. When I think of our condition, my heart is heavy. I see men of my own race treated as outlaws and driven from country to country, or shot down like animals.

Whenever the white man treats the Indian as they treat each other, then we shall have no more wars. We shall all be alike—brothers of one father and mother, with one sky above us and one country around us and one government for all. Then the Great Spirit Chief who rules above will smile upon this land and send rain to wash out the bloody spots made by brothers' hands upon the face of the earth. For this time, the Indian race are waiting and praying. I hope no more groans of wounded men and women will ever go to the ear of the Great Spirit Chief above, and that all people may be one people.

For eight years, Chief Joseph worked on behalf of his people. Finally, in 1885, his band of Nez Percé were allowed to return to the Northwest. Unable to join the treaty bands on the Idaho reservation, Joseph and the others went to the Colville Reservation in the Washington Territory. It was there that Joseph died in 1904, reportedly from a broken heart.

COMPREHENSION

Recalling details
1. Where did the Nez Percé originally live?

   They lived where the states of Washington, Oregon,

   and Idaho now meet.

Recalling details
2. Why did the white settlers want the Nez Percé land?

   They were searching for gold.

Identifying cause and effect
3. What event divided the Nez Percé into two groups?

   Several chiefs sold reservation land and signed a treaty

   with the U.S. government. Other bands of Nez Percé

   were angry about it.

Identifying cause and effect
4. Why did Chief Joseph's band run away instead of going to the reservation in 1877?

   Several of the Nez Percé killed some white settlers in

   revenge. They were afraid the U.S. government would

   punish them.

Recalling details
5. Why did the U.S. soldiers think that Chief Joseph was a great leader?

   His people never killed without a reason, did not destroy

   the property of settlers, and fought in self-defense.

Recalling details
6. When and why was Chief Joseph's band allowed to return to the Northwest?

   They returned in 1885 because Chief Joseph had

   worked with the U.S. government on behalf of his

   people.

Using context clues
7. Write the letter of the correct meaning next to each word.

   __c__ retreat   **a.** following in order to capture

   __a__ pursuit   **b.** to give up

   __b__ surrender   **c.** going to a safe place

Drawing conclusions

A. For each pair of sentences below, circle the letter next to the statement that expresses Chief Joseph's thoughts and opinions in his speech.

1. (**a.**) The white man can live in peace with the Indian if all men are treated alike under the same law.

   b. Because so many promises have been broken, there can never be peace between the white man and the Indian.

2. **a.** There will be no more wars when the settlers sign a peace treaty with the Indians.

   (**b.**) There will be no more wars when the settlers treat the Indians as they treat each other.

Drawing conclusions

B. Decide whether Chief Joseph is a great and honorable leader. To reach a conclusion, look carefully at Chief Joseph's actions below. For each action Chief Joseph takes, explain his reasons.

1. Chief Joseph first agrees to lead his people to the reservation without a fight.

   He knows that the small number of Nez Percé cannot win against the army.

2. Chief Joseph decides to lead his people to Bitterroot Valley in Canada.

   He wants to escape the U.S. army's punishment for some of his warriors' actions. Also, in Canada,

   they would not be put on reservations.

3. Chief Joseph will fight the U.S. army only if they try to stop him.

   He knows that the battle will end only in defeat because his people are outnumbered by U.S. soldiers.

4. Chief Joseph leads his people on a twisting trail through the mountains for four months.

   He is trying to avoid battle and being captured by the soldiers who are pursuing him and his people.

5. During this time, Chief Joseph tries not to get into battles with the army.

   He knows that the U.S. army has more trained men and better weapons, so his people cannot win a battle.

6. Chief Joseph says that he will "fight no more, forever" and leads his people to the reservation.

   The army has trapped them. His people have suffered great losses. They are cold and hungry. They must either

   surrender or die.

7. Two years later, Chief Joseph speaks out against being "penned up" on a reservation, even though he led his people there.

   He believes that taking away a people's freedom is another kind of death. People, like animals, were not meant to live

   "penned up." Yet he has given his word, and he keeps it.

C. Decide if you think that Chief Joseph was a great and honorable leader. In your answer, first tell what you mean by the words *great* and *honorable.* Then tell why you think Chief Joseph was or was not a great and honorable leader. Give facts to support your view.

Answers will vary. All answers should include the following: (a) definitions of the words *great* and *honorable;* (b) a conclusion

about Chief Joseph that is consistent with the definitions of *great* and *honorable;* (c) facts from the selection and details from

Chief Joseph's speech that support the conclusion.

SKILL FOCUS: USING A PRIMARY SOURCE

Reread Chief Joseph's speech. Pay special attention to what it tells you about Chief Joseph's feelings and motives. Then answer the questions below.

A. Find out all you can about the primary source.

1. What type of document is this? This document is a speech.

2. Who delivered it? Chief Joseph delivered the speech.

3. Was the speaker involved in the events described in the document? Yes.

4. When were the words in the document presented? The speech was delivered in 1879.

B. Study the primary source to learn about a past event.

1. What facts can you learn from this document? Indian lands were being overrun by white settlers. Many Indians were dying and being treated as outlaws.

2. What was the author's opinion about what was reported? Chief Joseph believed that the Indians and white men could live in peace if all were subject to the same laws. He thought that his people would prosper if they could be moved back to their homelands in the Pacific Northwest.

Reading-Writing Connection

In a library or on the Internet, find a primary source that was written by a settler in the American West in the 1800s. On a separate sheet of paper, write a speech from the point of view of the settler that summarizes the facts and opinions expressed by this person.

LESSON 45

For ESL/ELL support, see highlighted words, page T100, and pages T28–T30.

Skill: Main Idea and Supporting Details

For lesson support, see page T100.

BACKGROUND INFORMATION

In "Saving Parks and Wilderness Areas," you will read about problems facing our national parks. National parks and wilderness areas are places set aside by the government for everyone to enjoy. The first national park in the world was Yellowstone National Park. It was established by the U.S. government in 1872. Other U.S. national parks include Sequoia, Yosemite, and Mount Rainier. During the twentieth century, the National Park Service began to set aside hundreds of recreation areas, historic sites and monuments, and scenic areas. They attract millions of visitors every year.

SKILL FOCUS: Main Idea and Supporting Details

The **main idea** is the most important idea expressed in a paragraph. The other sentences in a paragraph contain **supporting details**. Supporting details tell more about the main idea.

Read the following paragraph.

> There are beautiful national parks in every region of the United States. Acadia National Park preserves the beauty of the Maine coast. Michigan's Isle Royale National Park is a beautiful wilderness island on Lake Superior. In California's Redwood National Park, visitors see the world's oldest, tallest trees.

The first sentence states the main idea. *There are beautiful national parks in every region of the United States.* The next three sentences support this idea. They all give details about national parks in different regions of the United States.

You can use a chart to keep track of main ideas and supporting details.

▶ Underline the main idea in the paragraph.

> *Yellowstone Canyon provides some of the most beautiful sights in Yellowstone National Park.* Twenty miles long and 2,000 feet deep, the canyon is an awesome sight. The beautiful yellow stones in its walls give the park its name. As the Yellowstone River flows through the canyon, it creates two grand waterfalls.

CONTEXT CLUES: Details

Details in surrounding sentences give important clues to the meaning of a new word. In the sentences below, look for details that help you figure out what *heritage* means.

> Our national parks are a treasure from the past. Beautiful trees and ponds have been handed down to us by people who cared about nature. Efforts to save our natural **heritage** began more than one hundred years ago.

The details show that *heritage* means "treasures from the past that are handed down to us."

▶ In the following sentences, underline the details that show the meaning of the word *artifacts*.

> Museums display valuable <u>paintings</u>, <u>jewels</u>, <u>books</u>, and <u>clothing</u>. There is always the chance these **artifacts** will be damaged.

As you read this selection, use details to figure out the meaning of *vandalism*, *defacement*, and *extinct*.

Strategy Tip

As you read, look for the main idea of each paragraph and the details that support it.

Main Idea: There are beautiful national parks in every region of the United States.		
Supporting Detail	**Supporting Detail**	**Supporting Detail**
Acadia National Park in Maine is in the Northeast.	Isle Royale in Michigan is in the central region.	Redwood National Park in California is in the West.

Saving Parks and Wilderness Areas

1. For many years, people have been changing the earth, but the changes have not always been good ones. For example, many beautiful wilderness areas are disappearing. Every summer, millions of people take outdoor vacations to enjoy nature. Often they find parks crowded with people, fast-food restaurants, and gift shops.

2. Our national parks are a treasure from the past. Efforts to save our natural heritage began more than 100 years ago. In 1872, the U.S. Congress passed a law setting up Yellowstone National Park. Since then, Congress has set up 200 other national parks. They are run by the National Park Service. The United States also has hundreds of state parks. Today, many parks are overcrowded. Over the years, more and more people are visiting national parks.

3. Because of vandalism, it is hard to keep up the parks. Some people choose to destroy or spoil beautiful things in the parks. For example, some people throw litter in park areas. Others spoil old buildings by writing on them. They use paint or lipstick that is hard to remove. The defacement of historic buildings has become a big problem. The government spends millions of dollars each year to repair damage caused by vandals.

4. In addition to national parks, the government has created many wildlife **sanctuaries** (SANK chew AI reez) and other wilderness areas. These are places where it is against the law to hunt birds and other animals. These sanctuaries protect natural **habitats** (HAB ə tats). A habitat is an area where a certain type of animal can live. Animals that lose their habitat may die in large numbers, becoming **endangered** (in DAYN jərd). If all of one kind of animal dies, that type of animal becomes extinct. Without these sanctuaries to protect wildlife, some habitats and animal species would be destroyed.

5. Some ranchers would like to raise cattle in wilderness areas. Some mining companies would like to dig for minerals there. Some people also want to build roads through these areas. They want to build homes and businesses in them. As a result, animals would have to move to a different habitat or die. Fewer people could enjoy the natural beauty of these wilderness areas. There are many serious effects of destroying natural habitats.

The government has protected wilderness areas like this one since the late 1800s.

COMPREHENSION

Recalling details
1. When did Congress set up Yellowstone National Park?

Congress set up Yellowstone National Park in 1872.

Identifying cause and effect
2. Why is it difficult to keep up the parks?

Vandalism destroys or spoils many parks.

Recalling details
3. What is a wildlife sanctuary?

A wildlife sanctuary is a place where it is against the

law to hunt birds and other animals.

Recalling details
4. What do some mining companies want to do in wilderness areas?

They want to dig for minerals.

Using context clues
5. Decide if each of the following statements is true or false. Write *true* or *false* on the lines.
   a. Picking up trash on the sidewalk is an example of vandalism. _____false_____

   b. Dinosaurs have been extinct for centuries. _____true_____

   c. Sticking chewing gum on the seat of a bus is an example of defacement. _____true_____

CRITICAL THINKING

Inferring cause and effect
1. Explain how wilderness areas disappear.

People cut down trees, dig for minerals, and build roads

and homes.

Making inferences
2. Discuss why the building of roads and homes in wildlife sanctuaries might ruin animal habitats.

To build roads and houses, people need to clear away

trees and other plants that animals need for food and

shelter.

SKILL FOCUS: MAIN IDEA AND SUPPORTING DETAILS

The main idea of each numbered paragraph in the selection is given below and on page 132. Write the supporting details on the lines below each main idea. Use your own words. Leave out any details that do *not* support the main idea. The first one is done for you.

Paragraph 1

Main Idea: For many years, people have been changing the earth, but the changes have not always been good ones.

Supporting Details:

a. Many beautiful wilderness areas are disappearing.

b. Millions of people take outdoor vacations to enjoy nature.

c. Parks and wilderness areas are crowded with people, restaurants, and shops.

Paragraph 2

Main Idea: Efforts to save our natural heritage began more than 100 years ago.

Supporting Details:

a. In 1872, Congress set up Yellowstone National Park.

b. Congress has set up 200 other national parks.

c. The national parks are run by the National Park Service.

d. The United States also has hundreds of state parks.

Paragraph 3

Main Idea: It is difficult to keep up the parks because of vandalism.

Supporting Details:

a. Some people throw litter in parks.

b. Some people destroy old buildings by writing on them.

c. They use paint or lipstick that is hard to remove.

d. Repairing damage caused by vandalism costs millions of dollars each year.

Paragraph 4

Main Idea: Without wildlife sanctuaries to protect wildlife, some habitats and animal species would be destroyed.

Supporting Details:

a. Wildlife sanctuaries are places where it is against the law to hunt birds and other animals.

b. These sanctuaries protect natural habitats.

c. Animals that lose their habitat might die.

d. Some animals become endangered or extinct.

Paragraph 5

Main Idea: There are many serious effects of destroying natural habitats.

Supporting Details:

a. Some ranchers want to raise cattle in wilderness areas.

b. Mining companies want land for digging minerals.

c. Some people want to build roads, homes and businesses in wilderness areas.

d. As a result, animals must move to a different habitat or die.

e. Fewer people could enjoy the natural beauty.

Reading-Writing Connection

What is more important in your community—building more houses or saving wilderness areas? On a separate sheet of paper, write an editorial to persuade people to accept your opinion.

Skill: Reading a Table

For ESL/ELL support, see highlighted words, page T101, and pages T28–T30.

For lesson support, see page T101.

BACKGROUND INFORMATION

"A Growing Population" shows you how to read information on a table. A table organizes information in columns and rows. Tables make everyday life much easier. A timetable, for example, is one type of table. You use it to find out when a bus or train reaches a certain stop. A table of contents is another type of table. It shows the page numbers on which the chapters of a book begin. Your school schedule—on which you list your classes, teachers, and room numbers—is a type of table, too.

SKILL FOCUS: Reading a Table

Information can be presented in many ways. A map is often the best way to show details about a place. A diagram shows the parts of an object or a process. A **table** is a good way to present number facts.

A table organizes facts in rows and columns. Usually, it is easier to find number facts in a table than in a paragraph of text.

To use a table, first read the title. The **title** gives you an idea of the kind of facts shown in the table. Next read the **labels** for the rows and columns. These labels will help you find the exact number fact you need.

▶ Look at the table below. Use it to answer the questions that follow.

U.S. Population: 1880–1900	
Year	**Population**
1880	50,156,000
1890	62,948,000
1900	75,994,000

What is the title of the table?

U.S. Population: 1880–1900

What was the U.S. population in 1890?

62,948,000

CONTEXT CLUES

Synonyms are words with the same or similar meanings. Often a synonym can help you figure out the meaning of a new word. Synonyms are often found in the same sentence as a new word. They might also appear in the sentence before or after the new word.

In the sentence below, look for a synonym that explains the meaning of the underlined word.

*Then miners **discovered**, or found, gold in California in 1849.*

If you don't know the meaning of *discovered*, the word *found* will help you. *Found* is a synonym for *discovered*.

▶ Read the following sentence. Circle the synonym that helps you figure out the meaning of the underlined word.

*These states were the first ones to be **colonized**, or (settled,) after the first 13 colonies in the East.*

In "A Growing Population," look for the underlined words *migration*, *asterisk*, and *data*. Use synonym context clues in the surrounding sentences to understand their meanings.

Strategy Tip

When reading a mathematics selection, you will often find facts presented in tables. To find the fact you need, be sure to read both across the rows and down the columns.

A Growing Population

When European settlers came to the New World, they established 13 colonies. These colonies later became states. They were New Hampshire, Rhode Island, Massachusetts, Connecticut, New York, New Jersey, Pennsylvania, Delaware, Maryland, Virginia, North Carolina, South Carolina, and Georgia.

Over time, though, people began to look toward the West. Soon some brave people loaded their belongings into wagons and moved to the West. Then miners discovered gold in California in 1849. As a result, the westward migration (meye GRAY shən), or movement, grew more quickly. The number of people moving to the West grew again during the gold rushes of 1860 and 1874.

The number of people living in an area is called its population (pahp yoo LAY shən). The table below shows the populations of some states from 1790 to 1830. These states were the first ones to be settled after the first 13 colonies in the East.

The title of the table tells what the table shows. Always read the title before studying a table. In the table below, the column on the far left lists the states. The top row of the table shows different years. In the column under each year is the number of people living in each state in that year.

✔ When reading a table, you can use a sheet of paper or a ruler to make sure that you are looking at the correct row. Place a sheet of paper below the word *Indiana*. Now look across until you find the number in the column labeled *1830*. The number is 343,000. There were 343,000 people living in Indiana in 1830.

Now read across from *Kentucky*. In the year 1790, 73,600 people lived in Kentucky. In 1800, 221,000 people lived there. Keep reading across. Find Kentucky's population in 1810, 1820, and 1830. Notice that the number of people living in Kentucky grew quickly.

Now look down the column on the far left until you find *Illinois*. Did the number of people living in Illinois also grow quickly?

Look for Michigan's population in 1800. The star, or asterisk, in that column tells you to look at the bottom of the table. In the lower left corner of the table, find the words *no data available*. These words tell you that we have no information about the population of Michigan in the year 1800. There are no written records of how many people lived in Michigan then.

Population Growth in the West 1790–1830					
Year	**1790**	**1800**	**1810**	**1820**	**1830**
Alabama	*	1,250	9,050	127,900	309,500
Arkansas	*	*	1,060	14,300	30,400
Illinois	*	*	12,300	55,200	157,400
Indiana	*	5,600	24,500	148,200	343,000
Kentucky	73,600	221,000	406,500	564,300	687,900
Louisiana	*	*	76,600	153,400	215,700
Michigan	*	*	4,760	8,900	31,400
Mississippi	*	7,600	31,300	75,400	136,600
Missouri	*	*	19,800	66,600	140,500
Ohio	*	45,400	230,800	581,400	937,900
Tennessee	35,690	105,600	261,700	422,800	681,900

* No data available

Use the table on page 134 to answer the following questions.

Reading a table
1. Which state had the largest population in 1820?

   Ohio

Reading a table
2. Which state had the smallest population in 1800?

   Alabama

Reading a table
3. For Missouri, what does the asterisk mean under 1790?

   No record of population is available.

Reading a table
4. Which state had the lowest population in 1830?

   Arkansas

Recalling details
5. In studying a table, what should you read first?

   the title

Recalling details
6. When reading a table, what can you use to make sure that you are looking at the correct row?

   a sheet of paper or a ruler

Identifying the main idea
7. Reread the paragraph with a ✔ next to it. Draw a line under the sentence that has the main idea.

Using context clues
8. Write the letter of the correct synonym next to each word.

   _c_ asterisk   **a.** movement

   _a_ migration   **b.** information

   _b_ data   **c.** star

Use the table on page 134 to answer the following questions.

Making inferences
1. Explain why the states are listed in the table in alphabetical order.

   Listing the states in alphabetical order makes it easier to find a particular state.

Making inferences
2. Tell why you think there is more information available in later years than in early years.

   The government probably counted the people in later years.

Making inferences
3. Evaluate why the population of the Western states might have increased faster than the population in Northeastern states from 1790 to 1830.

   People from the Northeast moved to the West, where more land was available.

A. Use the table below to answer the questions.

| American Indian Population by Selected States, 2000 ||
State	Population
Florida	53,000
Colorado	44,000
New Mexico	173,000
California	333,000

1. What is the title of the table?

   American Indian Population by Selected States, 2000

2. What was the American Indian population of Colorado in 2000?

   44,000

3. Which state shows an American Indian population of 173,000?

   New Mexico

4. Which of the four states has the largest American Indian population?

   California

5. What was the total American Indian population of Colorado and New Mexico in 2000?

   217,000

6. What is the difference between the American Indian populations of Florida and Colorado?

   9,000

B. The following paragraph gives information about growth in the American Indian population from 1990 to 2000. Use the information to complete the table below.

In 1990, about 203,000 American Indians lived in Arizona. By 2000, the population had grown to 256,000. Massachusetts had an American Indian population of about 12,000 in 1990. By 2000, the population had grown to about 15,000. In 1990, about 63,000 American Indians lived in New York. By 2000, the number had grown to about 82,000. The American Indian population of Wyoming grew from about 9,000 in 1990 to about 11,000 in 2000.

| Growth in American Indian Population in Selected States, 1990-2000 |||
State	1990	2000
Arizona	203,000	256,000
Massachusetts	12,000	15,000
New York	63,000	82,000
Wyoming	9,000	11,000

Reading-Writing Connection

Research the population growth of your own state or community over the last ten years. Use a library or the Internet. On a separate sheet of paper, make a table to show facts about the population growth.

Skill: Syllables

For lesson support, see page T102.

Words With Two Consonants Between Two Sounded Vowels

You will learn a rule to help you divide words into **syllables**. It shows you how to divide words that have two consonants between two sounded vowels.

A. The words in the chart have been divided into syllables. Fill in the chart. Then complete the rule below it.

Word	Number of sounded vowels	Number of consonants between the vowels	Where the word is divided
dan ger	2	2	between the two consonants
bas ket	2	2	between the two consonants
mar ket	2	2	between the two consonants
har bor	2	2	between the two consonants
don key	2	2	between the two consonants
pic ture	2	2	between the two consonants

RULE: A word that has two ___consonants___ between two sounded ___vowels___ is usually divided

into syllables between the two ___consonants___.

B. Divide each word below into two syllables. Write each syllable on the line next to the word.

1. winter ___win ter___
2. turban ___tur ban___
3. number ___num ber___
4. shelter ___shel ter___
5. jersey ___jer sey___
6. larva ___lar va___

7. magnet ___mag net___
8. seldom ___sel dom___
9. practice ___prac tice___
10. circus ___cir cus___
11. barber ___bar ber___
12. surface ___sur face___

13. sentence ___sen tence___
14. monkey ___mon key___
15. furnace ___fur nace___
16. service ___ser vice___
17. entire ___en tire___
18. compare ___com pare___

Skill: Syllables

For lesson support, see page T102.

Words With One Consonant Between Two Sounded Vowels

You will learn a rule that will help you divide words into **syllables.** It shows you how to divide words that have one consonant between two sounded vowels. The rule has two parts.

A. The words in the chart below have been divided into syllables. Fill in the chart. Then complete the rule below it.

Word	Number of sounded vowels	Number of consonants between the vowels	Is the first vowel long or short?	Is the word divided before or after the consonant?
spi der	2	1	long	before
me ter	2	1	long	before
to tal	2	1	long	before

RULE: A word that has one ____consonant____ between two sounded ____vowels____, with the first vowel long, is usually divided into syllables before the ____consonant____.

B. Divide each word below into two syllables. Write each syllable on the line next to the word.

1. tiger ____ti ger____
2. local ____lo cal____
3. pilot ____pi lot____
4. moment ____mo ment____
5. silent ____si lent____
6. minus ____mi nus____

C. To understand the second part of the rule, fill in the chart below. Then complete the rule.

Word	Number of sounded vowels	Number of consonants between the vowels	Is the first vowel long or short?	Is the word divided before or after the consonant?
cab in	2	1	short	after
top ic	2	1	short	after
riv er	2	1	short	after

RULE: A word that has one ____consonant____ between two sounded vowels, with the first vowel ____short____, is usually divided into syllables ____after____ the ____consonant____.

Words with Blends

The word *betray* has two consonants between the two sounded vowels, but you do not divide the word between the two consonants. Since *tr* is a consonant blend, it is treated in the same way that one consonant would be treated. So the word is divided before the blend.

be tray

If three consonants are in the middle of a word, it is possible that two of those consonants are a blend. You treat the blend as one consonant. For example, *compress* has a *pr* blend. You divide the word between the consonant and the consonant blend.

com press

In words ending with a consonant and *-le*, these letter groups are treated as one syllable.

tum ble

D. Circle the blend or consonant and *-le*, in each word below. Then divide the word into syllables. Write each syllable separately on the line next to the word.

1. replied — re plied	11. cradle — cra dle	21. Pilgrim — Pil grim
2. congress — con gress	12. matron — ma tron	22. microbe — mi crobe
3. declare — de clare	13. central — cen tral	23. muscle — mus cle
4. children — chil dren	14. reply — re ply	24. hustle — hus tle
5. explain — ex plain	15. secret — se cret	25. tremble — trem ble
6. control — con trol	16. surprise — sur prise	26. between — be tween
7. increase — in crease	17. curdle — cur dle	27. circle — cir cle
8. complain — com plain	18. substance — sub stance	28. emblem — em blem
9. purple — pur ple	19. complete — com plete	29. comprise — com prise
10. subtract — sub tract	20. stable — sta ble	30. paddle — pad dle

E. Fill in the words necessary to complete the following rule.

RULE: Do not split a consonant ___blend___ or a consonant and ___-le___. Treat a consonant blend or a ___consonant___ and *-le* as if it were one consonant.

For ESL/ELL support, see page T103.

Skill: Making Inferences

For lesson support, see page T103.

In many of the paragraphs that you read, information is given about a subject. You can use this information to **infer** other information. When you infer, you put together what you read in the selection with what you already know about a topic to figure out something new.

Read the following selection about Ada E. Deer. Answer the questions by making inferences about what you read.

Ada E. Deer was born and raised in a one-room log cabin on the Menominee Indian Reservation in Wisconsin. All during her childhood, Ada Deer believed that education was very important. When she was ready for college, her American Indian nation gave her a scholarship. She became the first Menominee to graduate from the University of Wisconsin. Later she was the first American Indian to obtain a master's degree in social work from Columbia University in New York City.

Deer's education included law school, but in the 1970s, she dropped out to help her people. In 1961, the reservation was terminated, which brought many

hardships to the Menominee nation. The Menominee were struggling for survival. She wrote: "As a teenager, I saw the poverty of the people—poor housing, poor education, poor health. I thought, this isn't the way it should be… I wanted to help the tribe in some way…."

Ada Deer became a Menominee chief and a social worker. In helping American Indians, she has kept her promise to repay her nation for sending her to college. From 1993 to 1997, she worked for the U.S. government at the Bureau of Indian Affairs as its assistant secretary. In 2000, she became director of the American Indian Studies Program at the University of Wisconsin.

1. Explain why you think Ada Deer's nation gave her a college scholarship. The nation knew that she valued education. The tribe believed that a member with a higher education could help the Menominee.

2. Illustrate how you know that Ada Deer works hard. She has two college degrees. She helped the Menominee people. She became a chief and a social worker.

3. In what ways did Ada Deer repay her nation for making her college education possible? She became a chief and a social worker. She worked at the Bureau of Indian Affairs. She directs an American Indian Studies Program.

4. Assess how Ada Deer feels about American Indians. She respects and honors them. She wants to improve conditions for them.

5. Conclude how Ada Deer feels about the ability of people to improve their lives. She is positive and optimistic because she helped change conditions for the Menominee. She also worked hard to be successful in her own life.

Skill: Alphabetical Order

For lesson support, see page T103.

A. Below are 24 words you might find in a science textbook. On the numbered lines, write the words in alphabetical order according to the first letter in each word. Cross out each word in the list after you write it.

kerosene	tide	1. ant	13. moon
nectar	lake	2. bees	14. nectar
underground	jet	3. cell	15. ocean
equator	bees	4. dew	16. planet
planet	ocean	5. equator	17. quartz
Venus	star	6. fish	18. root
quartz	wind	7. germ	19. star
fish	cell	8. hail	20. tide
hail	moon	9. insect	21. underground
dew	X-ray	10. jet	22. Venus
insect	ant	11. kerosene	23. wind
root	germ	12. lake	24. X-ray

In a dictionary, you see many pages of words that begin with the same letter. What if you are looking up a word that begins with letter *p*? To find the word, turn to the *p* section of the dictionary, and use the second letter of the word as a guide. For example, the word *pattern* is listed before the word *platter* because *a* comes before *l* in the alphabet. When several words begin with the same letter, they are arranged in alphabetical order according to the second letter in the word.

B. Below are 14 words you might find in a social studies textbook. On the numbered lines, write the words in alphabetical order according to the first two letters in each word. Cross out each word in the list after you write it.

arctic	atlas	1. adobe	8. arctic
age	aviation	2. Africa	9. Asia
Asia	Africa	3. age	10. atlas
axis	automobile	4. airplanes	11. automobile
alfalfa	Andes	5. alfalfa	12. aviation
airplanes	Aztec	6. Amazon	13. axis
adobe	Amazon	7. Andes	14. Aztec

Skill: Using Guide Words

For lesson support, see page T104.

At the top of each dictionary page are two words by themselves. These words are called **guide words.** Guide words help you find entry words easily and quickly. They tell you the first entry word on the page and the last entry word on the page. All the other entry words on that page come between these two words in alphabetical order.

Below are two pairs of guide words that might appear on two dictionary pages. Following each pair is a list of entry words. If an entry word would be on the same page as the guide words, write *yes* next to the word. If an entry word would appear on an earlier page, write *before*. If an entry word would appear on a later page, write *after*. Some of the entry words in each list begin with the same first two letters. You will need to look at the third letters to complete this activity.

A. pencil/polite

1.	percent	yes	9.	pool	after	17.	pedal	before
2.	pouch	after	10.	pebble	before	18.	porcupine	after
3.	pepper	yes	11.	petunia	yes	19.	pester	yes
4.	pay	before	12.	pocket	yes	20.	play	yes
5.	pearl	before	13.	pelican	before	21.	patient	before
6.	power	after	14.	point	yes	22.	perch	yes
7.	permit	yes	15.	pony	after	23.	polish	yes
8.	pigeon	yes	16.	poet	yes	24.	poodle	after

B. gem/goose

1.	gear	before	9.	general	yes	17.	gone	yes
2.	geography	yes	10.	goggle	yes	18.	gourd	after
3.	graduate	after	11.	got	after	19.	gaze	before
4.	giant	yes	12.	geranium	yes	20.	gift	yes
5.	gown	after	13.	geese	before	21.	good	yes
6.	golf	yes	14.	goat	yes	22.	genius	yes
7.	gather	before	15.	gently	yes	23.	gate	before
8.	gelatin	before	16.	govern	after	24.	gorilla	after

For ESL/ELL support, see page T104.

Skill: Reading a Dictionary Entry

For lesson support, see page T104.

In a dictionary, the entry word and all the information about it is called the **entry**. The entry word always appears in boldface type. If the word has more than one syllable, it is divided into syllables to show where the word can be divided at the end of a line of writing.

The entry word is followed by a **respelling** of the word in parentheses. The respelling shows you how to pronounce the word.

The **part-of-speech label** follows the respelling. The labels are usually abbreviated as follows: *adj.* for adjective, *adv.* for adverb, *conj.* for conjunction, *interj.* for interjection, *n.* for noun, *prep.* for preposition, *pron.* for pronoun, and *v.* for verb.

The meanings are arranged according to parts of speech. For example, if an entry has noun meanings, they are grouped together and numbered following the *n.* label. Any meanings the word may have for other parts of speech are numbered and placed after the appropriate labels. When an entry has only one meaning for any part of speech, the definition is not numbered.

At the end of some entries are phrases, or idioms. An **idiom** is a group of words that has a meaning different from the meaning the individual words have by themselves. In some dictionaries, idioms have a dash in front of them, and they appear in boldface type.

Use the dictionary entry in the box to answer the questions below.

wear (wer) *v.* **1** to have or carry on the body [*Wear* your coat. Do you *wear* glasses?] **2** to have or show in the way one appears [She *wore* a frown. He *wears* his hair long.] **3** to make or become damaged, used up, etc., by use or friction [She *wore* her jeans to rags. The water is *wearing* away the river bank.] **4** to make by use or friction [He *wore* a hole in his sock.] **5** to last in use [This cloth *wears* well.] **6** to pass gradually [The year *wore* on.]–**wore, worn, wear′ ing** ◆ *n.* **1** the act of wearing or the condition of being worn [A dress for holiday *wear.*] **2** clothes; clothing [men's *wear*]. **3** the damage or loss from use or friction [These shoes show a little *wear.*] **4** the ability to last in use [There's a lot of *wear* left in that tire.] –**wear down,** **1** to become less in height or thickness by use or friction **2** to overcome by continuing to try [to *wear down* an enemy] –**wear off**, to pass away gradually [The effects of the medicine *wore off.*] –**wear out**, **1** to make or become useless from much use or friction **2** to tire out; exhaust.

1. What is the entry word? _____ wear _____

2. Write the respelling of the entry word. _____ (wer) _____

3. How many verb meanings follow the part-of-speech label *v.*? _____ 6 _____

4. How many noun meanings follow the part-of-speech label *n.*? _____ 4 _____

5. What is the first noun meaning? the act of wearing or the condition of being worn

6. What is the fifth verb meaning? to last in use

7. Write the idioms with the same meanings as the underlined words below.

   a. Jane is trying to *overcome by continuous effort* her dad's resistance to buying her a car. _____ wear down _____

   b. A full day at the amusement park was enough to *tire out* Jill. _____ wear out _____

For ESL/ELL support, see page T105.

Skill: Using a Library Catalog

For lesson support, see page T105.

To locate a book in the library quickly and easily, use the **library catalog**. In most cases, the catalog will be a computer database. You find the information you want by choosing items from a **menu,** or list. On the main, or first, menu, one of the numbered items will be the library catalog. When you choose that item, a second menu will appear. Now you can choose to search for a book by the **title**, the **author's name**, or the **subject** that it is about. If you don't have exact information about the book, you may be able to choose an item called **key words**. The computer will search its database using only one or two important words that you give it.

The catalog gives more information than just the author, title, and subject of a book. Usually each entry gives a summary of the book and describes it (size, number of pages, kinds of illustrations). It also gives the publisher, the date of publication, and a list of related subjects. It may also tell how many copies of the book there are, which libraries have the book, and whether it is available.

Suppose you want to find a book about space flight. First, you choose *Subject* from the catalog menu to do a **subject search**. Then you enter the words *space flight.* (You could also enter words such as *space exploration, outer space,* or *astronauts.*) A list of books about that topic will appear. Then you can choose a particular book from the list to find out more about it.

If you want to find a list of books written by a particular author, you can do an **author search**. Choose *Author* from the catalog menu and enter

the author's name, last name first (for example, Scott, Elaine). A list of his or her books will appear. You can then choose a particular book to find out more about it.

If you already know what book you want, you can do a **title search**. Choose *Title* from the catalog menu and enter the exact title. Information about your book will appear.

In each kind of search, the last step is to choose a particular book. When you do, a screen like the one below will appear:

Public Library

[HOME] [SEARCH AGAIN]

Call Number	Children's Nonfiction	Status: In
J500.22 SCOTT (1998)		

Author: Scott, Elaine

Title: Close Encounters: Exploring the Universe With the Hubble Space Telescope

Publisher: New York: Hyperion Books, ©1998

Description: 64 pages; ill. (some color); 24x26 cm

Summary: Describes what scientists have learned about our solar system and the universe based on data collected by the Hubble telescope.

Subjects: Hubble space telescope; Spacecraft; Outer space–Exploration; Solar system

Notice the call number at the top of the screen on page 144. This number appears on the spine, or narrow back edge, of the book. Every nonfiction book has its own call number that tells where it is shelved in the library. Nonfiction books are kept in numerical order. The *J* stands for *juvenile*. It tells you that this book is for young readers. It can be found in the Children's or Young Adult section of the library. Across from the call number is the word *status*. This tells you whether the book is on the shelf or checked out.

A. **Now use the screen on page 144 to do the following.**

   1. Draw a line below the name of the author of the book.

   2. How new is the information in this book? Circle the year that the book was published.

   3. Does the book have pictures? Draw two lines below the information that tells you.

   4. The subject used for this search was *space flight*. Draw a box around other subjects that you could use in your search.

B. **Circle the kind of search that you would do to answer each question.**

   1. Who wrote the book *Animals in Orbit: Monkeynauts and Other Pioneers in Space*?

      author search   (title search)   subject search

   2. Does the library have any books about smoke jumpers?

      author search   title search   (subject search)

   3. What books by Roberto Terpilauskas are in the library?

      (author search)   title search   subject search

C. **Use the information on the screen below to answer each question.**

Call Number	Children's Nonfiction	Status: Checked out
J629.441 KALLEN		

Author:	Kallen, Stuart A.
Title:	Space Shuttles
Series:	Giant Leaps
Publisher:	Edina, Minnesota: Abdo & Daughters, ©1996
Description:	32 pages; color ill.; 26 cm
Summary:	Describes the physical characteristics of space shuttles and life aboard them, and provides a history of the NASA space shuttle program.
Subjects:	Space shuttle program; Space shuttles; Space flight

   1. Is this book currently available at the library? _____ no

   2. Will this book most likely tell you what astronauts do on the space shuttle? _____ yes

   3. What is the call number of this book? _____ J629.441 KALLEN

   4. This book is one of several books in a series. What is the name of the series? _____ Giant Leaps

Skill: Using a Bus Route Map

For lesson support, see page T105.

Suppose you want to visit a friend who lives so far away from your home that you decide to take a bus. However, it is the first time that you have to take a bus, and you have no idea which bus to take. What should you do? Your local bus company, perhaps called the Transit Authority, prints a map showing bus routes. Bus routes are the ways different buses travel in your city. Using a **route map**, you can find the best way to travel by bus from place to place.

Look at the bus route map below. The map shows some of the main streets in a city. Different bus routes are shown on the map. The key on the map will help you read and understand the bus route.

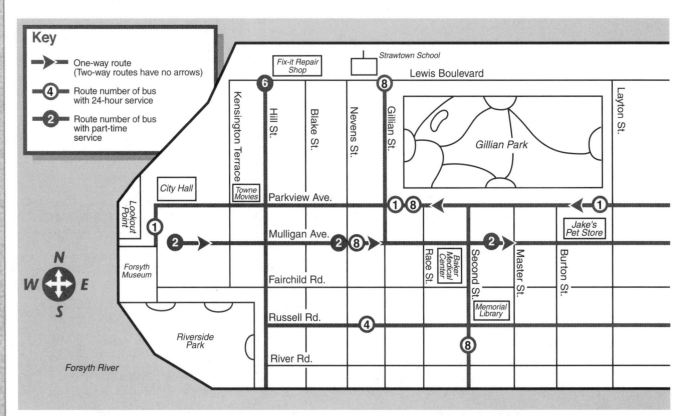

A. Read each statement about the bus route map. Fill in the circle before *true* or *false*.

1. Six bus routes are shown on the map.
   ○ true   ● false

2. Buses on Route 6 travel on Hill Street.
   ● true   ○ false

3. Buses on Route 6 run north and south.
   ● true   ○ false

4. Buses on Route 2 travel in two directions.
   ○ true   ● false

5. Buses on Route 8 run north and south on Second Street and west on Parkview Avenue.
   ● true   ○ false

6. Buses on Route 6 travel 24 hours a day.
   ○ true   ● false

7. Buses on Routes 6 and 8 travel past Gillian Park.
   ○ true   ● false

8. Buses on Route 2 travel east on Mulligan Avenue.

    ● true   ○ false

9. Bus Route 8 runs south on Gillian Street, east on Mulligan Avenue, and south again on Second Street.

    ● true   ○ false

10. Buses on Route 8 travel on four different streets.

    ● true   ○ false

11. Buses on Routes 6 and 8 travel past Riverside Park.

    ○ true   ● false

12. You can travel from Gillian Park to City Hall without changing buses.

    ● true   ○ false

13. To go from the corner of Hill Street and River Road to the corner of Mulligan Avenue and Layton Street, you must take three buses.

    ○ true   ● false

14. You cannot go on one bus from the corner of Gillian Street and Russell Road to the corner of Mulligan Avenue and Hill Street.

    ● true   ○ false

B. **Use the route map to answer each question.**

Answers will vary.

1. Rachel lives at the corner of Kensington Terrace and Mulligan Avenue. She wants to go to the library. Which bus routes should she use?

She can take Route 2 to Second Street and then take Route 8 south to Russell Road.

2. Timothy and his sisters are at the movie theater on the corner of Parkview Avenue and Hill Street. Which bus route can they take to go to Riverside Park? _____Route 6_____

3. How can Dr. Chin get to City Hall from the Medical Center?

Dr. Chin can take Route 8 to Gillian Street and Parkview Avenue and then take Route 1 west on

Parkview Avenue to City Hall.

4. Marvin wants to go from his house on Nevens Street and Parkview to the Forsyth Museum. What is the closest bus route? _____Route 1_____ What other route can he use to return home? _____Route 2_____

5. What two ways could Rosa travel from Strawtown School to Jake's Pet Store?

She could take an 8 bus and get off when it reaches Mulligan Avenue, changing to a 2 bus to Burton Street.

Or she could take an 8 bus to Second Street, changing to a 2 bus.

6. How can Mr. Goldman get from Master Street near River Road to the Fix-it Repair Shop?

He can walk to Russell Road and ride the 4 bus to Hill Street. Then he can change to the 6 bus

and ride it all the way to Lewis Boulevard.

unit six

For ESL/ELL support, see highlighted
words, page T106, and pages T28–T30.

Africa

For theme support, see page T26.

LESSON 55

Skill: Setting and Dialogue

For lesson support, see page T106.

BACKGROUND INFORMATION

"Talk" is a West African folktale that tells about strange events and talking objects. The main characters in the story are people who do everyday things near Accra, the capital city of Ghana. Here, Asante weavers are known for creating *kente* cloth. This colorful, patterned fabric is used to make clothing. Yams, or sweet potatoes, are another main product of this region.

SKILL FOCUS: Setting and Dialogue

Setting is the time and place of a story. A story can be set in the city or in the country, in a forest or on a boat at sea. The time could be the past, present, or future. The details of the setting may be stated directly. They can also be implied, or suggested, from the details in the story. Details about the setting can help the reader better imagine events and people in the story.

The characters in a story often talk to each other. This is called **dialogue**. In a novel or short story, quotation marks surround dialogue. Dialogue usually uses words of saying, such as *he said* or *she asked*. These words tell who is speaking. Both setting and dialogue help readers understand what happens in the story.

▶ Use the following lines from the story to answer the questions. Use complete sentences.

The farmer turned around and looked at his cow in amazement. The cow was chewing her cud and looking at him.

"Did you say something?" he asked.

The cow kept chewing and said nothing, but the man's dog spoke up.

"It wasn't the cow who spoke to you," the dog said. "It was the yam. The yam says leave him alone."

1. Who are the speakers of these lines?

A farmer and a dog speak the lines.

2. What can you tell about the setting?

The story takes place on a farm in the country. It is a

climate where yams can be found.

CONTEXT CLUES: Using a Dictionary

Sometimes there are not enough context clues in a story for you to understand a new word. When this happens, use a dictionary to learn a word's meaning. A **dictionary** is a book that tells how to pronounce words. It also tells what the words mean.

Read the following sentence from the story. Do you know what the underlined word means?

Once, not far from the city of Accra on the <u>Gulf</u> of Guinea, a country man went out to his garden to dig up some yams to take to market.

You might be able to tell from the context clues that a *gulf* is a landform. However, no clues tell you what kind of landform it is. You can use a dictionary to find out. You may want to finish what you are reading first and then look up the word.

▶ Look up the word *gulf* in a dictionary. Find the definition that describes a landform. Write the definition on the lines below.

The dictionary gives several definitions. The one that fits best

here is "a part of an ocean or sea extending into the land."

As you read the story "Talk," use a dictionary to look up the meaning of the underlined words *ford, wheezed,* and *refrain.*

Strategy Tip

As you read "Talk," notice who speaks as the story continues. Let the details help you imagine the setting.

Talk

Once, not far from the city of Accra on the Gulf of Guinea, a country man went out to his garden to dig up some yams to take to market. While he was digging, one of the yams said to him:

"Well, at last you're here. You never weeded me, but now you come around with your digging stick. Go away and leave me alone!"

The farmer turned around and looked at his cow in amazement. The cow was chewing her cud and looking at him.

"Did you say something?" he asked.

The cow kept chewing and said nothing, but the man's dog spoke up.

"It wasn't the cow who spoke to you," the dog said. "It was the yam. The yam says leave him alone."

The man became angry, because his dog had never talked before, and he didn't like his tone besides. So he took his knife and cut a branch from a palm tree to whip his dog. Just then the palm tree said:

"Put that branch down!"

The man was getting very upset about the way things were going, and he started to throw the palm branch away, but the palm branch said:

"Man, put me down softly!"

He put the branch down gently on a stone, and the stone said:

"Hey, take that thing off me!"

This was enough, and the frightened farmer started to run for his village. On the way he met a fisherman going the other way with a fish trap on his head.

"What's the hurry?" the fisherman asked.

"My yam said, 'Leave me alone!' Then the dog said, 'Listen to what the yam says!' When I went to whip the dog with a palm branch the tree said, 'Put that branch down!' Then the palm branch said, 'Do it softly!' Then the stone said, 'Take that thing off me!'"

"Is that all?" the man with the fish trap asked. "Is that so frightening?"

"Well," the man's fish trap said, "did he take it off the stone?"

"Wah!" the fisherman shouted. He threw the fish trap on the ground and began to run with the farmer, and on the

trail they met a weaver with a bundle of cloth on his head.

"Where are you going in such a rush?" he asked them.

"My yam said, 'Leave me alone!'" the farmer said. "The dog said, 'Listen to what the yam says!' The tree said, 'Put that branch down!' The branch said, 'Do it softly!' And the stone said, 'Take that thing off me!'"

"And then," the fisherman continued, "the fish trap said, 'Did he take it off?'"

"That's nothing to get excited about," the weaver said, "no reason at all."

"Oh yes it is," his bundle of cloth said. "If it happened to you you'd run too!"

"Wah!" the weaver shouted. He threw his bundle on the trail and started running with the other men.

They came panting to the <u>ford</u> in the river and found a man bathing.

"Are you chasing a gazelle?" he asked them.

The first man said breathlessly:

"My yam talked at me, and it said, 'Leave me alone!' And my dog said, 'Listen to your yam!' And when I cut myself a branch the tree said, 'Put that branch down!' And the branch said, 'Do it softly!' And the stone said, 'Take that thing off me!'"

The fisherman panted:

"And my trap said, 'Did he?'"

The weaver <u>wheezed</u>:

This illustration shows an Asante, or Ashanti, colony in Ghana during the 1800s.

"And my bundle of cloth said, 'You'd run too!'"

"Is that why you're running?" the man in the river asked.

"Well, wouldn't you run if you were in their position?" the river said.

The man jumped out of the water and began to run with the others. They ran down the main street of the village to the house of the chief. The chief's servants brought his stool out, and he came and sat on it to listen to their complaints. The men began to recite their troubles.

"I went out to my garden to dig yams," the farmer said, waving his arms. "Then everything began to talk! My yam said, 'Leave me alone!' My dog said, 'Pay attention to your yam!' The tree said, 'Put that branch down!' The branch said, 'Do it softly!' And the stone said, 'Take if off me!'"

"And my fish trap said, 'Well, did he take it off?'" the fisherman said.

"And my cloth said, 'You'd run too!'" the weaver said.

"And the river said the same," the bather said hoarsely, his eyes bulging.

The chief listened to them patiently, but he couldn't <u>refrain</u> from scowling.

"Now this is really a wild story," he said at last. "You'd better all go back to your work before I punish you for disturbing the peace."

So the men went away, and the chief shook his head and mumbled to himself, "Nonsense like that upsets the community."

"Fantastic, isn't it?" his stool said. "Imagine, a talking yam!"

COMPREHENSION

Recalling details
1. Who is the first character to speak?

The yam is the first character to speak.

Drawing conclusions
2. What is the setting at the beginning of the story?

The setting is the countryside near Accra, Ghana, on the Gulf of Guinea in Africa.

Drawing conclusions
3. Who told the farmer to put down the palm branch?

The palm tree told the farmer to put down the branch.

Making inferences
4. How did the fisherman feel when his fish trap spoke to him? How can you tell?

The fisherman felt frightened. He dropped his trap and ran away with the farmer.

Identifying cause and effect
5. Why did the men run to the village?

They wanted to speak with the village chief.

Recalling details
6. Where did the chief sit to listen to the men's story? He sat on his stool.

Making inferences
7. What did the chief think about their story?

He did not believe their story. He might have thought

they were crazy or were trying to fool him.

Recalling details
8. Who is the last character to speak?

The chief's stool is the last character to speak.

Making inferences
9. What is surprising about the ending?

The stool says it is fantastic to think that a yam could

talk.

Using context clues
10. On each line below, write the letter of the correct meaning in front of each word.

_c_ ford   **a.** to keep oneself from doing something

_b_ wheezed   **b.** breathed with difficulty, creating a whistling sound

_a_ refrain   **c.** a low spot in a river where it is easy to cross

CRITICAL THINKING

Making inferences
1. Why did the farmer ask if the cow had said something?

When the farmer looked around, the cow was looking at him.

Drawing conclusions
2. What kind of tone did the dog probably use when speaking?

Answers will vary. Possible answer: The dog probably spoke in a disrespectful or bossy tone.

Making inferences
3. Why was the weaver carrying cloth on his head?

The cloth is heavy and hard to balance. Carrying it on his head helps him walk and balance the cloth farther.

Drawing conclusions
4. Why did the bather ask if the farmer, fisherman, and weaver were chasing gazelles?

They were running fast, which is how gazelles run. A gazelle is a type of animal found in Africa.

Analyzing character
5. Why did the farmer, weaver, and others run away when animals and other things spoke?

It was strange to hear them and they did not know what to think. They were afraid and ran to seek help.

Drawing conclusions
6. Do you think the characters reacted in a normal or unusual way?

Answers will vary. Possible response: The characters reacted in a normal way because they were afraid and wanted to get

away. or The characters reacted in an unusual way because they ran from the problem instead of solving it.

7. Identify the message of this story. Put a ✔ in front of the sentence that best states the theme.

_____ It is scary when animals or nonliving things talk.

_✔_ People may be frightened when strange things happen.

_____ Village elders can listen to people's complaints.

SKILL FOCUS: SETTING AND DIALOGUE

Setting and dialogue are common parts of short stories. Use the dialogue and setting clues from the story "Talk" to fill in the correct settings and events below and on page 154.

1. Writers describe the setting and present different events to move the story along. Briefly tell about the setting and the important events in each part of the story.

A. **With the farmer:**

Setting: a garden outside of Accra

Characters: farmer, dog, cow, yam, palm tree, palm branch, stone

Event: The yam is angry at the farmer, who proposes to whip his dog.

B. **With the fisherman:**

Setting: on the way to the village

Characters: fisherman, farmer, fish trap

Event: The farmer tells what happened to him, the fish trap speaks, and both men run away.

C. **With the weaver:**

Setting: on the trail to the village

Characters: farmer, fisherman, weaver, bundle of cloth

Event: The farmer and fisherman tell what happened to them, the bundle of cloth speaks, and all three men run away.

D. **With the bather:**

Setting: a ford in the river

Characters: farmer, fisherman, weaver, bather, river

Event: The farmer, fisherman, and weaver tell their stories, the river speaks, and all four men run to the village.

E. With the chief:

Setting: outside the chief's house in the village

Character: farmer, fisherman, weaver, bather, chief, servants, stool

Event: The farmer, fisherman, weaver, and bather tell their stories to the chief, hoping he will do something about it; the chief scolds them for making up stories and sends them back to work; the stool makes a comment to the chief.

2. Reread the dialogue between the men and the village chief. Then answer the questions.

A. Who is in charge? What does the chief threaten to do to the men?

The chief is in charge and threatens to punish the men for making up nonsense.

B. What happens to the men? The chief sends them back to their work.

3. Match the character with the object each uses. Then describe what these details tell you about the people's way of life.

b	1. farmer	a.	trap
a	2. fisherman	b.	cow
e	3. weaver	c.	stool
d	4. bather	d.	river
c	5. chief	e.	cloth

Way of Life: Answers will vary. These details show that the people live a simple life. It shows that they live off the land.

Leaders have bigger and stronger things, such as stools, than other people.

Reading-Writing Connection

Imagine a situation in your own life in which a nonliving thing talks. Write a brief dialogue between you and the thing. Remember to use words of saying. Add details that describe the setting.

Skill: Reading a Map

For lesson support, see page T107.

BACKGROUND INFORMATION

The next selection is about the Great Rift Valley, a series of deep valleys that cut through eastern Africa. It runs north to south, from Ethiopia to Mozambique. In some places, the valley's steep walls rise a mile (1.6 kilometers) high. The valleys were formed millions of years ago by shifts deep within the Earth. Today the region is known for its beautiful lakes, grasslands, and mountains.

SKILL FOCUS: Reading a Map

Two types of maps—physical maps and political maps—are often found in newspapers, magazines, and textbooks. A **physical map** shows features on the Earth's surface, such as mountains, lakes, rivers, plains, and plateaus. These features are often shown by different colors or shades of one color. A **political map** shows the location and boundaries of countries, states, capital cities, and other important cities. When a map combines the features of both types of maps, it is called a **physical/political map.**

Most maps have a scale of distance and a key. A scale helps you measure distances between two points on a map. A key explains the colors and symbols used on a map.

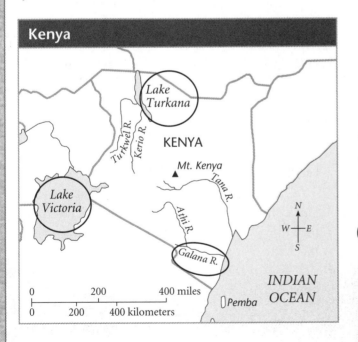

Kenya

Reading a map along with a text will give you more information than either one could provide alone.

▶ Is the map of Kenya on this page a physical map or a political map? How do you know? Circle three surface features on the map.

Physical map; it shows features on the Earth's surface.

CONTEXT CLUES: Appositives

If you don't know the meaning of a word as you read, often a word that follows it will help you figure out the unknown word. This word is called an **appositive.**

Read the sentence below. Look for an appositive that explains the underlined word.

Most of the volcanoes near the valley are now ***extinct****, or dead.*

If you do not know the meaning of *extinct* in this instance, the appositive *or dead* will help. Usually an appositive is set off by commas or dashes.

▶ Read these sentences from the selection. Circle the appositive, and answer the question below.

As these plates move apart, they tear the continent above. This creates a rift, or crack, in the Earth's crust.

What word does the appositive explain?

rift

While reading the next selection, look for the underlined words *dormant*, *craters*, and *savannas*. Use appositives as context clues to help you figure out the meanings of the words.

Strategy Tip

As you read "The Great Rift Valley," look at the physical and political maps. What surface features does the physical map show? What countries and cities do you see? Be sure to use the map keys to learn more about the Great Rift Valley.

THE GREAT RIFT VALLEY

The continent of Africa is tearing apart. Deep below eastern Africa, **tectonic plates** (tek TAHN ik playts) are moving away from each other. Tectonic plates are giant sections of rock that make up the Earth. As these plates move apart, they tear the continent above. This creates a rift, or crack, in the Earth's crust. As sections of the continent move in opposite directions, the land between them stretches thin. Then it drops, creating deep valleys.

These movements in the Earth have created a dramatic landscape. It is called the Great Rift Valley. The rift cuts across eastern Africa for about 2,800 miles (4,500 kilometers). It goes all the way from Ethiopia to Mozambique.

Astronauts orbiting the Earth can spot the Great Rift Valley. It is between 30 and 50 miles (50 and 80 kilometers) wide. In some places, the rift is about 3,000 feet (900 meters) deep.

A close look at a map shows that the Great Rift Valley has two branches. The Eastern Rift runs through Ethiopia, Kenya, and Tanzania to Malawi.

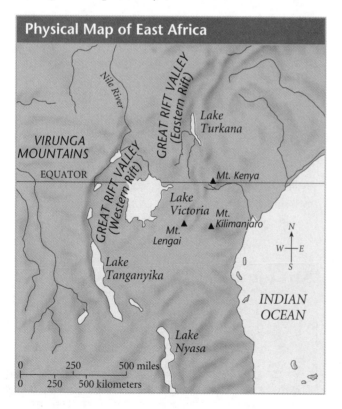

Physical Map of East Africa

Nile River

GREAT RIFT VALLEY (Eastern Rift)

VIRUNGA MOUNTAINS

GREAT RIFT VALLEY (Western Rift)

EQUATOR

Lake Turkana

Mt. Kenya

Lake Victoria

Mt. Kilimanjaro

Mt. Lengai

Lake Tanganyika

INDIAN OCEAN

Lake Nyasa

N W E S

0   250   500 miles
0   250   500 kilometers

The Western Rift runs along the border of the Republic of the Congo, Uganda, Rwanda, and Tanzania. The two branches come together in Malawi.

Formed by Fire

The Great Rift Valley has been growing for a long time. More than 20 million years ago, earthquakes first split the Earth's crust there. **Lava** (LAHV ə) poured out, piling up volcanoes. Today the process continues deep underground. The Great Rift Valley widens by 0.04 inch (1 millimeter) a year. That is only 4 inches (10 centimeters) a century. Still, if the process continues for millions of years, the rift could break the continent apart. Then an ocean might cover Kenya and Tanzania. Somalia to the east could become an island.

Most of the volcanoes near the valley are now extinct, or dead. The two highest mountains in Africa, Mount Kilimanjaro in Tanzania and Mount Kenya in Kenya, for example, are extinct volcanoes. Other volcanoes in the region are dormant, or resting. They could erupt again some day. Mount Lengai in Tanzania last erupted in 1966. It covered the Great Rift Valley with ash.

Some of the volcanoes collapsed millions of years ago. They left behind deep craters, or holes, in the Earth. These craters can be more than 12 miles (19 kilometers) across. Dotted with ponds and marshes, they are a favorite habitat, or home, for many animals.

Fertile Grasslands

One African myth says that the first animals on Earth emerged from an extinct volcano. From there, the animals spread out on the green plains. In a way, the myth is true. Over time, volcanic ash formed rich soil in the Great Rift Valley. Some of Africa's most fertile and rich land is in this valley.

The savannas, or grasslands, of the Great Rift Valley are home to a huge number of animals. Antelopes and wildebeests, elephants and zebras all graze here. Giraffes and antelopes browse on the bushes and treetops. Lions, leopards, and other big cats prey on the grazing animals.

The savannas of the Great Rift Valley are home to many animals.

Beyond the savannas are the steep slopes of the valley walls. If you hiked up these slopes, you would pass through jungles. Next you would reach cool forests. Higher still, you would reach ice glaciers. The mountains along the Great Rift Valley are covered with snow all year.

A Land of Lakes

Almost all of Africa's large lakes lie in the Great Rift Valley, where water flows naturally into the deep parts of the valley. Lake Tanganyika, for example, is the second deepest lake on Earth. It fills a tremendous **fault**, or crack, in the Earth. Lake Victoria is found between the Eastern Rift and the Western Rift. Lake Victoria is the source of the Nile River and has the largest surface area of any African lake.

You wouldn't want to swim in most lakes in eastern Africa. The water is very salty and filled with minerals from volcanic rock. Some lakes are so salty that they would blind you if you swam in them.

Often the lakes are dark green. Only tiny plants, called algae, live in them. Other lakes support only shrimp. Millions of flamingos swirl in pink clouds over these lakes. The birds get their pink color from eating the shrimp.

A Living Lab for Scientists

Kenya, Tanzania, and other African countries have created many national parks in the Great Rift Valley. The parks preserve the land and animals for all time. At Gombe National Park in Tanzania, the scientist, Dr. Jane Goodall, studied chimpanzees for 30 years. In Kenya's Amboseli National Park, Dr. Cynthia Moss lived with elephants to study them. Dian Fossey worked to save the gorillas in the volcanic mountains. The African parks are a living lab for scientists.

The Great Rift Valley holds many fossils, too. As the rift widened, ancient bones were brought close to the surface. The ash that covers the fossils helps scientists tell the age of the bones.

Olduvai Gorge in Tanzania is a famous fossil site. Scientists have found many human bones there. One set of human footprints there is 3.5 million years old. Scientists also found a four-million-year-old skeleton of a boy. For a long, long time, the Great Rift Valley has provided a dramatic and rich habitat for humans as well as animals.

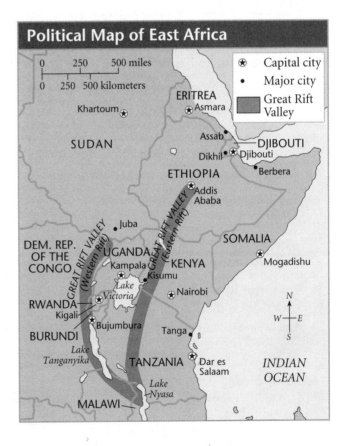

Recalling details
1. How long and how wide is the Great Rift Valley in eastern Africa?

The valley is 2,800 miles (4,500 kilometers) long and

between 30 and 50 miles (50 and 80 kilometers) wide.

Recalling details
2. About how long ago did the rift in Eastern Africa first begin to develop?

The rift began developing more than 20 million years

ago.

Recalling details
3. Through which countries does the Eastern Rift pass?

The Eastern Rift passes through Ethiopia, Kenya,

Tanzania, and Malawi.

Comparing and contrasting
4. How are Lake Tanganyika and Lake Victoria different from each other?

Lake Tanganyika is deeper; Lake Victoria has more

surface area.

Comparing and contrasting
5. How are Mount Kilimanjaro and Mount Lengai different from each other?

Mount Kilimanjaro is an extinct volcano. Mount Lengai

is dormant and last erupted in 1966.

Identifying cause and effect
6. Why is the soil of the Great Rift Valley so rich?

Over the years, the volcanic ash has added many

minerals to the soil.

Identifying cause and effect
7. Why is the Great Rift Valley a good place to search for fossils?

The movement of the earth has brought very old fossils

close to the surface.

Recalling details
8. Which scientist is well known for her study of chimpanzees in eastern Africa?

Dr. Jane Goodall is well known for studying

chimpanzees in eastern Africa.

Identifying the main idea
9. Reread the paragraph that has an ✗ next to it. Underline the sentence in the paragraph that states its main idea.

Using context clues
10. Underline the word that correctly completes each sentence.

a. The collapsing volcanoes left deep

_____ in the valley floor.

    <u>craters</u>   algae   savannas

b. The wide grasslands of eastern Africa

are called _____.

    rifts   craters   <u>savannas</u>

c. A volcano that could erupt after years of

silent is said to be _____.

    <u>dormant</u>   extinct   volcanic

Drawing conclusions
1. The Great Rift Valley is said to be widening by about 1 millimeter a year. How do you think scientists know this for sure?

Answers will vary. Scientists have probably taken careful measurements at various points in the valley.

By measuring the same distance year after year, they can note small changes.

Making inferences
2. Discuss why you think the countries of East Africa have created so many national parks in the Great Rift Valley.

Answers will vary. They realize that the valley is a unique and beautiful landscape.

or They want to preserve the land and the animals that live there.

Making inferences
3. The selection mentions an African myth about the first animals emerging from a volcano. Explain why the author says, "In a way, the myth is true."

Answers will vary. Ash from the volcanoes made the soil very rich. This created the

fertile savannas that support many animals.

Inferring cause and effect
4. Why do you think many lakes in the Great Rift Valley support only algae or small shrimp?

The water is too salty for most fish to survive.

Inferring main idea and supporting details
5. Only one of the following statements expresses the unstated main idea of the selection you just read. Underline this statement that identifies the unstated main idea.

   a. The Great Rift Valley is a region of many contrasts that is slowly being torn apart.

   b. The Great Rift Valley in Africa is a land of earthquakes and volcanoes.

   c. The Great Rift Valley is a dramatic and rich natural environment formed by movements under the Earth.

   d. The Great Rift Valley cuts across East Africa for about 2,800 miles.

Inferring main idea and supporting details
6. On the lines below, write at least five supporting details that tell about the unstated main idea. You can go back to the selection to find the supporting details. Answers will vary.

   a. Even astronauts in space can see the Great Rift Valley.

   b. The highest mountains in Africa are in the valley.

   c. Almost all of Africa's largest lakes lie within the Great Rift Valley.

   d. Millions of flamingos swirl over the lakes in pink clouds.

   e. The grasslands of the Great Rift Valley support many grazing animals.

SKILL FOCUS: READING A MAP

Use the maps on pages 156 and 157 to answer the following questions.

1. Which city is Kenya's capital? How do you know?

   The capital of Kenya is Nairobi. It is marked by a ⊛.

2. Name a city in Tanzania that is not the capital. How do you know it is a city?

   Tanga; it is marked by a •.

3. From north to south, about how long is Lake Tanganyika? What feature of the map will you use to find out?

   Lake Tanganyika is about 400 miles (640 kilometers) long. The distance scale shows this.

4. Locate Mount Kilimanjaro and Mount Kenya on the map. Which mountain is north of the equator? Which is south of the equator?

   Mount Kenya is north of the equator; Mount Kilimanjaro is south of the equator.

5. Based on the map scale, what is the greatest distance between the eastern and western branches of the Great Rift Valley?

   The two branches are about 400 miles (640 kilometers) apart.

6. With which other African countries does Kenya share borders?

   Somalia, Ethiopia, Sudan, Uganda, and Tanzania all border Kenya.

7. In what direction would you sail across Lake Victoria to get from Kisumu in Kenya to Kampala in Uganda?

   You would sail west.

8. Which capital city is directly east of Khartoum? Of which country is it the capital?

   Asmara; it is the capital of Eritrea.

9. Why would it be difficult to measure the exact length of the Great Rift Valley using the distance scale?

   The Rift system has several branches. The branches curve and twist. Since the valleys are not straight,

   it would be hard to measure their length.

10. What lake is found near where the Eastern and Western Rifts come together in Malawi?

   Lake Nyasa is found near where the Rifts come together.

Reading-Writing Connection

What mountains, deserts, oceans, rivers, or lakes are in your part of the country? What landforms are important there? How do these features of the land affect the way people live and work? On a separate sheet of paper, write a few paragraphs describing the landforms of your region.

LESSON 57

For ESL/ELL support, see highlighted
words, page T108, and pages T28–T30.

Skill: Making Inferences

For lesson support, see page T108.

BACKGROUND INFORMATION

"Antelopes" is about the many kinds of swift, graceful antelopes that live on the plains of Africa. These include gazelles (gə ZELZ), elands (EE ləndz), and impalas (im PAL əz). You may be surprised to learn that these graceful animals belong to the same family as cows. Like cows on a farm, antelopes eat mainly grass. Also, both antelopes and cows have a special four-part stomach.

SKILL FOCUS: Making Inferences

Writers don't tell you everything in a text. Sometimes you have to **make inferences**, or figure out information that is not stated. To make an inference, you need to combine the details in a selection with what you already know.

Read the following paragraph. As you read, try to make inferences about lions and antelopes.

> *A group of female lions sneaks up on a herd of antelopes. The lions keep low, blending in with the dry grass around them. The lions quietly surround their prey. The lions stay downwind of the antelopes, so that the creatures cannot smell them. At the last minute, the lions attack with a short burst of speed.*

The paragraph tells you that the lions blend in with the dry grass around them. You know from your own experience that dry grass turns yellow or brown. Therefore you can infer that lions are the same yellowish-brown color as dry grass.

To make inferences, think carefully about the details in a text. Then think about what you already know. Combine the details in the text with your own knowledge. In that way, you can infer something that the author does not state directly.

(Details from text) + (What I know) = (Inference)

▶ Read the paragraph about lions and antelopes again. Then think about what you already know about wild animals. Fill in the chart in the next column to make an inference about why the

lions sneak up on the antelopes and attack only at the last minute.

Details from text		What I know		Inference
Lions hide and attack antelopes at the last minute with a burst of speed.	+	Lions prey on antelopes. Antelopes run faster and for longer periods of time.	=	Lions need to sneak up on antelopes or the antelopes would be able to run away from them.

CONTEXT CLUES: Definitions

Some context clues are **definitions**. Authors of science articles, for example, will often tell you the exact meaning of an unfamiliar word.

Look for the definition of the underlined word in these sentences.

> *Some antelopes have **spiral** horns. Spiral means "turned or twisted."*

If you don't know the meaning of *spiral*, the second sentence tells you its definition. A definition of a new word may appear before or after the word.

▶ In the sentences below, circle the definition of the underlined word.

> *Like deer, antelope are **herbivorous** animals. Herbivorous means (eating only grass, leaves, and fruit.)*

While reading "Antelopes," look for the definitions of the underlined words *permanent*, *chambers*, and *digestive*.

Strategy Tip

As you read "Antelopes," pay close attention to the facts and details. Combine this information with what you already know to make inferences about antelopes.

Antelopes

1. Antelopes are deerlike animals that live in the grassy plains of eastern and southern Africa and in parts of Asia. Like deer, antelopes are **herbivorous** (hər BIV ər əs) animals. Herbivorous means eating only grass, leaves, and fruit. All antelopes have two-toed hoofs and hollow horns. Some antelopes have spiral horns. *Spiral* means "turned or twisted." Others have straight horns. Antelope horns are different from a deer's antlers. A deer sheds its antlers every year and grows new ones. Antelopes have underline{permanent} horns. *Permanent* means "lasting for a long time."

✔ 2. There are more than 150 different kinds of antelopes. Most of them live in Africa. Antelopes range in size from the large eland to the tiny dik-dik.

The eland may stand up to 6 feet (1.8 meters) tall at the shoulder. It may weigh up to 1,500 pounds (680 kilograms). The dik-dik is about 2 feet long (61 centimeters), roughly the size of a jack rabbit.

3. All antelopes are built for running. They use speed to get away from their enemies. They can usually outrun wild dogs, cheetahs, leopards, and lions. Antelopes can run at high speeds for a longer time than the big cats can.

4. Gazelles and impalas are two of the fastest and most graceful antelopes. Gazelles are 2 to 3 feet (60 to 90 centimeters) tall at the shoulder. They can run as fast as 60 miles (96 kilometers) per hour for short distances. Impalas are about 3 feet

Eland

Dik-dik

Gazelle

Impala

(90 centimeters) tall at the shoulder. Impalas can cover 30 feet (9 meters) in one leap.

5. Antelopes are in the animal group called **ruminants** (ROO mə nənts). Ruminants include cattle, goats, deer, and giraffes. Most of these animals have horns and split hoofs. What makes ruminants different from other hoofed animals is that their stomachs have four <u>chambers</u>. A chamber is a closed space.

6. When a ruminant eats grass or leaves, it swallows them without much chewing. The food is then stored in the first chamber of the stomach. This chamber is called the **rumen** (ROO min). The food then slowly moves to the second chamber. The second chamber is called the **reticulum** (re TIK yə ləm). In the reticulum, the food is changed to a sticky substance called **cud**. Later, when the animal is relaxed, the muscles of the reticulum send the cud back up to the mouth. The animal chews its cud thoroughly and swallows a second time. Then the cud passes through the rumen and the reticulum again and moves into a third chamber. The third chamber is called the **omasum** (oh MAY səm). From the omasum, the cud goes into the fourth chamber. This chamber is called the **abomasum** (AB ə MAY səm). In the abomasum, the cud mixes with <u>digestive</u> fluids and is completely

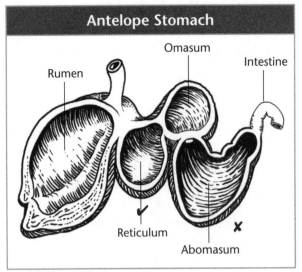

Antelope Stomach

Rumen · Omasum · Intestine · Reticulum · Abomasum

This diagram shows the four chambers of an antelope's stomach.

broken down. *Digestive* means "helping to break down food so that it can be used by the body." Finally the digested food enters the small intestine, where it is sent into the animal's bloodstream.

7. Certain types of antelopes are now in danger of being wiped out because cattle now graze on more and more land that was once used by wild animals. Hunters kill antelopes for meat. However laws are being passed to prevent antelopes from becoming extinct.

COMPREHENSION

Recalling details
1. What do herbivorous animals eat?

   Herbivorous animals eat grass, leaves, and fruit.

Recalling details
2. Contrast a deer's antlers with an antelope's horns.

   A deer's antlers are shed every year. An antelope's

   horns are permanent.

Recalling details
3. What is the largest type of antelope?

   The eland is the largest type of antelope.

Identifying the main idea
4. Reread the paragraph with a ✔ next to it. Underline the sentence that has the main idea.

Reading text with diagrams
5. On the diagram of a ruminant's stomach, put a ✔ next to the chamber where the food is changed to cud. Put an ✘ next to the chamber where the cud mixes with digestive fluids.

Using context clues
6. Underline the word or words that correctly complete each sentence.

   a. Something that is permanent _____.

   changes often   <u>lasts a long time</u>
   breaks easily

   b. A closed-off area is a _____.

   <u>chamber</u>   digestive   ruminant

   c. Digestive juices help to _____.

   dissolve metal   burn oxygen
   <u>break down food</u>

CRITICAL THINKING

Circle the letter next to each correct answer.

Making inferences

1. If an antelope could not outrun its enemy, it could use its _____ to defend itself.

   a. sharp teeth   **c.** horns

   b. antlers   **d.** sharp claws

Inferring cause and effect

2. A wild dog probably wouldn't hunt an eland because _____.

   a. elands are too strong for them

   b. elands are too fast for them

   c. elands are too difficult to see

   d. elands are not very tasty

Inferring the unstated main idea

3. Which of the following sentences states the main idea of Paragraph 6?

   a. Ruminants often have digestive problems because their stomachs have four chambers.

   b. Ruminants eat many different types of food.

   c. The digestive process of ruminants is complicated.

   d. Ruminants swallow grass or leaves without much chewing.

SKILL FOCUS: MAKING INFERENCES

Read the following group of statements. Put a ✔ next to the statement or statements that can be inferred from the paragraph listed. Then, on the lines that follow, write details from the paragraph and what you already know that helped you make the inferences.

Paragraph 1 (check two)

_✔_ Most antelopes live in a warm climate.

_✔_ Most antelopes have long, slim legs.

_____ Most antelopes have pointed teeth.

Details From Paragraph: Antelopes live in parts of Asia and in the dry, grassy plains of eastern and southern Africa.

What I Know: Answers will vary. These areas have a warm climate.

Details From Paragraph: Antelopes are deerlike animals.

What I Know: Answers will vary. Deer have long, slim legs.

Paragraph 3 (check two)

_✔_ Some antelopes hide from their enemies.

_✔_ Antelopes need to be very alert because they have many enemies.

_____ If a cheetah can't catch an antelope in the first few minutes of a chase, the antelope will escape.

Details From Paragraph: They can usually outrun wild dogs, cheetahs, leopards, and lions.

What I Know: Answers will vary. Animals that have many enemies must constantly be on guard.

Details From Paragraph: Antelopes can run at high speeds for a longer time than the big cats.

What I Know: Answers will vary. Because an antelope can keep up a high speed for a longer time,

it would escape if the cheetah didn't catch it quickly.

Paragraph 6 (check one)

  ✔   A ruminant's way of eating and digesting its food helps it to survive when enemies are nearby.

_____ Ruminants are larger than other hoofed animals.

_____ Ruminants prefer grass to leaves.

Details From Paragraph: When a ruminant eats grass or leaves, it swallows them without chewing.

What I Know: Answers will vary. When enemies are near, a ruminant can eat quickly and be ready

to run away if necessary. It can then chew its cud later when it knows that it is safe.

Paragraph 7 (check one)

_____ Cattle do not like antelopes.

  ✔   Africa is becoming more developed.

_____ Grazing cattle is against the law in Africa.

Details From Paragraph: Cattle are grazed on more and more land that was once used by wild animals.

What I Know: Answers will vary. More cattle ranches are being set up in Africa.

Reading-Writing Connection

On a separate sheet of paper, write a paragraph comparing and contrasting deer and antelope. Tell ways in which the two animals are alike and ways in which they are different.

LESSON 58

For ESL/ELL support, see highlighted
words, page T109, and pages T28–T30.

Skill: Reading Fractions

For lesson support, see page T109.

BACKGROUND INFORMATION

In the next selection, you will learn how to read
fractions. When you understand fractions, you will be
able to solve many types of problems in real life, in
math class, and in other subject areas. For example,
suppose you were in a supermarket. Two pounds of
hamburger are more than you need, and 1 pound is
not enough. You might need to buy $1\frac{1}{2}$ pounds.

Sometimes you will need to measure things in
fractions, or parts, of whole numbers. A recipe, for
example, might call for $\frac{1}{2}$ cup of sugar or $\frac{1}{3}$ cup of
milk. A gas tank that is less than half full will need
to be filled.

SKILL FOCUS: Reading Fractions

A **fraction** is part of a whole. In a fraction, one
number is written above a line and another is
written below, like the following.

$$\frac{3}{4}$$

You read these two numbers together as *three-fourths*.

The bottom number in a fraction tells how many
equal parts there are in the whole. The top number
tells how many equal parts of the whole are being
used. The following square, for example, shows the
fraction $\frac{3}{4}$. In all, there are four equal parts. Three of
the parts are shaded, or being used.

The following circle shows the fraction $\frac{1}{3}$. In all,
there are three equal parts. One of the parts is
shaded, or being used.

This rectangle shows the fraction $\frac{2}{5}$. There are five
equal parts. Two of the parts are shaded.

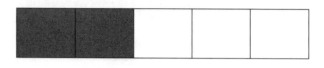

▶ Shade the rectangle below so that it shows the
fraction $\frac{1}{3}$.

Shade in 1
of the three
sections.

WORD CLUES

A mathematics selection will often include
definitions of new terms. When you come to a
word you don't understand, check to see if its
definition is nearby.

In "How to Read Fractions," there are two words
that are important for you to understand. They are
numerator and *denominator*. Both of these math
words are defined in the selection. Look for the
definitions to help you read and understand fractions.

Strategy Tip

When reading about fractions, it is important to
study the diagrams closely. The diagrams show
what the text means. Read the text and look at
the diagrams several times if necessary.

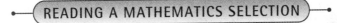
How to Read Fractions

✔ A fraction shows a part of a whole. Suppose that you broke a stick into three equal parts. The fraction $\frac{1}{3}$ describes each part. You read this as *one-third*. If you have two of the parts, you have $\frac{2}{3}$ (two-thirds) of the whole stick. The fraction $\frac{2}{3}$ is larger than $\frac{1}{3}$. If you have $\frac{2}{3}$ of the stick, you have more parts of the whole than someone with $\frac{1}{3}$.

In the fraction $\frac{2}{3}$, the bottom number shows the number of parts into which the whole has been divided. It is called the <u>denominator</u> (di NAHM ə nay tər). The top number shows the number of parts that you have. It is called the <u>numerator</u> (NOO mə ray tər).

FIGURE 1.

In Figure 1, the whole has been divided into three equal parts. Two of these parts are shaded. The fraction $\frac{2}{3}$ (two-thirds) can stand for the shaded parts of the whole.

Remember that in order to show fractions, the whole must first be divided into *equal* parts. Each part must be exactly the same size. Look at the diagrams in Figure 2. Into how many parts has each whole been divided?

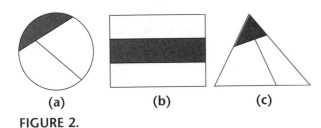

    (a)   (b)   (c)

FIGURE 2.

Only one diagram is divided into three *equal* parts. Only Figure 2(b) shows the fraction $\frac{1}{3}$ (one-third).

Look at Figure 3. Into how many equal parts has the whole been divided? How many parts are shaded? What fraction shows how many of the parts are shaded?

The fraction $\frac{2}{6}$ (two-sixths) is correct.

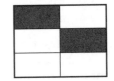

FIGURE 3.

Figures 4–6, below, show three more fractions. Study the diagrams and labels carefully.

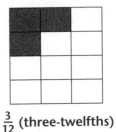

$\frac{3}{12}$ (three-twelfths)

FIGURE 4.

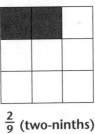

$\frac{2}{9}$ (two-ninths)

FIGURE 5.

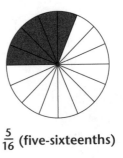

$\frac{5}{16}$ (five-sixteenths)

FIGURE 6.

MATHEMATICS

Recalling details
1. A fraction shows a ____part____ of a whole.

Recalling details
2. The bottom number in a fraction is called the ____denominator____.

Recalling details
3. The top number in a fraction is called the ____numerator____.

Recalling details
4. A fraction shows a whole divided into ____equal____ parts.

Identifying the main idea
5. Reread the paragraph that has a ✔ next to it. Underline the sentence that has the main idea.

Using context clues
6. The denominator shows _the number of parts into_ _which the whole has been divided_ _____.

Making inferences
7. The numerator shows _the number of parts you_ _have_ _____.

CRITICAL THINKING

Put a ✔ on the line next to the two situations in which you would use fractions.

_____ a. when you go through the check-out counter at a grocery store

__✔__ b. when you want to share a pie equally among several people

_____ c. when you keep track of weekly attendance

__✔__ d. when you are measuring cooking ingredients

_____ e. when you read a bus schedule

SKILL FOCUS: READING FRACTIONS

A. Look at the diagrams below. Put a check mark below the diagram in which the whole has been divided into equal parts.

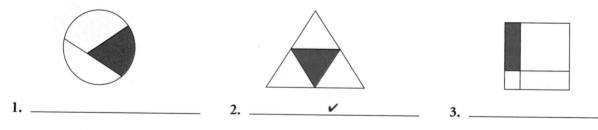

1. _____   2. ____✔____   3. _____

B. Look at the diagrams below. In each diagram, a whole has been divided into equal parts. Write the fraction that stands for the shaded parts of the whole. Write your answer on the line below each diagram.

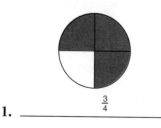 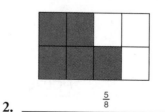

1. ____$\frac{3}{4}$____   2. ____$\frac{5}{8}$____   3. ____$\frac{2}{4}$____

C. Shade in each diagram below to show the fraction next to it.

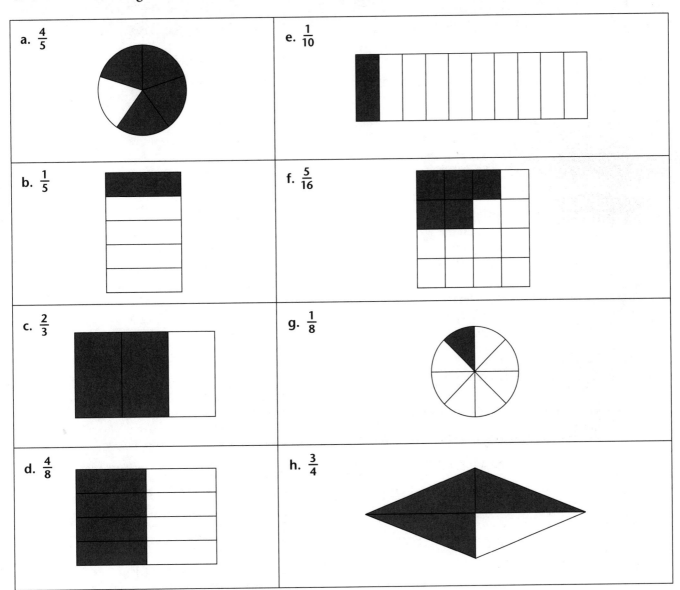

a. $\frac{4}{5}$

e. $\frac{1}{10}$

b. $\frac{1}{5}$

f. $\frac{5}{16}$

c. $\frac{2}{3}$

g. $\frac{1}{8}$

d. $\frac{4}{8}$

h. $\frac{3}{4}$

Reading-Writing Connection

On a separate sheet of paper, write a paragraph to describe two recent situations in which you used fractions. In what ways did you use them?

Skill: Multiple-Meaning Words

For lesson support, see page T110.

Sometimes words that we use every day have entirely different meanings when used in science, geography, history, or mathematics. Some words with **multiple meanings** are listed below.

bed	crop	bank	cape	date	scale
pole	yard	bark	check	mouth	school

Read the two definitions for number 1 below. One definition is its everyday meaning. The other is its meaning in science, mathematics, or social studies. Choose a word from the list above that goes with those two definitions. Write the word on the line. Complete the rest of the lesson the same way.

1. **Everyday Meaning:** opening in the head through which food is taken in
Geography Meaning: place where a river empties into a larger body of water
Word: _____ mouth _____

2. **Everyday Meaning:** written order to the bank to pay money to someone
Mathematics Meaning: test the answers to problems to make sure that they are right
Word: _____ check _____

3. **Everyday Meaning:** long, thin piece of wood
Geography Meaning: point farthest north or south on Earth
Word: _____ pole _____

4. **Everyday Meaning:** fruit of a type of palm tree
History Meaning: exact point in time at which an event takes place
Word: _____ date _____

5. **Everyday Meaning:** piece of furniture to sleep on
Geography Meaning: bottom of a river
Word: _____ bed _____

6. **Everyday Meaning:** short, sharp noise made by dogs
Science Meaning: outer covering of a tree
Word: _____ bark _____

7. **Everyday Meaning:** ground around or next to a house or other building
Mathematics Meaning: measure of length
Word: _____ yard _____

8. **Everyday Meaning:** sleeveless article of clothing worn around the shoulders
Geography Meaning: piece of land extending into water
Word: _____ cape _____

9. **Everyday Meaning:** place to deposit money
Geography Meaning: land along the edge of a river
Word: _____ bank _____

10. **Everyday Meaning:** place for learning
Science Meaning: large number of fish traveling in a group
Word: _____ school _____

11. **Everyday Meaning:** weighing machine
Science Meaning: small, flat, hard plate forming part of the covering of fishes and reptiles
Word: _____ scale _____

12. **Everyday Meaning:** the grain, fruit, or vegetables grown during one season
Science Meaning: a pouch in the throat of some birds
Word: _____ crop _____

Skill: Prefixes

For lesson support, see page T110.

In your reading, you will often find a word that has a **prefix** added to the beginning of it. A prefix is a word part that changes the meaning of a word. Look at the following four prefixes and their meanings.

Prefix	Meaning
un-	not
in-	in, toward
re-	back, again
pre-	before

A. Write one of the prefixes above on the line next to each word below. Make the new word mean the same thing as the phrase that follows it.

1. ___un___ fastened = not fastened
2. ___re___ check = to check again
3. ___pre___ view = to view before
4. ___in___ land = toward the land
5. ___re___ appear = to appear again

6. ___re___ call = to call back
7. ___un___ covered = not covered
8. ___re___ view = to view again
9. ___pre___ test = before the test
10. ___un___ pleasant = not pleasant

B. Below are some words that contain prefixes. Think about the meaning of the prefix at the beginning of each word. Then write the meaning of the word.

1. uneven ___not even___
2. redo ___to do again___
3. unable ___not able___
4. unusual ___not usual___
5. inland ___in the land___
6. repaint ___to paint again___
7. preheat ___to heat before___
8. redraw ___to draw again___
9. unsafe ___not safe___
10. inset ___to set in___

11. preschool ___before regular school___
12. prejudge ___to judge before___
13. input ___to put in___
14. unbend ___to not bend___
15. reread ___to read again___
16. prearrange ___to arrange before___
17. reclaim ___to claim again___
18. rearrange ___to arrange again___
19. inshore ___toward the shore___
20. unselfish ___not selfish___

Skill: Suffixes

For lesson support, see page T111.

Many words have **suffixes** added to the ends of them. A suffix is a word part that changes the meaning of the word. The meanings of five suffixes are given below. Suffixes often have several meanings. The most common meanings are given here.

Suffix	Meaning
-er	one who does
-en	made of, to become
-ful	full of
-ly	like in appearance or manner
-ness	quality or state of

A. Write one of the suffixes above on the line next to each base word below. Make the new word mean the same thing as the phrase that follows it.

1. wonder ___ful___ = full of wonder

2. hard ___en___ = to become hard

3. quick ___ly___ = in a quick manner

4. dark ___ness___ = the state of being dark

5. sing ___er___ = one who sings

6. spoon ___ful___ = a full spoon

7. buy ___er___ = one who buys

8. earth ___en___ = made of earth

9. brother ___ly___ = like a brother

10. own ___er___ = one who owns

B. Below are some words that contain suffixes. Think about the meaning of the suffix at the end of each word. Then write the meaning of the word.

1. worker ___one who works___

2. queenly ___like a queen___

3. thickness ___the quality of being thick___

4. sisterly ___like a sister___

5. teacher ___one who teaches___

6. powerful ___full of power___

7. wooden ___made of wood___

8. planter ___one who plants___

9. fatherly ___like a father___

10. fighter ___one who fights___

11. kindness ___the quality of being kind___

12. rancher ___one who owns a ranch___

13. leader ___one who leads___

14. friendly ___like a friend___

15. darkness ___the quality of being dark___

16. strengthen ___to become strong___

17. joyful ___full of joy___

18. loudness ___the state of being loud___

Skill: Using an Encyclopedia

For lesson support, see page T111.

As you study science, social studies, and mathematics, you will need to look up more information about a topic. An excellent source for additional information is a set of books called an **encyclopedia**.

Look at the picture of an encyclopedia. The volumes are numbered in alphabetical order. Each volume has one or more letters on its spine showing that topics beginning with the letter or letters are in that volume.

For example, words beginning with *a* would be found in Volume 1. Words beginning with *t, u,* and *v* would be found in Volume 14.

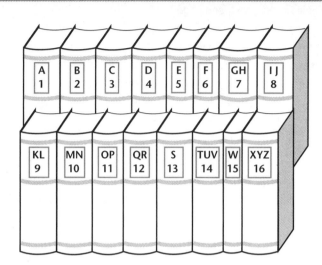

Use the picture of the encyclopedia to answer the following questions. Fill in the circle next to the correct answer.

1. Ken looked at Volume 5. What do you think he was looking up?

    ○ **a.** butterflies   ● **c.** elephants

    ○ **b.** giraffes   ○ **d.** antelopes

2. Felipe wanted to find information about reptiles. Which volume did he need?

    ○ **a.** 5   ○ **b.** 9   ● **c.** 12   ○ **d.** 0

3. After he read about reptiles, Abdul decided to look up crocodiles and snakes. Which two volumes did he use?

    ● **a.** 3 and 13   ○ **c.** 14 and 3

    ○ **b.** 3 and 10   ○ **d.** 4 and 13

4. Shannon had Volume 10. What might she have looked up?

    ○ **a.** parrots and plants

    ○ **b.** seals and snakes

    ● **c.** mammals and moss

    ○ **d.** nuts and owls

5. At the end of the article on salmon, Yuan found a note that read "*See fish.*" Which volume did he need next?

    ○ **a.** 3   ● **b.** 6   ○ **c.** 8   ○ **d.** 4

6. Belicia wanted to find out all about dogs. What three topics might she have looked up?

    ○ **a.** dogs, cats, and birds

    ● **b.** dogs, pets, and mammals

    ○ **c.** dogs, reptiles, and snakes

    ○ **d.** dogs, lions, and tigers

7. Bob had to do a report on salmon. Which volume did he need?

    ○ **a.** 6   ○ **b.** 11   ○ **c.** 15   ● **d.** 13

8. Sue looked at Volume 14. What might she have looked up?

    ○ **a.** airplanes   ○ **c.** canals

    ● **b.** tunnels   ○ **d.** bridges

9. Carla had to write a report on Meriwether Lewis and William Clark for social studies. Which two volumes did she need?

    ○ **a.** 4 and 9   ○ **c.** 10 and 15

    ● **b.** 9 and 3   ○ **d.** 9 and 14

10. Safar chose the explorer Robert LaSalle for his report. Which volume did he use?

    ○ **a.** 12   ○ **b.** 15   ○ **c.** 16   ● **d.** 9

Skill: Using a Mall Floor Plan

For lesson support, see page T112.

You probably have visited a shopping center or mall. Some malls are quite large, with many stores. How can you find one particular store? Most malls have a **floor plan** that shows the location of all the stores in the mall. If you use the floor plan, you don't have to waste time walking up and down the mall looking for a certain store.

Examine the floor plan below. It shows where each store in the Randolph Road Shopping Mall is located. Look for the arrow (⬆) on the floor plan. If you were looking at the floor plan in this mall, you would be standing at the place marked by the arrow. You would be able to find your way around the mall by using the floor plan.

Notice the numbers and the symbols on the floor plan. The numbers identify the stores in the mall. The symbols indicate other important places in the mall.

The key below the floor plan lists the stores in alphabetical order and indicates the number of the store on the floor plan. The key also explains what the symbols on the floor plan mean.

To locate a store, first find the name of the store in the alphabetical listing. Notice the numeral assigned to the store. Then find that numeral on the floor plan.

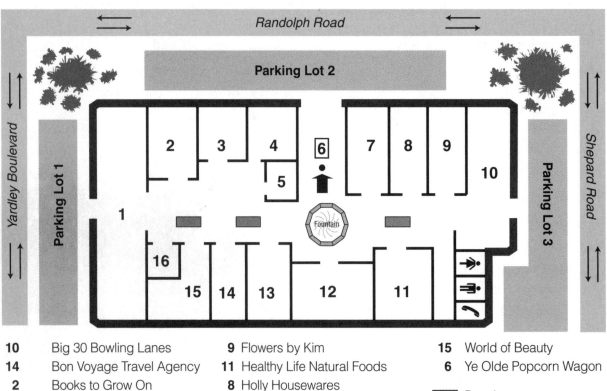

Randolph Road Shopping Mall

10 Big 30 Bowling Lanes	**9** Flowers by Kim	**15** World of Beauty
14 Bon Voyage Travel Agency	**11** Healthy Life Natural Foods	**6** Ye Olde Popcorn Wagon
2 Books to Grow On	**8** Holly Housewares	
5 Cardon Computers	**12** Nile Furniture Company	▭ Bench
13 Clothes Closet	**7** Pretty Pets, Inc.	
16 Dilly's Donuts	**1** Rupert's Department Store	✆ Public telephones
4 Fancy Feet Shoes	**3** Sports Scene	🚻 Restrooms

A. Use the floor plan to complete each sentence.

1. The store labeled 8 is ___Holly Housewares___.

2. The number ___7___ on the floor plan stands for Pretty Pets, Inc.

3. The public telephones in the mall are next to the ___restrooms___.

4. The store closest to the Big 30 Bowling Lanes is called ___Flowers by Kim___.

5. If you park in Parking Lot 1, you will have to walk through ___Rupert's Department Store___ to get to Books to Grow On.

6. To go to the Big 30 Bowling Lanes, it is best to park in ___Parking Lot 3___.

7. If you want to go to Cardon Computers, park in ___Parking Lot 2___.

8. You can sit down on one of the ___3___ benches in the mall.

9. Between World of Beauty and Clothes Closet is ___Bon Voyage Travel Agency___.

10. The three ways to enter the mall include going through Rupert's Department Store, going through ___Big 30 Bowling Lanes___, and coming in the ___Randolph___ Road entrance.

11. Walking from Books to Grow On to Cardon Computers, you pass ___Sports Scene___ and ___Fancy Feet Shoes___.

12. The only restrooms in the mall are located close to Parking Lot ___3___.

B. Decide if each of the following questions can be answered using the mall's floor plan. Write *yes* if you can find an answer on the floor plan or *no* if you cannot find an answer on the floor plan.

1. Where can I get something to eat? ___yes___

2. Does the pet shop sell parakeets? ___no___

3. Where can I find Fancy Feet Shoes? ___yes___

4. Is the mall open on Sundays? ___no___

5. Is the furniture store having a sale? ___no___

6. Where is the closest public telephone? ___yes___

7. Where is the travel agency? ___yes___

8. Is there a donut shop in the mall? ___yes___

C. Use the floor plan to answer the following questions.

1. If you were leaving the mall through the Randolph Road exit and wanted to eat a snack on the way out, where would you stop?

   Ye Olde Popcorn Wagon

2. If you were shopping at World of Beauty and Books to Grow On, what would be the closest exit?

   Go through Rupert's Department Store.

3. What is the name of one store located between Pretty Pets, Inc. and the Big 30 Bowling Lanes?

   Holly Housewares (or Flowers by Kim)

4. Which two stores are on either side of the Clothes Closet?

   Bon Voyage Travel Agency and Nile Furniture

   Company

5. If you are looking at the mall floor plan, which store is directly behind you?

   Nile Furniture Company

CONTEXT CLUE WORDS

The following words are treated as context clue words in the lessons indicated. Each lesson provides instruction in a particular context clue type and includes an activity that requires you to use context clues to find word meanings. Context clue words typically appear in the literature, social studies, and science selections and are underlined or footnoted.

Word	Lesson
ambergris	2
asterisk	46
barging	33
chambers	57
charts	1
chassis	34
courageous	43
course	1
crackling	43
craters	56
crisp	24
data	46
defacement	45
denominator	58
digestive	57
digit	36
dormant	56
eased	33
embarrassed	24
exhaust stroke	35
exhibits	45
flare	1
flywheel	35
forsake	26
gear	43
glared	13
habitation	15
harpoons	2
hoists	55
ignorant	55
innovations	34
interrupt	33
jet stream	14
jolt	13
lobsters	3
meteorology	14
migration	46
numerator	58
orbiting	15
permanent	57
power stroke	35
pursuit	44
reproachfully	55
retreat	44
savannas	56
scallops	3
scavenge	26
semiconductors	15
spermaceti	2
standardizing	25
stratosphere	14
surrender	44
suspension	34
trudged	13
unsustainable	25
urban	25
vandalism	45
vendors	24
voraciously	26

CONCEPT WORDS

In lessons that feature social studies, science, or mathematics selections, words that are unique to the content and whose meanings are important in the selection are treated as concept words. These words appear in boldface type and are often followed by a phonetic respelling and a definition.

Word	Lesson
abomasum	57
assembly line	34
baleen whales	2
biologists	15
Celsius	27
centi-	16
cosmonauts	15
councils	44
crankshaft	35
crustaceans	3
cud	57
cylinder	35
deca-	16
deci-	16
degrees	27
estimate	4
ethanol	34
explosion	35
Fahrenheit	27
fault	56
gram	16
gravity	15
habitats	45
hecto-	16
helium	14
herbivorous	57
imported	34
kilo-	16
lava	56
liter	16
mass production	25
meter	16
milli-	16
mollusks	3
omasum	57
parallel of latitude	14
physicists	15
piston	35
place holder	36
place value	36
pollute	26
post-war	25
predators	26
radiator	35
reservation	44
restricted	14
reticulum	57
rumen	57
ruminants	57
sanctuaries	45
suburbanites	25
suburban sprawl	25
tectonic plates	56
territorial	26
toothed whales	2
treaty	44
vertebrates	3